## Preface

Welcome to the world of Database Management System. This book is your gateway to understanding the fundamental concepts, principles, and practices that underpin the efficient and effective management of data in modern information systems.

In today's data-driven age, where information is often referred to as the new oil, the role of DBMS cannot be overstated. Whether you are a student embarking on a journey of discovery, a professional seeking to enhance your knowledge, or an entrepreneur aiming to harness the power of data for your business, this book will serve as your comprehensive guide.

This Book Matters because Databases are the backbone of nearly every organization, from multinational corporations to small start-ups. They store, organize, and retrieve data critical for decision-making, customer service, product development, and more. Understanding how to design, implement, and manage databases is a vital skill in the digital age.

## Table of Contents

Preface ..... 1
Chapter 1: Introduction to Databases ..... 3
Chapter 2: The Structured Query Language (SQL) ..... 55
Chapter 3: Database Design ..... 99
Chapter 4: Database Administration ..... 149
Chapter 5: Data Modelling ..... 177
Chapter 6: Transactions ..... 196
Chapter 7: Implementation Techniques ..... 242
Chapter 8: Advanced Topics ..... 278
Chapter 9 : Advanced Database Management Systems ..... 325
Chapter 10: Data Security and Privacy ..... 355
Chapter 11: Data Analytics and Business Intelligence ..... 362
Chapter 12: Emerging Trends in Database Management ..... 374
Chapter 13: Laboratory Practical's ..... 382
Chapter 14: VivaQuestions ..... 416

# Chapter 1: Introduction to Databases

Databases are the backbone of modern information systems, playing a pivotal role in storing, organizing, and managing data efficiently. This section provides a fundamental understanding of databases, their significance, and the distinction between data and information.

## Purpose of Database Systems

Information systems are complex networks of hardware, software, data, and people that work together to collect, process, store, and disseminate information for various purposes within an organization. Databases play a pivotal role in information systems, serving as their foundational backbone. Let's delve into the intricate details of how databases contribute to the functionality of information systems:

**Efficiency in Data Storage:**

Databases efficiently store vast amounts of data in a structured and organized manner. This ensures that data is readily accessible when needed, eliminating the need for paper-based or scattered electronic records.

**Data Integration:**

Information systems often gather data from multiple sources, such as sales, inventory, customer records, and more. Databases allow for the integration of this diverse data into a unified and coherent structure.

**Data Retrieval and Reporting:**

Databases provide powerful querying capabilities, allowing users to retrieve specific data or generate complex reports. This is crucial for decision-making processes, as it enables users to extract relevant information from large datasets.

**Data Security:**

Information systems deal with sensitive and critical data. Databases include security features such as user authentication, access controls, and encryption to protect data from unauthorized access and ensure data integrity.

**Data Consistency:**

Databases enforce data consistency by maintaining relationships between different data elements. This ensures that data remains accurate and coherent throughout the system, even when multiple users access it simultaneously.

**Redundancy Reduction:**

Redundancy in data storage can lead to inconsistencies and increased storage costs. Databases are designed to minimize data redundancy by storing each piece of information in one location, thus reducing the risk of conflicting data.

**Data Scalability:**

As organizations grow, their data needs increase. Databases are scalable, allowing organizations to expand their data storage and processing capabilities seamlessly, ensuring the information system can accommodate future growth.

**Data Recovery and Backup:**

Databases include mechanisms for data backup and recovery. This is crucial for disaster recovery and ensuring that data is not lost due to hardware failures, errors, or other unforeseen events.

**Data Analysis and Business Intelligence:**

Databases serve as the foundation for data analysis and business intelligence tools. They enable organizations to derive insights, make data-driven decisions, and gain a competitive edge in the market.

**Streamlined Workflows:**

Information systems leverage databases to automate and streamline workflows. This includes processes such as order processing, inventory management, and customer relationship management.

**Decision Support:**

Databases facilitate decision support systems by providing historical and real-time data, enabling organizations to make informed decisions based on accurate and up-to-date information.

In summary, databases are the linchpin of information systems, serving as the repositories that house data critical to an organization's operations. Their role extends far beyond mere data storage; they enable data integration, retrieval, security, and analysis, contributing significantly to the efficiency, effectiveness, and competitiveness of modern organizations. Understanding the pivotal role of databases in information systems is essential for anyone involved in designing, managing, or using these systems.

## Views of Data

In a Database Management System (DBMS), views of data refer to virtual representations or subsets of the underlying database that present data in a specific way to users or applications. Views are created to simplify data access, enhance security, and provide a customized perspective on the database. Here are several aspects of views of data in DBMS:

**Abstraction and Simplification**: Views abstract the complex underlying database structure, presenting users with a simplified and user-friendly interface. This simplification hides the technical complexities of the database schema, making it easier for users to interact with the data.

**Data Security**: Views are often used to enforce data security by limiting access to sensitive or confidential information. Database administrators can create views that only expose certain columns or rows of data to specific users or roles, ensuring that users can only see the data they are authorized to access.

**Customized Perspectives**: Different users or applications may require customized perspectives of the data. Views allow database administrators to tailor data presentations to meet the specific needs of different user groups or software components. For example, a sales team may have a view that focuses on customer information, while a logistics team may have a view that emphasizes inventory and shipping details.

**Data Restructuring**: Views can restructure data to present it in a more logical or meaningful way. This can involve joining multiple tables, calculating derived values, or aggregating data. Views enable users to work with data in a format that aligns with their requirements.

**Data Consistency**: Views can ensure data consistency by providing a centralized location for managing data transformations. This prevents redundancy and discrepancies that may arise when different users or applications independently manipulate the same data.

**Performance Optimization**: Database administrators can use views to optimize query performance. By creating views that store the results of complex or frequently used queries, the system can avoid reprocessing the same data, resulting in faster response times.

**Query Simplification**: Views simplify the process of writing queries. Users can interact with views using straightforward SQL queries without needing to understand the underlying database schema. This is particularly valuable for non-technical users who may not be familiar with the database structure.

**Version Control**: Views can act as version control mechanisms for data. They allow organizations to maintain different versions or snapshots of data for auditing, reporting, or historical analysis purposes.

**Data Partitioning**: Views can be used to partition data logically, helping users or applications access relevant subsets of data based on specific criteria. This is especially useful in large databases where efficiently managing and accessing data is essential.

In summary, views of data in a DBMS provide a versatile mechanism for presenting data in a manner that aligns with the needs of users, enhances security, and simplifies data access and manipulation. They serve as a crucial tool for managing data complexity and ensuring that users interact with the database in a way that maximizes efficiency and usability.

## Keys

In a Database Management System (DBMS), keys play a fundamental role in organizing and identifying data within a database. They are essential for maintaining data integrity, ensuring data uniqueness, and establishing relationships between tables. Here's an in-depth look at keys in DBMS:

**Primary Key (PK):**

A primary key is a unique identifier for each record (row) in a table.

It ensures data integrity by guaranteeing that each record has a distinct and non-null identifier.

A table can have only one primary key, and it is typically implemented as an indexed column.

Primary keys are used as references (foreign keys) in other tables to establish relationships between tables.

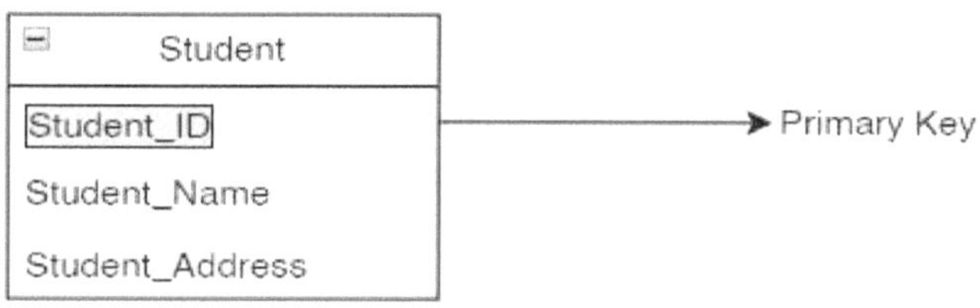


**Candidate Key:**

A candidate key is a set of one or more columns that could potentially serve as the primary key of a table.

Like the primary key, candidate keys must ensure uniqueness and integrity.

When there are multiple candidate keys, one is chosen as the primary key, and the others become alternate keys.

**Alternate Key:**

An alternate key is a candidate key that is not selected as the primary key.

While it is not the primary means of identifying records, it can still be used for unique identification.

Alternate keys can provide additional options for querying and indexing data.

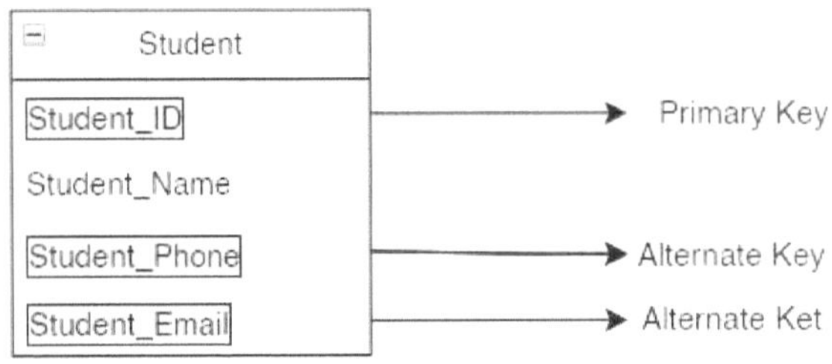


**Composite Key:**

A composite key consists of two or more columns used together as a single key.

It is employed when no single column can uniquely identify records, but a combination of columns can.

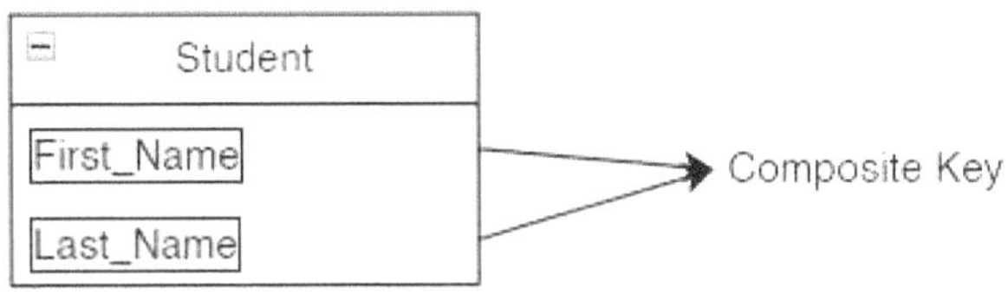


Composite keys are often used in junction tables for many-to-many relationships.

**Foreign Key (FK):**

A foreign key is a column or a set of columns in one table that refers to the primary key of another table.

It establishes relationships between tables, enforcing referential integrity.

Foreign keys ensure that values in the referencing table (child table) correspond to values in the referenced table (parent table).

They help maintain data consistency and enforce data relationships.

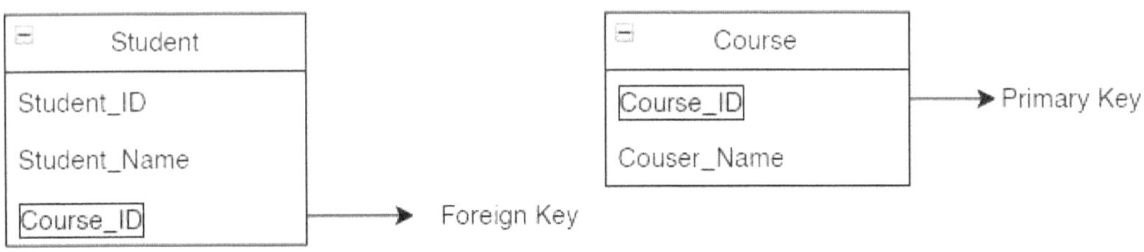


**Super Key:**

A super key is a set of one or more columns that can uniquely identify a record within a table.

It can include more columns than required for a minimal identifier.

A super key is a broader concept than a candidate key because it can contain additional attributes.

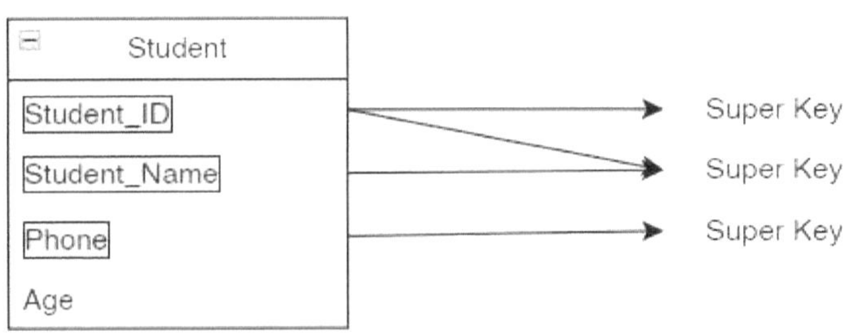

**Natural Key vs. Surrogate Key:**

A natural key is a key composed of existing, meaningful data attributes (e.g., a person's social security number).

A surrogate key is a system-generated key, often an auto-incremented number, used as a primary key to ensure uniqueness. It has no inherent meaning.

**Unique Key:**

A unique key is similar to a primary key in that it enforces uniqueness but may allow null values.

Unlike a primary key, a table can have multiple unique keys.

Unique keys are often used when you need to ensure data integrity without enforcing a primary key constraint.

In summary, keys in DBMS are crucial for maintaining data integrity, enforcing relationships, and identifying records uniquely within tables. Each type of key serves a specific purpose in database design, and their correct usage is essential for effective data management and retrieval.

**Integrity Constraints**

In a database management system (DBMS), integrity constraints are rules or conditions that are enforced to maintain the accuracy, consistency, and reliability of the data stored in the database. They define the limits and boundaries of the data and ensure that it adheres to specific criteria or conditions. Integrity constraints help in preventing data inconsistencies and errors within the database.

There are several types of integrity constraints commonly used in DBMS:

**Entity Integrity Constraint (Primary Key Constraint):**

Ensures that each row in a table is uniquely identified by a primary key field.

Prevents duplicate or null values in the primary key field.

**Referential Integrity Constraint (Foreign Key Constraint):**

Defines relationships between tables by enforcing referential links between them.

Ensures that foreign key values in one table match primary key values in another table.

Prevents the creation of orphaned records.

**Domain Integrity Constraint**:

Defines the valid range of values for a column or attribute.

Ensures that data entered into a column conforms to a specified data type, format, or range of values.

Helps maintain data accuracy and consistency.

**Check Constraint**:

Specifies a condition that data values in a column must meet.

Allows the definition of custom business rules or conditions.

Ensures that only valid data is stored in the database.

**Unique Constraint**:

Enforces the uniqueness of values in a column or a set of columns.

Prevents the insertion of duplicate values within the specified column(s).

**Default Constraint:**

Provides a default value for a column when no value is explicitly specified during insertion.

Ensures that each row has a predefined default value for the column.

**Assertion Constraint**:

Defines a condition that applies to a table as a whole.

Enforces complex integrity rules or constraints that involve multiple columns or tables.

**Key Constraint**:

Ensures that a specific column or set of columns contains unique values, similar to a unique constraint.

May be used when a key other than the primary key needs to be unique.

**Null Constraint:**

Specifies whether a column can contain null (missing or undefined) values or not.

Enforces whether a column is mandatory or optional.

**Types of Constraints**

Here are explanations of the common types of constraints:

**Primary Key Constraint**: A primary key uniquely identifies each record in a table. Violating this constraint occurs when you try to insert a duplicate value into a primary key column, which would result in multiple records having the same identifier.

**Unique Constraint**: A unique constraint ensures that values in a specified column or set of columns are unique across all records in the table. A violation happens when you attempt to insert or update a value that already exists in the unique column(s).

**Foreign Key Constraint**: A foreign key constraint establishes a relationship between two tables by referencing the primary key of one table as a foreign key in another. A violation occurs when you try to insert a value into the foreign key column that does not exist in the referenced primary key column.

**Check Constraint**: A check constraint enforces a condition that must be true for a row to be inserted or updated. A violation takes place when the condition defined in the check constraint evaluates to false.

**Default Constraint**: A default constraint specifies a default value for a column. A violation might occur if an insert operation doesn't provide a value for a column with a default constraint, and the default value cannot be generated or is not valid.

**NotNull Constraint**: A NotNull constraint ensures that a column cannot contain null (empty) values. Violating this constraint happens when you try to insert or update a row with a null value in a column that has a NotNull constraint.

## Relational Algebra

Relational Algebra in Database Management Systems (DBMS) is a mathematical system used for manipulating and querying data stored in relational databases. It provides a formal and theoretical framework for performing operations on the data within a relational database. The key operations in relational algebra are:

**Selection (σ):** This operation is used to retrieve rows from a relation (table) that satisfy a specific condition. It is akin to the SQL WHERE clause. For example, selecting all employees with a salary greater than $50,000 would be expressed as $\sigma$ (salary > 50000) (Employees).

**Projection (π):** Projection is used to select specific columns from a relation while discarding others. It is similar to the SQL SELECT statement but focuses on columns rather than rows. For instance, projecting only the "name" and "age" columns from the "Persons" relation would be written as π(name, age)(Persons).

**Union (∪):** The union operation combines two relations with the same schema (attributes) to create a new relation that contains all unique rows from both input relations. For example, if we have two sets of students, A and B, the union of these sets would include all distinct students from both sets.

**Intersection (∩):** The intersection operation combines two relations to create a new relation containing only the rows that appear in both input relations. It is like finding common elements between two sets.

**Difference (-):** The difference operation is used to find the rows that are unique to one relation and do not appear in another. For example, if we have two sets of students, A and B, the difference between A and B would include students who are in set A but not in set B.

**Cartesian Product (◊):** The Cartesian product combines every row from the first relation with every row from the second relation, resulting in a new relation with a combination of rows from both relations. It generates all possible pairs of rows from the input relations.

**Join (⋈):** Join operations are used to combine rows from two or more relations based on a related column (attribute). Different types of join include inner join, outer join (left, right, and full outer joins), and natural join. They are similar to SQL join operations.

**Rename(ρ):** The rename operation is used to rename the output relation. It is denoted by rho (ρ). Example: We can use the rename operator to rename STUDENT relation to STUDENT1.

Relational algebra serves as the foundation for query languages like SQL and helps database systems understand and process user queries. It provides a precise and systematic way of expressing operations on relational data, facilitating efficient data retrieval and manipulation in relational database management systems.

**Cartesian Product:**

The Cartesian product is an operation that combines all rows from one table with all rows from another table to produce a result set. It's also known as the cross product or simply "times."

For two tables, A and B, the Cartesian product, denoted as A ◊ B, generates a new table where each row from table A is paired with every row from table B. The resulting table contains (number of rows in A) ◊ (number of rows in B) rows.

Example:

Let's illustrate the Cartesian product with a simple example. Consider two tables, "Customers" and "Products," as follows:

Customers Table:

| CustomerID | CustomerName |
|---|---|
| 1 | Alice |
| 2 | Bob |

Products Table:

| ProductID | ProductName |
|---|---|
| **101** | Laptop |
| **102** | Smartphone |

Now, let's find the Cartesian product of these two tables (Customers ◊ Products):

Resulting Table (Customers ◊ Products):

| CustomerID | CustomerName | ProductID | ProductName |
|---|---|---|---|
| 1 | Alice | 101 | Laptop |
| 1 | Alice | 102 | Smartphone |
| 2 | Bob | 101 | Laptop |
| 2 | Bob | 102 | Smartphone |

In the resulting table, each row from the "Customers" table is paired with every row from the "Products" table, creating all possible combinations.

**Division Operator:**

The division operator, denoted as ˜, is a relational algebra operation used to retrieve records from one table that are related to all records in another table without any remaining related records. In other words, it finds those tuples in a relation (table) that are associated with all the values in another relation.

The division operation is typically used when dealing with many-to-many relationships in a database. It helps identify entities that have relationships with all specified related entities.

Example of Division Operator:

Let's consider two tables: "Students" and "Courses."

Students Table:

| Student_ID | Student_Name |
|---|---|
| 1 | Alice |
| 2 | Bob |
| 3 | Carol |

Courses Table:

| Course_ID | Course_Name |
|---|---|
| **101** | Math |
| **102** | Physics |

Suppose we want to find students who have taken all the courses in the "Courses" table. The result of the division operation will be an empty set because no student has taken all the courses.

**Set Difference Operator:**

The set difference operator, denoted as "-", is used to retrieve records from one table that do not have matching records in another table. It returns the difference between two sets of records, where the records in one set are not present in the other set.

Example of Set Difference Operator:

Let's consider two tables: "Employees" and "Managers."

Employees Table:

| Employee_ID | Employee_Name |
|---|---|
| 1 | Alice |
| 2 | Bob |
| 3 | Carol |
| 4 | David |

Managers Table:

| Manager_ID | Manager_Name |
|---|---|
| 2 | Bob |
| 4 | David |

If we want to find employees who are not managers, we can use the set difference operator. The result will be:

| Employee_ID | Employee_Name |
|---|---|
| 1 | Alice |
| 3 | Carol |

These employees are not present in the "Managers" table.

**Query optimization**

Query optimization is a crucial component of database management systems (DBMS) that aims to improve the efficiency and performance of database queries. It involves selecting the most efficient execution plan for a given query from a set of possible execution plans. The primary goal of query optimization is to minimize the query's execution time and resource usage while producing the correct and desired results.

The process of query optimization typically involves the following steps:

Parsing and Validation: The first step is parsing and validating the SQL query to ensure its correctness and adherence to the database schema.

Query Rewriting: This step involves transforming the query into an equivalent but more optimized form. Techniques like query rewriting can simplify complex queries and make them more amenable to optimization.

Candidate Plan Generation: The query optimizer generates multiple candidate execution plans, each representing a different way to retrieve the required data. These plans consider various factors, such as the order of table access, join methods, and index usage.

Cost Estimation: The optimizer estimates the cost associated with each candidate execution plan. The cost includes factors like I/O operations, CPU usage, and network communication.

Plan Selection: Based on the cost estimates, the optimizer selects the execution plan with the lowest estimated cost. This plan is considered the optimal plan for executing the query.

Plan Execution: Finally, the selected execution plan is executed to retrieve the query results.

**Relationship to Join Operation:**

The Cartesian product operation is related to the join operation in that it forms the foundation for certain types of joins. Specifically, the Cartesian product is used as an intermediate step in the calculation of a cross join (also known as a Cartesian join) and certain types of outer joins.

Cross Join (Cartesian Join): A cross join is a join operation that produces the Cartesian product of two tables. In SQL, you can achieve this using the CROSS JOIN keyword. For example, SELECT * FROM Customers CROSS JOIN Products; would produce the same result as the Cartesian product of the two tables shown earlier.

Outer Joins: While the Cartesian product itself is not directly used for inner joins (they generally involve conditions for matching rows), it becomes relevant when performing outer joins. Outer joins involve keeping unmatched rows from one table, and the Cartesian product can be used to determine which rows are unmatched.

In summary, the Cartesian product operation forms the basis for the cross join operation and plays a role in certain scenarios involving outer joins in SQL and relational databases.

## Data vs. Information

Data and information are related concepts, but they have distinct characteristics and meanings in the context of databases and information systems. Understanding the difference between data and information is fundamental in data management and decision-making processes. Here's a detailed exploration of these two concepts:

**Data:**

**Raw Facts and Figures**: Data represents raw facts, numbers, text, symbols, or values. It is the unprocessed and unorganized input that is typically collected or generated during various activities.

**Lacks Context**: Data lacks context on its own. For example, the number "42" is data. Without additional information, it's unclear what this number represents.

**Objective**: Data is objective and neutral. It does not carry any inherent meaning or interpretation. It is up to humans or computer systems to interpret and derive meaning from data.

**Abundance**: Data can be abundant and overwhelming, especially in today's digital age, where vast amounts of data are generated continuously.

**Examples of Data**: Examples of data include individual numbers, names, dates, measurements, or individual pieces of text.

**Unprocessed:** Data is typically unprocessed and may require further actions, such as sorting, filtering, or analysis, to become meaningful.

**Information:**

**Processed Data**: Information results from the processing, interpretation, and organization of data. It is data that has been transformed into a meaningful context.

**Contextualized**: Information provides context to data. It answers questions like "what," "when," "where," "who," and "why." It adds meaning and relevance to raw data.

**Subjective**: Information can be subjective and context-dependent. Different individuals or systems may derive different information from the same data, depending on their objectives and perspectives.

**Purposeful**: Information serves a purpose. It is used to make decisions, gain insights, communicate, or support specific tasks or objectives.

**Examples of Information**: Examples of information include reports, summaries, charts, conclusions, and insights derived from data analysis.

**Actionable**: Information is often actionable. It guides actions, informs decisions, or contributes to problem-solving.

**Data vs. Information in Practice:**

To illustrate the difference, consider a database of sales transactions:

**Data**: In the database, individual data points may include customer names, purchase dates, product IDs, and transaction amounts. These are raw facts and figures.

**Information**: An information report generated from this data could include a summary of total sales for a specific period, customer preferences, or trends in product sales. This report transforms the raw data into meaningful insights that can guide business decisions.

## Types of Data

Data comes in various forms, each with its unique characteristics, properties, and use cases. Understanding the different types of data is crucial in data management and database design. Here, we delve into the details of the most common types of data:

**Structured Data:**

Structured data is highly organized and follows a specific format or structure. It is typically stored in tables with rows and columns.

**Characteristics:**

Consistent format and schema.

Easily searchable and queryable.

Commonly used in relational databases.

**Examples**: Employee records in a database, financial transactions, product catalog with attributes like name, price, and description.

**Unstructured Data:**

Unstructured data lacks a specific format or structure. It is often in the form of text, images, audio, or video and does not fit neatly into traditional databases.

**Characteristics:**

No predefined schema.

Varied and flexible in content.

Challenging to query and analyse without advanced tools.

**Examples**: Social media posts, email messages, multimedia content, documents, and sensor data.

**Semi-Structured Data:**

Semi-structured data falls between structured and unstructured data. It has some level of structure but does not conform to a rigid schema like structured data.

**Characteristics:**

Organized with minimal structure.

Often represented in formats like XML, JSON, or YAML.

Supports nested or hierarchical elements.

**Examples**: JSON files containing configuration data, XML documents with hierarchical information.

**Binary Data:**

Binary data consists of sequences of binary digits (0s and 1s) and can represent various types of content, including images, audio, executables, and more.

**Characteristics:**

Requires specific applications or codecs to interpret.

Compact storage of non-textual data.

**Examples:** Image files (JPEG, PNG), audio files (MP3, WAV), executable programs (EXE), and video files (MP4).

**Time-Series Data:** Time-series data records observations or measurements at specific time intervals. It is commonly used for tracking changes over time. Examples: Maps, GPS coordinates, geographic information system (GIS) data.

**Geospatial Data:** Geospatial data contains information related to geographic locations and spatial relationships between objects. Examples: Maps, GPS coordinates, geographic information system (GIS) data.

**Categorical Data:** Categorical data represents discrete categories or labels. It is used for classification and grouping. Examples: Nominal - colours, vehicle types; Ordinal - education levels (e.g., high school, bachelor's, master's).

**Numerical Data:** Numerical data consists of measurable quantities represented as numbers. It can be further categorized as continuous or discrete. Numerical data consists of measurable quantities represented as numbers. It can be further categorized as continuous or discrete.

**Text Data:** Text data includes written or typed characters, words, sentences, or paragraphs. Examples: Books, articles.

## Characteristics of a Database

Databases are critical components of modern information systems, offering a structured and efficient way to store, manage, and retrieve data. Understanding the characteristics of a database is essential for effective data management and utilization. Here are the key characteristics in detail:

**Data Integrity:** Data integrity refers to the accuracy and consistency of data stored in the database. It ensures that data is reliable and trustworthy.

**Data Consistency:** Data consistency ensures that data remains uniform and coherent across the database, even when multiple users or applications access it simultaneously.

**Data Security:** Data security safeguards data from unauthorized access, modification, or disclosure. It protects sensitive information from breaches and unauthorized use.

**Data Accessibility**: Data accessibility ensures that authorized users can access data when needed. It involves making data available while maintaining security and privacy.

**Data Scalability**: Scalability refers to the database's ability to handle growing volumes of data and increasing user demands without significant performance degradation.

**Data Recovery and Backup:** Data recovery and backup features ensure that data can be restored in case of hardware failures, data corruption, or accidental deletions.

**Data Redundancy Reduction:** Redundancy reduction minimizes the duplication of data within the database. It helps maintain data consistency and reduces storage costs.

**Transaction Management**: Transaction management ensures that database operations (e.g., insert, update, delete) are carried out reliably and maintain data consistency.

**Data Backup and Recovery:** Data backup and recovery mechanisms provide safeguards against data loss due to hardware failures, errors, or unforeseen events.

**Data Modelling and Schema**: Data modelling involves creating a logical representation of the database's structure using schema design, defining tables, relationships, and constraints.

Understanding and implementing these characteristics is crucial in designing, managing, and utilizing databases effectively. Databases that exhibit these qualities are reliable, secure, and efficient, supporting a wide range of applications and information systems.

**Relationship between Data Security and Data Integrity:**

**Protection Mechanisms:** Data security mechanisms, such as access controls, encryption, and authentication, are employed to prevent unauthorized users from tampering with data. By restricting access to authorized personnel and ensuring data is encrypted in transit and at rest, security measures contribute to data integrity by reducing the risk of unauthorized changes.

**Data Auditing:** Data security measures often include auditing and logging capabilities. Auditing tracks and records who accessed the data and what changes were made. Auditing not only enhances security by detecting unauthorized activities but also aids in maintaining data integrity by providing a record of data modifications for review and verification.

**Backup and Recovery**: Data security practices often involve regular data backup and recovery procedures. Backups are essential for data recovery in case of security incidents, such as data breaches or ransomware attacks. Having reliable backups contributes to data integrity by ensuring that data can be restored to its original, unaltered state.

**Access Controls**: Access controls, a key aspect of data security, prevent unauthorized users from making unintended or malicious changes to data. By enforcing strict access controls, data security measures contribute to maintaining data integrity by ensuring that only authorized users with the proper permissions can modify data.

Here's a simplified diagram illustrating the relationship between data security and data integrity:

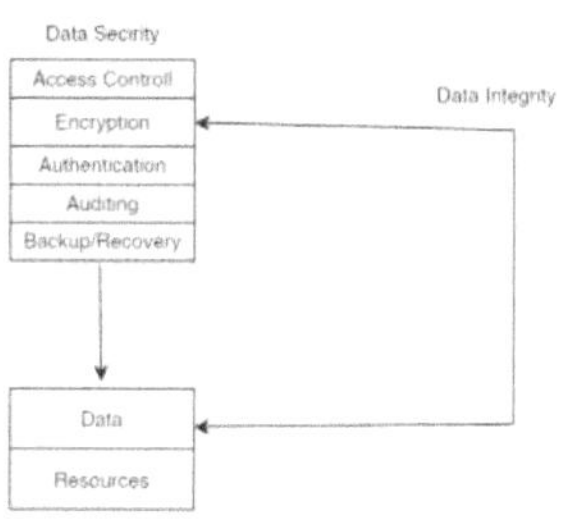

In this diagram, data security measures, represented in the left box, include access control, encryption, authentication, auditing, and backup/recovery. These measures protect data resources (e.g., databases) from unauthorized access and tampering. The protected data resources contribute to data integrity (right box) by ensuring the accuracy and consistency of the data stored within them.

In summary, data security and data integrity are interconnected, with data security measures helping to protect data resources and maintain data integrity. Together, they ensure that data remains secure, accurate, and reliable, ultimately supporting the trustworthiness of the database system.

**Exercise**

**Exercise 1 – MCQ**

Q 1. The primary role of databases in information systems is to:

A) Process data

B) Collect data

C) Store, manage, and retrieve data

D) Transmit data

Q 2. Which of the following best describes the difference between data and information?

A) Data is unprocessed, while information is processed and meaningful.

B) Data is qualitative, while information is quantitative.

C) Data is structured, while information is unstructured.

D) Data and information are synonymous terms.

**Exercise 2 – True/ False**

Q 1. Databases play a secondary role in information systems, primarily focused on data storage.

Q 2.True or False? Unstructured data, such as text documents and multimedia content, is easy to query and analyse in a database.

**Exercise 3 – Fill in the blanks**

Q 1. In information systems, databases serve as ___________ for storing, managing, and retrieving data efficiently.

Q 2. Data is raw facts and figures, while information is data that has been ___________ and given meaning.

**Exercise 4 – Match case**

Types of Data:

1. Structured Data
2. Unstructured Data
3. Semi-Structured Data

a. Data lacking a specific format or structure.

b. Highly organized and follows a specific format.

c. Falls between structured and unstructured data, with some level of structure.

**Exercise 5 – One word answer**

Q 1. What type of data is highly organized and follows a specific format?

Q 2. What is the primary role of databases in information systems?

**Exercise 6 – Small answer**

Q 1. What is the fundamental difference between data and information?

Q 2. What is the purpose of data redundancy reduction in a database?

**Exercise 7 – Long answer**

Q 1. Describe the various types of data, including structured, unstructured, semi-structured, and provide real-world examples of each type. Explain why understanding these data types is important in data management and database design.

Q 2. Explain the fundamental difference between data and information. Provide examples to illustrate the concept and discuss why this distinction is important in the context of data management and decision-making.

**Answer**

**Exercise 1**

Answer 1.C), **2.** A).

**Exercise**

Answer 1.False.**2.** False.

**Exercise 3**

Answer 1.Repositories.**2.** Processed.

**Exercise 4**

Answer 1. 1- b, 2- a, 3- c

**Exercise 5**

Answer 1.Structured, **2.**Storage.

**Previous Years Questions**

Q1. List and explain all the types of constraints which can be violated while modifying database values. (IGNOU MCA 2010)

Q2. Differentiate between the followings: Equi join and Natural join (IGNOU MCA 2010)

Q3. What is Cartesian product. Explain using an example. How Cartesian product operation is related to the join operation. (IGNOU MCA 2010)

Q4. Explain the following relational algebraic operations with the help of an example. (IGNOU MCA 2010)

Division operator

Set Difference operator

Q5. Explain following operators in Relational Algebra with the help of an example (IGNOU MCA 2011)

Select

Project

Join

Q6. Determine the output when following operations are applied on relations R1, R2 and R3 given below. (IGNOU MCA 2011 & 2021)

R1:

| A | B |
|---|---|
| A1 | B1 |
| A2 | B2 |
| A3 | B3 |
| A4 | B4 |

R2:

| X | Y |
|---|---|
| A1 | B1 |
| A7 | B7 |
| A2 | B2 |
| A4 | B4 |

R3:

| A |
|---|
| empty |

Union (R1 ∪ R2)

Intersection (R1 ∩ R2)

Difference (R1 - R2)

Cartesian cross – section (R1 x R2)

Division (R1 ˜ R3)

Q7. What do you mean by integrity constraints? Briefly describe the various types of integrity constraints. (IGNOU MCA 2011)

Q8. Define primary key, candidate key, super key and foreign key, Alternate key (IGNOU MCA 2012 & 2021)

Q9. Define foreign key. Explain its significance. (IGNOU MCA 2013)

Q10. What is an outer join? Discuss the different types of outer joins with the help of example. (IGNOU MCA 2013)

Q11. Explain the following terms: Equi Join, Data Replication, Entity Integrity Constraints. (IGNOU MCA 2013)

Q12. What is a join in DBMS? Explain three types of join with the help of an example for each. (IGNOU MCA 2014)

Q13. What are integrity constraints? Explain two types of integrity constraint with the help of an example. (IGNOU MCA 2014)

Q14. What is a view? What are the major advantages of views? Explain with the help of an example. (IGNOU MCA 2015) (Pune University MCA 2013) (ANNA University MCA 2010)

Q15. Define a view. How is it different from a table? Write the SQL syntax for creating a view (IGNOU MCA 2016)

Q16. What are integrity constraints? Discuss the various types of integrity constraints that can be imposed on databases. (IGNOU MCA 2017)

Q17.What is the role of views in DBMS? Can we perform delete, modify or insert operations, if the view contains group function? Justify. (IGNOU MCA 2018)

Q18. What do you understand by the term "closure of any relation"? How is closure used to determine key of relation? Explain with an example. (IGNOU MCA 2018)

Q19. What is Query Optimization? Discuss the role of Relational Algebra in query optimization. (IGNOU MCA 2018)

Q20. What are the advantages of a view? What are its limitations with respect to applying DM2 operations? (IGNOU MCA 2018)

Q21. Describe the relationship between Data Security and Data Integrity, with the help of a diagram. (IGNOU MCA 2020)

Q22. What are integrity constraints? What for they are required in databases? Briefly discuss the different types of integrity constraints. (IGNOU MCA 2020)

Q23. What is Relational Algebra? What is the utility of relational algebra? Is SQL related to relational algebra? Comment on it. Explain the following operations in the relational algebra with the help of an example for each: (i) Select (ii) Project (iii) Join (IGNOU MCA 2020)

Q24. Write short note on: Joins. (Pune University MCA 2013)

**Previous Years Questions with Answers**

Q1. What is candidate key? (RU BCA 2022)

**Answer:**

In the context of a relational database, a candidate key is a minimal superkey for a table (relation) that uniquely identifies each row (tuple) within that table. A superkey is a set of one or more attributes (columns) that can be used to uniquely identify rows, but a candidate key is a minimal superkey, meaning that it is a superkey with the fewest possible attributes. This makes candidate keys a fundamental concept in database design and the implementation of the relational model.

Here are some key points about candidate keys:

**Uniqueness:** A candidate key ensures that no two rows in the table will have the same combination of values in the attributes that make up the key. This property is essential for maintaining data integrity.

**Minimality:** A candidate key is minimal, meaning that if any attribute were removed from the key, it would no longer be unique. In other words, it's the smallest set of attributes that can still uniquely identify each row.

**Candidate Key Selection:** In practice, multiple candidate keys may exist for a table. Database designers choose one of these candidate keys as the primary key, which is used as the main means of uniquely identifying rows in the table.

**Primary Key:** The primary key is the chosen candidate key used as the main identifier for a table. The primary key is used in foreign key constraints in other tables to establish relationships between tables.

**Alternate Keys:** The remaining candidate keys (those not chosen as the primary key) are referred to as alternate keys. Although not used as the primary means of identifying rows, they are still unique and may have other uses in queries and constraints.

Candidate keys are a critical concept in relational database design because they help ensure the integrity and accuracy of data by preventing duplicate or ambiguous data. By selecting the appropriate candidate key as the primary key, you establish the foundation for well-structured and efficient databases.

Q2. What is weak entity set? (RU BCA 2022)

**Answer:**

In a relational database, a weak entity set (or simply a weak entity) is an entity that does not have a primary key attribute of its own. Instead, it relies on a related strong entity, known as the owner entity, for its identity. Weak entities are typically identified by a combination of their attributes and a partial key attribute from the owner entity, which is known as the discriminant or partial key. This means that the existence of a weak entity is dependent on its relationship with the owner entity.

Key characteristics of weak entities:

**No Standalone Identity:** A weak entity cannot be uniquely identified by its attributes alone. It requires the context of the owning entity to establish its identity.

**Partial Key:** To distinguish one weak entity from another, a weak entity typically uses a partial key, which is an attribute that is part of its own set of attributes. This partial key is combined with some additional attributes (if necessary) from the owner entity.

**Parent-Child Relationship:** There is a strong relationship between the owner entity and the weak entity. The owner entity is sometimes referred to as the parent entity, and the weak entity as the child entity.

**Dependent Existence:** The existence of a weak entity depends on its relationship with the owner entity. If the owner entity is deleted or ceases to exist, the weak entity associated with it may also be deleted.

**Double Diamond Notation:** In an Entity-Relationship Diagram (ERD), a weak entity is represented using a double diamond shape.

For example, consider a database for a library. In this context, a "Book" entity might be considered a strong entity because it has attributes like ISBN, title, and author that can uniquely identify each book. On the other hand, a "BookCopy" entity that represents individual physical copies of books in the library might be a weak entity. It depends on the "Book" entity for identification through attributes such as copy number and book ISBN (partial key) in combination with the "Book" entity.

Weak entities are essential in modeling real-world scenarios where certain entities have attributes or characteristics that are specific to their relationship with another entity. They help maintain data integrity by ensuring that related entities are properly linked and identified within the database system.

Q3. What is specialization in DBMS? (RU BCA 2022)

**Answer:**

Specialization in a database management system (DBMS) is a process of defining one or more subtypes of an entity, which inherits the attributes and relationships of a higher-level entity called a supertype. This is used to represent a specific subset of instances from the broader entity, often because those instances have unique characteristics that are not shared by all instances of the supertype. Specialization is a fundamental concept in the Entity-Relationship Model (ER Model) for database design.

Key points about specialization in DBMS:

**Supertype:** The higher-level entity, from which one or more subtypes are derived, is called the supertype. The supertype includes common attributes and relationships that are shared by all its subtypes.

**Subtype:** Each specialized subset of the supertype is referred to as a subtype. Subtypes inherit the attributes and relationships from the supertype and can have additional attributes specific to their characteristics.

**Disjoint vs. Overlapping Subtypes:** Specialization can be either disjoint or overlapping:

**Disjoint Subtypes:** Instances of the supertype can belong to only one subtype. For example, a "Vehicle" supertype may have disjoint subtypes like "Car" and "Bike," and an instance can belong to either "Car" or "Bike," but not both.

**Overlapping Subtypes:** Instances of the supertype can belong to multiple subtypes simultaneously. For example, a "Person" supertype may have overlapping subtypes like "Employee" and "Customer," where an instance can be both an employee and a customer at the same time.

**Specialization Hierarchy:** Specialization can be organized in a hierarchy, where there can be further subtypes of subtypes. This hierarchy can extend to multiple levels, creating a tree-like structure.

**Total vs. Partial Specialization:** Specialization can be total or partial:

**Total Specialization:** Every instance of the supertype must belong to at least one subtype. In a total specialization, the subtype categories are collectively exhaustive.

**Partial Specialization:** Instances of the supertype may not belong to any subtype. In a partial specialization, the subtype categories are not collectively exhaustive.

**Attributes and Relationships:** Subtypes inherit the attributes and relationships of the supertype. They can also have their own additional attributes and relationships.

**Entity-Subtype Relationship:** A relationship exists between the supertype and its subtypes, which indicates the specialization relationship.

Specialization is an important concept in database design because it allows for the representation of entities with diverse characteristics in a structured and organized manner. It helps ensure that each subtype can be uniquely identified while sharing common attributes and relationships with the supertype. This modeling technique is particularly useful when dealing with complex and diverse real-world scenarios.

Q4. What are the different types or relationship in DBMS? (RU BCA 2022)

**Answer:**

In a database management system (DBMS), relationships define how two or more database tables are connected or linked. These relationships are established using keys, such as primary keys and foreign keys. There are several types of relationships commonly used in DBMS, including:

**One-to-One (1:1) Relationship:**

In a one-to-one relationship, each record in one table is related to one and only one record in another table.

This relationship is relatively rare and is typically used to break down a large table with many columns into smaller, more manageable tables.

For example, you might have a "Person" table and a "Driver's License" table. Each person can have only one driver's license, and each driver's license is associated with a unique individual.

**One-to-Many (1:N) Relationship:**

In a one-to-many relationship, each record in one table can be related to one or more records in another table.

This is the most common type of relationship in relational databases.

For example, consider a "Customer" table and an "Order" table. Each customer can have multiple orders, but each order is associated with a single customer.

**Many-to-One (N:1) Relationship:**

In a many-to-one relationship, many records in one table are related to a single record in another table.

This relationship is essentially the reverse of a one-to-many relationship.

An example of this relationship is a "Product" table and a "Supplier" table. Many products can be supplied by a single supplier.

**Many-to-Many (N:N) Relationship:**

In a many-to-many relationship, multiple records in one table can be related to multiple records in another table.

This type of relationship is implemented using a junction table or associative table that acts as a bridge between the two tables.

An example of this relationship is a "Student" table and a "Course" table. Many students can be enrolled in multiple courses, and each course can have multiple students.

**Self-Referencing Relationship:**

A self-referencing relationship occurs when records in a single table are related to other records within the same table.

This is often used to represent hierarchical or recursive structures.

An example is an "Employee" table where each employee may have a supervisor who is also an employee within the same table.

**Identifying Relationship vs. Non-Identifying Relationship:**

An identifying relationship is one in which the primary key of the child table includes the primary key of the parent table, and it uniquely identifies the child record.

A non-identifying relationship is one in which the primary key of the child table is not derived from the parent table's primary key and is not unique across all child records.

**Recursive Relationship:**

A recursive relationship occurs when records in a table are related to other records in the same table.

This is often used to represent hierarchical structures, such as organizational charts or family trees.

An example is a "Person" table where each person can have a parent who is also a person in the same table.

Understanding and correctly modeling relationships between tables is crucial in database design, as it ensures data integrity and efficient data retrieval when querying the database.

Q5. Differentiate the following: (RU BCA 2022)

DROP, TRUNCATE and DELETE commands

UNION AND UNION ALL

Primary key and unique key

**Answer:**

**DROP, TRUNCATE, and DELETE commands:**

**DROP Command:**

The DROP command is used to remove an entire database object, such as a table, index, or view.

It permanently deletes the object from the database, and the structure, as well as the data within it, are completely removed.

It is a Data Definition Language (DDL) command.

Example:

DROP TABLE TableName;

**TRUNCATE Command:**

The TRUNCATE command is used to delete all the rows from a table while keeping the table structure intact.

It is faster than the DELETE command because it doesn't log individual row deletions.

It resets identity columns (auto-increment columns) to their initial seed values.

It is also a DDL command.

Example:

TRUNCATE TABLE TableName;

**DELETE Command:**

The DELETE command is used to remove specific rows from a table based on a condition.

It is slower than TRUNCATE for deleting all rows because it logs each row's deletion.

It doesn't reset identity columns.

It is a Data Manipulation Language (DML) command.

Example:

DELETE FROM TableName WHERE Condition;

**UNION AND UNION ALL:**

**UNION:**

The UNION operator is used to combine the result sets of two or more SELECT queries into a single result set.

It removes duplicate rows from the combined result set, ensuring that each row is unique.

It is often used when you want to merge rows from two or more tables or queries, and you want to eliminate duplicate records.

Example:

SELECT column1 FROM table1

UNION

SELECT column1 FROM table2;

**UNION ALL:**

The UNION ALL operator is also used to combine the result sets of multiple SELECT queries into a single result set.

Unlike UNION, it does not remove duplicate rows, so all rows from all SELECT statements are included.

It is generally faster than UNION because it doesn't perform the duplicate elimination.

Example:

```
SELECT column1 FROM table1
UNION ALL
SELECT column1 FROM table2;
```

**Primary Key and Unique Key:**

**Primary Key:**

A primary key is a column (or set of columns) in a relational database table that uniquely identifies each row or record in the table.

It enforces the entity integrity constraint, ensuring that each value in the primary key column(s) is unique and not null.

There can be only one primary key in a table.

A primary key also automatically creates a unique clustered index in many database systems.

**Unique Key:**

A unique key is a column (or set of columns) that enforces the uniqueness constraint, ensuring that each value in the column(s) is unique across the table.

Unlike a primary key, a unique key can contain null values.

A table can have multiple unique keys, but only one primary key.

Unique keys are used when you want to ensure the uniqueness of values but don't need the additional constraints imposed by a primary key.

Example:

```
CREATE TABLE TableName
(
ID INT PRIMARY KEY,   -- Primary Key
Email VARCHAR(255) UNIQUE,   -- Unique Key
...
);
```

Q6. What are the different types of languages that are available in the DBMS. (RU BCA 2022)

**Answer:**

In the context of Database Management Systems (DBMS), there are primarily four types of languages used:

**Data Definition Language (DDL):**

DDL is used to define and manage the structure of the database, including creating, altering, and deleting tables, indexes, and other database objects.

Common DDL commands include **CREATE**, **ALTER**, **DROP**, and **TRUNCATE**.

Example: **CREATE TABLE TableName (column1 datatype, column2 datatype);**

**Data Manipulation Language (DML):**

DML is used to retrieve, insert, update, and delete data in the database. It deals with the manipulation of data stored in the database.

Common DML commands include **SELECT, INSERT, UPDATE**, and **DELETE**.

Example: **SELECT column1 FROM TableName WHERE condition;**

**Data Query Language (DQL):**

DQL is a subset of DML that focuses specifically on data retrieval. It is used to query the database and retrieve information without modifying it.

The primary DQL command is **SELECT**.

Example: **SELECT column1, column2 FROM TableName WHERE condition;**

**Data Control Language (DCL):**

DCL is used to control access to the database. It includes commands that grant or revoke privileges and permissions to users or roles.

Common DCL commands include **GRANT** and **REVOKE**.

Example: **GRANT SELECT ON TableName TO User;**

It's important to note that different database management systems may have variations in the specific commands and syntax used for DDL, DML, DQL, and DCL, but the general categories of languages remain consistent across most relational database systems.

Q7. Write short notes on:

Primary key and foreign key (RU BCA 2022)

Join, union and intersection in SQL (RU BCA 2021)

**Answer:**

**Primary Key and Foreign Key:**

**Primary Key:** A primary key is a column or a set of columns in a database table that uniquely identifies each row or record in that table. It enforces entity integrity, ensuring that each row in the table is unique. Primary keys are used as a reference point for other tables that have relationships with the table containing the primary key.

Example: In a "Customers" table, the "CustomerID" column can serve as the primary key, ensuring that each customer has a unique identifier.

**Foreign Key:** A foreign key is a column or a set of columns in a table that is used to establish a link between the data in two tables. It creates referential integrity between the tables by referencing the primary key of another table. A foreign key in one table is linked to the primary key in another table.

Example: In an "Orders" table, the "CustomerID" column may serve as a foreign key referencing the "CustomerID" in the "Customers" table, indicating which customer placed the order.

**Join, Union, and Intersection in SQL:**

**Join:** A SQL join is used to combine rows from two or more tables based on a related column between them. SQL supports different types of joins, including INNER JOIN (returns matching rows), LEFT JOIN (returns all rows from the left table and matching rows from the right table), RIGHT JOIN (returns all rows from the right table and matching rows from the left table), and FULL OUTER JOIN (returns all rows when there is a match in either table).

Example: **SELECT Orders.OrderID, Customers.CustomerName FROM Orders INNER JOIN Customers ON Orders.CustomerID = Customers.CustomerID;**

**Union:** The SQL UNION operator is used to combine the result sets of two or more SELECT queries into a single result set. It removes duplicate rows by default, and it is used when you want to combine rows from different tables with the same structure.

Example: **SELECT column1 FROM table1 UNION SELECT column1 FROM table2;**

**Intersection:** SQL does not have a specific operator for set intersection. However, you can achieve an intersection effect using appropriate SQL queries. For example, to find rows common to two tables, you can use an INNER JOIN to identify matching rows, effectively achieving the intersection of the two sets.

Example:

SELECT column1 FROM table1

INTERSECT

SELECT column1 FROM table2;

Please note that the exact SQL syntax may vary slightly depending on the specific database management system you are using (e.g., MySQL, PostgreSQL, SQL Server).

Q8. Define database? (RU BCA 2021)

**Answer:**

A **database** is a structured collection of data that is organized and stored electronically in a computer system. It is designed to efficiently store, manage, and retrieve data. Databases are a fundamental part of modern information systems and are widely used in various applications and industries, including business, education, healthcare, government, and more.

Key characteristics of a database include:

**Structured Data:** Databases store data in a structured format, typically organized into tables, rows, and columns. Each column represents an attribute or field, and each row represents a record or entry.

**Data Integrity:** Databases enforce data integrity rules, such as ensuring data consistency, accuracy, and reliability. These rules are defined using constraints and data types.

**Data Retrieval:** Users can query databases to retrieve, filter, and analyze data based on their specific needs. SQL (Structured Query Language) is commonly used to interact with relational databases.

**Concurrency Control:** Databases support multiple users accessing and modifying data concurrently. Concurrency control mechanisms ensure that data remains consistent even when multiple users are interacting with the database.

**Data Security:** Databases provide mechanisms for securing data through user authentication, authorization, and access control. Data encryption and auditing may also be used for enhanced security.

**Scalability:** Databases can scale vertically (adding more resources to a single server) or horizontally (distributing data across multiple servers) to accommodate growing data and user demands.

**Redundancy and Backup:** To ensure data availability and fault tolerance, databases may incorporate redundancy and backup strategies.

There are various types of databases, including:

**Relational Databases:** Organize data into structured tables with predefined schemas and relationships between tables. Examples include MySQL, PostgreSQL, Oracle, and SQL Server.

**NoSQL Databases:** Designed for unstructured or semi-structured data and provide flexibility in data storage. Types of NoSQL databases include document stores, key-value stores, column-family stores, and graph databases.

**In-Memory Databases:** Store data primarily in RAM (random-access memory) for exceptionally fast data retrieval, suitable for applications that require real-time processing.

**Distributed Databases:** Store data across multiple servers or locations and provide mechanisms for data distribution and replication.

**Object-Oriented Databases:** Store data in an object-oriented manner, often used in software development where objects can be directly stored and retrieved.

Databases play a crucial role in managing and organizing data, enabling efficient data analysis, and supporting various applications that rely on accurate and consistent information.

Q9. Discuss the various types of keys. (RU BCA 2021)

**Answer:**

In the context of databases, various types of keys are used to uniquely identify and manage data within tables. Each type of key serves a specific purpose, and understanding these keys is crucial for database design and data integrity. Here are some of the key types:

**Primary Key (PK):** A primary key is a column or set of columns in a table that uniquely identifies each row. It ensures that there are no duplicate rows in the table and enforces data integrity. A primary key must have unique values and cannot contain NULL values.

**Unique Key (Unique Constraint):** A unique key is similar to a primary key but allows NULL values. It enforces the uniqueness of values in a column or set of columns, except for NULL values. Unlike the primary key, a table can have multiple unique keys.

**Foreign Key (FK):** A foreign key is a column or set of columns in one table that refers to the primary key of another table. It establishes a relationship between tables and ensures referential integrity, meaning that the values in the foreign key column must exist in the referenced primary key column.

**Composite Key:** A composite key consists of two or more columns used together to uniquely identify rows in a table. It is used when no single column can provide a unique identifier. In relational databases, composite keys are often used to model complex relationships.

**Super Key:** A super key is a set of one or more columns that can be used to uniquely identify rows in a table. It may contain extra columns that are not strictly necessary for uniqueness. A super key is a broader concept that includes primary keys, unique keys, and other candidate keys.

**Candidate Key:** A candidate key is a minimal super key, meaning it is a set of columns that uniquely identifies rows without any unnecessary columns. In a table, there can be multiple candidate keys, and one of them is chosen as the primary key.

**Alternate Key:** An alternate key is a candidate key that is not selected as the primary key. While it can uniquely identify rows, it is not used as the primary means of identification for data retrieval.

**Natural Key:** A natural key is a key that is derived from the inherent characteristics of the data it represents. For example, using a person's Social Security Number as a key in a table.

**Surrogate Key:** A surrogate key is an artificially generated key, typically an auto-incremented integer, used as the primary key. It has no inherent meaning but is easier to manage and provides better performance than natural keys.

**Compound Key:** A compound key is a key that consists of multiple columns. It is often used in cases where a single column cannot provide a unique identifier.

**Functional Dependency Key:** A functional dependency key is derived from the functional dependencies between attributes in a relation. It represents the dependencies between the attributes and is used for normalization in database design.

Choosing the right types of keys and defining them appropriately is a critical aspect of relational database design, as it ensures data integrity, efficient data retrieval, and the establishment of relationships between tables.

Q10. What is mean by aggregation? (RU BCA 2021)

**Answer:**

In the context of databases and data analysis, aggregation refers to the process of combining and summarizing multiple data values into a single value or set of values. Aggregation is typically used to obtain meaningful insights from large datasets, simplify data analysis, and reduce the volume of data while preserving essential information.

Key points about aggregation include:

**Combining Data:** Aggregation involves taking multiple data records or values and applying a function or operation to condense them into a more manageable or meaningful form.

**Summarization:** The aggregated result provides a summary or overview of the data, allowing for easier interpretation and analysis.

**Grouping:** Aggregation often involves grouping data by specific attributes or categories, such as time periods, geographic regions, or product categories. The data within each group is then aggregated separately.

**Common Aggregation Functions:** Common aggregation functions include SUM (for adding values), AVG (for calculating the average), COUNT (for counting the number of records), MAX (for finding the maximum value), and MIN (for finding the minimum value).

**Aggregated Data Types:** Aggregated data can take various forms, including sums, averages, counts, percentages, or any other statistical or mathematical summary that makes sense for the dataset and the analysis goals.

Examples of Aggregation:

**Sales Data:** Aggregating daily sales data to calculate monthly or yearly totals.

**Website Analytics:** Aggregating website visitor data to calculate daily, weekly, or monthly page views.

**Financial Reporting:** Aggregating transaction data to generate balance sheets and income statements.

**Social Media Metrics:** Aggregating user engagement metrics (likes, comments, shares) for a specific post or over a period.

In databases, aggregation is often performed using SQL (Structured Query Language) commands, and aggregated data is presented in the form of query results. Aggregation plays a crucial role in data analysis, reporting, and decision-making processes, as it allows for the extraction of insights and patterns from large datasets.

Q11. What is meant by primary key? (RU BCA 2019)

**Answer:**

A primary key in a relational database is a column or a set of columns that uniquely identifies each row (record) within a table. It serves as a fundamental concept in database design and plays several critical roles:

**Uniqueness:** Every value in the primary key column (or columns) must be unique. This uniqueness constraint ensures that no two rows in the table have the same primary key value.

**Uniquely Identifying Rows:** The primary key is used to identify and retrieve specific rows from the table. It provides a way to pinpoint a particular record within the dataset.

**Enforcing Data Integrity:** By enforcing uniqueness, a primary key helps maintain data integrity. It prevents duplicate or inconsistent data from being entered into the table.

**Supporting Relationships:** Primary keys are often used in establishing relationships between tables in a relational database. They serve as a reference point for foreign keys in related tables, enabling the creation of meaningful connections between data.

**Indexed for Efficiency:** Most database systems automatically create an index on the primary key column(s). This index speeds up data retrieval operations, making queries more efficient.

**Constraints:** The primary key constraint is a fundamental part of ensuring data quality. When defining a primary key, the database management system (DBMS) enforces the uniqueness and not-null constraints on the designated column(s).

Typical examples of primary keys include:

An employee table might use an employee ID (emp_id) as the primary key.

A customer table could use a unique customer number (cust_no) as the primary key.

An inventory table may use a combination of product ID and location ID (product_id, location_id) as the composite primary key, ensuring that each product is uniquely identified within each location.

In some cases, a primary key is a single column with an auto-incrementing integer (or a similar mechanism) to guarantee uniqueness. In other cases, especially in complex data models, a composite primary key consists of multiple columns that together must be unique.

Defining an appropriate primary key is a crucial step in the design of a relational database, as it affects data integrity, relationships between tables, and the overall performance of data retrieval operations.

Q12. What is join statement? (RU BCA 2017)

**Answer:**

In the context of databases and SQL (Structured Query Language), a "JOIN" statement is used to combine rows from two or more tables based on a related column between them. The JOIN operation allows you to create a single result set that includes columns from all the tables involved. It's a fundamental SQL operation used to retrieve and manipulate data from multiple tables.

There are several types of JOIN operations, including:

**INNER JOIN:** This is the most common type of join. It returns only the rows where there is a match between the columns being joined. If there's no match, those rows are excluded from the result set. INNER JOIN is the default type of join if you simply use the "JOIN" keyword.

```
SELECT employees.name, departments.department_name
FROM employees
INNER JOIN departments ON employees.department_id = departments.department_id;
```

**LEFT JOIN (or LEFT OUTER JOIN):** This returns all rows from the left table (the first table listed) and the matching rows from the right table. If there is no match in the right table, NULL values are returned for the right table's columns.

```
SELECT customers.name, orders.order_date
FROM customers
LEFT JOIN orders ON customers.customer_id = orders.customer_id;
```

**RIGHT JOIN (or RIGHT OUTER JOIN):** This is the reverse of a LEFT JOIN. It returns all rows from the right table and the matching rows from the left table. If there's no match in the left table, NULL values are returned for the left table's columns.

```
SELECT orders.order_date, customers.name
FROM orders
RIGHT JOIN customers ON orders.customer_id = customers.customer_id;
```

**FULL JOIN (or FULL OUTER JOIN):** This returns all rows from both tables, with NULL values in columns where there is no match. It's less common than INNER, LEFT, or RIGHT JOIN but can be useful for specific scenarios.

```
SELECT employees.name, departments.department_name
FROM employees
FULL JOIN departments ON employees.department_id = departments.department_id;
```

**CROSS JOIN:** This type of join returns the Cartesian product of two tables. It combines each row from the first table with every row from the second table. Be cautious when using CROSS JOIN, as it can result in a large number of rows.

```
SELECT employees.name, products.product_name
FROM employees
CROSS JOIN products;
```

The choice of which JOIN type to use depends on the specific requirements of your query and the data you're working with. Understanding how these JOINs work is crucial for creating complex SQL queries and retrieving data from related tables.

Q13. Differentiate between following: (RU BCA 2017)
Strong and weak entity
Referential integrity and domain integrity
Single valued and multi valued attributes

**Answer:**

**Strong and Weak Entity**:

**Strong Entity**: A strong entity is an entity that has a primary key attribute, which uniquely identifies each instance of the entity. It can exist independently of any other entity and does not depend on another entity for its identification. For example, in a database for a library, the "Book" entity can be a strong entity because it has a unique ISBN as its primary key.

**Weak Entity**: A weak entity, on the other hand, does not have a primary key attribute that can uniquely identify instances of the entity. It depends on a related strong entity, known as the "owning" or "parent" entity, for its identification. A weak entity is often identified by a partial key, which is a set of attributes that, when combined with the primary key of the owning entity, becomes a unique identifier. For example, in the same library database, a "BookCopy" entity could be a weak entity, depending on the "Book" entity for its identity.

**Referential Integrity and Domain Integrity**:

**Referential Integrity**: Referential integrity is a database concept that ensures that relationships between tables (entities) are maintained correctly. It enforces that the foreign key values in one table match the primary key values in another table. In other words, it ensures that relationships between tables are consistent and that you cannot insert data that violates these relationships. For example, if you have a "Customer" table with a foreign key linking to an "Order" table, referential integrity ensures that you cannot create an order for a non-existent customer.

**Domain Integrity**: Domain integrity refers to the validity and consistency of data values within a specific column (attribute) of a table. It ensures that data in a column conforms to predefined data types, constraints, and business rules. For example, domain integrity ensures that a "Date of Birth" column only contains valid dates or that a "Price" column only contains positive numeric values.

**Single-Valued and Multi-Valued Attributes**:

**Single-Valued Attribute**: A single-valued attribute is an attribute that holds a single value for each entity in a database. It represents atomic, indivisible data. For example, in a "Person" entity, the "Age" attribute is typically single-valued because a person has only one age.

**Multi-Valued Attribute**: A multi-valued attribute is an attribute that can hold multiple values for each entity. It represents non-atomic, composite, or structured data. For example, in the same "Person" entity, the "Phone Number" attribute might be multi-valued because a person can have more than one phone number.

Q14. What is the difference between primary key and unique key? (RU BCA 2016)

**Answer:**

**Primary Key** and **Unique Key** are both used to enforce the uniqueness of values in a column (or a set of columns) within a relational database. However, there are some differences between them:

**Primary Key**:

**Uniqueness**: A primary key enforces the uniqueness of values in a column or a combination of columns within a table. No two rows can have the same primary key value.

**Required**: Every table should have a primary key. It is used to identify each record uniquely and is crucial for the table's integrity.

**NULL Values**: A primary key column does not allow NULL values. Every row in the table must have a valid value for the primary key column.

**One per Table**: A table can have only one primary key.

**Clustered Index**: In some database management systems, the primary key automatically creates a clustered index on the table, which affects how data is physically stored on disk.

**Unique Key**:

**Uniqueness**: A unique key also enforces the uniqueness of values in a column or a combination of columns. It ensures that no duplicate values exist within the specified columns.

**Optional**: Unlike the primary key, a table can have multiple unique keys, but they are not mandatory for every table. They are used when you need to ensure uniqueness on a column, but it doesn't necessarily serve as the main identifier.

**NULL Values**: A unique key allows NULL values, but a NULL value in a unique key column is not considered a duplicate, so it doesn't violate the uniqueness constraint. As a result, multiple rows can have NULL values in that column.

**Non-Clustered Index**: A unique key typically creates a non-clustered index on the table in most database management systems, improving search performance but not impacting the physical storage of data.

In summary, both primary keys and unique keys serve the purpose of ensuring data integrity by enforcing the uniqueness of values. However, primary keys have additional constraints such as non-null values and are often used as the main identifier for a table. Unique keys, on the other hand, can be applied to columns where you want to maintain uniqueness without the additional constraints of a primary key.

Q15. What is relational algebra? Explain types of operation performed in relational algebra. (RU BCA 2016)

**Answer:**

**Relational algebra** is a formal mathematical system used to query and manipulate data stored in a relational database. It provides a set of operations that can be applied to one or more database tables or relations to produce a result as a new relation. Relational algebra serves as the foundation for database query languages like SQL (Structured Query Language). The main operations in relational algebra include:

**Selection (σ)**: The selection operation is used to retrieve rows from a relation that satisfy a specified condition. It is similar to the SQL WHERE clause. For example, you can use σSalary > 50000(Employee) to select employees with a salary greater than 50,000.

**Projection (π)**: The projection operation extracts specified columns from a relation, creating a new relation with a subset of the original attributes. It is similar to the SQL SELECT clause. For example, you can use πName,Salary(Employee) to project only the Name and Salary columns from the Employee relation.

**Union (∪)**: The union operation combines two relations (usually with the same schema) to produce a new relation that contains all distinct rows from both relations. For example, R ∪ S would result in a relation containing all rows from R and S with duplicates removed.

**Intersection (∩)**: The intersection operation returns a new relation containing all rows that appear in both of the input relations. For example, R ∩ S would result in a relation with rows that exist in both R and S.

**Set Difference (-)**: The set difference operation retrieves rows from one relation that are not present in another. For example, R - S returns a relation with rows that are in R but not in S.

**Cartesian Product (◊)**: The Cartesian product operation combines every row in one relation with every row in another relation, resulting in a new relation that has a combination of all rows. It is rarely used on its own but often as part of other operations.

**Renaming (ρ)**: The renaming operation is used to change the name of a relation or its attributes. It is used to avoid naming conflicts and make queries more readable.

These relational algebra operations allow you to perform various tasks in database queries, such as filtering rows, selecting specific columns, combining data, and more. These operations serve as the foundation for query languages like SQL, and by using them in combination, you can express complex queries and retrieve the desired data from a relational database.

Q16. Discuss the fundamental operations of relational algebra. (RU BCA 2021)

**Answer:**

Relational algebra is a formal system for manipulating and querying relational databases. It consists of several fundamental operations that allow you to retrieve, filter, combine, and transform data in a relational database. The fundamental operations of relational algebra include:

**Selection (σ - Sigma)**:

Selection is used to filter rows from a relation based on a specified condition.

It is similar to the SQL **SELECT** statement with a **WHERE** clause.

The result of the selection operation is a new relation containing only the rows that satisfy the condition.

For example, σSalary > 50000(Employee) retrieves employees with a salary greater than 50,000.

**Projection (π - Pi)**:

Projection is used to extract specific columns (attributes) from a relation, creating a new relation with a subset of the original attributes.

It is similar to the SQL **SELECT** statement with specific column names.

The result of the projection operation is a new relation with only the specified columns.

For example, $\pi$Name, Salary(Employee) retrieves only the "Name" and "Salary" attributes from the Employee relation.

**Union (∪ - Union)**:

Union combines two relations (usually with the same schema) to produce a new relation that contains all distinct rows from both relations.

It is similar to the SQL **UNION** operator.

The result of the union operation is a new relation with all rows from both input relations, and duplicates are automatically removed.

**Intersection (∩ - Intersection)**:

Intersection returns a new relation containing rows that appear in both of the input relations.

It is similar to the SQL **INTERSECT** operator.

The result of the intersection operation is a relation with rows that exist in both input relations.

**Set Difference (- - Minus)**:

Set difference retrieves rows from one relation that are not present in another.

It is similar to the SQL **EXCEPT** operator.

The result of the set difference operation is a relation with rows that are in the first input relation but not in the second.

**Cartesian Product (◊ - Cross Product)**:

The Cartesian product combines every row in one relation with every row in another relation, resulting in a new relation that has a combination of all rows.

It is used for joining two relations and is the basis for other join operations.

The result is a large relation with all possible combinations of rows from the input relations.

These fundamental operations serve as the building blocks for more complex queries and operations in relational algebra. By combining these operations and nesting them, you can express a wide range of queries to retrieve and manipulate data from a relational database.

Q17. What do you understand by DBMS? (RU BCA 2019)

**Answer:**

A Database Management System (DBMS) is software designed to manage, store, retrieve, and manipulate data in a database. It acts as an intermediary between the users and the physical database, providing an efficient and organized way to store and access data. Here are some key points to understand about DBMS:

**Data Organization**: DBMS provides a structured way to organize and store data in databases. Data is stored in tables (relations) where each table consists of rows (records) and columns (attributes).

**Data Retrieval**: Users can easily retrieve data from the database by using query languages like SQL (Structured Query Language). SQL allows users to specify what data they want to retrieve, and the DBMS handles the complexity of finding and returning the data.

**Data Security**: DBMSs offer mechanisms for securing data. Access controls and permissions can be set to restrict who can view, modify, or delete data. This ensures data privacy and prevents unauthorized access.

**Data Integrity**: DBMS enforces data integrity by defining rules and constraints on data. This ensures that data is accurate and consistent. Common integrity constraints include primary keys, foreign keys, and unique constraints.

**Concurrency Control**: In multi-user environments, a DBMS manages concurrent access to data. It ensures that multiple users can work with the data simultaneously without interfering with each other's operations.

**Data Recovery**: DBMS systems include features for data backup, recovery, and transaction management. In case of system failures or errors, data can be restored to a consistent state.

**Data Abstraction**: DBMS provides data abstraction, which means that users and applications interact with a high-level view of the data without needing to understand the underlying physical storage details.

**Scalability**: DBMSs are designed to handle large amounts of data and provide scalability. As data grows, the system can be adapted to accommodate increased data volume and user loads.

**Data Independence**: DBMS offers data independence. This means that changes to the database structure (e.g., adding or modifying attributes) do not affect the applications that use the database.

**Query Optimization**: DBMSs include query optimizers that analyze SQL queries and determine the most efficient way to execute them. This helps in improving query performance.

Common examples of database management systems include Oracle Database, Microsoft SQL Server, MySQL, PostgreSQL, and MongoDB (a NoSQL database). Each of these systems provides features tailored to specific data storage and retrieval needs.

In summary, a DBMS is a critical component of modern information systems, enabling the efficient management of data, ensuring data accuracy and security, and simplifying data retrieval and manipulation.

Q18. Discuss the advantages and disadvantages of DBMS. (RU BCA 2018)

**Answer:**

**Advantages of DBMS:**

**Data Centralization:** All data is stored in one location, making it easy to access and manage.

**Data Integrity:** DBMS enforces data integrity constraints (e.g., primary keys, foreign keys), ensuring data accuracy and consistency.

**Data Security:** Access controls and permissions protect data from unauthorized access.

**Concurrency Control:** DBMS handles multiple users accessing data simultaneously, preventing conflicts and ensuring data consistency.

**Data Recovery:** DBMS systems offer backup and recovery features, protecting data against loss.

**Reduced Data Redundancy:** Data is stored efficiently without duplication, reducing redundancy and saving storage space.

**Data Abstraction:** Users interact with high-level data models without needing to understand the underlying database structure.

**Query Optimization:** DBMS automatically optimizes query execution for improved performance.

**Scalability:** DBMS can handle growing data volumes and user loads, making it suitable for both small and large-scale applications.

**Data Independence:** Changes to the database structure do not affect application programs, providing flexibility.

**Data Consistency:** DBMS ensures that data remains consistent across the database.

**Disadvantages of DBMS:**

**Complexity:** DBMS systems are complex and may require a skilled database administrator to set up and maintain them.

**Cost:** Licensing and support costs can be significant, especially for commercial DBMS systems.

**Resource Intensive:** DBMS systems can consume a significant amount of system resources (CPU, memory, disk space), potentially affecting system performance.

**Security Vulnerabilities:** If not properly configured, DBMS systems can be vulnerable to security breaches.

**Learning Curve:** Users and administrators need to learn how to use and manage the DBMS effectively.

**Vendor Lock-In:** Some commercial DBMS systems may lock organizations into a specific vendor's technology, limiting flexibility.

**Data Loss:** If not backed up and maintained properly, data can be lost in case of system failures or errors.

**Customization Challenges:** Adapting a DBMS to meet specific requirements can be challenging, especially for unique or complex applications.

**Potential for Performance Bottlenecks:** Poorly designed databases or inefficient queries can lead to performance bottlenecks.

**Data Privacy Concerns:** Organizations must ensure that sensitive data is adequately protected, as any data breach can have severe consequences.

Q19. List any four advantages of using DBMS? (RU BCA 2017)

**Answer:**

Using a Database Management System (DBMS) offers several advantages, but here are four of the key benefits:

**Data Centralization:** A DBMS centralizes data in one location, making it easier to access, manage, and maintain. This eliminates the need for redundant data storage and simplifies data management.

**Data Integrity:** DBMS enforces data integrity constraints, such as primary keys and foreign keys, to maintain the accuracy and consistency of data. This ensures that data adheres to predefined rules.

**Security and Access Control:** DBMS provides robust security features, including authentication and authorization mechanisms. It allows administrators to control who can access data and what operations they can perform, helping to protect data from unauthorized access and potential security breaches.

**Concurrent Access and Multi-User Support:** DBMS systems handle concurrent access by multiple users or applications to the same data. They manage data concurrency, prevent conflicts, and maintain data consistency, allowing multiple users to work with the data simultaneously without issues.

These advantages highlight the efficiency, reliability, and security that DBMS brings to data management, making it a valuable tool for various applications and organizations.

Q20. What is relational calculus? What is difference between tuple relational calculus (TRC) and Domain Relational calculus (DRC). (RU BCA 2022)

**Answer:**

**Relational calculus** is a non-procedural query language used to retrieve data from relational databases. It specifies what data should be retrieved rather than how to retrieve it. There are two main variants of relational calculus: Tuple Relational Calculus (TRC) and Domain Relational Calculus (DRC).

**Tuple Relational Calculus (TRC):**

In TRC, you specify the desired results by defining a set of tuples (rows) that satisfy the conditions of the query.

It focuses on the selection of tuples from the relations based on the conditions in the query.

TRC uses variables that stand for tuples, and the query is formulated as an expression involving these variables.

For example, if you want to find all employees with a salary greater than 50,000, the TRC query might be written as: $\{E \mid \exists E \in \text{Employee} (E.\text{salary} > 50000)\}$.

**Domain Relational Calculus (DRC):**

In DRC, you specify the desired results by defining the attributes or domains of the tuples that satisfy the query.

It focuses on the selection of attributes or domains from the relations based on the conditions in the query.

DRC uses variables that stand for attributes or domains, and the query is formulated as an expression involving these variables.

For example, if you want to find the names of all employees with a salary greater than 50,000, the DRC query might be written as: $\{E.\text{name} \mid \exists E \in \text{Employee} (E.\text{salary} > 50000)\}$.

In summary, TRC focuses on selecting tuples that meet certain criteria, while DRC focuses on selecting specific attributes or domains of the tuples that satisfy the query. Both variants provide a declarative way to express queries, leaving the database management system to determine how to retrieve the data efficiently.

Q21. Explain the different integrity constraints with example. (RU BCA 2022)

**Answer:**

Integrity constraints are rules that are enforced by a database management system (DBMS) to maintain the accuracy, consistency, and reliability of the data stored in a database. There are several types of integrity constraints, each serving a specific purpose. Here are some common integrity constraints with examples:

**Entity Integrity Constraint:**

Ensures that the primary key attribute(s) in a relation do not contain NULL values.

Example: In a "Students" table, the "StudentID" is defined as the primary key. The entity integrity constraint ensures that each student record has a unique and non-null StudentID.

**Referential Integrity Constraint:**

Maintains the relationships between tables by ensuring that foreign key values in one table match primary key values in another table.

Example: In a "Orders" table, the "CustomerID" is a foreign key referencing the "Customers" table's "CustomerID" as the primary key. The referential integrity constraint ensures that every "CustomerID" in the "Orders" table corresponds to a valid "CustomerID" in the "Customers" table.

**Domain Integrity Constraint:**

Enforces the permissible values and data types for attributes in a table.

Example: In an "Employees" table, the "Salary" attribute must be a positive numeric value. The domain integrity constraint ensures that no negative values or non-numeric data are stored in the "Salary" column.

**Check Constraint:**

Defines a condition that must be satisfied for data to be inserted or updated in a table.

Example: In a "Products" table, a check constraint can ensure that the "UnitPrice" of a product is greater than or equal to zero.

**Unique Constraint:**

Guarantees that the values in a column (or a combination of columns) are unique across all rows in a table.

Example: In a "Books" table, a unique constraint on the "ISBN" column ensures that no two books share the same ISBN.

**Check Constraint:**

Defines a condition that must be satisfied for data to be inserted or updated in a table.

Example: In a "Users" table, a check constraint can ensure that the "Birthdate" attribute contains dates in the past and not in the future.

**Default Constraint:**

Specifies a default value to be used when no explicit value is provided for an attribute during insertion.

Example: In an "Employees" table, you can define a default constraint for the "MaritalStatus" attribute, setting it to "Single" by default unless otherwise specified.

These integrity constraints help maintain data accuracy, consistency, and reliability in a database, preventing the entry of invalid or inconsistent data. They are essential for ensuring data quality and reliability in a database system.

Q22. Describe the structure of DBMS in detail. (RU BCA 2019)

**Answer:**

A Database Management System (DBMS) is a software system that manages, organizes, and provides efficient access to databases. The structure of a DBMS is designed to handle various aspects of database management, including data storage, data retrieval, security, and data integrity. Here's a detailed description of the structure of a typical DBMS:

**User Interface:**

The user interface provides a means for users and applications to interact with the DBMS.

It includes command-line interfaces, graphical user interfaces (GUIs), and programming interfaces (APIs) that allow users to interact with the database.

**Query Processor:**

The query processor receives and processes queries or requests from users and applications.

It includes a query parser that checks the syntax of queries and a query optimizer that generates efficient execution plans for query processing.

**Transaction Manager:**

The transaction manager is responsible for ensuring the integrity and consistency of the database.

It manages concurrent access to the database, enforces the rules of the database, and ensures that transactions are executed in an atomic, consistent, isolated, and durable (ACID) manner.

**Storage Manager:**

The storage manager is responsible for managing the physical storage of data on the storage devices.

It includes a file manager, buffer manager, and disk space manager.

The file manager manages files and data structures used to store the database.

The buffer manager manages a cache of data in memory to improve data retrieval performance.

The disk space manager allocates and manages space on storage devices.

**Data Dictionary:**

The data dictionary (also known as a system catalog) stores metadata about the database.

It contains information about the structure of the database, such as tables, columns, indexes, constraints, and relationships.

It is used by the DBMS to validate queries and ensure data consistency.

**Query Engine:**

The query engine executes the optimized query plans generated by the query optimizer.

It interacts with the storage manager to fetch and write data as needed.

**Concurrency Control:**

Concurrency control mechanisms manage simultaneous access to the database by multiple users and transactions.

They ensure that transactions do not interfere with each other and maintain data consistency.

**Security and Authorization:**

DBMS provides security features to control access to the data.

This includes authentication to verify the identity of users and authorization to specify what actions users are allowed to perform on the data.

**Backup and Recovery:**

Backup and recovery mechanisms are responsible for data protection and disaster recovery.

They create backups of the database to restore it in case of data loss or system failures.

**Transaction Log:**

The transaction log records all changes made to the database to support recovery and rollbacks in case of system failures.

It is crucial for maintaining the ACID properties of transactions.

**Data Storage:**

The actual data storage is where the database files are stored on disk or other storage devices.

The structure of data storage can include various data files, indexes, and other data structures.

**Database Engine:**

The database engine is the core component that manages the overall functioning of the DBMS.

It coordinates the activities of various components, manages system resources, and ensures data integrity.

This structured organization of components and layers within a DBMS ensures efficient data management, data retrieval, and data security. The DBMS provides a consistent and reliable interface for users and applications to interact with the underlying database, abstracting the complexities of data storage and management.

Q23. What is mean by mapping constraints? (RU BCA 2018)

**Answer:**

Mapping constraints, in the context of database design, refer to the rules and relationships that define how data from one entity or table in a database is associated or mapped to data in another entity or table. These constraints ensure that the data is properly connected and consistent within the database. Mapping constraints play a crucial role in maintaining data integrity and enforcing business rules.

There are two main types of mapping constraints:

**Referential Integrity Constraint:**

Referential integrity constraints define the relationships between tables in a database. They ensure that foreign key values in one table correspond to primary key values in another table.

Key components of referential integrity include primary keys and foreign keys.

Examples:

A foreign key in the "Orders" table referencing the primary key in the "Customers" table ensures that each order is associated with a valid customer.

A foreign key in the "OrderDetails" table referencing the primary key in the "Products" table ensures that each order detail is linked to an existing product.

**Cardinality Constraints:**

Cardinality constraints specify how many instances of one entity can be related to instances of another entity.

Common cardinality notations include one-to-one (1:1), one-to-many (1:N), and many-to-many (N:N).

Examples:

In a one-to-many relationship between "Authors" and "Books," one author can write many books, but each book is authored by only one author.

In a many-to-many relationship between "Students" and "Courses," each student can enroll in many courses, and each course can have many students.

Mapping constraints ensure that data remains consistent, prevents data anomalies, and enforces business rules when relationships between entities or tables are established in a database schema. Violating these constraints can lead to data inconsistency and integrity issues.

Q24. What is relational algebra? Explain different types of join and aggregation operations of relational algebra. Give appropriate example. (RU BCA 2017)

**Answer:**

**Relational algebra** is a formal query language used to perform operations on relational databases. It consists of a set of operations that can be applied to relations (database tables) to retrieve or manipulate data. The main operations in relational algebra include selection, projection, union, set difference, Cartesian product, and join. Two important subsets of relational algebra are the join operations and the aggregation operations. Let's explore these operations with examples in table format:

**Sample Relations:**

Consider two relations - Employees and Departments, with the following data:

**Employees (EmpID, EmpName, Salary, DeptID):**

| EmpID | EmpName | Salary | DeptID |
|---|---|---|---|
| 1 | Alice | 50000 | 101 |
| 2 | Bob | 60000 | 102 |
| 3 | Carol | 55000 | 101 |
| 4 | Dave | 62000 | 103 |
| 5 | Eve | 53000 | 102 |

**Departments (DeptID, DeptName):**

| DeptID | DeptName |
|---|---|
| 101 | HR |
| 102 | Sales |
| 103 | IT |

**Relational Algebra Operations:**

**Join Operation:**

Join operations combine rows from two or more relations based on a related column (attribute). Common join types are inner join, left outer join, and right outer join.

**Inner Join (σ):** The inner join returns rows that have matching values in both relations.

**Example:**

σ(EmpID = DeptID)(Employees ⋈ Departments)

| EmpID | EmpName | Salary | DeptID | DeptName |
|---|---|---|---|---|
| 1 | Alice | 50000 | 101 | HR |
| 2 | Bob | 60000 | 102 | Sales |
| 3 | Carol | 55000 | 101 | HR |
| 4 | Dave | 62000 | 103 | IT |
| 5 | Eve | 53000 | 102 | Sales |

**Left Outer Join (⋈):** The left outer join returns all rows from the left relation and matching rows from the right relation. If there's no match, NULL values are included.

**Example:**

Employees⋈ Departments

| EmpID | EmpName | Salary | DeptID | DeptName |
|---|---|---|---|---|
| 1 | Alice | 50000 | 101 | HR |
| 2 | Bob | 60000 | 102 | Sales |
| 3 | Carol | 55000 | 101 | HR |
| 4 | Dave | 62000 | 103 | IT |
| 5 | Eve | 53000 | 102 | Sales |

**Right Outer Join (⋈):** The right outer join returns all rows from the right relation and matching rows from the left relation. If there's no match, NULL values are included.

**Example:**

Employees⋈ Departments

| EmpID | EmpName | Salary | DeptID | DeptName |
|---|---|---|---|---|
| 1 | Alice | 50000 | 101 | HR |
| 2 | Bob | 60000 | 102 | Sales |
| 3 | Carol | 55000 | 101 | HR |
| 4 | Dave | 62000 | 103 | IT |
| 5 | Eve | 53000 | 102 | Sales |

**Aggregation Operations:**

Aggregation operations allow you to perform calculations on groups of rows, resulting in a single summary value. Common aggregation functions include SUM, COUNT, AVG, MAX, and MIN.

**Example:**

Find the total salary for each department.

π(DeptName, SUM(Salary))(Employees ⋈ Departments)

| DeptName | SUM(Salary) |
|---|---|
| HR | 105000 |
| Sales | 113000 |
| IT | 62000 |

These are just a few examples of how relational algebra operations can be used to retrieve and manipulate data from relations. These operations serve as the foundation

Q25. What is metadata? (RU BCA 2016)

**Answer:**

**Metadata** is data that describes other data. It provides information about various aspects of data, such as its structure, meaning, relationships, origin, usage, and more. Metadata plays a crucial role in data management, database systems, and information systems in general. Here are some key points about metadata:

**Description of Data:** Metadata provides descriptions and context for data. It helps users and systems understand what the data represents, how it's organized, and its significance.

**Data Dictionary:** Metadata often serves as a data dictionary, which is a repository of metadata information about data elements in a system, including data definitions, data types, lengths, and permissible values.

**Database Management:** In database management systems (DBMS), metadata is used to store information about database objects such as tables, columns, indexes, constraints, and relationships. It helps the DBMS manage and optimize data storage and retrieval.

**Data Integration:** In data integration and data warehousing, metadata is used to track the source, transformations, and history of data as it moves from various source systems into a data warehouse. This helps in data quality and lineage analysis.

**Data Governance:** Metadata is crucial for data governance. It includes information about data ownership, data lineage, access controls, and compliance requirements.

**Search and Discovery:** In content management systems and search engines, metadata is used for tagging and categorizing content, making it easier to search and discover relevant information.

**Data Interoperability:** Metadata standards and schemas (e.g., Dublin Core for describing web resources) enable data interoperability between systems and across organizations.

**Data Quality:** Metadata can include information about data quality, such as data validation rules, data profiling results, and data cleansing history.

**Security and Access Control:** Metadata can describe who has access to data, access permissions, and encryption methods used to secure data.

**Data Lineage:** Metadata can trace the lineage of data, showing how it was created, transformed, and used throughout its lifecycle.

**Data Versioning:** In data versioning systems, metadata helps track different versions of data and their relationships.

**Data Catalogs:** Metadata catalogs are used to store and manage metadata across an organization. These catalogs help users discover and access the data they need.

Metadata is essential for data understanding, management, and governance. It ensures that data is used effectively, accurately, and securely in various applications and systems.

Q26. List database programming language that is procedural and non-procedural? (RU BCA 2016)

**Answer:**

Database programming languages can be categorized as procedural and non-procedural. Here are examples of both types:

**Procedural Database Programming Languages:**

**SQL (Structured Query Language)**: While SQL is primarily a declarative language for querying and manipulating data, it does support procedural elements in the form of SQL/PSM (Persistent Stored Modules) and PL/SQL (Procedural Language/SQL). These extensions allow for the creation of stored procedures, functions, and triggers, which include procedural logic.

**PL/SQL**: PL/SQL is Oracle's procedural extension to SQL. It is used for writing stored procedures, functions, and triggers within Oracle Database.

**T-SQL (Transact-SQL)**: T-SQL is Microsoft's procedural extension to SQL. It is used with Microsoft SQL Server and Azure SQL Database to create stored procedures, functions, and triggers.

**PL/pgSQL**: PL/pgSQL is a procedural language for PostgreSQL, allowing the creation of stored procedures, functions, and triggers.

**Non-Procedural Database Programming Languages:**

**SQL (Structured Query Language)**: SQL is primarily a non-procedural language for querying and manipulating data. Users specify what data they want and let the database management system (DBMS) figure out how to retrieve it.

**Datalog**: Datalog is a declarative logic programming language used in some database systems for querying and deductive databases. It's non-procedural because users describe the desired results without specifying how to obtain them.

**Query by Example (QBE)**: QBE is a non-procedural language that allows users to specify their queries by providing examples or patterns of data they want to retrieve from the database.

**LINQ (Language-Integrated Query)**: LINQ is a .NET-based non-procedural language that allows developers to use a consistent query syntax to access and manipulate data stored in various types of data sources, including databases.

It's important to note that many modern database systems support a combination of both procedural and non-procedural approaches. While SQL provides a non-procedural way to express queries, it also includes features for embedding procedural code, such as stored procedures, within the database. This flexibility allows developers and database administrators to choose the most appropriate approach based on their requirements.

Q27. What is referential integrity and entity integrity? (RU BCA 2016)

**Answer:**

Referential integrity and entity integrity are two important concepts in the context of relational databases:

**Entity Integrity:**

**Entity integrity** ensures that each row or record in a database table is uniquely identifiable. It is primarily associated with the concept of primary keys.

In entity integrity, the primary key attribute(s) of a table must contain unique values and cannot contain NULL values. This means that every record in the table must be uniquely identified by its primary key.

Entity integrity is enforced by defining one or more primary keys for a table. A primary key is a column or set of columns that uniquely identifies each record in the table. It helps maintain data accuracy and consistency by preventing duplicate or NULL values in the primary key column(s).

For example, in an "Employees" table, the "EmployeeID" column can be designated as the primary key, ensuring that each employee has a unique identifier, and no employee records have NULL EmployeeIDs.

**Referential Integrity:**

**Referential integrity** is a set of rules that ensures the relationships between tables are maintained consistently. It is often associated with foreign keys.

In referential integrity, foreign key values in one table must match the primary key values in another table. This constraint ensures that relationships between tables are valid and that data consistency is maintained.
Referential integrity also enforces actions such as cascading updates and deletes, which automatically update or delete related records in other tables when changes are made to the primary key.
For example, in a database with "Customers" and "Orders" tables, the "CustomerID" column in the "Orders" table may be a foreign key referencing the primary key "CustomerID" in the "Customers" table. Referential integrity ensures that for each order in the "Orders" table, there is a corresponding customer in the "Customers" table with a matching "CustomerID."
In summary, entity integrity guarantees the uniqueness and non-null property of primary keys within a single table, while referential integrity guarantees the consistency of relationships between tables through primary keys and foreign keys. These constraints are essential for maintaining the integrity and quality of data in a relational database.

Q28. What is join? Explain types of join with suitable examples. (RU BCA 2016)

**Answer:**

An **outer join** is a type of join operation in relational databases that combines rows from two or more tables based on a related column between them. Unlike an inner join, which returns only the rows with matching values in both tables, an outer join returns all rows from one table and the matching rows from the other table. If there's no match for a row in one table, the result will include null values for the columns from that table.
There are three main types of outer joins:

**Left Outer Join (or Left Join)**:

A left outer join returns all the rows from the left (or first) table, along with the matching rows from the right (or second) table.
If there's no match in the right table, the result will include null values for the right table's columns.
This is useful when you want to keep all records from the left table and get additional data from the right table when available.

**Example - Left Outer Join**: Consider two tables, **Employees** and **Departments**. A left outer join between these tables will return all employees and their respective department names.

SELECT Employees.Name, Departments.Name AS Department FROM Employees LEFT JOIN Departments ON Employees.DepartmentID = Departments.ID;

**Right Outer Join (or Right Join)**:

A right outer join returns all the rows from the right (or second) table, along with the matching rows from the left (or first) table.
If there's no match in the left table, the result will include null values for the left table's columns.
This is less commonly used than the left join but can be useful when you want to keep all records from the right table and get additional data from the left table when available.

**Example - Right Outer Join**: Using the same **Employees** and **Departments** tables, a right outer join will return all departments and the employees working in them, if any.

SELECT Employees.Name, Departments.Name AS Department FROM Employees RIGHT JOIN Departments ON Employees.DepartmentID = Departments.ID;

**Full Outer Join (or Full Join)**:

A full outer join returns all the rows when there is a match in either the left or the right table. It combines the results of both left and right outer joins.

If there's no match in one of the tables, the result will include null values for the columns from that table.

This type of join is useful when you want to keep all records from both tables.

**Example - Full Outer Join**: Continuing with the **Employees** and **Departments** tables, a full outer join will return all employees along with their department names and all departments, whether they have employees or not.

SELECT Employees.Name, Departments.Name AS Department FROM Employees FULL JOIN Departments ON Employees.DepartmentID = Departments.ID;

Outer joins are especially valuable when working with data where not every row in one table has a corresponding match in the other table. They help you preserve all the data from one table while associating relevant data from another.

Q29. Discuss the aggregation function with example. (RU BCA 2021)

**Answer:**

In the context of SQL and relational databases, an **aggregation function** (also known as an aggregate function) is used to perform calculations on a set of values and return a single value as the result. Aggregation functions are often used in combination with the **GROUP BY** clause to calculate summary statistics for groups of rows. Here are some common aggregation functions and examples of how they work:

**SUM**: Calculates the sum of a numeric column.

Example: Calculate the total salary for each department.

SELECT Dept, SUM(Salary) AS TotalSalary

FROM Employees

GROUP BY Dept;

**AVG**: Calculates the average (mean) of a numeric column.

Example: Calculate the average age of employees in each department.

SELECT Dept, AVG(Age) AS AvgAge

FROM Employees

GROUP BY Dept;

**COUNT**: Counts the number of rows in a group.

Example: Count the number of employees in each department.

SELECT Dept, COUNT(*) AS NumberOfEmployees

FROM Employees

GROUP BY Dept;

**MIN**: Returns the minimum value in a numeric column.

Example: Find the minimum salary in each department.

```
SELECT Dept, MIN(Salary) AS MinSalary
FROM Employees
GROUP BY Dept;
```

**MAX**: Returns the maximum value in a numeric column.

Example: Find the maximum salary in each department.

```
SELECT Dept, MAX(Salary) AS MaxSalary
FROM Employees
GROUP BY Dept;
```

**SUM DISTINCT**: Calculates the sum of distinct (unique) values in a column.

Example: Calculate the sum of distinct salaries in each department.

```
SELECT Dept, SUM(DISTINCT Salary) AS DistinctSalarySum
FROM Employees
GROUP BY Dept;
```

These aggregation functions help you perform calculations and generate summary statistics based on the data in your database. They are especially useful when you need to analyze data and derive insights from it, such as when summarizing sales figures, calculating averages, or determining the count of specific items in a dataset.

Q30. Discuss the generalization and aggregation (RU BCA 2021)

**Answer:**

In the context of relational databases and data modeling, **generalization** and **aggregation** are two important concepts used in designing data models that accurately represent complex relationships and hierarchies. Let's explore each of these concepts:

**Generalization:**

Generalization is a modeling technique used to represent relationships between entities in a way that captures common characteristics or attributes. It is often employed in entity-relationship modeling, particularly when dealing with inheritance or hierarchical structures. Generalization allows for the creation of a more abstract, generalized entity from which one or more specialized entities inherit attributes and relationships.

**Superclass/Parent Entity:** The generalized entity that contains common attributes and relationships.

**Subclass/Child Entity:** Specialized entities that inherit attributes and relationships from the superclass. Each subclass can have its own additional attributes and relationships.

For example, consider a database for employees in an organization. You may have a generalized entity called "Employee" as the superclass, and subclasses such as "Manager," "Engineer," and "Salesperson." The superclass "Employee" may have common attributes like "EmployeeID" and "FirstName," while each subclass can have its own attributes. This modeling approach allows you to efficiently represent different types of employees while sharing common attributes.

**Aggregation:**

Aggregation is a modeling concept that represents a whole-part relationship between entities. It's used to indicate that an entity is composed of other entities. In an aggregation relationship, the whole entity contains one or more parts. Aggregation is often depicted as a diamond shape in entity-relationship diagrams.

**Whole/Aggregating Entity:** The entity that represents the whole or container.

**Part/Aggregated Entity:** Entities that are components or parts of the whole entity.

For example, in a university database, you can represent an aggregation relationship between a "Department" (whole) and "Professor" (part) entities. Each department contains multiple professors, and if the department is deleted, the professors may still exist, but they are no longer associated with any department. This represents an aggregation because the professors can exist independently, but they are also part of a department.

In summary, generalization helps model hierarchical relationships and inheritance, while aggregation is used to represent whole-part relationships. These modeling techniques are essential for designing effective database schemas that accurately reflect the structure and associations of the real-world data they represent.

Q31. What is aggregation? Give example. (RU BCA 2017)

**Answer:**

**Aggregation** in the context of databases and data modeling refers to a relationship between entities where one entity is composed of other entities, typically described as a whole-part relationship. This concept is used to represent the idea that an entity can be broken down into smaller, related entities. Here's an example to illustrate aggregation:

Consider a database for a library. You may have entities like "Library" and "Book." In this case, an aggregation relationship can be established between these two entities because a library is composed of multiple books. The "Library" entity is the whole (the container), and the "Book" entity is the part (the items within the container).

Let's break this down:

**Whole Entity (Aggregating Entity):** "Library"

**Part Entity (Aggregated Entity):** "Book"

The aggregation relationship here represents the fact that a library is made up of many individual books. It allows you to connect and associate books with a specific library. If you remove a book from the library, it still exists but is no longer part of that library's collection.

In an entity-relationship diagram, you might represent this aggregation relationship using a diamond shape connecting the "Library" and "Book" entities, indicating that a library contains books. This diagrammatic representation makes it clear that books are part of the library.

Q32. Explain fundamental operations of Relational Algebra. (RU BCA 2019)

**Answer:**

Relational algebra is a formal system used to manipulate relations (tables) in a relational database. It consists of a set of operations that can be applied to one or more relations to retrieve, filter, combine, and transform data. The fundamental operations of relational algebra are as follows:

**Selection (σ):** The selection operation is used to retrieve rows from a relation that satisfy a given condition (predicate). The syntax for selection is σ_condition(relation), where "condition" is the predicate that specifies the criteria for selecting rows.

Example: σ(Salary > 50000)(Employee) selects all rows from the "Employee" relation where the salary is greater than 50,000.

**Projection (π):** The projection operation is used to retrieve specific columns (attributes) from a relation while discarding others. The syntax for projection is π_attribute1, attribute2, ... (relation).

Example: π(EmployeeName, Department)(Employee) retrieves only the "EmployeeName" and "Department" attributes from the "Employee" relation.

**Cross Product (◊):** The cross product operation combines all rows from one relation with all rows from another relation, creating a new relation with every possible combination of rows.

Example: R ◊ S combines all rows from relation R with all rows from relation S, generating a new relation.

**Set Union (∪):** The union operation takes two relations with the same schema and returns a new relation that includes all distinct rows from both relations.

Example: R ∪ S returns a relation containing all distinct rows from R and S.

**Set Difference (-):** The set difference operation takes two relations with the same schema and returns a new relation containing all rows present in the first relation but not in the second relation.

Example: R - S returns a relation containing all rows from R that are not in S.

**Set Intersection (∩):** The set intersection operation takes two relations with the same schema and returns a new relation containing all rows present in both relations.

Example: R ∩ S returns a relation containing all rows that are common to both R and S.

**Join (⋈):** The join operation combines rows from two relations based on a common attribute, creating a new relation. Various types of joins exist, including inner join, left outer join, right outer join, and full outer join, which define how non-matching rows are handled.

Example: R ⋈ S, where R and S share a common attribute, joins rows from R and S based on that attribute.

These fundamental operations can be used in combination to perform complex queries and transformations on relational data. Relational algebra provides a formal foundation for query languages like SQL used in relational databases.

Q34. What is Database system? [Marks: 2] (RTU MCA 2022)

**Answer:**

A database system refers to a complex system designed to enable the storage, retrieval, and management of data in a structured and efficient manner. It typically consists of two main components: the database management system (DBMS) and the actual databases themselves.

**Database Management System (DBMS):** This is the software that interacts with end users, applications, and the database itself to capture and analyze the data. The DBMS software allows for data to be defined, created, maintained, and controlled access. It ensures that the data is consistent, secure, and easily accessible to authorized users. DBMS can support various database models, such as relational, document, key-value, graph, or object-oriented models.

**Databases:** These are the collections of data that are organized in a way that facilitates efficient data retrieval, insertion, update, and delete operations. The data can be organized in tables, documents, graphs, or objects, depending on the type of DBMS being used.

Together, the DBMS and the databases form a database system that provides an efficient and secure way to store, manage, and query data. Database systems are crucial in various applications, ranging from small systems like personal address books to complex systems like national identity card databases, financial systems, and internet-based applications that handle billions of transactions each day.

Q35. What is PL/SQL? [Marks: 2] (RTU MCA 2022)

**Answer:**

PL/SQL stands for "Procedural Language extensions to SQL," and it is Oracle Corporation's procedural extension for SQL and the Oracle relational database. PL/SQL is integrated into the Oracle Database (since version 7), and it adds programming constructs that are not available in standard SQL, making it a powerful tool for managing the data in Oracle databases.

PL/SQL seamlessly integrates with SQL, the standard query language used for managing and manipulating databases. It allows developers to write complex database applications using control structures, variables, and procedures that are not possible with standard SQL alone. Here are some key features and capabilities of PL/SQL:

**Block Structure:** PL/SQL is executed in blocks, which may contain declarations, executable commands, and exception handling parts. This structure helps organize and encapsulate logic for reuse and readability.

**Procedural Constructs:** Unlike SQL, which is declarative, PL/SQL includes procedural constructs such as loops, conditional statements (IF-THEN-ELSE), and error handling (EXCEPTIONS), allowing for sophisticated flow control and complex processing logic.

**Integration with SQL:** PL/SQL allows for the embedding of SQL statements within its blocks, enabling seamless data manipulation and querying within a procedural framework.

**Stored Procedures and Functions:** PL/SQL supports stored procedures and functions, which are stored in the database for reuse. These can be called from SQL statements, other PL/SQL blocks, or externally from client applications.

**Triggers:** PL/SQL can be used to write triggers, which are stored procedures that automatically execute in response to specific events on a particular table or view in the database, such as insertions, updates, or deletions.

**Packages:** PL/SQL allows developers to group related procedures, functions, variables, and other elements into packages, improving organization and encapsulation.

PL/SQL is specifically designed for the Oracle Database and is used extensively in enterprise environments for developing robust, secure, and efficient database applications. Its tight integration with SQL, combined with the power of procedural programming, makes it a critical tool for Oracle database developers.

Q36. Explain the data types available in PL/SQL. [Marks: 4] (RTU MCA 2022)

**Answer**

PL/SQL, Oracle Corporation's procedural language extension to SQL, supports a variety of data types that allow programmers to define variables, constants, and parameters. These data types provide the flexibility to work with different kinds of data, from simple numeric and string data to complex records and collections. Here's an overview of the main data types available in PL/SQL:

**Scalar Data Types**

These are simple data types that hold a single value:

**Numeric Types:**

**NUMBER**: Stores fixed and floating-point numbers. You can specify precision and scale.

**PLS_INTEGER** or **BINARY_INTEGER**: Stores integers in the range of -2^31 to 2^31-1, offering faster arithmetic operations compared to **NUMBER**.

**FLOAT**: Specifies a floating-point number with binary precision.

**BINARY_FLOAT** and **BINARY_DOUBLE**: Provide single and double precision floating-point numbers, respectively, conforming to IEEE standards.

**Character Types:**

**CHAR**: Fixed-length character data, with a maximum size of 2000 bytes.

**VARCHAR2**: Variable-length character data, with a maximum size of 4000 bytes.

**NCHAR** and **NVARCHAR2**: Used for Unicode character data. **NCHAR** is fixed-length, and **NVARCHAR2** is variable-length.

**Date and Time Types:**

**DATE**: Stores date and time information including the year, month, day, hour, minute, and second.

**TIMESTAMP**, **TIMESTAMP WITH TIME ZONE**, **TIMESTAMP WITH LOCAL TIME ZONE**: Provide more precise control over time and timezone information than the **DATE** type.

**Boolean Type:**

**BOOLEAN**: Represents logical values **TRUE**, **FALSE**, and **NULL**.

**Large Object (LOB) Data Types**

These types are designed to store large amounts of data:

**BLOB**: Stores binary large objects without character set semantics.

**CLOB** and **NCLOB**: Store large blocks of character data, with **CLOB** using the database's default character set and **NCLOB** supporting Unicode.

**Composite Data Types**

These types allow multiple values:

**RECORD**: A composite type that can contain multiple fields, each with its own data type. Records are similar to structures in C or objects in Java without methods.

**TABLE** and **VARRAY (Variable-size array)**: Collections of elements that can be of the same data type. **TABLE** types are unbounded, while **VARRAYs** have a fixed maximum size but can contain a varying number of elements up to that maximum.

**Reference Data Types**

**REF CURSOR**: A pointer to a cursor that can be dynamically defined and opened for fetching rows from a database. Useful for returning result sets from stored procedures and functions.

**Other Types**

PL/SQL also supports user-defined types (object types), which can encapsulate both data and related behaviors (methods) as a single entity, much like classes in object-oriented programming languages.

This wide range of data types in PL/SQL provides the tools necessary for developers to handle various data management tasks efficiently and effectively, enabling the development of robust database applications.

Q37. Write a PL/SQL procedure for an application using user-defined and pre-defined exceptions. [Marks: 10] (RTU MCA 2022)

Answer:

```
CREATE OR REPLACE PROCEDURE TransferFunds (
p_from_account_id IN NUMBER,
p_to_account_id IN NUMBER,
p_amount IN NUMBER
) AS
User-defined exception for an invalid account
e_invalid_account EXCEPTION;
User-defined exception for insufficient funds
e_insufficient_funds EXCEPTION;
Variables to hold account balances
v_from_account_balance NUMBER;
v_to_account_balance NUMBER;
BEGIN
Check if from_account exists and retrieve balance
SELECT balance INTO v_from_account_balance
FROM accounts
WHERE account_id = p_from_account_id
FOR UPDATE; -- Lock the row for update

Check if to_account exists and retrieve balance
SELECT balance INTO v_to_account_balance
FROM accounts
```

```
WHERE account_id = p_to_account_id
FOR UPDATE; -- Lock the row for update

Check for sufficient funds in from_account
IF v_from_account_balance < p_amount THEN
RAISE e_insufficient_funds;
END IF;

Deduct the amount from the from_account
UPDATE accounts SET balance = balance - p_amount
WHERE account_id = p_from_account_id;

Add the amount to the to_account
UPDATE accounts SET balance = balance + p_amount
WHERE account_id = p_to_account_id;

Commit the transaction
COMMIT;

DBMS_OUTPUT.PUT_LINE('Transfer successful.');

EXCEPTION
WHEN NO_DATA_FOUND THEN
RAISE e_invalid_account;
WHEN e_insufficient_funds THEN
DBMS_OUTPUT.PUT_LINE('Error: Insufficient funds in the from_account.');
ROLLBACK; -- Roll back the transaction
WHEN e_invalid_account THEN
DBMS_OUTPUT.PUT_LINE('Error: One or both account IDs are invalid.');
ROLLBACK; -- Roll back the transaction
WHEN OTHERS THEN
DBMS_OUTPUT.PUT_LINE('An unexpected error occurred: ' || SQLERRM);
ROLLBACK; -- Roll back the transaction
END TransferFunds;
/
```

## ONLINE RESOURCES

**Practice Paper Link:** https://forms.gle/w31oBA33kTaZw7RH8

**QR Code:**

**Video Content:** https://www.youtube.com/playlist?list=PLzlh_31VWEFpHf2teQUBkgicMGxz1s3vV

**QR Code:**

# Chapter 2: The Structured Query Language (SQL)

## Data Manipulation Language (DML)

Data Manipulation Language (DML) is a subset of SQL (Structured Query Language) used to interact with and manipulate data stored in a relational database management system (DBMS). DML primarily consists of SQL statements for querying, inserting, updating, and deleting data within database tables. Below are detailed explanations of common DML statements:

**SELECT Statement (Data Retrieval):**

Purpose: The SELECT statement retrieves data from one or more tables in the database.

Syntax:
```
SELECT column1, column2, ...
FROM table_name
WHERE condition;
```

Explanation:

SELECT: Specifies the columns to retrieve or use `*` to select all columns.

FROM: Specifies the table(s) from which to retrieve data.

WHERE (optional): Filters rows based on a specified condition.

**INSERT Statement (Data Insertion):**

Purpose: The INSERT statement adds new records (rows) to a table.

Syntax:
```
INSERT INTO table_name (column1, column2, ...)
VALUES (value1, value2, ...);
```

Explanation:

INSERT INTO: Specifies the target table.

(column1, column2, …): Lists the columns to insert data into.

VALUE: Provides corresponding values for each column.

**UPDATE Statement (Data Modification):**

Purpose: The UPDATE statement modifies existing records in a table.

Syntax:
```
UPDATE table_name
SET column1 = value1, column2 = value2, ...
WHERE condition;
```

Explanation:

UPDATE: Specifies the table to be updated.

SET: Assigns new values to columns.

WHERE (optional): Specifies the rows to be updated based on a condition.

**DELETE Statement (Data Deletion):**

Purpose: The DELETE statement removes records from a table.

Syntax:
```
DELETE FROM table_name
WHERE condition;
```

Explanation:

DELETE FROM: Specifies the table from which to delete data.

WHERE (optional): Filters rows to be deleted based on a condition.

**MERGE Statement (Upsert Operation):**

Purpose: The MERGE statement performs an "upsert" operation, which means it inserts a row if it doesn't exist or updates it if it does.

Syntax:
```
MERGE INTO target_table AS target
USING source_table AS source
ON condition
WHEN MATCHED THEN
UPDATE SET column1 = value1, ...
WHEN NOT MATCHED THEN
 INSERT (column1, column2, ...)
VALUES (value1, value2, ...);
```

Explanation:

MERGE INTO: Specifies the target table and aliases it as "target."

USING: Specifies the source table and aliases it as "source."

ON: Defines the condition to match records.

WHEN MATCHED and WHEN NOT MATCHED clauses allow for different actions based on whether a match is found or not.

DML statements are essential for manipulating the data stored in a relational database. These statements enable you to query for specific information, insert new data, update existing data, and remove data as needed. Properly constructed DML statements ensure data accuracy, integrity, and consistency within the database.

**Procedural DML:**

Specifies How: Procedural DMLs are designed to specify not only "what" data operations should be performed but also "how" they should be carried out. They involve detailed step-by-step instructions to achieve a specific data manipulation task.

Precise Control: Programmers using procedural DMLs have precise control over the sequence of operations. They need to specify every detail, including iteration and conditional logic, for achieving the desired outcome.

Complexity: Procedural DMLs tend to be more complex and require a deeper understanding of programming concepts. Developers need to handle data access and control flow explicitly.

Examples: SQL/PSM (SQL/Persistent Stored Modules) and PL/SQL (Procedural Language/SQL) are examples of procedural DMLs used in relational database systems like Oracle and PostgreSQL.

**Non-Procedural DML:**

Specifies What: Non-procedural DMLs focus solely on "what" data operations should be performed, leaving the "how" to the database management system (DBMS). Instead of specifying a step-by-step procedure, users declare their data requirements.

Higher Abstraction: Non-procedural DMLs provide a higher level of abstraction. Users describe their data needs in a declarative manner without getting into implementation details.

Simplicity: They are often simpler for end-users because they don't need to be concerned with programming logic. Users state what data they want without specifying how to retrieve it.

Examples: SQL (Structured Query Language) is a prime example of a non-procedural DML. Users write SQL queries that declare what data they want from the database, and the DBMS's query optimizer determines the most efficient way to retrieve it.

In summary, the key difference between procedural and non-procedural DMLs lies in how they approach data manipulation. Procedural DMLs require developers to specify both "what" and "how," providing precise control but with added complexity. Non-procedural DMLs, like SQL, focus on "what" and leave the "how" to the DBMS, offering a higher level of abstraction and simplicity for users.

**DML precompiler**

A DML (Data Manipulation Language) precompiler is a software tool or program that processes SQL statements embedded within a host programming language. Its primary purpose is to enable the seamless integration of database manipulation operations, such as inserting, updating, deleting, and querying data, within a larger application written in a host programming language.

Here's a breakdown of the key components and functions of a DML precompiler:

Integration with Host Programming Language: A DML precompiler is designed to work with a specific host programming language, such as C, C++, COBOL, or Java. It allows SQL statements to be embedded directly into the code of the host program, making it easier to perform database operations from within the application.

Preprocessing SQL Statements: When a program containing embedded SQL statements is compiled or processed, the DML precompiler performs an initial preprocessing step. During this phase, the precompiler identifies SQL statements, validates their syntax, and prepares them for execution.

Binding Variables: DML precompilers facilitate the binding of program variables to SQL parameters. This binding allows values from the host program to be passed to the SQL statements dynamically at runtime. It ensures that data can be exchanged between the application and the database.

Error Handling: DML precompilers often provide mechanisms for handling database errors that may occur during SQL statement execution. They allow programmers to define error-handling routines or conditions to gracefully manage exceptions.

Optimization: Some DML precompilers offer query optimization capabilities. They can analyze SQL statements and generate efficient query plans for database access, improving overall performance.

Code Generation: After preprocessing and optimization, the DML precompiler generates the necessary code for database access. This code typically includes calls to database libraries or APIs that execute the SQL statements.

Compilation: The resulting code, which combines the host programming language and SQL statements, is then compiled using the appropriate compiler for the host language. This generates an executable program that can interact with the database.

Execution: When the compiled program runs, it can execute the embedded SQL statements as part of its operations. This allows the application to perform CRUD (Create, Read, Update, Delete) operations on the associated database. DML precompilers are valuable tools for developers working on applications that require database connectivity. They help streamline the integration of database operations into application code, ensuring data can be accessed and manipulated efficiently while maintaining compatibility with the host programming language.

**Data Definition Language (DDL)**

Data Definition Language (DDL) is a subset of SQL (Structured Query Language) that focuses on defining and managing the structure of a relational database. DDL statements are used to create, modify, and delete database objects, such as tables, indexes, and constraints. DDL is essential for database schema design and maintenance. Below are detailed explanations of common DDL statements and their roles:

CREATE Statement (Creating Database Objects):

Purpose: The CREATE statement is used to create new database objects, including tables, indexes, views, and more.

Syntax: CREATE object_type object_name

(column1 datatype1, column2 datatype2, ...);

Explanation:

CREATE: Specifies the creation of a new object.

object_type: Defines the type of object to create (e.g., TABLE, INDEX, VIEW).

object_name: Specifies the name of the object being created.

(column1 datatype1, column2 datatype2, ...): Specifies the columns and their data types for tables, or other relevant parameters for other object types.

ALTER Statement (Modifying Database Objects):

Purpose: The ALTER statement is used to modify existing database objects, such as adding, modifying, or deleting

Syntax: ALTER object_type object_name

action;

columns in a table.

Explanation:

ALTER: Specifies the modification of an existing object.

object_type and object_name: Define the type and name of the object to be altered.

action: Specifies the action to perform, such as adding or modifying columns.

**DROP Statement (Deleting Database Objects):**

Purpose: The DROP statement is used to delete database objects, including tables, indexes, and views.

Syntax: DROP object_type object_name;

Explanation:

DROP: Specifies the removal of an existing object.

object_type and object_name: Define the type and name of the object to be dropped.

TRUNCATE Statement (Emptying Tables):

Purpose: The TRUNCATE statement is used to delete all rows from a table, effectively emptying the table.

Syntax: TRUNCATE TABLE table_name;

Explanation:

TRUNCATE TABLE: Specifies the emptying of a table.

table_name: Specifies the name of the table to be truncated.

**COMMENT Statement (Adding Comments):**

Purpose: The COMMENT statement is used to add comments or descriptions to database objects for documentation purposes.

Syntax: COMMENT ON object_type object_name IS 'comment_text';

Explanation:

COMMENT ON: Specifies the addition of comments.

object_type and object_name: Define the type and name of the object to be commented.

comment_text: Provides the descriptive comment.

RENAME Statement (Renaming Database Objects):

Purpose: The RENAME statement is used to change the name of an existing database object.

Syntax: ALTER object_type object_name RENAME TO new_name;

Explanation:

ALTER: Specifies the modification of an existing object.

object_type and object_name: Define the type and current name of the object to be renamed.

RENAME TO new_name: Specifies the new name for the object.

DDL statements are essential for defining and managing the database schema. They allow database administrators and designers to create, modify, and delete database objects, ensuring the database structure remains accurate and aligned with application requirements. Care should be taken when using DDL statements, as they can have a significant impact on the database structure and data.

**How DDL is different from DML**

DDL (Data Definition Language) and DML (Data Manipulation Language) are two categories of SQL (Structured Query Language) used for interacting with relational databases. They serve distinct purposes in managing and manipulating the database. Here's how DDL differs from DML:

Purpose:

DDL (Data Definition Language): DDL is used for defining, modifying, and managing the structure of the database schema. It deals with tasks related to creating, altering, and dropping database objects like tables, indexes, and constraints.

DML (Data Manipulation Language): DML, on the other hand, is used for manipulating the data stored within the database. It handles tasks like inserting, updating, retrieving, and deleting data from database tables.

Examples:

DDL Examples:

CREATE TABLE: Defines a new table structure.

ALTER TABLE: Modifies an existing table structure.

DROP TABLE: Deletes an existing table.

CREATE INDEX: Defines an index on one or more table columns.

DML Examples:

SELECT: Retrieves data from one or more tables.

INSERT INTO: Adds new rows of data to a table.

UPDATE: Modifies existing data within a table.

DELETE FROM: Removes rows from a table.

Impact:

DDL: DDL statements impact the database schema's structure. When you execute DDL statements, you are making structural changes to the database, which may involve creating, altering, or deleting database objects. These changes are permanent and affect the database's overall design.

DML: DML statements affect the actual data stored within the database. When you execute DML statements, you are adding, modifying, or deleting data in the database tables. These changes are temporary and can be rolled back if needed.

Transaction Control:

DDL: DDL statements typically result in an implicit commit of the current transaction. This means that changes made using DDL are immediately permanent and cannot be rolled back within the same transaction.

DML: DML statements are part of a transaction and can be explicitly committed or rolled back. This allows for more fine-grained control over data changes and transaction management.

User Privileges:

DDL: DDL statements often require higher-level privileges because they involve making structural changes to the database. Users may need special permissions to execute DDL commands.

DML: DML statements typically require regular data manipulation privileges, which are often granted to a wider range of users.

DDL and DML are two distinct categories of SQL commands. DDL is used for defining and managing the database's structure, while DML is used for manipulating the data stored within the database. They serve different purposes, have different impacts on the database, and are used by different types of users with varying levels of privileges.

## SQL Functions and Operators

SQL functions and operators are essential components of the Structured Query Language (SQL) used for data manipulation and transformation within a relational database management system (DBMS). They allow you to perform various operations on data, from simple arithmetic calculations to string manipulation and aggregation. Below, we provide a detailed explanation of common SQL functions and operators:

**SQL Functions:**

**Aggregate Functions**

Purpose: Aggregate functions operate on sets of rows and return a single result. Common aggregate functions include:

COUNT(): Counts the number of rows in a set.

SUM(): Calculates the sum of numeric values in a set.

AVG(): Computes the average of numeric values in a set.

MIN(): Retrieves the minimum value in a set.

MAX(): Retrieves the maximum value in a set.

Example: To find the average salary of employees in a department:

SELECT AVG(Salary) FROM Employees WHERE Department = 'HR';

**String Functions:**

Purpose: String functions manipulate character strings, such as:

CONCAT(): Concatenates two or more strings.

SUBSTRING(): Extracts a portion of a string.

UPPER(): Converts a string to uppercase.

LOWER(): Converts a string to lowercase.

LENGTH(): Returns the length of a string.

Example: To concatenate first and last names:

SELECT CONCAT(FirstName, ' ', LastName) FROM Employees;

**Date and Time Functions:**

Purpose: Date and time functions manipulate date and time values, including:

NOW(): Retrieves the current date and time.

DATE_FORMAT(): Formats a date in a specific way.

DATE_ADD(): Adds a specified interval to a date.

DATEDIFF(): Calculates the difference between two dates.

Example: To find the number of days between two dates:

SELECT DATEDIFF('2023-09-15', '2023-08-01') AS DaysDifference;

**Mathematical Functions:**

Purpose: Mathematical functions perform calculations on numeric values, such as:

ABS(): Returns the absolute value of a number.

ROUND(): Rounds a number to a specified decimal place.

CEIL(): Rounds a number up to the nearest integer.

FLOOR(): Rounds a number down to the nearest integer.

Example: To calculate the square root of a number:

SELECT SQRT(25) AS SquareRoot;

**SQL Operators:**

**Arithmetic Operators:**

Arithmetic operators (+, -, *, /) perform mathematical calculations on numeric values.

Example: To calculate the total cost of items in an order:

```
SELECT Quantity * UnitPrice AS TotalCost FROM OrderDetails;
```

**Comparison Operators:**

Comparison operators (=, <>, <, >, <=, >=) are used to compare values in expressions.

Example: To find employees with a salary greater than $50,000:

```
SELECT * FROM Employees WHERE Salary > 50000;
```

**Logical Operators:**

Logical operators (AND, OR, NOT) are used to create complex conditions in SQL queries.

Example: To find employees in the HR department who are managers:

```
SELECT * FROM Employees WHERE Department = 'HR' AND JobTitle = 'Manager';
```

**Concatenation Operator:**

The concatenation operator (|| or + in some DBMS) combines strings.

Example: To create a full address from multiple columns:

```
SELECT Street || ', ' || City || ', ' || State AS FullAddress FROM Addresses;
```

SQL functions and operators are powerful tools for transforming and manipulating data within a database. They enable you to perform calculations, manipulate strings, format dates, and create complex conditions to retrieve and process data effectively. Understanding and using these functions and operators is essential for SQL query development and database management.

## SQL Fundamentals

SQL (Structured Query Language) is a domain-specific language used for managing and manipulating relational databases in Database Management Systems (DBMS). SQL serves as the primary means of interacting with databases, allowing users to perform various operations such as data retrieval, insertion, updating, and deletion. Here are the fundamentals of SQL:

**Data Retrieval (SELECT):**

SELECT: The core SQL command for retrieving data from one or more database tables.

FROM: Specifies the table(s) from which to retrieve data.

WHERE: Filters data based on specified conditions.

ORDER BY: Sorts the result set in ascending or descending order.

GROUP BY: Groups rows with similar values into summary rows.

HAVING: Filters grouped rows based on specified conditions.

**Data Manipulation (INSERT, UPDATE, DELETE):**

INSERT INTO: Adds new rows to a table.

UPDATE: Modifies existing data in a table.

DELETE: Removes rows from a table.

**Table Operations:**

CREATE TABLE: Creates a new table with specified columns and data types.

ALTER TABLE: Modifies an existing table, adding or removing columns or constraints.

DROP TABLE: Deletes an entire table and its data.

**Data Constraints:**

PRIMARY KEY: Enforces uniqueness of values in a column, typically used to identify each row uniquely.

FOREIGN KEY: Establishes relationships between tables by referencing a column in another table.

UNIQUE: Ensures that values in a column are unique.

CHECK: Defines conditions that must be met for data to be valid.

DEFAULT: Specifies a default value for a column if no value is provided during insertion.

**Joins:**

INNER JOIN: Combines rows from two or more tables based on a related column, returning only matching rows.

LEFT (OUTER) JOIN: Combines rows from two or more tables, returning all rows from the left table and matching rows from the right table.

RIGHT (OUTER) JOIN: Similar to the left join but returns all rows from the right table.

FULL (OUTER) JOIN: Combines all rows from both tables, filling in missing values with NULLs.

**Aggregate Functions:**

COUNT: Counts the number of rows in a result set.

SUM: Calculates the sum of values in a column.

AVG: Computes the average of values in a column.

MIN: Retrieves the minimum value in a column.

MAX: Retrieves the maximum value in a column.

**Subqueries:** Nested queries that can be used within other SQL statements to retrieve data based on the results of the subquery.

**Views:** Virtual tables created from the result of a SELECT query, allowing users to access and manipulate data without altering the underlying tables.

**Transactions:** A set of SQL statements that are treated as a single unit of work, ensuring that either all statements are executed successfully or none of them are, maintaining data consistency.

SQL is a powerful tool for working with relational databases, and its understanding is fundamental for database administrators, developers, and data analysts. It provides the means to manage data effectively, extract meaningful insights, and maintain data integrity within a DBMS.

**Disadvantages of SQL**

SQL (Structured Query Language) is a widely used language for managing and querying relational databases. While SQL offers numerous advantages, it also comes with some disadvantages, including:

Complex Syntax: SQL queries can become complex, especially for tasks involving multiple tables and complex joins. Writing and understanding complex SQL queries can be challenging for some users.

Vendor-Specific Implementations: Different database management systems (DBMS) have their own variations and extensions of SQL. Code that works on one DBMS may not work on another without modification. This can lead to vendor lock-in and compatibility issues.

Performance Overhead: SQL queries can introduce performance overhead, especially for complex queries or when working with large datasets. Inefficient queries, improper indexing, and lack of query optimization can slow down database operations.

Limited Scalability: Traditional relational databases can face scalability challenges when dealing with massive amounts of data and high-velocity data streams. Scaling SQL databases horizontally can be complex and expensive.

Lack of Support for Unstructured Data: SQL is primarily designed for structured data, making it less suitable for handling unstructured or semi-structured data types such as JSON, XML, or free text.

Normalization Complexity: While normalization is a best practice in database design, it can lead to complex schema designs with numerous tables and relationships. This complexity can make it harder to work with the data.

Learning Curve: SQL can have a steep learning curve for beginners. Mastering SQL requires understanding various concepts like data modeling, schema design, and query optimization.

Limited Support for Hierarchical Data: SQL databases are not well-suited for handling hierarchical or tree-like data structures. Managing hierarchical data can be cumbersome.

Security Concerns: SQL databases can be vulnerable to security threats like SQL injection attacks if not properly protected. Ensuring data security requires implementing appropriate security measures.

Cost: Some commercial SQL database systems come with licensing costs, which can be a significant expense for businesses. Open-source alternatives are available but may lack certain features.

Data Type Limitations: SQL databases may have limitations in handling certain data types or custom data structures. This can be a constraint when dealing with specialized data.

## Advanced SQL Features

Advanced SQL features in a Database Management System (DBMS) go beyond the basic operations and provide powerful capabilities for data manipulation and querying. Here are some advanced SQL features:

**Stored Procedures and Functions:**

Stored Procedures: Sets of SQL statements that can be executed as a single unit. They are stored in the database and can be called by applications.

Functions: Similar to stored procedures but return a single value. They are often used in SQL queries.

**Triggers:**

Database Triggers: Are automatic actions that occur in response to certain database events, such as INSERT, UPDATE, or DELETE operations on specific tables. Triggers are often used to enforce data integrity rules or perform auditing.

**Dynamic SQL:**

Dynamic SQL Statements: SQL statements that are constructed and executed at runtime. This allows for flexibility in creating queries based on variable conditions.

**Common Table Expressions (CTEs):**

CTEs: Temporary result sets that can be referenced within a SELECT, INSERT, UPDATE, or DELETE statement. They simplify complex queries and make them more readable.

**Window Functions:**

Window Functions: Analytic functions that perform calculations across a set of table rows related to the current row. They are useful for tasks such as calculating running totals and ranking results.

**Recursive Queries:**

Recursive Queries: SQL queries that can reference their own output, enabling hierarchical data retrieval. They are particularly useful for working with tree structures or organizational hierarchies.

**Pivoting and Unpivoting:**

Pivoting: Transforms rows into columns, making it easier to analyze data in a cross-tabular format.

Unpivoting: The reverse operation of pivoting, converting columns into rows for more flexible data analysis.

**XML and JSON Support:**

XML: SQL databases often provide functions and operators for querying and manipulating XML data.

JSON: Similar to XML, SQL databases can work with JSON data, allowing for storage and querying of structured document data.

**Full-Text Search:**

Full-Text Search: Allows for efficient searching of text data within database columns, making it suitable for applications like search engines and content management systems.

**Materialized Views:**

Materialized Views: Precomputed result sets stored as tables, which can be periodically refreshed. They are used to improve query performance for complex and frequently executed queries.

**User-Defined Types (UDTs):**

UDTs: Custom data types defined by users to encapsulate complex or domain-specific data structures.

**Advanced Joins:**

Self-Joins: Joining a table with itself to create relationships within the same table.

Non-Equi Joins: Joining tables using operators other than equality (e.g., greater than or less than).

Outer Joins with Filtering: Combining outer joins with additional filtering conditions for complex result sets.

These advanced SQL features empower database professionals to perform sophisticated data operations, optimize query performance, and handle complex data scenarios effectively. They are essential tools for working with large and complex databases in various application domains.

## Embedded SQL

Embedded SQL is a powerful feature in Database Management Systems (DBMS) that allows SQL statements to be included directly within a programming language's source code. It enables seamless interaction between application code and a database, making it easier to retrieve and manipulate data. Here are the key aspects of Embedded SQL:

**Integration with Programming Languages:** Embedded SQL is typically integrated with popular programming languages like C/C++, COBOL, Java, and others. This integration allows developers to embed SQL statements directly within their code.

**Preprocessing:** Before the application code is compiled, a preprocessor scans it for embedded SQL statements. These statements are identified and separated from the host language code.

**Variable Binding:** Embedded SQL allows for the binding of program variables to SQL placeholders. This means that values can be passed between the program and the SQL statement dynamically, making applications highly flexible.

**SQL Execution:** When the program runs, the embedded SQL statements are executed by the DBMS. The results are returned to the program, which can then process and use the data as needed.

**Error Handling:** Embedded SQL provides mechanisms for handling database errors within the host language code. This enables developers to implement error-checking and error-handling routines.

**Static and Dynamic SQL:** Embedded SQL supports both static and dynamic SQL statements. Static SQL statements are known at compile time, while dynamic SQL statements are constructed at runtime, often based on user input or other variables.

**Security:** Embedded SQL helps ensure that SQL statements are properly parameterized, reducing the risk of SQL injection attacks. By binding variables to placeholders, developers can prevent malicious input from compromising database security.

**Performance:** Embedded SQL can lead to better performance in database operations compared to using external SQL queries because the SQL statements are optimized by the DBMS at compile time.

**Portability:** Applications with embedded SQL statements can be ported to different DBMSs with minimal code changes. This makes it easier to switch to a different database system if needed.

**Use Cases:** Embedded SQL is commonly used in applications where direct database interaction is required, such as banking systems, enterprise resource planning (ERP) software, and real-time data processing applications.

Overall, embedded SQL streamlines the development of database-driven applications by allowing developers to work with both programming logic and database operations in a unified environment. It enhances the security, performance, and maintainability of applications that rely on database connectivity.

## Dynamic SQL

Dynamic SQL is a powerful feature in Database Management Systems (DBMS) that allows SQL statements to be constructed and executed dynamically at runtime within an application or stored procedure. Unlike static SQL, where the query is known and fixed at compile time, dynamic SQL allows for flexibility in query generation. Here are key aspects of Dynamic SQL:

**Runtime Query Construction:** With Dynamic SQL, you can build SQL statements as strings in your application code or stored procedure based on runtime conditions or user inputs. This dynamic construction enables you to create queries tailored to specific requirements.

**Parameterized Queries:** Dynamic SQL supports parameterized queries, where placeholders are used in the SQL statement for values that will be supplied later. This helps prevent SQL injection attacks by separating SQL code from user input.

**Query Execution:** Once the dynamic SQL statement is constructed, it can be executed by the DBMS. The DBMS parses, optimizes, and executes the query, just as it would with static SQL.

**Flexibility:** Dynamic SQL is particularly useful when dealing with complex or conditional queries. It allows you to adapt your queries based on changing criteria, user selections, or other dynamic factors.

**Dynamic Cursors:** Dynamic SQL can also be used to create dynamic cursors, which are particularly helpful when dealing with unknown or changing result sets.

**SQL Injection Prevention:** When used correctly with parameterized queries, Dynamic SQL helps prevent SQL injection attacks because user inputs are treated as data, not executable code.

**Database Portability:** Dynamic SQL can enhance database portability by allowing the generation of SQL statements that are compatible with different DBMSs. This can simplify the process of migrating applications to different database platforms.

**Performance Considerations:** While Dynamic SQL offers flexibility, it may introduce some performance overhead, as the DBMS needs to dynamically compile and optimize queries at runtime. Caching and query plan reuse can help mitigate this.

**Use Cases:** Dynamic SQL is commonly used in scenarios where the structure or content of SQL queries needs to change dynamically, such as in report generation tools, search functionality, and data-driven applications.

**Security:** Care must be taken to properly validate and sanitize user inputs when using Dynamic SQL to prevent malicious input from compromising security.

In summary, Dynamic SQL provides a flexible and adaptable way to work with SQL statements in applications and stored procedures. It allows developers to create dynamic, parameterized queries that can respond to changing conditions or user input, making it a valuable tool in building data-driven applications.

**Exercise**

**Exercise 1 – MCQ**

Q 1. Which category of SQL is primarily used for querying and manipulating data?

A) DDL

B) DML

C) Data Modelling

D) Data Validation

Q 2. What does DDL stand for in SQL?

A) Data Definition Language

B) Data Manipulation Language

C) Database Design Language

D) Database Modelling Language

**Exercise 2 – True/ False**

Q 1. SQL is a programming language used exclusively for data manipulation and querying.

Q 2. Data Definition Language (DDL) in SQL is used for inserting, updating, and deleting data in a database.

**Exercise 3 – Fill in the blanks**

Q 1. In SQL, the abbreviation DML stands for Data __________ Language, which is used for querying and manipulating data in a database.

Q 2. The abbreviation DDL in SQL stands for Data __________ Language, which is used for defining and managing the structure of database objects.

**Exercise 4 – One word answer**

Q 1.What does DML stand for?

Q 2.Which SQL component is primarily used for creating, altering, and dropping database objects?

**Exercise 5 – Small answer**

Q 1. What is the primary purpose of Data Manipulation Language (DML) in SQL?

Q 2. Explain the role of Data Definition Language (DDL) in SQL.

**Exercise 6 – Long answer**

Q 1. Explain the key components and concepts of Data Manipulation Language (DML) in SQL. How do DML statements like SELECT, INSERT, UPDATE, and DELETE facilitate the manipulation of data within a relational database?

Q 2. Describe the key components of Data Definition Language (DDL) in SQL. How do DDL statements like CREATE, ALTER, DROP, and TRUNCATE contribute to the design and management of a relational database?

**Answer**

**Exercise 1**

Answer 1. B), 2. A)

**Exercise 2**

Answer 1: False, 2: False

**Exercise 3**

Answer 1: Manipulation, 2: Definition

**Exercise 4**

Answer 1: Data Manipulation Language, 2: DDL (Data Definition Language)

**Previous Years Questions**

Q1. Consider the following tables: (IGNOU MCA 2010)

Working (P_name, C_name, Salary)

Living (P_name, Street, City)

Located (C_name, city)

When P_name = Professor name,

C-name = College name.

Write the SQL Queries for the following.

a) List the names and cities they live in, of the professors who are working for the college C1

b) Find the name, street and city of the professors who are working for the college C2 and are having a salary more than 60000/-.

c) Find the names of professors who live and work in the same city.

d) Find the names of the professors who do not work for college C3.

e) Find the professors whose salaries are less than that of all of the college C4 employees.

f) Display college wise total salary.

Q2. Define the term DML precompiler. (IGNOU MCA 2010)

Q3. Differentiate between the followings: Procedural and Non-Procedural DMLs. (IGNOU MCA 2010)

Q4. Explain insert, delete and update anomalies for a relation (R), with examples. (IGNOU MCA 2011)

Q5. Write SQL statements to perform following queries on the given relations i.e. Employee (Empid, Emp_name, Dept_id)

a) Department (Dept_id, Dept_name, Dept_loc, Emp_id)

b) List the names of employees whose name starts with 'S'

c) To sort the employee data, in the alphabetic descending order.

d) Find total number of employees.

e) Find the department number and number of employees working in each department. (IGNOU MCA 2011)

Q6. Describe the following: Disadvantages of SQL (IGNOU MCA 2011)

Q7. Consider the following Tables:

Works (Pname, Cname, salary)

LIVES (Pname, street, city)

LOCATED (Cname, city)

MANAGER (Pname, Mname)

Write queries in SQL for the following

a) List the names of the people who work for the company Wipro along with the cities they live in.

b) Find the people who work for the company 'Infosys' having salary greater than Rs - 50000/-

c) List the names of the people, along with the street and city addresses.

d) Find the persons whose salaries are more than that of all of the 'Oracle' employees.

e) And the name of the persons who do not work in 'Infosys'.

f) Find the average salary of the employee in company named `accenture'.

g) Create a table for the above relation using SQL - DDL (viii) Create a view consisting of the person's name along with their manager's name and company name. (IGNOU MCA 2011)

Q8. Explain the GROUPBY clause. What is the differences between the WHERE and HAVING clause in SQL? (IGNOU MCA 2013)

Q9. Define a view? How is it different from a table? Write the SQL Syntax for creating a view. (IGNOU MCA 2013)

Q10. What is DDL? How it is different from DML? Briefly explain guidelines for creation of table (IGNOU MCA 2014)

Q11. What are nested queries? explain with the help of an example. (IGNOU MCA 2014)

Q12. Consider the following relations

STUDENT (Name, Roll_Number, Teacher_ID, Programme, Semester, Subject)

DEPARTMENT (Dep_ID, Programme, Teacher_ID)

TEACHER(Teacher_ID,Dep_ID, Name, Subject)

Write the following queries using SQL:

a) List name of all the teachers who belong to Dep_ID ='4' and take "Graph Theory", subject.

b) List names of all the students who study in Semester-II of BCA programme and are taught by Teacher_ID = '1'.

c) Find the name of all the teachers who teaches to the student whose ROLL Number ='101'.

d) Find the name of all the students who are in Is' semester of MCA programme and are taught by Prof. Ajay. (IGNOU MCA 2014)

Q13. A bookshop has a huge collection of books to sell them online and therefore requires a database to track its sales. For each book they store the Title, Author(s) name, Publisher, Volume, ISBN No., Price, Stock (no. of copies), Year of publication, etc. To help the customers to search the book, they require that each book is assigned to one or more categories such as Engineering, Sciences, Fiction, Literature, Applications, etc. If at all, any discounts that are there for certain books, need to be notified on the site (best-buy offer). To buy a book, a customer needs to register on the site. Also, it maintains the profile of the user and also their earlier purchases. The bookshop also sends "Newsletter" to all the registered users to update them about the publications.

Identify the entities, relationships, constraints and cardinality and construct an ER diagram for the above-mentioned specifications. (IGNOU MCA 2015)

Q14. Explain the working of GROUP BY clause. What is the difference between the WHERE and HAVING clause in SQL? (IGNOU MCA 2016)

Q15. Consider the Relational Database Schema given below:

Employee (empcode, empname, empaddress, salary)

Department (deptcode, deptname, deptlocation)

Perform the following queries using SQL and Relational Algebra:

a) Find details of the departments located in Delhi.

b) Find the names of employees whose salary is more than 4 lakhs per annum. (IGNOU MCA 2016)

Q16. With the help of a suitable example, discuss the insertion, deletion and updation anomalies that can occur in a database. Briefly discuss the mechanism to remove such anomalies. (IGNOU MCA 2017)

Q17. Write SQL commands for each of the following. Also illustrate the usage of each command through suitable example. (i) Creation of views (ii) Creation of sequences (iii) Outer join (iv) To give access permission to any user. (IGNOU MCA 2017)

Q18. Consider the following relational schema: Student (Student_ID, student_name, program) Course (Course_ID, Course_name, school_of studies) Taught (Student_ID, Course_ID, Year, Instructor ID) Write SQL statements for the following:

a) To retrieve the names of all 3rd year students of MCA Program who have done courses under Instructor ID-001

b) To retrieve the names of all courses taught by instructor-002 between 1996-2001 and total number of students attended the courses.

Q19. Compare Embedded SQL with dynamic SQL. (ANNA University M.Sc 2013)

**Previous Years Questions with Answer**

Q1 Define instance and schema in DBMS? (RU BCA 2022)

**Answer:**

In a database management system (DBMS), the terms "instance" and "schema" are used to describe different aspects of the database:

**Instance:Database Instance:** The term "instance" in a DBMS context refers to the actual data stored in the database at a specific point in time. It represents the current state or snapshot of the data within the database. The instance includes all the rows and columns of data as they exist in the database tables.

**Database Server Instance:** In some cases, "instance" can also refer to a specific running instance of a DBMS, particularly in the context of database servers. A DBMS may support multiple databases, and each database may have its own instance of the DBMS server running. These instances allow multiple databases to coexist and operate independently on the same DBMS server.

**Schema:Database Schema:** A database schema is a logical container or structure that defines the organization of the database objects, such as tables, views, indexes, and relationships. It specifies the design and layout of the database, including the structure of tables, data types, constraints, and relationships between tables. A schema provides a blueprint for how data is stored and organized within the database.

**Schema Objects:** Within a database schema, there are various schema objects, such as tables, views, indexes, stored procedures, and functions. These objects define the structure and functionality of the database. Each schema object belongs to a specific schema, and this organization helps in managing and accessing database objects.

In summary, the "instance" of a database refers to the current data content, while the "schema" defines the logical structure, organization, and design of the database objects. The schema specifies how data is stored and the relationships between data elements. Understanding the distinction between instance and schema is crucial in the context of managing and querying a database.

Q2 What is purpose of SQL? (RU BCA 2022)

**Answer:**Structured Query Language (SQL) serves as a powerful and standardized tool for managing, querying, and manipulating relational databases. Its primary purpose is to provide a means for users and applications to interact with relational database management systems (RDBMS) to achieve several key objectives:

Data Querying: SQL allows users to retrieve data from a database using SELECT statements. Users can specify criteria to filter, sort, and aggregate the data, making it easy to extract specific information from large datasets.

Data Manipulation: SQL enables users to insert, update, and delete data in a database using INSERT, UPDATE, and DELETE statements. This facilitates data maintenance and ensures the accuracy and integrity of the information stored.

Data Definition: SQL supports the creation, modification, and deletion of database structures and objects, including tables, indexes, views, and constraints, using CREATE, ALTER, and DROP statements.

Data Security: SQL provides mechanisms for defining user access privileges and roles, allowing database administrators to control who can perform specific operations on the data, ensuring data security and integrity.

Data Integrity: SQL supports the enforcement of data integrity constraints through the use of unique constraints, primary keys, foreign keys, and check constraints, helping maintain the quality and consistency of data.

Data Transactions: SQL transactions (BEGIN, COMMIT, and ROLLBACK) ensure that a series of database operations are executed as a single unit of work, guaranteeing that either all the changes are applied or none of them are, preventing data inconsistencies.

Data Aggregation and Reporting: SQL offers powerful aggregation functions (e.g., SUM, AVG, COUNT) and grouping capabilities (GROUP BY) to analyze and summarize data, making it ideal for generating reports and analytics.

Data Joins: SQL supports the ability to combine data from multiple tables using JOIN operations, facilitating complex data retrieval and analysis across related datasets.

Data Validation: SQL can be used to validate and enforce data quality by defining rules and constraints, reducing the risk of erroneous data entry.

Data Migration: SQL is essential for transferring data between different databases or systems, making it possible to import/export data and maintain data consistency during the migration process.

Data Optimization: SQL allows for the optimization of database queries through techniques like indexing, query tuning, and performance analysis, ensuring efficient data retrieval.

Data Triggers and Stored Procedures: SQL can be used to define triggers and stored procedures, which are pre-defined sets of actions that can automatically execute in response to specific events, improving automation and data consistency.

In summary, SQL serves as a comprehensive and essential tool for managing and interacting with relational databases, making it possible to store, retrieve, manipulate, and secure data effectively. Its versatility and widespread adoption make it a fundamental skill for anyone working with databases or data-driven applications.

Q3 What is difference between CHAR and VARCHAR2 data type in SQL? (RU BCA 2022)

**Answer:**

In SQL, CHAR and VARCHAR2 are two different data types used to store character strings, but they have some key differences in terms of storage and behavior:

Length and Storage:

CHAR: The CHAR data type stores fixed-length character strings. When you define a CHAR column with a specific length, it always uses that length, padding the stored value with spaces to fill the entire length. For example, if you define a CHAR(10) column and store "hello" in it, it will be stored as "hello " (with six spaces at the end).

VARCHAR2: The VARCHAR2 data type stores variable-length character strings. It only uses as much storage as needed for the actual data. For example, if you define a VARCHAR2(10) column and store "hello" in it, it will be stored as "hello" (without any extra spaces).

Space Efficiency:

CHAR consumes more storage space because it always reserves the defined length, even if the actual data is shorter. This can be inefficient when storing strings with varying lengths, as you may end up with a lot of wasted space.

VARCHAR2 is more space-efficient as it only uses as much storage as required by the actual data. It's a better choice for variable-length strings.

Performance:

CHAR can be slightly faster for exact-match searches because the lengths are always fixed, which simplifies comparison operations.

VARCHAR2 is generally more efficient when dealing with varying-length data, as it saves storage space and can improve query performance by reducing I/O and memory usage.

Trailing Spaces:

CHAR columns always pad the data with spaces to the defined length, which means that trailing spaces are included in the stored value.

VARCHAR2 does not pad the data with spaces, so trailing spaces are not included in the stored value.

In practice, you would choose between CHAR and VARCHAR2 based on your specific needs. If you have a column with a fixed length for which data length will not vary, CHAR may be appropriate. However, for most scenarios where data lengths can vary, VARCHAR2 is the more commonly used and space-efficient choice.

Q4 What is (Data manipulation language)? (RU BCA 2022)

**Answer:**Data Manipulation Language (DML) is a subset of SQL (Structured Query Language) that is used for managing data within a relational database management system (RDBMS). DML focuses on the following key operations:

**SELECT**: DML allows you to retrieve data from one or more tables. The SELECT statement is used to specify the columns you want to retrieve and apply conditions to filter the data. You can also perform operations like sorting and grouping data. It is primarily used for querying and reporting purposes.

**INSERT**: DML enables you to add new records (rows) to a table using the INSERT statement. You provide values for each column when inserting a new row.

**UPDATE**: DML allows you to modify existing records in a table using the UPDATE statement. You specify which columns to change and the new values, as well as a condition to identify the rows to be updated.

**DELETE**: DML allows you to remove records from a table using the DELETE statement. You provide a condition to identify the rows to be deleted.

These DML operations are crucial for managing the data stored in a database. They provide the means to add, modify, retrieve, and delete data, which are fundamental tasks when working with relational databases.
DML statements are often used in conjunction with Data Definition Language (DDL) statements, which are responsible for defining and managing the structure of the database, such as creating tables, indexes, and constraints. Together, DML and DDL statements form the core of SQL for managing and interacting with relational databases.

Q5 Write short notes on: (RU BCA 2022)
Operation of relation algebra
Loss-less decomposition
Advantages of SQL
**Answer:**Operation of Relation Algebra:
Relation algebra is a formal system for manipulating and querying sets of data in a relational database. It consists of various operations that can be applied to relations (tables) to retrieve, filter, and transform data. Some common operations include:
Selection (σ): This operation selects rows from a relation that satisfy a given condition.
Projection (π): Projection selects specific columns from a relation, creating a new relation with a subset of the original columns.
Union (∪) and Intersection (∩): These set operations combine or find common elements between two relations, respectively.
Join (⋈): The join operation combines two relations based on a specified condition, often used to relate data from multiple tables.
Rename (ρ): Renaming is used to provide alternate names for relations or attributes.
These operations are essential for performing queries, data manipulation, and database design in the context of relational databases.
Loss-less Decomposition:
Loss-less decomposition is a property of the process of decomposing a relational schema into smaller, related schemas (tables) while ensuring that no information is lost in the process.
When a relational schema is decomposed, the goal is to create smaller tables that are still able to represent all the information from the original schema.
Loss-less decomposition is crucial to maintain the integrity and consistency of data. It ensures that you can reconstruct the original data by joining the decomposed tables without any loss of information.
One common method to achieve loss-less decomposition is to decompose tables so that the join of the resulting smaller tables is equivalent to the original table (this property is known as the "join property").
Advantages of SQL:
SQL (Structured Query Language) is a powerful and widely used language for managing relational databases. Its advantages include:

**Data Retrieval**: SQL provides a straightforward and efficient way to retrieve data from databases, making it easy to query and report on large datasets.

**Data Manipulation**: SQL allows for data modification using INSERT, UPDATE, and DELETE statements, enabling the maintenance and integrity of data.

**Data Definition**: SQL supports the creation, modification, and deletion of database structures like tables, indexes, views, and constraints using CREATE, ALTER, and DROP statements.

**Data Security**: SQL provides fine-grained access control, allowing administrators to define user privileges, ensuring data security and privacy.

**Data Integrity**: SQL enforces data integrity through constraints, ensuring the quality and consistency of data.

**Data Aggregation and Reporting**: SQL offers powerful aggregation functions and grouping capabilities, making it suitable for generating reports and analytics.

**Data Optimization**: SQL allows for query optimization through techniques like indexing, improving query performance.

**Data Portability**: SQL is a standardized language, ensuring that SQL-based databases are interoperable and can be migrated to different database systems.

**Data Automation**: SQL supports stored procedures and triggers for automating tasks and maintaining data consistency.

These advantages make SQL an essential tool for working with relational databases, and it is widely used in various applications, including web development, business intelligence, and data analysis

Q6 Define entities and attributes? (RU BCA 2021)

**Answer:**In the context of database management and data modeling, "entities" and "attributes" are fundamental concepts:

**Entity**:

An entity represents a distinct object, concept, or thing in the real world that can be uniquely identified. In a database, an entity typically corresponds to a table or a class in an entity-relationship model.

Entities are used to organize and categorize data. They are defined by their properties, which are represented by attributes.

For example, in a database for a library, entities could include "Books," "Authors," "Customers," and "Transactions." Each of these entities represents a specific category of information, and each instance of an entity (e.g., a specific book or author) can be uniquely identified within that category.

**Attribute**:

An attribute is a property or characteristic that describes an entity and provides details about it. Attributes are the specific data elements or fields that define the entity's properties.

In a database table or entity-relationship diagram, attributes are represented as columns. Each row (record) in the table represents an instance of the entity, and the values in the columns (attributes) provide information about that instance.

For example, in the "Books" entity, attributes might include "Title," "Author," "Publication Year," "ISBN," and "Genre." These attributes provide specific information about each book in the database.

In summary, entities are the high-level categories or objects that represent distinct concepts in a database, while attributes are the specific characteristics or properties associated with those entities, used to describe and organize the data within those categories. Together, entities and attributes help structure and manage data in a way that makes sense for the specific domain or application.

Q7 What is SQL. (RU BCA 2021)

**Answer:**

SQL stands for Structured Query Language. It is a domain-specific programming language used for managing and manipulating relational databases. SQL provides a standardized way to interact with relational database management systems (RDBMS) and is essential for tasks such as data retrieval, data insertion, data updates, and data deletion. It is also used for defining and modifying the structure of databases, including creating and altering tables, indexes, and constraints.

Here are some key aspects of SQL:

**Data Querying**: SQL allows users to retrieve data from a database using SELECT statements. You can specify conditions to filter, sort, and aggregate the data.

**Data Manipulation**: SQL enables users to insert new records, update existing data, and delete records using INSERT, UPDATE, and DELETE statements.

**Data Definition**: SQL is used to define the structure of a database, including creating tables (CREATE TABLE), modifying table structures (ALTER TABLE), and deleting tables (DROP TABLE).

**Data Control**: SQL provides tools for controlling and securing data access, such as defining user permissions and access privileges.

**Data Integrity**: SQL enforces data integrity through constraints like unique keys, primary keys, foreign keys, and check constraints, ensuring data accuracy and consistency.

**Data Transaction Management**: SQL supports transactions (BEGIN, COMMIT, ROLLBACK) to ensure that a series of operations are executed as a single unit of work, allowing for data consistency and reliability.

**Data Optimization**: SQL allows for query optimization techniques, such as indexing, to improve the performance of database queries.

SQL is used in various applications and industries, including web development, data analysis, business intelligence, and more. Different database management systems (e.g., MySQL, PostgreSQL, Oracle, Microsoft SQL Server) implement SQL with some variations, but the core SQL language remains consistent, making it a valuable skill for working with relational databases.

Q8 Define view. (RU BCA 2021)

**Answer:**

In the context of relational databases, a "view" is a virtual table that is derived from the data in one or more physical tables. It does not store data itself but instead provides a way to present data from one or more underlying tables in a structured and easily accessible format. Views are defined by SQL queries and are used to simplify data access, enhance security, and improve the manageability of a database. Here are some key characteristics and purposes of views:

**Virtual Table**: A view is not a physical table; it is a logical representation of data. It is created by defining a SELECT statement that specifies how data from one or more base tables should be displayed.

**Data Abstraction**: Views provide a level of abstraction, allowing users to work with data without needing to understand the underlying table structures or the complexity of the data relationships.

**Data Security**: Views can be used to restrict access to sensitive data. By defining views that show only specific columns or rows, you can control what data users are allowed to see, even if they have access to the underlying tables.

**Simplification**: Views simplify complex data by presenting a subset of columns or rows, or by joining multiple tables into a single view. This can make it easier to write queries and reports.

**Data Integrity**: Views can enforce data integrity by filtering out rows that do not meet certain criteria or by aggregating data in a meaningful way.

**Performance Optimization**: Views can also be used to precompute and store aggregated or calculated data, reducing the need to perform complex calculations in queries, which can improve query performance.

**Ease of Maintenance**: Views can make database maintenance easier because changes to the underlying tables can be abstracted from the users, and modifications to the view definition can be made without affecting applications that use the view.

**Reusability**: Views can be reused in multiple queries or applications, providing a consistent way to access and present data.

Creating a view typically involves using a CREATE VIEW statement in SQL. To query data from a view, you use the view's name just like you would with a regular table. The database system processes the view definition and returns the result as if it were a physical table.

Q9 Explain advantages and disadvantages of DBMS. (RU BCA 2021)

**Answer:** A Database Management System (DBMS) is a software system that allows users to store, manage, and retrieve data efficiently in a structured way. DBMS offers numerous advantages, but it also comes with some disadvantages. Here is an overview of both:

**Advantages of DBMS:**

**Data Integrity**: DBMS enforces data integrity by defining constraints and relationships, ensuring that data remains accurate and consistent.

**Data Security**: DBMS provides user authentication and authorization features, allowing control over who can access and modify data, improving data security.

**Data Redundancy Reduction**: DBMS minimizes data redundancy by promoting a central repository for data, reducing the chances of inconsistencies.

**Data Sharing**: Multiple users and applications can access the data concurrently, promoting data sharing and collaboration.

**Data Independence**: DBMS separates the physical data storage from the logical data model, making it easier to change the database structure without affecting applications.

**Data Query Language**: DBMS offers a structured query language (SQL) for efficient data retrieval and manipulation.

**Concurrent Access and Transactions**: DBMS manages concurrent access to data and ensures that transactions are ACID-compliant (Atomic, Consistent, Isolated, Durable).

**Data Backup and Recovery**: DBMS includes features for data backup and recovery, reducing the risk of data loss due to hardware failures or other issues.

**Data Scalability**: DBMS systems can scale to handle larger datasets and more users as an organization's needs grow.

**Centralized Management**: A DBMS centralizes database management tasks like backup, security, and optimization, making it easier to maintain data.

**Disadvantages of DBMS:**

**Cost**: DBMS software can be expensive to purchase and maintain. Smaller organizations may find it challenging to afford these systems.

**Complexity**: Setting up and managing a DBMS can be complex, requiring expertise and resources, which can be a disadvantage for small businesses.

**Performance Overhead**: DBMS introduces some performance overhead due to query processing, transaction management, and other system processes.

**Data Security Concerns**: While DBMS systems offer security features, they can also be vulnerable to security breaches if not configured and managed properly.

**Data Backup and Recovery Complexity**: While DBMS provides backup and recovery mechanisms, the process can be complex and time-consuming, especially for large databases.

**Data Size Limitations**: Some DBMS systems may have limitations on the size of the database they can handle.

**Vendor Lock-In**: Organizations may become dependent on a specific DBMS vendor, making it difficult and costly to switch to another system.

**Resource Consumption**: DBMS systems can consume significant system resources, including memory and processing power.

**Learning Curve**: Users and administrators need to learn how to use and manage the specific DBMS, which can have a learning curve.

**Potential for Data Corruption**: Misconfigurations or software errors in the DBMS can lead to data corruption or loss.

In summary, while DBMS offers many advantages for efficient and structured data management, it also comes with some inherent complexities and costs that organizations need to consider when deciding whether to implement a database management system. The choice of a DBMS should be based on the specific needs and resources of the organization.

Q10 Write short note: (RU BCA 2021)

Characteristics of SQL

Type of SQL commands

**Answer:**

**Characteristics of SQL**:

SQL (Structured Query Language) is a domain-specific language for managing and manipulating relational databases. Its characteristics include:

**Declarative Language**: SQL is a declarative language, meaning you specify what you want to achieve rather than how to achieve it. You describe the desired results, and the database system determines the most efficient way to execute the query.

**Standardized**: SQL is an industry-standard language, and most relational database management systems (RDBMS) support it to some extent. While there are variations in SQL dialects across RDBMS platforms, the core SQL syntax remains fairly consistent.

**Data Query and Manipulation**: SQL supports a wide range of operations, including data retrieval (SELECT), data insertion (INSERT), data modification (UPDATE), and data deletion (DELETE), making it versatile for working with data.

**Set-Based Operations**: SQL operates on sets of data, allowing you to manipulate multiple records at once. This makes it powerful for querying and manipulating large datasets.

**Data Integrity and Constraints**: SQL provides mechanisms for defining data integrity constraints like primary keys, foreign keys, unique constraints, and check constraints to maintain data quality and consistency.

**Data Control**: SQL offers features for managing user access and privileges, allowing administrators to control who can access and modify data.

**Transaction Support**: SQL supports transactions, ensuring that a series of database operations are executed as a single unit of work. This guarantees data consistency and reliability.

**Joins**: SQL enables the combining of data from multiple tables through various join operations, facilitating complex queries that retrieve related data.

**Aggregation and Grouping**: SQL provides aggregation functions like SUM, COUNT, and AVG, as well as grouping capabilities (GROUP BY) for summarizing and analyzing data.

**Types of SQL Commands**:

SQL commands can be categorized into several types based on their purpose:

**Data Query Language (DQL)**:

SELECT: Retrieves data from one or more tables based on specified conditions.

**Data Definition Language (DDL)**:

CREATE: Defines new database objects such as tables, indexes, and views.

ALTER: Modifies the structure of existing database objects.

DROP: Deletes database objects.

TRUNCATE: Removes all data from a table, but retains the table structure.

**Data Manipulation Language (DML)**:

INSERT: Adds new records (rows) to a table.

UPDATE: Modifies existing data in a table.

DELETE: Removes records from a table.

**Data Control Language (DCL)**:

GRANT: Provides specific privileges to users or roles.

REVOKE: Removes specific privileges from users or roles.

**Transaction Control Language (TCL)**:

COMMIT: Saves changes made during the current transaction.

ROLLBACK: Reverts changes made during the current transaction.

SAVEPOINT: Sets a point within a transaction to which you can later roll back.

These types of SQL commands cover a wide range of tasks, from defining the database structure to querying and managing data, as well as controlling access and transactions.

Q11 Explain DML in SQL. (RU BCA 2019)

**Answer:**

DML, or Data Manipulation Language, is a subset of SQL (Structured Query Language) that focuses on manipulating and managing data within a relational database. DML consists of a set of commands that allow you to perform various operations on the data stored in database tables. The primary purpose of DML is to insert, update, and delete data, as well as to retrieve data from tables. Some common DML commands and their explanations include:

**INSERT**:

The INSERT statement is used to add new records (rows) to a table.

You specify the table in which you want to insert data and provide values for each column in the form of a new row.

For example:

sqlCopy code INTO employees (employee_id, first_name, last_name) VALUES (101, 'John', 'Doe');

**UPDATE**:

The UPDATE statement is used to modify existing data in a table.

You specify the table, set new values for one or more columns, and use a WHERE clause to specify the condition that identifies the rows to be updated.

For example:

UPDATE customers SET email = 'newemail@example.com' WHERE customer_id = 123;

**DELETE**:

The DELETE statement is used to remove records from a table.

You specify the table and use a WHERE clause to determine which rows should be deleted.

For example:

DELETE FROM orders WHERE order_id = 456;

**SELECT**:

While SELECT is often considered a Data Query Language (DQL) command, it is a critical part of data manipulation as well. The SELECT statement retrieves data from one or more tables.

You specify the columns you want to retrieve, apply conditions to filter the data, and can perform various operations like sorting and aggregation.

For example:

SELECT first_name, last_name FROM employees WHERE department = 'HR';

DML commands are essential for maintaining the accuracy and integrity of data in a relational database. They are used to insert new data, update existing records, delete unnecessary information, and retrieve specific data for reporting and analysis. In conjunction with Data Definition Language (DDL) commands, which are used to define and manage the structure of the database, DML forms the core set of commands for interacting with relational databases

Q12 Describe types of SQL commands. (RU BCA 2019)

**Answer:**

SQL (Structured Query Language) commands can be categorized into several types based on their purpose and functionality. The primary types of SQL commands are as follows:

**Data Query Language (DQL) Commands**:

**SELECT**: DQL commands are used to retrieve data from one or more tables. The SELECT statement allows you to specify the columns you want to retrieve and apply conditions to filter, sort, and aggregate the data.

**Data Definition Language (DDL) Commands**:

**CREATE**: DDL commands are used for defining and managing the structure of the database. The CREATE statement is used to create new database objects such as tables, indexes, and views.

**ALTER**: The ALTER statement modifies the structure of existing database objects. You can use it to add, modify, or drop columns, constraints, and other attributes.

**DROP**: The DROP statement is used to delete existing database objects, including tables, indexes, views, and more.

**TRUNCATE**: The TRUNCATE command removes all data from a table, but it retains the table structure, such as columns and constraints.

**Data Manipulation Language (DML) Commands**:

**INSERT**: DML commands are used to insert new records (rows) into a table. The INSERT statement allows you to specify the table and provide values for each column.

**UPDATE**: The UPDATE statement is used to modify existing data in a table. You specify the table, set new values for one or more columns, and use a WHERE clause to specify the condition that identifies the rows to be updated.

**DELETE**: The DELETE statement is used to remove records from a table. You specify the table and use a WHERE clause to determine which rows should be deleted.

**Data Control Language (DCL) Commands**:

**GRANT**: DCL commands are used for controlling user access and privileges. The GRANT statement provides specific privileges to users or roles, allowing them to perform actions on specific database objects.

**REVOKE**: The REVOKE statement removes specific privileges from users or roles, restricting their access to certain database objects.

**Transaction Control Language (TCL) Commands**:

**COMMIT**: TCL commands are used to manage transactions. The COMMIT command is used to save changes made during the current transaction, making the changes permanent.

**ROLLBACK**: The ROLLBACK command is used to revert changes made during the current transaction, restoring the data to its previous state.

**SAVEPOINT**: The SAVEPOINT command sets a point within a transaction to which you can later roll back. It provides a way to partially undo changes within a transaction.

These types of SQL commands cover a wide range of tasks, from defining the database structure to querying and managing data, controlling access and transactions, and specifying user privileges. SQL commands are essential for interacting with relational databases and managing data effectively.

Q13 What do you understand by view and index in SQL? Explain each with suitable example. (RU BCA 2019)

**Answer:**

In SQL, "view" and "index" are two database objects that serve different purposes:

**View**:

A view is a virtual table that is derived from the data in one or more physical tables (base tables). It does not store data itself but provides a way to present data from one or more underlying tables in a structured and easily accessible format.

Views are primarily used for simplifying data access, enhancing data security, and improving the manageability of a database.

Views can be used to restrict the visibility of certain columns, join tables, or aggregate data in a way that makes querying more convenient.

A view is defined by a SQL query, and users can query it as if it were a regular table.

Here's an example of creating a simple view:

Let's assume we have two tables: **employees** and **departments**. We want to create a view that shows the names of employees and their corresponding department names.

```
CREATE VIEW EmployeeDepartment AS
SELECT e.employee_name, d.department_name
```

```
FROM employees e
JOIN departments d ON e.department_id = d.department_id;
```

Once the view is created, you can query it just like a table:

```
SELECT * FROM EmployeeDepartment;
```

**Index**:

An index is a database object used to improve the speed of data retrieval operations on database tables. It is an optional structure that enhances the efficiency of queries by providing a faster way to access data.

Indexes work like the index in a book, where you can quickly locate specific information without reading the entire book. In a similar way, database indexes allow the database management system to quickly locate rows of data without scanning the entire table.

Indexes are typically created on one or more columns of a table. When you perform a query that involves the indexed column(s), the database can use the index to find the data more efficiently.

Here's an example of creating an index:

Let's assume we have a table named **products**, and we frequently search for products by their name. To speed up these searches, you can create an index on the **product_name** column.

```
CREATE INDEX idx_product_name ON products(product_name);
```

With this index in place, when you search for a product by name, the database can use the index to locate the data more quickly:

```
SELECT * FROM products WHERE product_name = 'Example Product';
```

Indexes can significantly improve query performance for read-heavy operations. However, they come with some trade-offs, such as increased storage requirements and potential overhead for write operations, so they should be used judiciously based on the specific needs of the database.

Q14 Write a note on type of SQL commands and SQL operators. (RU BCA 2018)

**Answer:**

**Types of SQL Commands**:

SQL commands are categorized into several types based on their functionality:

**Data Query Language (DQL) Commands**:

**SELECT**: DQL commands are used to retrieve data from one or more tables. The SELECT statement allows you to specify the columns you want to retrieve and apply conditions to filter, sort, and aggregate the data.

**Data Definition Language (DDL) Commands**:

**CREATE**: DDL commands are used for defining and managing the structure of the database. The CREATE statement is used to create new database objects such as tables, indexes, and views.

**ALTER**: The ALTER statement modifies the structure of existing database objects. You can use it to add, modify, or drop columns, constraints, and other attributes.

**DROP**: The DROP statement is used to delete existing database objects, including tables, indexes, views, and more.

**TRUNCATE**: The TRUNCATE command removes all data from a table, but it retains the table structure, such as columns and constraints.

**Data Manipulation Language (DML) Commands**:

**INSERT**: DML commands are used to insert new records (rows) into a table. The INSERT statement allows you to specify the table and provide values for each column.

**UPDATE**: The UPDATE statement is used to modify existing data in a table. You specify the table, set new values for one or more columns, and use a WHERE clause to specify the condition that identifies the rows to be updated.

**DELETE**: The DELETE statement is used to remove records from a table. You specify the table and use a WHERE clause to determine which rows should be deleted.

**Data Control Language (DCL) Commands**:

**GRANT**: DCL commands are used for controlling user access and privileges. The GRANT statement provides specific privileges to users or roles, allowing them to perform actions on specific database objects.

**REVOKE**: The REVOKE statement removes specific privileges from users or roles, restricting their access to certain database objects.

**Transaction Control Language (TCL) Commands**:

**COMMIT**: TCL commands are used to manage transactions. The COMMIT command is used to save changes made during the current transaction, making the changes permanent.

**ROLLBACK**: The ROLLBACK command is used to revert changes made during the current transaction, restoring the data to its previous state.

**SAVEPOINT**: The SAVEPOINT command sets a point within a transaction to which you can later roll back. It provides a way to partially undo changes within a transaction.

**SQL Operators**:

SQL operators are used to perform operations on data in SQL queries. Some common SQL operators include:

**Arithmetic Operators**:

+ (Addition)

- (Subtraction)

* (Multiplication)

/ (Division)

% (Modulo)

**Comparison Operators**:

= (Equal to)

!= or <> (Not equal to)

< (Less than)

> (Greater than)

<= (Less than or equal to)

>= (Greater than or equal to)

**Logical Operators**:

**AND** (Logical AND)

**OR** (Logical OR)

**NOT** (Logical NOT)

**Concatenation Operator**:

|| (Concatenates two or more strings)

**Assignment Operator**:

= (Assigns a value to a variable or column)

**IS NULL Operator**:

**IS NULL** (Tests if a value is NULL)

**LIKE Operator**:

**LIKE** (Performs pattern matching in text data)

These SQL operators are used in SELECT statements to perform various operations on data, including mathematical calculations, comparisons, logical operations, and text manipulation. They are an essential part of SQL queries for filtering, sorting, and transforming data.

Q15 Define Instances. (RU BCA 2018)

**Answer:**

Database management systems (DBMS), an "instance" refers to a specific occurrence or realization of a database at a particular point in time. More specifically:

**Database Instance**:

A database instance is a running, operational database system. It includes the database's data, metadata, and the processes necessary for the database to function.

A database instance can be thought of as the database in its active state, with data accessible for queries and updates.

In the context of some DBMSs, like Oracle Database, a database instance is a collection of memory structures and background processes that manage the physical data files on disk.

**Object Instance**:

In object-oriented programming and data modeling, an object instance represents a single occurrence or realization of a class or object type. It is an individual, unique instance of a class, with its own set of attributes and values.

For example, if you have a class "Person," an object instance of that class might represent a specific individual with attributes like name, age, and address.

**Software Instance**:

In a broader sense, a software instance refers to a running copy of a software application or service. It represents the execution of the software at a particular point in time.

For example, in a cloud-based environment, you might have multiple instances of a web application running to handle different user requests.

In summary, "instance" can refer to different concepts depending on the context. In the database context, it usually refers to a running database system, while in object-oriented programming, it represents a specific occurrence of a class, and in a broader software context, it denotes the running state of a software application or service.

Q16 Discuss the characteristics and advantages of SQL. (RU BCA 2018)

**Answer:**

SQL (Structured Query Language) is a domain-specific language used for managing and manipulating relational databases. It offers several characteristics and advantages that make it a powerful tool for working with data. Here are some key characteristics of SQL and its associated advantages:

**Characteristics of SQL**:

**Declarative Language**: SQL is a declarative language, meaning you specify what you want to achieve rather than how to achieve it. You describe the desired results, and the database system determines the most efficient way to execute the query. This abstraction simplifies database querying and management.

**Standardized Language**: SQL is an industry-standard language, and most relational database management systems (RDBMS) support it to some extent. While there are variations in SQL dialects across RDBMS platforms, the core SQL syntax remains fairly consistent. This standardization promotes interoperability and portability of database solutions.

**Data Query and Manipulation**: SQL supports a wide range of operations, including data retrieval (SELECT), data insertion (INSERT), data modification (UPDATE), and data deletion (DELETE). It is versatile for working with data in various ways.

**Set-Based Operations**: SQL operates on sets of data, allowing you to manipulate multiple records at once. This makes it powerful for querying and manipulating large datasets, promoting efficiency and simplicity.

**Data Integrity and Constraints**: SQL provides mechanisms for defining data integrity constraints like primary keys, foreign keys, unique constraints, and check constraints. These constraints ensure that data remains accurate and consistent.

**Data Control**: SQL offers features for managing user access and privileges, allowing administrators to control who can access and modify data. This is critical for data security and privacy.

**Transaction Support**: SQL supports transactions, ensuring that a series of database operations are executed as a single unit of work. This guarantees data consistency and reliability by ensuring that all operations succeed or fail as a unit.

**Joins**: SQL enables the combining of data from multiple tables through various join operations. This is essential for performing complex queries that retrieve related data from multiple sources.

**Advantages of SQL**:

**Data Retrieval**: SQL provides a straightforward and efficient way to retrieve data from databases, making it easy to query and report on large datasets.

**Data Manipulation**: SQL allows for data modification using INSERT, UPDATE, and DELETE statements, enabling the maintenance and integrity of data.

**Data Definition**: SQL supports the creation, modification, and deletion of database structures like tables, indexes, views, and constraints using CREATE, ALTER, and DROP statements.

**Data Security**: SQL provides fine-grained access control, allowing administrators to define user privileges, ensuring data security and privacy.

**Data Integrity**: SQL enforces data integrity through constraints, ensuring the quality and consistency of data.

**Data Aggregation and Reporting**: SQL offers powerful aggregation functions and grouping capabilities, making it suitable for generating reports and analytics.

**Data Optimization**: SQL allows for query optimization through techniques like indexing, improving query performance.

**Data Portability**: SQL is a standardized language, ensuring that SQL-based databases are interoperable and can be migrated to different database systems.

**Data Automation**: SQL supports stored procedures and triggers for automating tasks and maintaining data consistency.

These advantages make SQL an essential tool for working with relational databases. It is widely used in various applications, including web development, business intelligence, data analysis, and more.

Q17 What is mean by minus in SQL? (RU BCA 2018)

**Answer:**

In SQL, the **MINUS** operator is used to retrieve the result set from the first query, excluding any rows that are also returned by a second query. Essentially, it performs a set difference operation on the result sets of two SELECT statements.

Here is the basic syntax of the **MINUS** operator:

```
SELECT column1, column2, ...
FROM table1
WHERE condition
MINUS
SELECT column1, column2, ...
FROM table2
WHERE condition;
```

The first **SELECT** statement retrieves data from **table1**, and the second **SELECT** statement retrieves data from **table2**. The **MINUS** operator then returns all rows from the first query that are not present in the second query. The columns and conditions in both queries must be compatible for the operation to work correctly.

For example, suppose you have two tables, "employees" and "contractors," and you want to find employees who are not also contractors. You can use the **MINUS** operator like this:

```
SELECT employee_id, first_name, last_name
FROM employees
MINUS
```

SELECT contractor_id, first_name, last_name

FROM contractors;

The result would be a list of employees who are not in the "contractors" table.

It's important to note that the **MINUS** operator is specific to certain database systems, such as Oracle. In other database systems like MySQL or PostgreSQL, you may use the **EXCEPT** operator to achieve the same result, and the syntax may vary slightly. Additionally, not all database systems support set difference operations directly, so you might need to use alternative methods to achieve the same result in those systems.

Q18 Explain the structure of SQL SELECT statement? (RU BCA 2017)

**Answer:**

The SQL **SELECT** statement is used to retrieve data from one or more tables in a relational database. It is one of the most commonly used SQL statements for querying data. The basic structure of the **SELECT** statement consists of several clauses that allow you to specify the data you want to retrieve, filter, and manipulate. Here is the general structure of a SQL **SELECT** statement:

```
SELECT
[DISTINCT | ALL] column1, column2, ...
FROM
table_name
WHERE
condition
GROUP BY
column1, column2, ...
HAVING
condition
ORDER BY
column1 [ASC | DESC], column2 [ASC | DESC], ...
LIMIT
n;
```

Now, let's break down each part of the **SELECT** statement:

**SELECT Clause**:

The **SELECT** clause specifies the columns you want to retrieve from the table. You can list one or more column names, or you can use * to select all columns.

**DISTINCT | ALL (Optional)**:

The **DISTINCT** keyword is used to retrieve distinct (unique) values for the specified columns, removing duplicates. If omitted, all rows are returned, including duplicates.

The **ALL** keyword is the default and is rarely used. It explicitly states that all rows should be returned, including duplicates.

**FROM Clause**:

The **FROM** clause specifies the table or tables from which you want to retrieve data. You can specify one or more tables, and you can use table aliases for brevity.

**WHERE Clause (Optional)**:

The **WHERE** clause is used to filter the rows that meet a specified condition. Rows that satisfy the condition are included in the result set, and those that don't are excluded.

**GROUP BY Clause (Optional)**:

The **GROUP BY** clause is used to group the result set into subsets based on the values of one or more columns. It is typically used with aggregate functions to perform calculations on each group.

**HAVING Clause (Optional)**:

The **HAVING** clause is used to filter the groups generated by the **GROUP BY** clause. It acts like a **WHERE** clause for grouped data.

**ORDER BY Clause (Optional)**:

The **ORDER BY** clause is used to specify the order in which the result set should be sorted. You can specify one or more columns, and you can use the **ASC** (ascending) or **DESC** (descending) keywords to control the sort order.

**LIMIT Clause (Optional)**:

The **LIMIT** clause limits the number of rows in the result set to a specified number (n). It is often used for pagination or to retrieve a sample of rows from the result set.

The clauses can be combined and customized to perform complex queries that retrieve, filter, aggregate, and sort data from one or more tables. The specific usage and combinations of these clauses depend on the requirements of your query.

Q19 Explain the data types available in SQL. Also explain various aggregate functions in SQL with suitable examples. (RU BCA 2017)

**Answer:**

**Data Types in SQL**:

SQL supports a variety of data types to represent different kinds of data. These data types are used when defining the structure of tables and columns in a database. The specific data types available can vary slightly between different database management systems (DBMS), but there are common data types shared among most SQL database systems. Here are some of the commonly used data types in SQL:

**Numeric Data Types**:

**INT** or **INTEGER**: Represents whole numbers.

**NUMERIC(p, s)** or **DECIMAL(p, s)**: Represents fixed-point numbers with 'p' total digits and 's' decimal places.

**FLOAT(p)**: Represents floating-point numbers with 'p' bits of precision.

**REAL** or **DOUBLE PRECISION**: Represents double-precision floating-point numbers.

**Character String Data Types**:

**CHAR(n)**: Represents fixed-length character strings of 'n' characters.

**VARCHAR(n)**: Represents variable-length character strings with a maximum length of 'n' characters.

**TEXT**: Represents variable-length character strings without a specified maximum length.

**Date and Time Data Types**:

**DATE**: Represents a date (year, month, and day).

**TIME**: Represents a time of day.

**TIMESTAMP**: Represents a combination of date and time.

**INTERVAL**: Represents a time interval.

**Boolean Data Type**:

**BOOLEAN**: Represents true or false values.

**Binary Data Types**:

**BINARY(n)**: Represents fixed-length binary data of 'n' bytes.

**VARBINARY(n)**: Represents variable-length binary data with a maximum length of 'n' bytes.

**BLOB**: Represents large binary objects.

**Miscellaneous Data Types**:

**ENUM**: Represents a predefined set of values.

**JSON**: Represents JSON (JavaScript Object Notation) data.

**UUID**: Represents a universally unique identifier.

**Spatial Data Types**:

**GEOMETRY**, **POINT**, **LINESTRING**, **POLYGON**, etc.: Used for representing spatial data in geographical information systems (GIS).

**Aggregate Functions in SQL**:

Aggregate functions in SQL are used to perform calculations on sets of values or rows and return a single result. These functions are often used in conjunction with the **GROUP BY** clause to perform calculations on groups of rows. Here are some common aggregate functions in SQL:

**SUM**: Calculates the sum of a set of values.

Example: **SELECT SUM(salary) FROM employees;**

**AVG**: Calculates the average (mean) of a set of values.

Example: **SELECT AVG(age) FROM customers;**

**COUNT**: Counts the number of rows in a result set or the number of non-null values in a column.

Example: **SELECT COUNT(*) FROM orders;**

**MIN**: Returns the minimum value from a set of values.

Example: **SELECT MIN(price) FROM products;**

**MAX**: Returns the maximum value from a set of values.

Example: **SELECT MAX(score) FROM students;**

**GROUP_CONCAT** (or equivalent functions, e.g., **STRING_AGG** in SQL Server): Concatenates values from multiple rows into a single string, typically used with a **GROUP BY** clause.

Example: **SELECT department, GROUP_CONCAT(employee_name) FROM employees GROUP BY department;**

**COUNT DISTINCT**: Counts the number of distinct (unique) values in a column.

Example: **SELECT COUNT(DISTINCT category) FROM products;**

**Variance and Standard Deviation Functions**:

**VAR_POP** and **VAR_SAMP**: Calculate population and sample variances.

**STDDEV_POP** and **STDDEV_SAMP**: Calculate population and sample standard deviations.

Example: **SELECT VAR_POP(salary) FROM employees;**

These aggregate functions are powerful tools for summarizing and analyzing data in SQL queries, especially when you need to generate reports or calculate statistics on grouped data. The specific availability and syntax of these functions may vary between different database systems.

Q20 What is embedded SQL? (RU BCA 2016)

**Answer:**

Embedded SQL is a technique that allows SQL statements to be embedded within a program or application written in a high-level programming language, such as C, C++, Java, or COBOL. The purpose of embedded SQL is to enable the seamless integration of database operations and data manipulation within an application's code, allowing developers to access and interact with a database from within their programming language of choice. This integration combines the power of a general-purpose programming language with the data management capabilities of a database management system (DBMS).

Here are some key points about embedded SQL:

**Integration**: Embedded SQL allows developers to seamlessly integrate SQL statements into their application code, making it possible to interact with a database without needing a separate, standalone SQL script or program.

**Preprocessing**: To execute SQL statements embedded within a program, they need to be preprocessed. This involves taking the embedded SQL statements and translating them into the appropriate function calls or API (Application Programming Interface) calls that the DBMS understands. This preprocessing is typically done by a precompiler.

**Type Checking**: Embedded SQL provides type checking and validation of SQL statements within the program code, ensuring that the SQL statements are syntactically correct and that data types match properly.

**Efficiency**: Embedded SQL can improve application efficiency because database queries can be executed directly from the program, reducing the need for data transfer between the application and the database.

**Security**: Embedded SQL can provide a level of security, as it allows for the use of parameterized queries, which can help prevent SQL injection attacks by sanitizing user input.

**Portability**: Embedded SQL can make applications more portable because the SQL code is not tied to a specific DBMS. If the application is designed with embedded SQL, it can be adapted to work with different DBMSs by changing the preprocessing and API calls.

**Maintenance**: Managing the application's SQL statements within the code can make it easier to maintain and understand the application, as all related logic is in one place.

**Error Handling**: Embedded SQL enables developers to handle database errors directly in the program code, providing the flexibility to respond to errors in a way that suits the application's needs.

The specific syntax for embedded SQL varies based on the programming language and the DBMS being used. Popular programming languages like C and C++ have well-defined standards and libraries for working with embedded SQL.

Overall, embedded SQL is a valuable approach for developing database-driven applications, as it simplifies the interaction with databases and promotes the integration of data management into application logic.

Q21 What are different SQL operators? (RU BCA 2016)

**Answer:**

SQL operators are special symbols or keywords used in SQL statements to perform operations on data. These operators allow you to filter, combine, and manipulate data in your SQL queries. Here are some common SQL operators:

**Arithmetic Operators**:

+ (Addition)

- (Subtraction)

* (Multiplication)

/ (Division)

% (Modulo, returns the remainder of a division)

Example:

SELECT salary * 1.1 AS increased_salary FROM employees;

**Comparison Operators**:

= (Equal to)

!= or <> (Not equal to)

< (Less than)

> (Greater than)

<= (Less than or equal to)

>= (Greater than or equal to)

Example:

SELECT product_name FROM products WHERE price > 100;

**Logical Operators**:

**AND** (Logical AND)

**OR** (Logical OR)

**NOT** (Logical NOT)

Example:

SELECT employee_name FROM employees WHERE department = 'HR' AND salary > 50000;

**Concatenation Operator**:

|| (Concatenates two or more strings together)

Example:

SELECT first_name || ' ' || last_name AS full_name FROM employees;

**LIKE Operator**:

Used for pattern matching in text data. You can use wildcard characters:

% (Matches any sequence of characters)

_ (Matches any single character)

Example:

SELECT product_name FROM products WHERE product_name LIKE 'Widget%';

**IS NULL Operator**:

Used to test whether a value is NULL.

Example:

SELECT product_name FROM products WHERE description IS NULL;

**IN Operator**:

Tests whether a value is equal to any value in a list.

Example:

SELECT employee_name FROM employees WHERE department IN ('Sales', 'Marketing');

**BETWEEN Operator**:

Tests whether a value is within a specified range.

Example:

SELECT order_date FROM orders WHERE order_date BETWEEN '2023-01-01' AND '2023-12-31';

These SQL operators are used in combination with SQL statements such as **SELECT**, **WHERE**, **UPDATE**, and **DELETE** to perform various operations on data in a relational database. The choice of operator depends on the specific data manipulation or filtering task you want to accomplish.

Q22 Explain normalization and its different forms. Give appropriate examples. (RU BCA 2017)

**Answer:**

Normalization is a database design technique that aims to minimize data redundancy and improve data integrity by organizing data into separate related tables. The goal of normalization is to reduce data anomalies (such as insertion, update, and deletion anomalies) and improve the efficiency of data retrieval in a relational database. It involves breaking down large, complex tables into smaller, more manageable ones, each with a specific purpose and set of relationships.

Normalization is typically carried out in multiple stages or forms, each represented by a normal form (e.g., 1NF, 2NF, 3NF, BCNF, and 4NF). The higher the normal form, the more rigorously the data is organized and the fewer data anomalies are present. Let's briefly discuss the different normal forms and provide examples for each:

**First Normal Form (1NF):**

A table is in 1NF if it has no repeating groups or arrays. Each column contains atomic (indivisible) values.

Example: A table of students and their course enrollments is not in 1NF because the "Courses" column contains multiple values.

**Before 1NF:**

| Student ID | Name | Courses |
|---|---|---|
| 1 | Alice | Math, History |
| 2 | Bob | Science, Math |

**After 1NF:**

| Student ID | Name | Course |
|---|---|---|
| 1 | Alice | Math |
| 1 | Alice | History |
| 2 | Bob | Science |
| 2 | Bob | Math |

**Second Normal Form (2NF):**

A table is in 2NF if it is in 1NF, and all non-key attributes are functionally dependent on the entire primary key (no partial dependencies).

Example: A table with composite primary keys where non-key attributes depend on only part of the key.

**Third Normal Form (3NF):**

A table is in 3NF if it is in 2NF and all attributes are functionally dependent on the primary key (no transitive dependencies).

Example: A table with an attribute that depends on another non-key attribute.

**Boyce-Codd Normal Form (BCNF):**

A table is in BCNF if it is in 3NF, and for every non-trivial functional dependency ($X \rightarrow Y$), X is a superkey. In other words, every non-key attribute is functionally dependent on the primary key.

Example: A table with a composite candidate key where a non-key attribute depends on only part of the key.

**Fourth Normal Form (4NF):**

A table is in 4NF if it is in BCNF, and it does not have multi-valued dependencies.

Example: A table with multi-valued dependencies, where the presence of one value in a row implies the presence of another value in the same row.

Normalization is an iterative process, and not all databases require reaching the highest normal form. The choice of normal form depends on the specific requirements and trade-offs of the database design. Each normal form eliminates certain types of data redundancy and anomalies, making the database more efficient and reliable.

Q23 What is query and sub query in DBMS? (RU BCA 2022)

**Answer:**

In a database management system (DBMS), a query is a request for data or information from the database. It is typically expressed using SQL (Structured Query Language) and is used to retrieve, update, or manipulate data stored in the database. Queries can range from simple requests for specific data to complex operations involving multiple tables, filtering, sorting, and aggregating data.

A subquery, on the other hand, is a query that is nested inside another query. It is also known as a subselect or inner query. Subqueries are used to retrieve data that will be used by the main or outer query to further filter or process the results. Subqueries are enclosed within parentheses and are often used in the following scenarios:

**Filtering**: Subqueries can be used to filter the results of the main query based on conditions that depend on data from other tables or subqueries.

Example: Find all employees who earn more than the average salary in their department.

```
SELECT employee_name, salary
FROM employees
WHERE salary > (SELECT AVG(salary) FROM employees WHERE department_id = employees.department_id);
```

**Inclusion**: Subqueries can be used to check if a value exists in a list of values retrieved by another query.

Example: Find all products that have been ordered.

```
SELECT product_name
FROM products
WHERE product_id IN (SELECT product_id FROM order_details);
```

**Correlation**: Correlated subqueries are subqueries that reference columns from the outer query. They are used to compare values between the main query and the subquery on a row-by-row basis.

Example: Find all employees who earn more than the average salary in their department, and display the department name in the result.

```
SELECT employee_name, salary
FROM employees e
WHERE salary > (SELECT AVG(salary) FROM employees WHERE department_id = e.department_id);
```

Subqueries provide a way to break down complex tasks into more manageable steps and make SQL queries more flexible and powerful. They are a fundamental concept in SQL and are used extensively for various data retrieval and manipulation operations in a database.

Q24. Differentiate between DDL and DML. [Marks: 2] (RTU MCA 2022)

**Answer:**

DDL (Data Definition Language) and DML (Data Manipulation Language) are two types of languages used within SQL (Structured Query Language) for database management and manipulation. They serve different purposes in the context of managing and interacting with databases.

**DDL (Data Definition Language)**

DDL statements are used for defining, altering, and managing the structures of database objects such as tables, schemas, indexes, views, triggers, etc. The main operations performed using DDL include:

**CREATE:** To create new database objects.

**ALTER:** To modify existing database structures.

**DROP:** To delete objects from the database.

**RENAME:** To rename database objects.

**TRUNCATE:** To remove all records from a table, including all spaces allocated for the records are removed.

DDL commands do not manipulate data itself, rather they define or change the schema of the database. Operations performed using DDL commands are auto-committed, meaning they cannot be rolled back.

**DML (Data Manipulation Language)**

DML statements are used for managing data within database objects like tables. This includes the manipulation of data in existing objects. The main operations performed using DML include:

**SELECT:** To retrieve data from the database.

**INSERT:** To add new rows (records) to a table.

**UPDATE:** To modify existing data within a table.

**DELETE:** To remove rows from a table.

Unlike DDL, DML commands directly affect the data itself, allowing for the addition, deletion, or modification of data in a database. Operations performed with DML can be rolled back if the database is operating in a transaction mode that supports rollbacks.

In summary, DDL focuses on the structure and schema of the database, whereas DML focuses on the data itself. DDL commands result in changes to the structure of the database, which are automatically saved and cannot be undone, while DML commands modify the data and can often be rolled back if necessary.

Q25. Define instance and schema. [Marks: 2] (RTU MCA 2022)

**Answer:**

**Schema**

A schema is the structural design or blueprint of a database that defines how data is organized and how the relationships among data are associated. It specifies the tables, fields (attributes), data types, constraints, and relationships between tables. A schema is more about the logical structure of the database and does not contain any data itself. It acts as a template that describes the organization of data and standard rules for how the data can be accessed and manipulated. The schema is designed during the database design phase and usually does not change frequently.

**Instance**

An instance, on the other hand, refers to the data in the database at a particular moment in time. It is a snapshot of the database that includes all the data currently stored within its structures. An instance changes every time the database is updated, such as when data is inserted, deleted, or modified. While the schema is the static aspect of the database that outlines its structure, instances are dynamic and represent the actual content of the database as it varies over time.

To summarize, the schema is the structural design of a database, whereas an instance is the data contained within the database at any given moment. The schema is like the architectural blueprint of a building, showing the layout and design, while the instance is like the building at a specific point in time, filled with people and furniture, which changes as people move in or out and furniture is added or removed.

Q26. Consider the following database schema -

Employee (ename, street, city)

Works (ename, company-name, salary)

Company (company-name, city)

Manager (ename, mgr-name)

Give regular expression for each of the following statements - [Marks: 10] (RTU MCA 2022)

**Find the company with most employees.**

```
SELECT company-name
FROM Works
GROUP BY company-name
ORDER BY COUNT(ename) DESC
LIMIT 1;
```

**Find the company with the smallest payroll.**

```
SELECT company-name
FROM Works
GROUP BY company-name
ORDER BY SUM(salary) ASC
LIMIT 1;
```

**Give all employees of ABC Company a IO-percent salary raise.**

```
UPDATE Works
SET salary = salary * 1.10
WHERE company-name = 'ABC Company';
```

**Delete all tuples in the works relation for employee of XYZ Company.**

```
DELETE FROM Works
WHERE company-name = 'XYZ Company';
```

**Find the names and cities of residence of all employee who work for ABC Company.**

```
SELECT Employee.ename, Employee.city
FROM Employee
JOIN Works ON Employee.ename = Works.ename
WHERE Works.company-name = 'ABC Company';
```

## ONLINE RESOURCES

**Practice Paper Link** : https://forms.gle/JgsFzbGtQ7ZqX7Sh8

**QR Code:**

**Video Content:** https://www.youtube.com/playlist?list=PLzlh_31VWEFqlTQ77B1DrjW-3sVOWrXE-

**QR Code:**

# Chapter 3: Database Design

## E-R Diagrams

ER diagrams are used to represent the E-R model in a database, which makes them easy to be converted into relations (tables).

ER diagrams provide the purpose of real-world modelling of objects which makes them intently useful.

ER diagrams require no technical knowledge and no hardware support.

These diagrams are very easy to understand and easy to create even for a naive user.

It gives a standard solution for visualizing the data logically.

**Symbols Used in ER Model**

ER Model is used to model the logical view of the system from a data perspective which consists of these symbols:

| Figures | Symbols | Represents |
|---|---|---|
| Rectangle | | Entities in ER Model |
| Ellipse | | Attributes in ER Model |
| Diamond | | Relationships among Entities |
| Line | | Attributes to Entities and Entity Sets with Other Relationship Types |
| Double Ellipse | | Multi-Valued Attributes |
| Double Rectangle | | Weak Entity |

Rectangles: Rectangles represent Entities in the ER Model.

Ellipses: Ellipses represent Attributes in the ER Model.

Diamond: Diamonds represent Relationships among Entities.

Lines: Lines represent attributes to entities and entity sets with other relationship types.

Double Ellipse: Double Ellipses represent Multi-Valued Attributes.

Double Rectangle: Double Rectangle represents a Weak Entity.

## Entity-Relationship Model

The Entity-Relationship (ER) model is a fundamental conceptual framework used in Database Management Systems (DBMS) to represent and design relational databases. It provides a visual and abstract representation of the data and its relationships within an organization or system. Here are key aspects of the Entity-Relationship Model:

**Entities:** Entities represent real-world objects, concepts, or things within the domain of the database. Examples of entities could include "Customer," "Product," "Employee," or "Order.

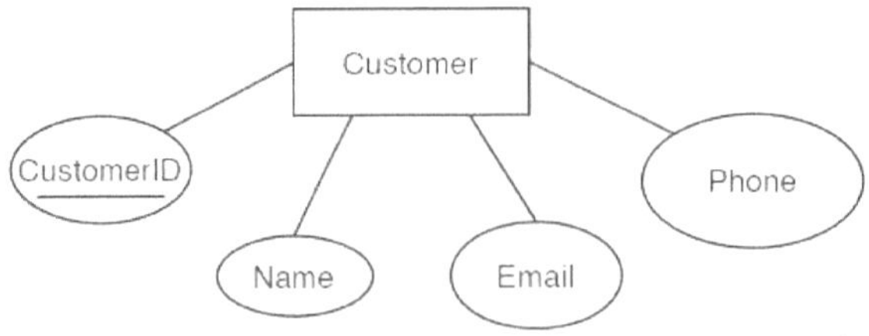


**Attributes:** Attributes are properties or characteristics of entities. Each entity has a set of attributes that describe its properties. For example, a "Customer" entity might have attributes like "CustomerID," "Name," "Email," and "Phone."

**Relationships:** Relationships define how entities are related to each other. They represent associations between entities. Relationships can have cardinality, which describes the number of instances of one entity that are related to another entity. Common cardinalities include one-to-one, one-to-many, and many-to-many.

**Key Attributes:** Each entity has one or more key attributes that uniquely identify instances of that entity. For example, in a "Customer" entity, the "CustomerID" attribute might serve as the primary key.

**Weak Entities:** Some entities may depend on other entities for their identity. These are called weak entities. They don't have a primary key attribute of their own but rely on a related strong entity for identification.

**Relationship Attributes:** In addition to entities having attributes, relationships themselves can have attributes. These attributes are specific to the relationship and describe additional information about the association between entities.

**Supertype and Subtype Entities:** In some cases, entities can be categorized into supertype and subtype entities. A supertype entity represents a general category, while subtype entities represent specific subcategories with additional attributes.

**ER Diagrams:** ER diagrams are graphical representations of the model. They use symbols like rectangles for entities, diamonds for relationships, and lines connecting them to depict the relationships and attributes.

**Normalization:** The ER model helps in the process of normalization, which is the method of organizing data in a database to minimize data redundancy and improve data integrity.

**Database Design:** The ER model serves as a blueprint for designing the relational database schema. It guides the creation of tables, defining relationships, and ensuring data consistency and accuracy.

**Communication:** ER diagrams provide a common language for communication between developers, designers, and stakeholders during the database design phase.

The Entity-Relationship model is a powerful tool for designing databases that accurately represent the real-world relationships and constraints of an organization or system. It helps in creating well-structured databases that can

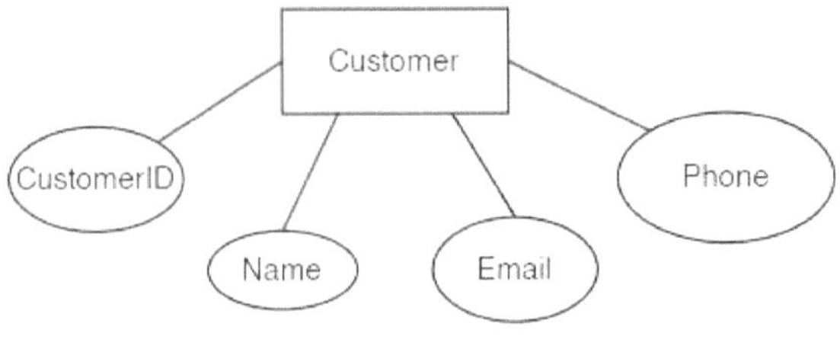

efficiently store and retrieve data, ensuring data integrity and usability.

**Generalization**

Generalization, is a process of organizing and structuring data to create higher-level, more abstract entities or concepts from lower-level, more specific ones. It is a fundamental concept in entity-relationship modelling and database design, particularly when dealing with complex and hierarchical data structures. Generalization is used to simplify the representation of data and to establish relationships between entities.

Hierarchy of Entities: Generalization involves organizing related entities into a hierarchy where higher-level entities (known as superclass or parent entities) encompass lower-level entities (known as subclass or child entities). This hierarchy represents an "is-a" relationship, where a subclass is a specific type of the superclass.

Inheritance: In the context of generalization, subclasses inherit attributes and relationships from their superclass. This means that the attributes and relationships defined for the superclass are also applicable to the subclasses. Subclasses can also have their own additional attributes and relationships that are specific to them.

Abstraction: Generalization allows for abstraction by creating more abstract, generalized entities at higher levels of the hierarchy. This abstraction simplifies the modelling of complex systems by grouping similar entities together and capturing common characteristics at the superclass level.

Example: Consider a database for a university. You might have a superclass entity called "Person," which represents individuals in the university community. "Person" can have attributes like "Name" and "Address." Below "Person," you can have subclasses like "Student" and "Faculty," each with its own specific attributes (e.g., "Student ID" for students and "Employee ID" for faculty). Both "Student" and "Faculty" inherit the "Name" and "Address" attributes from the "Person" superclass.

Use of Inheritance: Generalization and inheritance are essential in object-oriented databases and programming languages. They allow for the creation of class hierarchies, where subclasses inherit behavior and properties from their superclass. This promotes code reuse and maintains a consistent structure.

**Specialisation**

Specialization, is a process that allows you to create one or more subtypes (specialized entities) based on an existing entity type (superclass or parent entity). It is a concept used to represent hierarchies and categorizations within a database schema. Specialization is often employed when you want to model entities that share common attributes and relationships but also have distinct characteristics.

Superclass (Parent Entity): The superclass or parent entity is the original entity from which specialization is derived. It represents a generalization of entities that share common attributes and relationships.

Subtype (Specialized Entity): A subtype, also known as a specialized entity or subclass, is a more specific entity that inherits attributes and relationships from the superclass. Subtypes have their own unique attributes and relationships in addition to the inherited ones.

Attributes: Both the superclass and subtypes can have attributes. Attributes common to all subtypes are typically part of the superclass, while attributes specific to a subtype are added to that subtype.

Relationships: Relationships can exist between the superclass and other entities or between subtypes and other entities. Subtypes can also have relationships unique to them.

Specialization Hierarchy: In some cases, specialization can be further organized into a hierarchy where subtypes have their own sub-subtypes. This hierarchical structure allows for more granular categorization.

Total and Partial Specialization: Specialization can be total or partial. In total specialization, every entity of the superclass must belong to at least one subtype. In partial specialization, entities of the superclass may or may not belong to a subtype.

Example:

Consider a database for a university where you have a superclass called "Person" representing individuals. You can specialize "Person" into subtypes like "Student" and "Faculty." Each subtype (Student and Faculty) inherits attributes like "Name" and "Address" from the "Person" superclass. However, they have their own unique attributes. For example, "Student" may have attributes like "Student ID" and "Major," while "Faculty" may have attributes like "Employee ID" and "Department."

In this example, "Person" is the superclass, and "Student" and "Faculty" are subtypes.

Specialization is a powerful concept in database design as it allows you to model complex relationships and hierarchies in a structured manner. It helps ensure that the database accurately represents the real-world entities it is designed to capture while maintaining data integrity and consistency.

### Enhanced E-R Model

The Enhanced Entity-Relationship (EER) model is an extension of the traditional Entity-Relationship (ER) model used in Database Management Systems (DBMS). It includes additional concepts and features to help represent more complex relationships and constraints in a database. Here's an overview of the Enhanced E-R model:

**Entities and Attributes:** Like in the ER model, the EER model represents entities (objects or concepts) and their attributes. Entities are depicted as rectangles, and attributes are shown within ellipses connected to entities.

**Key Attributes**: EER allows you to specify key attributes within an entity, which are used to uniquely identify instances of that entity. Key attributes are typically underlined in the diagram.

**Relationships:** Relationships between entities are represented using diamond shapes connecting the related entities. The EER model supports various types of relationships, including one-to-one (1:1), one-to-many (1:N), and many-to-many (M:N) relationships.

**Generalization and Specialization**: EER introduces the concepts of generalization and specialization, which are used to model inheritance and hierarchy among entities. A generalization represents a higher-level, more abstract entity (superclass), while specialization represents lower-level, more specific entities (subclasses). This allows you to model entity hierarchies and inheritance relationships.

**Union Types:** In cases where an entity can belong to multiple entity types, union types can be used. These are represented as a combination of two or more entities, indicating that an instance can belong to any one of them.

**Aggregation:** Aggregation is a modeling concept that allows you to treat a group of related entities and their relationships as a single unit. It's represented using a diamond shape with a line connecting it to the aggregate entity.

**Constraints:** EER diagrams can include additional constraints, such as participation constraints (total or partial participation of entities in a relationship), disjointness constraints (whether subclasses are mutually exclusive), and completeness constraints (whether a superclass is complete or incomplete).

**Derived Attributes**: Derived attributes are attributes whose values can be calculated or derived from other attributes. They are typically indicated with a dashed ellipse.

**Multi-valued Attributes**: Multi-valued attributes are attributes that can have multiple values for a single entity instance. They are represented with double ellipses connected to the entity.

**Complex Relationships**: EER can represent complex relationships with additional characteristics. For example, a ternary relationship involves three entities, while recursive relationships involve an entity relating to itself.

The Enhanced E-R model provides a more expressive way to represent the structure and semantics of a database. It is particularly useful when dealing with complex data models, inheritance hierarchies, and advanced constraints. Designers use EER diagrams as a blueprint for creating the actual database schema, helping ensure that the database accurately reflects the real-world domain it represents.

## 3.4 ER-to-Relational Mapping

Entity-Relationship (ER) to Relational Mapping is the process of translating the conceptual design represented by an Entity-Relationship Diagram (ERD) into a relational database schema. In other words, it's the transformation of entities, relationships, and attributes from the ER model into tables, keys, and constraints in a relational database. Here's how ER-to-Relational Mapping works:

**Entities to Tables**: Each entity in the ERD is typically mapped to a corresponding table in the relational database. The table name usually reflects the entity's name.

**Attributes to Columns**: Attributes of entities are mapped to columns in the respective tables. The data type of each column is chosen based on the attribute's data type (e.g., text, integer, date).

**Primary Keys**: In the ERD, if an entity has a primary key attribute, it's mapped as the primary key of the corresponding table in the relational schema. This ensures that each row in the table is uniquely identifiable.

**Relationships to Foreign Keys:** Relationships between entities in the ERD are translated into foreign keys in the relational schema. A foreign key in one table references the primary key in another table, creating a link between them. This enforces referential integrity and maintains the integrity of the relationships.

**Associative Entities**: When dealing with many-to-many relationships or associative entities (junction tables), a new table is created to represent the relationship. This table typically contains foreign keys referencing the related entities.

**Cardinality Constraints**: Cardinality constraints (e.g., one-to-one, one-to-many, many-to-many) in the ERD are implemented using the foreign key constraints. For example, in a one-to-many relationship, the "one" side entity's primary key is referenced as a foreign key in the "many" sides entity's table.

**Derived Attributes**: Derived attributes from the ERD may or may not be included as columns in the tables. It depends on whether the derived attributes are needed for querying and whether they can be efficiently calculated during query execution.

**Composite Attributes**: Composite attributes in the ERD are typically mapped to individual columns representing their component parts.

**Multi-valued Attributes**: Multi-valued attributes are handled by creating a separate table to represent them. This table includes a foreign key referencing the owning entity and a column for each value of the multi-valued attribute.

**Generalization-Specialization**: When generalization-specialization hierarchies exist in the ERD, you have several options for mapping them to relational schemas. One common approach is to use a single table for the superclass and separate tables for each subclass, linked through primary keys and foreign keys.

**Aggregation**: Aggregation relationships may be represented using foreign keys, similar to how other relationships are handled.

**Constraints**: Constraints such as uniqueness constraints, not-null constraints, and check constraints can be implemented in the relational schema to enforce data integrity.

The process of ER-to-Relational Mapping is a critical step in database design as it translates the logical design into a concrete database schema. Careful consideration of the mapping ensures that the resulting relational database accurately reflects the structure and semantics of the original ERD, enabling efficient data storage and retrieval while maintaining data integrity.

## Functional Dependencies

Functional dependencies are a crucial concept in database management systems (DBMS) that describe the relationships between attributes (columns) in a relational database table. They help ensure data integrity and the elimination of data anomalies. A functional dependency (FD) exists when the value of one attribute (the dependent attribute) in a database table uniquely determines the value of another attribute (the determinant attribute) in the same table. In other words, knowing the value of the determinant uniquely identifies the value of the dependent.

Example:

In a table called "Student_Grades" with attributes 'Student_ID' and 'Grade,' we have the functional dependency:

Student_ID → Grade

This means that for every unique 'Student_ID,' there can be only one corresponding 'Grade' value.

**Notation**: Functional dependencies are typically represented as A → B, where A is the determinant attribute, and B is the dependent attribute. This notation signifies that for any two rows in the table where the values of A are the same, the values of B must also be the same.

Example: Consider a table 'Employees' with attributes (columns) 'Employee_ID,' 'First_Name,' and 'Last_Name.' If we have the functional dependency Employee_ID → First_Name, it means that for every unique 'Employee_ID,' there can be only one corresponding 'First_Name' value. In other words, Employee_ID uniquely determines First_Name.

In a table called "Customer_Info" with attributes 'Customer_ID' and 'Customer_Name,' we represent the functional dependency as:

Customer_ID → Customer_Name

**Keys and Superkeys**: Functional dependencies are closely related to keys and superkeys. A superkey is a set of attributes that, taken together, can uniquely identify a tuple (row) in a table. A key is a minimal superkey, meaning no subset of it can also uniquely identify a tuple. Keys often play a role in defining functional dependencies. For instance, the attributes that make up a key will have functional dependencies on all other attributes in the table.

Example:

In a table called "Orders" with attributes 'Order_ID,' 'Customer_ID,' and 'Order_Date,' the set {Order_ID, Customer_ID} is a superkey because it uniquely identifies each order. The functional dependency can be stated as:

{Order_ID, Customer_ID} → Order_Date

**Closure of Attributes**: The closure of attributes refers to the set of all attributes that can be functionally determined by a given set of attributes using a set of functional dependencies. This is essential for identifying candidate keys, superkeys, and other properties of a relational schema.

Example:

If we have the functional dependencies:

Student_ID → Student_Name

Student_ID → Student_Address

The closure of attributes for {Student_ID} includes {Student_ID, Student_Name, Student_Address}.

**Normalization:** Functional dependencies are instrumental in the process of database normalization. The goal of normalization is to reduce data redundancy and prevent anomalies (such as update anomalies, insertion anomalies, and deletion anomalies) by ensuring that a table is organized efficiently and that data is stored in a structured and consistent manner.

Example:

In a table called "Book_Authors" with attributes 'Book_ID,' 'Author_ID,' and 'Author_Name,' we can use functional dependencies to normalize the table. Here, 'Book_ID' and 'Author_ID' together form a candidate key, and the table can be normalized to eliminate redundancy.

**Types of Functional Dependencies**: There are various types of functional dependencies, including:

**Trivial Functional Dependencies**: These are dependencies where the determinant and dependent are the same attribute. For example, A → A is a trivial functional dependency.

Example of Trivial Functional Dependency:

Customer_Name → Customer_Name (trivial)

**Partial Dependencies**: These occur when a non-prime attribute (not part of any candidate key) is functionally dependent on part of a candidate key.

Example of Partial Dependency:

In a table called "Order_Details" with attributes 'Order_ID,' 'Product_ID,' 'Product_Name,' and 'Customer_Name,' where {Order_ID, Product_ID} is a candidate key, we have the partial dependency:

{Order_ID, Product_ID} → Product_Name

**Transitive Dependencies**: A transitive dependency occurs when a non-prime attribute is functionally dependent on another non-prime attribute through a candidate key.

Functional dependencies are a fundamental concept in database design, helping database designers create tables with minimal redundancy and maximum data integrity. They serve as the basis for normalizing a database schema to higher normal forms, ultimately leading to more efficient and maintainable database systems.

Example of Transitive Dependency:

In a table called "Student_Course_Grades" with attributes 'Student_ID,' 'Course_ID,' 'Course_Name,' and 'Course_Instructor,' we have a transitive dependency:

Student_ID → Course_ID

Course_ID → Course_Instructor

In this case, Student_ID → Course_Instructor is a transitive dependency through Course_ID.

**Data independence**

Data independence is a fundamental concept in database management systems (DBMS) that refers to the separation of the logical and physical aspects of data storage and retrieval. It is designed to provide several benefits, including data abstraction, flexibility, and ease of maintenance. Data independence is divided into two main types:

**Logical Data Independence**: This type of data independence focuses on insulating the application programs and queries (the logical level) from changes in the structure or organization of the data (the physical level). In other words, it allows you to modify the database's schema without affecting the applications that use the data.

Example: Suppose you have a database with a "Customers" table, and you decide to split it into two separate tables, "IndividualCustomers" and "BusinessCustomers." With logical data independence, you can make this change to the database schema without rewriting all the queries or application code that interact with customer data.

**Physical Data Independence**: This type of data independence shields the higher-level logical schema from changes in the physical storage and access methods. It allows you to modify how data is stored, indexed, or accessed without affecting the logical schema or the applications that use it.

Example: Let's say your database stores customer data in flat files, and you decide to switch to a more efficient storage mechanism, such as a B+ tree index. With physical data independence, you can make this change to the underlying storage without altering the logical schema or application code.

In summary, data independence in a DBMS ensures that changes made at the physical level (e.g., storage structures, access methods) or logical level (e.g., schema changes) do not disrupt the integrity and functionality of the data and applications. This separation of concerns makes it easier to adapt to evolving requirements, enhance performance, and maintain large-scale databases over time.

## Non-loss Decomposition

Non-loss decomposition in database management refers to a process of breaking down a relation (table) into multiple smaller relations, or decomposed tables, while ensuring that no information is lost in the process. This decomposition is typically done to improve the overall efficiency, integrity, and maintainability of a database schema. To achieve non-loss decomposition, the resulting smaller relations should still be able to represent all the original information.

Let's illustrate non-loss decomposition with an example:

Consider a relation "Employee_Info" with the following attributes: Employee_ID (Primary Key), Employee_Name, Employee_Address, and Department.

Original Relation: Employee_Info

| Employee_ID | Employee_Name | Employee_Address | Department |
|---|---|---|---|
| **101** | John Doe | 123 Main St | HR |
| **102** | Jane Smith | 456 Elm St | IT |
| **103** | Bob Johnson | 789 Oak St | Marketing |

Now, let's say we want to decompose this relation to improve database organization. We can perform non-loss decomposition by creating two smaller relations based on functional dependencies:

Employee_Info_1 (Contains Employee_ID and Employee_Name)

| Employee_ID | Employee_Name |
|---|---|
| **101** | John Doe |
| **102** | Jane Smith |
| **103** | Bob Johnson |

Employee_Info_2 (Contains Employee_ID, Employee_Address, and Department)

| Employee_ID | Employee_Address | Department |
|---|---|---|
| **101** | 123 Main St | HR |
| **102** | 456 Elm St | IT |
| **103** | 789 Oak St | Marketing |

In this decomposition, we have ensured that no information from the original "Employee_Info" relation is lost. We can still reconstruct the original relation by joining "Employee_Info_1" and "Employee_Info_2" using the common attribute "Employee_ID." This non-loss decomposition enhances data integrity, simplifies database maintenance, and may also lead to improved query performance in certain situations.

Non-loss decomposition is a crucial concept in database normalization, where the goal is to eliminate redundancy and anomalies while preserving data integrity and ensuring efficient data management.

## First, Second, Third Normal Forms

In database management, Normalization is a process of organizing data in a database to eliminate redundancy and improve data integrity. It involves dividing a database into two or more tables and defining relationships between the tables. The most common normal forms are the First Normal Form (1NF), Second Normal Form (2NF), and Third Normal Form (3NF), each with specific rules and objectives.

**First Normal Form (1NF):**

Rule: All attributes (columns) must contain atomic (indivisible) values. Each value in a column should be of a single data type.

Example: A table with a multi-valued attribute like "Skills" (e.g., "Java, Python, SQL") is not in 1NF. To achieve 1NF, you can create a separate table for skills and link it to the original table using a key.

Explanation: In the context of the First Normal Form (1NF), consider a table that stores information about books in a library. Each row represents a book, and the columns contain various attributes such as Book_ID, Title, Author, and Keywords.

| Book_ID | Title | Author | Keywords |
|---|---|---|---|
| 1 | Introduction | John Smith | Database, SQL, Management |
| 2 | Programming | Alice Johnson | Java, Python |
| 3 | Web Design | Robert Williams | HTML, CSS, JavaScript |

In this table, the "Keywords" column violates 1NF because it contains multiple values separated by commas. To bring it into 1NF, we should create a separate table for keywords and link it to the book table using a key. The revised tables might look like this:

Books Table:

| Book_ID | Title | Author |
|---|---|---|
| 1 | Introduction | John Smith |
| 2 | Programming | Alice Johnson |
| 3 | Web Design | Robert Williams |

Keywords Table:

| Keyword_ID | Keyword |
|---|---|
| 1 | Database |
| 2 | SQL |
| 3 | Management |
| 4 | Java |
| 5 | Python |
| 6 | HTML |
| 7 | CSS |
| 8 | JavaScript |

**Second Normal Form (2NF):**

Rule: It must be in 1NF, and all non-key attributes (attributes not part of the primary key) must be fully functionally dependent on the entire primary key.

Example: Consider an Orders table with attributes Order_ID, Product_ID, and Quantity. If Product_Name is functionally dependent only on Product_ID, it violates 2NF. To achieve 2NF, you can create a separate Products table with Product_ID as the primary key and Product_Name as an attribute.

Explanation: Consider an Orders table that records sales orders for products. The table has the following attributes: Order_ID, Product_ID, Product_Name, and Quantity.

| Order_ID | Product_ID | Product_Name | Quantity |
|---|---|---|---|
| **101** | 1 | Laptop | 2 |
| **101** | 2 | Smartphone | 3 |
| **102** | 1 | Laptop | 1 |

In this table, Order_ID and Product_ID together form the composite primary key. However, Product_Name is functionally dependent only on Product_ID, not on the entire primary key. This violates 2NF.

To achieve 2NF, we create two tables:

Orders Table:

| Order_ID | Product_ID | Quantity |
|---|---|---|
| **101** | 1 | 2 |
| **101** | 2 | 3 |
| **102** | 1 | 1 |

Products Table:

| Product_ID | Product_Name |
|---|---|
| 1 | Laptop |
| 2 | Smartphone |

**Third Normal Form (3NF):**

Rule: It must be in 2NF, and all attributes must be functionally dependent only on the primary key. There should be no transitive dependencies.

Example: In an Employee table with Employee_ID, Department, and Manager_Name, Manager_Name is transitively dependent on Department. To achieve 3NF, you can create a separate Department table with Department_ID (as the primary key) and Manager_Name as an attribute.

Explanation: Consider an Employee table with the following attributes: Employee_ID, Employee_Name, Department, and Manager_Name.

| Employee_ID | Employee_Name | Department | Manager_Name |
|---|---|---|---|
| **101** | Alice | HR | Sarah |
| **102** | Bob | IT | John |
| **103** | Carol | HR | Sarah |

In this table, Manager_Name depends on the Department, creating a transitive dependency. To achieve 3NF, we create two tables:

Employee Table:

| Employee_ID | Employee_Name | Department |
|---|---|---|
| **101** | Alice | HR |
| **102** | Bob | IT |
| **103** | Carol | HR |

Department Table:

| Department | Manager_Name |
|---|---|
| **HR** | Sarah |
| **IT** | John |

Now, Manager_Name is directly related to the Department, and both tables are in 3NF, eliminating transitive dependencies.

Achieving these normal forms reduces data redundancy, minimizes update anomalies, and simplifies data maintenance. However, it's important to note that higher normal forms like BCNF (Boyce-Codd Normal Form) and 4NF (Fourth Normal Form) may be required for complex databases with specific requirements. The choice of the appropriate normal form depends on the specific needs of the database design and the application it serves.

### Dependency Preservation

Dependency preservation refers to the property of maintaining certain dependencies or relationships between attributes or columns when performing operations such as decomposition or restructuring of database tables. These dependencies are typically functional dependencies or multivalued dependencies.

Here's a more detailed explanation:

Let's use a simple example to illustrate dependency preservation in the context of functional dependencies (FDs) and multivalued dependencies (MVDs) in a relational database.

Consider a hypothetical database for tracking course registrations at a university. We have a table called "Student_Course" with the following attributes:

Student_ID

Course_ID

Student_Name

Course_Name

Textbook

**Functional Dependencies (FDs):** Functional dependencies describe the relationships between attributes (columns) in a relational database. An FD states that the value of one attribute uniquely determines the value of another attribute. For example, if we have an attribute "Employee_ID" and "Employee_Name," we might have a functional dependency that Employee_ID uniquely determines Employee_Name.

Suppose we have the following functional dependencies in our "Student_Course" table:

Student_ID → Student_Name (Student ID uniquely determines the student's name).

Course_ID → Course_Name (Course ID uniquely determines the course name).

Now, let's say we want to decompose the "Student_Course" table into two tables for normalization purposes:

Table 1: "Student_Info"

Student_ID

Student_Name

Table 2: "Course_Info"

Course_ID

Course_Name

**Dependency Preservation:** When you decompose a relation (table) into multiple smaller relations (tables), you want to ensure that the functional dependencies that existed in the original relation are still valid in the decomposed

relations. This means that if a functional dependency existed in the original table, it should also exist in at least one of the decomposed tables. If this property is maintained, we say that dependency preservation has been achieved.
In this decomposition, both functional dependencies are preserved. The "Student_Info" table still maintains the Student_ID → Student_Name dependency, and the "Course_Info" table maintains the Course_ID → Course_Name dependency.

**Multivalued Dependencies (MVDs):** Multivalued dependencies describe relationships between attributes when an attribute can have multiple values for a single value of another attribute. For example, if we have an attribute "Course_ID" and "Textbook," a multivalued dependency might state that for each Course_ID, there can be multiple associated textbooks.

Suppose we have the following multivalued dependency in our "Student_Course" table:

Student_ID →> Textbook (A student can be associated with multiple textbooks for different courses).

Now, let's say we want to decompose the "Student_Course" table into two tables:

Table 1: "Student_Info"

Student_ID

Student_Name

Table 2: "Course_Textbooks"

Student_ID

Course_ID

Textbook

**Dependency Preservation:** When you decompose a relation that contains multivalued dependencies, you want to ensure that these dependencies are preserved in the decomposed relations. This means that if a multivalued dependency existed in the original relation, it should also exist in the decomposed relations.

In this decomposition, the multivalued dependency is preserved. The "Course_Textbooks" table maintains the Student_ID →> Textbook dependency. Each row in this table represents a specific textbook associated with a student for a particular course.

Achieving dependency preservation is important to maintain data integrity and consistency in a relational database. If dependencies are not preserved during decomposition or restructuring, it can lead to anomalies and incorrect query results when accessing the data.

In both examples, we ensured that the original dependencies (functional and multivalued) that existed in the "Student_Course" table were maintained in the decomposed tables. This ensures data integrity and consistency in the database, preventing anomalies and incorrect results when querying the data.

To ensure dependency preservation, designers and developers often use techniques like normalization, which involves decomposing tables into smaller, related tables while carefully maintaining the original functional and multivalued dependencies in the decomposed tables. This process helps ensure that the database remains in a consistent state and that data can be retrieved accurately according to the defined dependencies.

**Data redundancy**

Data redundancy in a Database Management System (DBMS) refers to the duplication of data within a database or between different databases in a system. It occurs when the same piece of data is stored in multiple places, which can lead to various issues and inefficiencies. Data redundancy can occur at different levels:

Within a Table: In a relational database, data redundancy can occur when the same information is stored in multiple rows of a table. For example, if customer information such as address is repeated for each purchase they make, it leads to redundancy.

Between Tables: Redundancy can also occur when similar data is stored in different tables within the same database. For instance, if customer details are stored in both a "Customers" table and an "Orders" table, it can result in redundancy.

Data redundancy can lead to several problems, including:

Data Inconsistency: When the same data is stored in multiple places, it becomes challenging to ensure that all copies of the data are consistent. Changes made in one place may not be reflected in others, leading to inconsistencies.

Wasted Storage: Storing the same data multiple times consumes unnecessary storage space, which can be costly, especially in large databases.

Update Anomalies: Redundancy can make it difficult to update data consistently. For example, updating a customer's address in one place but not in another can result in incorrect information.

Insertion and Deletion Anomalies: Redundancy can cause issues when inserting new data or deleting existing data, as it may affect other related data stored redundantly.

To mitigate data redundancy, database designers use techniques such as normalization. Normalization involves organizing data to minimize redundancy and improve data integrity. It typically results in a set of related tables with clear relationships between them, reducing data duplication and ensuring data consistency.

Overall, data redundancy is a critical consideration in database design and management to maintain data accuracy, efficiency, and integrity.

**Anomalies**

Anomalies refer to inconsistencies, inaccuracies, or undesirable outcomes that can occur when manipulating or maintaining data within a database. There are three main types of anomalies: insertion anomalies, update anomalies, and deletion anomalies. Let's explore each of them:

**Insertion Anomalies:**

Definition: Insertion anomalies occur when it is difficult to add new records (rows) to a database table because certain required attributes are not known or cannot be provided.

Example: Consider a database of students with separate tables for enrolled courses and students. If a student has not yet enrolled in any courses, adding their record to the database can be problematic because they won't have any corresponding course records to link to.

**Update Anomalies:**

Definition: Update anomalies occur when modifying data in a database leads to inconsistencies or unintended changes in other related records.

Example: Using the same student and course database, suppose a student changes their last name. If this change is only made in the student table and not in the enrolled courses table, it can lead to discrepancies when retrieving data, as the student's name may be inconsistent across records.

**Deletion Anomalies:**

Definition: Deletion anomalies arise when removing a record from a database causes unintended data loss or renders the database incomplete or inconsistent.

Example: In the student and course database, if a student decides to drop a course and their record is deleted from the enrolled courses table, it could result in the loss of information about the course itself if no other students are enrolled in it.

To address these anomalies and ensure data integrity, database designers use a process called normalization. Normalization involves breaking down database tables into smaller, related tables and establishing relationships between them. This minimizes redundancy and helps prevent anomalies by ensuring that data is stored in a structured and organized manner.

By structuring the database according to the principles of normalization, you can reduce the likelihood of anomalies, improve data consistency, and make it easier to add, update, and delete records without unintended side effects.

## Boyce/Codd Normal Form

Boyce-Codd Normal Form (BCNF) is a higher level of database normalization that deals with certain types of functional dependencies within a relational database. BCNF is a stricter form of normalization than the Third Normal Form (3NF). To understand BCNF, let's first define some terms:

**Superkey:** A superkey is a set of one or more attributes (columns) that can be used to uniquely identify a tuple (row) in a relation (table).

**Candidate Key**: A candidate key is a minimal superkey, meaning it's a superkey with no unnecessary attributes, and removing any attribute from it would cause it to lose its uniqueness property.

**Prime Attribute:** A prime attribute is an attribute that is part of a candidate key.

**Non-prime Attribute:** A non-prime attribute is an attribute that is not part of any candidate key.

Now, let's explain BCNF with an example:

**Example:**

Consider a relation (table) called "StudentCourses" that stores information about students and the courses they are enrolled in. The attributes of this relation are:

StudentID (Primary Key)

CourseID (Primary Key)

StudentName

CourseName

In this case, both (StudentID, CourseID) and (CourseID, StudentID) can be considered candidate keys because they uniquely identify each combination of student and course. However, we'll focus on (StudentID, CourseID) as the primary candidate key.

Now, let's say we have the following functional dependency:

StudentID → StudentName (A student's ID determines their name).

This functional dependency indicates that StudentID is a superkey, and StudentName is a non-prime attribute. However, we need to check if our relation is in BCNF.

To be in BCNF, every non-trivial functional dependency (where the left-hand side determines the right-hand side) must have the left-hand side be a superkey. In our case, StudentID is a superkey, so the functional dependency StudentID → StudentName satisfies the BCNF condition.

Therefore, our "StudentCourses" relation is in BCNF because all non-trivial functional dependencies have superkeys on the left-hand side. If it didn't satisfy BCNF, we would need to decompose the relation further to ensure BCNF compliance.

In summary, BCNF is a stricter level of normalization that ensures that non-trivial functional dependencies are based on superkeys. It helps eliminate redundancy and maintain data integrity in the database.

## Multi-valued Dependencies and Fourth Normal Form

Fourth Normal Form (4NF) is a level of database normalization that deals with multi-valued dependencies within a relational database. To understand 4NF, let's first define some terms:

**Multi-valued Dependency (MVD):** A multi-valued dependency exists when one or more attributes in a relation are multi-valued with respect to another set of attributes. In simpler terms, it occurs when a single value in one attribute determines multiple values in another attribute.

Now, let's explain 4NF with an example:

**Example:**

Consider a relation (table) called "StudentCourses" that stores information about students and the courses they are enrolled in. The attributes of this relation are:

StudentID (Primary Key)

CourseID (Primary Key)

StudentName

CoursesTaken

In this case, (StudentID, CourseID) is the primary key. However, we have a multi-valued dependency:

StudentID →> CoursesTaken (A student can enroll in multiple courses).

This means that for a given student, there can be multiple courses in the "CoursesTaken" attribute. To bring this relation to 4NF, we need to split it into two relations: one for student information and another for the courses they have taken.

New Relations:

"Students" Relation:

StudentID (Primary Key)

StudentName

"StudentCoursesTaken" Relation:

StudentID (Foreign Key referencing Students)

CourseID (Multi-valued attribute)

Now, let's consider some data:

In the "Students" relation:

| StudentID | StudentName |
|---|---|
| 1 | John |
| 2 | Sarah |

In the "StudentCoursesTaken" relation:

| StudentID | CourseID |
|---|---|
| 1 | Math |
| 1 | Science |
| 2 | History |

By splitting the original relation into these two, we eliminate multi-valued dependencies, and each relation contains atomic (indivisible) values. This conforms to 4NF.

In summary, Fourth Normal Form (4NF) addresses multi-valued dependencies in a relational database. It helps maintain data integrity and eliminates redundancy by splitting relations with multi-valued attributes into separate tables.

## Join Dependencies and Fifth Normal Form

Join Dependencies and Fifth Normal Form (5NF) are advanced concepts in database management that deal with complex relationships and dependencies between database tables.

**Join Dependencies:**

Join dependencies are a higher-level extension of functional dependencies, which are used to describe how attributes in a table depend on each other. A join dependency specifies how data from multiple tables can be combined or joined to form a new table. In essence, it describes situations where a table can be reconstructed by joining several other tables together. Join dependencies are important when dealing with denormalized databases or multidimensional data modeling.

For example, consider three tables:

Student (StudentID, StudentName)

Course (CourseID, CourseName)

Enrollment (StudentID, CourseID)

A join dependency can be expressed as:

{Student} ⋈ {Course} = Enrollment

This means that by joining the "Student" table with the "Course" table on their respective attributes, you can reconstruct the "Enrollment" table.

**Fifth Normal Form (5NF):**

Fifth Normal Form (5NF), also known as Project-Join Normal Form (PJNF), is a level of data normalization that addresses join dependencies. It is an advanced level of normalization that aims to eliminate redundancy and ensure that data can be efficiently reconstructed from multiple tables using join operations. Achieving 5NF is not common in practice and is usually reserved for specialized situations where data integrity and consistency are of utmost importance.

To achieve 5NF, you need to ensure that:

The database schema is in Fourth Normal Form (4NF).

There are no join dependencies in the database.

In practical terms, achieving 5NF often involves breaking down tables into smaller, more specialized tables and carefully managing join dependencies. It may require complex schema designs and is typically applied in scenarios where maintaining absolute data consistency is critical, such as scientific databases and financial systems.

In summary, join dependencies describe how tables can be joined together to reconstruct other tables, while Fifth Normal Form (5NF) is an advanced level of data normalization that deals with eliminating join dependencies and ensuring data integrity through complex schema designs. Achieving 5NF is rare and reserved for specific situations where data consistency is paramount.

**Here's an example of join dependencies and achieving Fifth Normal Form (5NF) in table format:**

Let's consider a database for a library:

Table 1: Books

| BookID | Title | Author |
|---|---|---|
| 1 | "Book 1" | "Author 1" |
| 2 | "Book 2" | "Author 2" |
| 3 | "Book 3" | "Author 1" |

Table 2: Authors

| AuthorID | AuthorName |
|---|---|
| 1 | "Author 1" |
| 2 | "Author 2" |
| 3 | "Author 3" |

Table 3: Book Authors (to represent the many-to-many relationship)

| BookID | AuthorID |
|---|---|
| 1 | 1 |
| 2 | 2 |
| 3 | 1 |

In this example, "Books" and "Authors" are two tables. The "Book Authors" table represents a many-to-many relationship between books and authors.

Join Dependency:

We can express a join dependency as follows:

{Books} ⋈ {Authors} = {Book Authors}

This means that by joining the "Books" table with the "Authors" table using their respective attributes, we can reconstruct the "Book Authors" table, which represents the relationship between books and authors.

To achieve 5NF, we need to ensure that there are no join dependencies. In this case, achieving 5NF would involve breaking down the tables into smaller, more specialized tables, eliminating redundancy, and managing the join dependencies more rigorously. Achieving 5NF in this example might result in a more complex schema that ensures data integrity and consistency, but it's not a common practice in typical library database scenarios.

## DBMS Architecture 1-level, 2-Level, 3-Level

A Database store a lot of critical information to access data quickly and securely. Hence it is important to select the correct architecture for efficient data management. DBMS Architecture helps users to get their requests done while connecting to the database. We choose database architecture depending on several factors like the size of the database, number of users, and relationships between the users. There are two types of database models that we generally use, are logical model and physical model.

### Types of DBMS Architecture

There are several types of DBMS Architecture that we use according to the usage requirements. Types of DBMS Architecture are discussed here.

1-Tier Architecture

2-Tier Architecture

3-Tier Architecture

### 1-Tier Architecture

In 1-Tier Architecture the database is directly available to the user, the user can directly sit on the DBMS and use it that is, the client, server, and Database are all present on the same machine. For Example: to learn SQL we set up an SQL server and the database on the local system. This enables us to directly interact with the relational database and execute operations. The industry won't use this architecture they logically go for 2-Tier and 3-Tier Architecture.

Advantages of 1-Tier Architecture

Simple Architecture: 1-Tier Architecture is the simplest architecture to set up, as only a single machine is required to maintain it.

Cost-Effective: No additional hardware is required for implementing 1-Tier Architecture, which makes it cost-effective.

Easy to Implement: 1-Tier Architecture can be easily deployed, and hence it is mostly used in small projects.

### 2-Tier Architecture

The 2-tier architecture is similar to a basic client-server model. The application at the client end directly communicates with the database on the server side. APIs like ODBC and JDBC are used for this interaction. The server side is responsible for providing query processing and transaction management functionalities. On the client side, the user interfaces and application programs are run. The application on the client side establishes a connection with the server side in order to communicate with the DBMS.

An advantage of this type is that maintenance and understanding are easier, and compatible with existing systems. However, this model gives poor performance when there are a large number of users.

Advantages of 2-Tier Architecture

Easy to Access: 2-Tier Architecture makes easy access to the database, which makes fast retrieval.

Scalable: We can scale the database easily, by adding clients or by upgrading hardware.

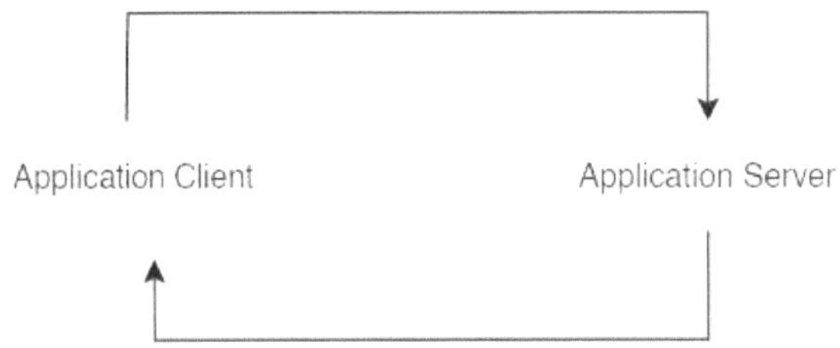


Low Cost: 2-Tier Architecture is cheaper than 3-Tier Architecture and Multi-Tier Architecture.

Easy Deployment: 2-Tier Architecture is easy to deploy than 3-Tier Architecture.

Simple: 2-Tier Architecture is easily understandable as well as simple because of only two components.

**3-Tier Architecture**

In 3-Tier Architecture, there is another layer between the client and the server. The client does not directly communicate with the server. Instead, it interacts with an application server which further communicates with the database system and then the query processing and transaction management takes place. This intermediate layer acts as a medium for the exchange of partially processed data between the server and the client. This type of architecture is used in the case of large web applications.

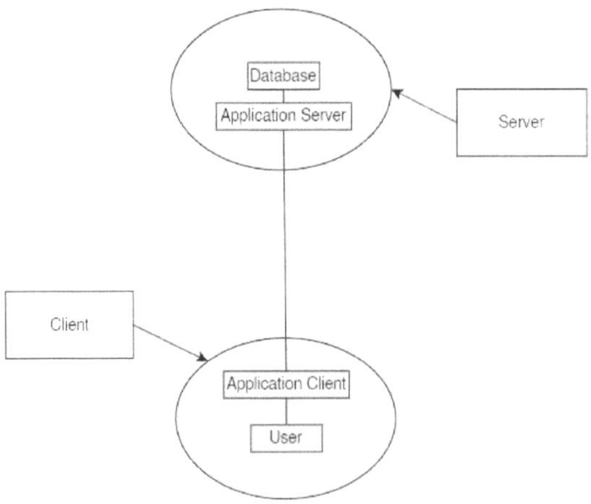


Advantages of 3-Tier Architecture

Enhanced scalability: Scalability is enhanced due to distributed deployment of application servers. Now, individual connections need not be made between the client and server.

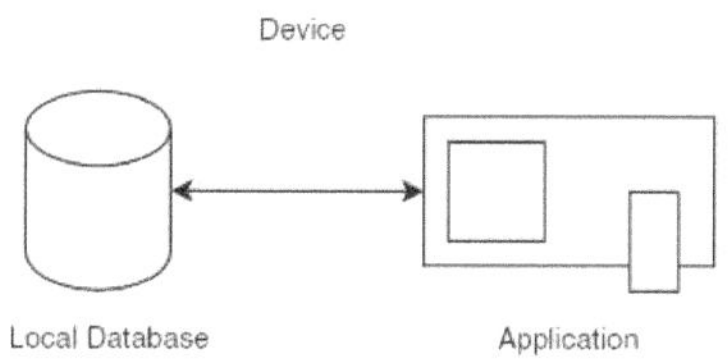


Data Integrity: 3-Tier Architecture maintains Data Integrity. Since there is a middle layer between the client and the server, data corruption can be avoided/removed.

Security: 3-Tier Architecture Improves Security. This type of model prevents direct interaction of the client with the server thereby reducing access to unauthorized data.

Disadvantages of 3-Tier Architecture

More Complex: 3-Tier Architecture is more complex in comparison to 2-Tier Architecture. Communication Points are also doubled in 3-Tier Architecture.

Difficult to Interact: It becomes difficult for this sort of interaction to take place due to the presence of middle layers.

**Exercise**

**Exercise 1 – MCQ**

Q 1. Which of the following is the primary objective of normalization in database design?

A) To increase data redundancy

B) To ensure faster query performance

C) To organize data efficiently and minimize data redundancy

D) To simplify the database schema

Q 2. Which type of database model is known for its flexibility and ability to handle semi-structured or unstructured data?

A) Relational Database Model

B) NoSQL Database Model

C) Entity-Relationship Model

D) Hierarchical Database Model

**Exercise 2 – True/ False**

Q 1. In the context of database design, normalization is the process of intentionally increasing data redundancy to improve query performance.

Q 2. Entity-Relationship Diagrams (ERDs) are graphical representations used to describe the physical structure of a database.

**Exercise 3 – Match case**

Q 1.Match the following principles of database design with their descriptions:

1. Principles of Database:
2. Data Independence
3. Data Redundancy
4. Data Consistency

Descriptions:

a. The concept that database structure can be modified without affecting the applications that use the data.

b. The undesirable situation where the same data is stored in multiple locations in a database.

c. Ensuring that data remains accurate and unchanged throughout its lifecycle.

**Exercise 4 – One word answer**

Q 1.What is the primary goal of normalization in database design?

Q 2. What type of data model is known for its flexibility in handling various data types?

**Exercise 5 – Small answer**

Q 1. What is the primary goal of normalization in database design?

Q 2. What is the primary goal of normalization in database design?

**Exercise 6 – Long answer**

Q 1. Explain the key principles of database design. How do these principles contribute to the creation of efficient and effective database systems?

Q 2. Explain the concept of data modelling in the context of database design. What role do data models play in creating a structured and organized database system?

**Answer**

**Exercise 1**

Answer 1: C), 2: B)

**Exercise 2**

Answer 1:False, 2: False

**Exercise 3**

Answer 1: A) Data Independence: 1, B) Data Redundancy: 2, C) Data Consistency: 3

**Exercise 4**

Answer 1: Efficiency, 2: NoSQL

**Previous Years Questions**

Q1. Define 3 NF. Justify whether the following relation satisfies 3 NF or not? In case it does not, decompose it into relations which do satisfy 3 NF. What advantages are gained by this decomposition? (IGNOU MCA 2010)

| Roll No. | Name | Department | Year | Hostel Name |
|---|---|---|---|---|
| R1 | N1 | D1 | 1 | H1 |
| R2 | N2 | D2 | 1 | H1 |
| R3 | N3 | D1 | 2 | H2 |
| R4 | N4 | D2 | 2 | H2 |
| R5 | N5 | D1 | 3 | H3 |
| R6 | N6 | D3 | 4 | H4 |

Q2. What is a weak entity? Explain with the help of an example. (IGNOU MCA 2010)

Q3. For the following statement, draw an E-R diagram. Make and state any reasonable assumptions. "A machine shop produces many parts which it takes on contract. It employs many operators who operate any of the machines. A part is produced using only one machine. A record is kept on the quantity of material needed for producing each part. The production of each part is tracked by giving a job number, start time and end time and operator's identification". (IGNOU MCA 2010)

Q4. Explain the following with the help of an example / diagram wherever needed:

BCNF

Conversion of relationships (in ER-Diagram) into relations. (IGNOU MCA 2010)

Q5. Explain the concept of data independence. (IGNOU MCA 2010)

Q6. Differentiate between the followings: 2 Tier and 3 Tier architecture (IGNOU MCA 2010)

Q7. Analyse the following Determine the output when following operations are applied on relations relations. Child (C-name, C-age, C-address) Parent (P-name, P-age, C-name, C-age) and identify the highest normal form possessed by them. If the relation is desired to be normalized then perform the task, otherwise justify with suitable arguments that "Normalization is not needed". (IGNOU MCA 2011)

Q8. Define Functional Dependency (FD). Find the valid FD's in the following relation. (IGNOU MCA 2011)

| A | B | C | D |
|---|---|---|---|
| a1 | b1 | c1 | d1 |
| a2 | b2 | c2 | d2 |
| a3 | b3 | c3 | d3 |
| a4 | b4 | c4 | d4 |

Q9. Explain physical data independence and logical data independence (IGNOU MCA 2011)

Q10. Draw E.R Diagram for the statement given below. Note: Use suitable notations at appropriate places. "Many teachers teaches many students in many institutes affiliated to many Universities, the institutes are categorised as Engineering, Medical and Management institutes". (IGNOU MCA 2011)

Q11. List the desirable properties of decomposition of a data base. (IGNOU MCA 2011)

Q12. Explain the following: 2-Tier Client/Server model. (IGNOU MCA 2011)

Q13. Decompose the relation R = (A, B, C, D, E) with the set of functional dependencies

A —> BC

CD --> E

B —> D into 3NF relation (IGNOU MCA 2012)

Q14. Justify the following statements: A Relation in BCNF is also in 3NF (IGNOU MCA 2012)

Q15. For the following problem definition: The book club has members. The book club sells books to its members. The members places orders for books, which the book club fulfils. Each order contains one or more than one books. The books are written by author (s). The publisher publishes the book. An author can write more than one book and a book can have more than one author. A book is published by a publisher, but a publisher publishes many books. A member can place more than one order. The member also can choose not to place an order. The book club sells many books.

Draw an E - R Diagram

Map the ER Diagram to Relational model. (IGNOU MCA 2012)

Q16. Consider the relation R (A, B, C, D, E) and the set of functional dependencies: - F (A —>D, {A, B} D —> E)

Which of the following are candidate keys? (A) (Al (B) (A, B} (C) {A, El

Consider the decomposition of R into {R1(A, B, C) and R2(A, D, E)}. Is this decomposition lossless? Justify? (IGNOU MCA 2012)

Q17. Is BCNF stronger than SNF? Justify your answer with the help of an example (IGNOU MCA 2013)

Q18. Define Data Independence? Explain the difference between physical and logical data independence. (IGNOU MCA 2013)

Q19. Construct on E-R diagram for the following problem definition: Each company operates four departments, and each department belongs to one company. Each department employs one or more employees, and each employee works for one department. Each of the employees may or may not have one or more dependents, and each dependent belongs to one employee. (IGNOU MCA 2013)

Q20. Explain Generalisation/Specialisation in a E-R diagram with the help of an example? (IGNOU MCA 2013)

Q21. How would you map the following ER constructs into relations? Give suitable example. Weak Entity, Generalization, Ternary Relationship (IGNOU MCA 2013)

Q22. Consider the following relation for published books:

Book (Book title, Author name, Book-type,
list price, Author-affil, Publisher)
(Author-affil referes to the affiliation of the
author.) Suppose the following dependencies exist:

Book-title —> Publisher, Book-type

Book-type y —> list price

Author-name —> Author-affil

What normal form is the above relation in? Justify.

Normalize the above relation to its highest Normal form. (IGNOU MCA 2013)

Q23. What is data independence? Explain two types of data independence with the help of an example for each. (IGNOU MCA 2013)

Q24. raw an ER diagram for the situation given below: Library consists of many books in different subject areas where books are written by different authors and are published by different publishers. A book is published by only one publisher. There are inside - members and outside - members who gets books issued for their uses. The issuing and return operation of the books are managed by the librarian. (IGNOU MCA 2013)

Q25. Explain 3NF. Also justify the statement "BCNF is stronger than 3NF" with the help of an example. (IGNOU MCA 2014)

Q26. What is data redundancy in DBMS ? How data redundancies are removed ? Explain whether the following relation named student is in 2NF or not with proper justification. STUDENT (Name, Course, Age, Sex) (IGNOU MCA 2014)

Q27. Construct an E-R diagram for the following problem definition: Each company operates four departments, and each department belongs to one company. Each department employs one or more employees, and each employee works for one department. Each of the employees may or may not have one or more dependants, and each dependant belongs to one employee. (IGNOU MCA 2016)

Q28. What are the different types of constraints which can be imposed on Generalization in an E-R diagram? (IGNOU MCA 2016)

Q28. How would you map the following E-R constructs into relations ? Give suitable examples. Aggregation, Inheritance, n-ary Relationship. (IGNOU MCA 2016)

Q29. Consider the following relation for published books:

Book (Book_title, Author_name, Book_type, Listprice, Author_affil, Publisher)

Author_affil refers to the affiliation of the author. Suppose the following dependencies exist :

Book_title —> Publisher, Book_type Book_type —> Listprice Author_name --> Author_affil

What Normal Form is the above relation in ? Justify.

Normalize the above relation till 3NF. (IGNOU MCA 2016)

Q30. Draw an ER diagram for the following situation : "An academic institution is affiliated to a University. The institution possesses several departments, each department offers several courses. Each department has its own infrastructure, where several teachers teach several students." Transform your ER diagram into Relational Database. (IGNOU MCA 2017)

Q31. Any relation in )3CNF is in 3NF, but the converse is not true." Justify the statement. (IGNOU MCA 2017)

Q32. Justify the statement "BCNF is stronger than 3NF" with the help of a suitable example. (IGNOU MCA 2018)

Q33. Construct an ER diagram for the loan management system of a finance company. Loans are given on the purchase of various items with different interest rates. The company keeps track of defaulters and takes appropriate steps against them. Make and state suitable assumptions (if any). (IGNOU MCA 2018)

Q34. Consider the following relation which keeps records of employees joining and leaving the projects. Employee can work on many projects : Project (emp_id emp_name, project_id, project_name, joining_date, leaving_date)

What are the anamolies in the relation above ? Explain with examples.

What are the functional dependencies in the relation ?

Normalize the above relation into 2NF. (IGNOU MCA 2019)

Q35. Design an E-R diagram for a Bank database schema for the following statement :

"Each bank can have multiple branches and each branch can have multiple accounts and loans." Convert the diagram into tables. (IGNOU MCA 2019)

Q36. What is the dependency preservation property for a decomposition ? Why is it important ? (IGNOU MCA 2019)

Q37. Prove the statement "Any relation which is in BCNF is in 3NF but the converse is not true". (IGNOU MCA 2019)

Q38. Explain the terms BCNF and 3NF and verify the statement "any relation in BCNF is in 3NF but converse is not true." (IGNOU MCA 2020)

Q39. Draw an E-R diagram of a manufacturing company that makes various kinds of products. The company has several customers. Some of whom have offices in multiple locations. The customers place the order on the company for shopping products to different offices. Assume reasonable attributes for the entities. (IGNOU MCA 2020)

Q40. What is the difference between strong and weak entities ? Specify strong and weak, entities in the above E-R diagram. (IGNOU MCA 2020)

Q41. What do you understand by the term "Normalization" in DBMS ? Write statement for second normal form (2NF), and discuss the insert, delete and update anomalies associated with 2 NF. (IGNOU MCA 2020) (ANNA University MCA 2010)

Q42. What do you understand by the term functional dependency ? Explain the following functional dependencies : (i) Full functional dependency (ii) Partial functional dependency (iii) Transitive functional dependency (iv) Trivial functional dependency. (IGNOU MCA 2020)

Q43. How do weak entities differ from strong entities ? Discuss with the help of an example. Briefly discuss the role of keys in identification of the entity type, i.e. weak or strong. (IGNOU MCA 2021)

Q44. What do you understand by functional dependency in a Relational DBMS ? For the relation given below, check whether the given functional dependencies hold or not. Give proper justification.

| J | K | L |
|---|---|---|
| x | 1 | 2 |
| x | 1 | 3 |
| y | 1 | 4 |
| y | 1 | 3 |
| z | 2 | 5 |
| p | 4 | 7 |

J → K (ii) K → J (iii) J, K → L (iv) K, L → J. (IGNOU MCA 2021)

Q45. Explain 3NF. Discuss the Insert, Delete and Update anomalies associated with 3NF. (IGNOU MCA 2021)

Q46. Differentiate the following: 2NF, 3NF and BCNF. (IGNOU MCA 2021) (ANNA University M.Sc 2013) (ANNA University MCA 2010)

Q47. Explain different Database Design approach. (Pune University MCA 2013)

Q48. Explain types of Function dependency in detail. (Pune University MCA 2013)

Q49. Relation { custno, custname, orderno, prodno, proddesc, qty_ordered,
custaddress,date +ordered, order descr, qty_available, price_per unit,
total cost}.

Normalize this relation upto 3NF with proper explanation. (Pune University MCA 2013)

Q50. Explain different Anomalies and data redundancy issues with unnormalized data. (Pune University MCA 2013)

Q51. Why certain functional dependencies called trivial functional dependencies? (ANNA University M.Sc 2013)

Q52. Construct an ER diagram for hospital management system with a set of patients and a set of doctors. Associate with each patient a log of the various tests and examinations conducted. (ANNA University M.Sc 2013)

Q53. Explain the architecture of database system. (ANNA University M.Sc 2013)

**Previous Years Questions with Answers**

Q1 Define the BCNF? (RU BCA 2022)

**Answer:**

BCNF, or Boyce-Codd Normal Form, is a level of database normalization in the field of relational database design. It is a more stringent form of normalization than the Third Normal Form (3NF). A table is in BCNF if it meets certain criteria that eliminate certain types of data anomalies and dependencies. Specifically, a table is in BCNF if it satisfies the following conditions:

It is already in the Third Normal Form (3NF).

For every non-trivial functional dependency (X → Y) in the table, X is a superkey.

Here's an explanation of these conditions:

**Third Normal Form (3NF)**: A table is in 3NF if it is in 2NF (Second Normal Form) and, in addition, it doesn't have any transitive dependencies. In other words, all non-prime attributes (attributes not part of any candidate key) are fully functionally dependent on the primary key.

**Superkey**: A superkey is a set of one or more attributes (columns) in a table that can be used to uniquely identify a row in that table. A superkey may contain more attributes than the primary key, but it must include the primary key. In BCNF, for every non-trivial functional dependency (X → Y), X must be a superkey, which means it is sufficient to uniquely identify rows.

The goal of BCNF is to ensure that there are no partial dependencies in a relational table. Partial dependency occurs when a non-prime attribute (an attribute not part of any candidate key) depends on only a part of a candidate key, as opposed to the entire candidate key. By enforcing BCNF, you eliminate such dependencies, which can cause anomalies in data manipulation.

BCNF is a higher level of normalization than 3NF and is used to ensure that a database design is free from certain types of data anomalies and inconsistencies. It promotes better data integrity, more efficient querying, and a more organized and efficient database structure.

Q2 What is E-R model? Describe the important components of an E-R diagrams. (RU BCA 2022)

**Answer:**

Important components of an E-R diagram include:

**Entities**:

Entities represent real-world objects or concepts about which data is stored in the database. They are typically represented by rectangles in E-R diagrams.

Example entities: "Customer," "Product," "Employee," "Order."

**Attributes**:

Attributes are the properties or characteristics of entities. They provide details about the entities in the database.

Attributes are typically represented by ovals connected to their respective entities in E-R diagrams.

Example attributes for the "Customer" entity: "Customer ID," "Name," "Email," "Phone."

**Relationships**:

Relationships represent associations or connections between entities. They describe how entities are related to each other.

Relationships are typically represented by diamond shapes in E-R diagrams and are labeled to indicate the nature of the relationship (e.g., "is married to," "works for," "places an order for").

**Cardinality**:

Cardinality defines the number of instances of one entity that can be associated with another entity in a relationship.

Common cardinality notations include "1" (one), "N" (many), and "0" (zero).

Example cardinality: "One customer places many orders," "One order is placed by one customer."

**Primary Key**:

A primary key is an attribute (or a combination of attributes) that uniquely identifies each instance of an entity. It is used to ensure that each entity has a unique identifier.

The primary key is underlined in the attribute oval in E-R diagrams.

**Foreign Key**:

A foreign key is an attribute that establishes a relationship between two tables by referencing the primary key of another table.

It is used to maintain referential integrity in the database by ensuring that the values in the foreign key match the values in the primary key.

**Associative Entity**:

An associative entity (also called a junction or linking entity) is an entity that represents a many-to-many relationship between other entities.

It typically includes attributes that describe the relationship between the connected entities.

**Derived Attribute**:

A derived attribute is an attribute whose value can be calculated or derived from other attributes.

It is represented by a dashed oval in E-R diagrams.

**Weak Entity**:

A weak entity is an entity that cannot be uniquely identified by its attributes alone. It depends on another entity, known as the owner entity, and is identified by a partial key.

It is represented by double rectangles in E-R diagrams.

**Inheritance/Generalization**:

In some E-R models, entities can be organized hierarchically through generalization/specialization, which represents inheritance relationships.

This is used to model entities with shared attributes and relationships.

E-R diagrams are essential for database design because they provide a clear and visual representation of the data structure and relationships within the database. They serve as a blueprint for creating the actual database schema and are a valuable communication tool between designers, developers, and stakeholders involved in the database project.

Q3 What is use of function dependency in DBMS. (RU BCA 2022)

**Answer:**

In a relational database management system (DBMS), functional dependency is a critical concept used to ensure data integrity, guide database design, and enforce rules that govern the relationships between attributes (columns) in a table. Functional dependency helps in the following ways:

**Data Integrity**:

Functional dependencies help maintain data integrity by defining rules that govern how data in one column is related to data in another column.

They ensure that the data in a table is consistent and that there are no inconsistencies or contradictions.

**Normalization**:

Functional dependency is fundamental in the process of database normalization. Normalization is the practice of structuring a relational database in a way that minimizes data redundancy and reduces the likelihood of data anomalies (such as insertion, update, and deletion anomalies).

Normal forms, such as First Normal Form (1NF), Second Normal Form (2NF), Third Normal Form (3NF), Boyce-Codd Normal Form (BCNF), and Fourth Normal Form (4NF), all rely on functional dependencies to guide the decomposition of tables into smaller, related tables.

**Query Optimization**:

By understanding the functional dependencies within the database, query optimization techniques can be applied. These techniques can help optimize query execution plans and improve the performance of data retrieval and manipulation operations.

**Data Validation and Constraints**:

Functional dependencies are used to define constraints on columns in a table. For example, a foreign key constraint is a type of functional dependency that ensures referential integrity between tables.

Check constraints, unique constraints, and primary key constraints are other types of constraints that rely on functional dependencies to validate data.

**Reducing Anomalies**:

Functional dependency rules can help eliminate data anomalies. For example, by specifying that a product's price should depend on the product ID, you can prevent situations where different products have the same price.

**Security and Privacy**:

Functional dependencies can be used to enforce security and privacy rules. For instance, certain attributes may be restricted based on the values of other attributes, ensuring sensitive data is accessible only to authorized users.

Q4 What is mean by data independence? (RU BCA 2021)

**Answer:**

Data independence is a concept in database management systems (DBMS) that refers to the separation of the logical and physical aspects of data. It is a fundamental principle in database design and management, and it ensures that changes made to the physical storage of data do not affect the logical structure of the data as perceived by users and applications. Data independence is typically categorized into two types:

**Logical Data Independence**:

Logical data independence refers to the ability to change the logical schema or structure of the database without affecting the application programs that use the data.

It allows changes to be made to the organization of data, such as adding, modifying, or deleting tables, columns, or relationships, without impacting the functionality of applications.

The goal is to shield the logical view of the data from changes in the underlying physical storage.

For example, if you add a new table to the database to store additional information, the application programs that query the existing data in other tables should continue to function without modification. This is logical data independence in action.

**Physical Data Independence**:

Physical data independence refers to the ability to change the physical storage structures and methods without affecting the logical schema or application programs.

It allows changes to be made to the storage mechanisms, such as moving data to a different storage device, changing indexing methods, or altering the file structure, without impacting the way data is accessed or manipulated.

For example, you might decide to migrate data from one type of storage system (e.g., hard disk drive) to another (e.g., solid-state drive) for performance reasons. With physical data independence, applications and users would still interact with the data in the same way, despite the change in storage technology.

Data independence provides several benefits:

**Flexibility**: It allows for changes in the database schema and storage methods without causing widespread disruptions to applications and users.

**Security**: It can enhance data security by isolating the underlying storage details from unauthorized access.

**Performance**: It enables optimizations in data storage and access methods without requiring changes in the application layer.

Q5 Discuss the architecture and 3-tier architecture. (RU BCA 2021)

**Answer:**

Database architecture and the 3-tier architecture model are two distinct but related concepts in the context of software and database design. Let's discuss each of them separately:

**Database Architecture**:

Database architecture refers to the structure, design, and organization of a database system, including its components, relationships, and how data is stored, accessed, and managed. The architecture of a database system influences its performance, scalability, and efficiency. Common components of a database architecture include:

**Data Storage**: This component deals with how data is physically stored on storage devices. It includes file structures, data organization, and access methods.

**Database Management System (DBMS)**: The DBMS is the core component that manages the database. It handles data storage, retrieval, and management, and it provides a set of tools and interfaces for users and applications to interact with the data.

**Data Access Interfaces**: These interfaces allow applications to connect to and interact with the DBMS. They include APIs (Application Programming Interfaces), SQL, and various query languages.

**Data Models**: The data model defines how data is structured and organized. Common data models include the relational model, hierarchical model, and network model.

**Query Processing and Optimization**: The database system processes and optimizes queries to retrieve data efficiently. This includes query parsing, query optimization, and query execution.

**Concurrency Control**: Database systems manage concurrent access to data by multiple users or applications to ensure data consistency and integrity.

**Security**: Security mechanisms, such as user authentication and access control, are in place to protect the database from unauthorized access and data breaches.

**Backup and Recovery**: Database systems implement mechanisms for data backup and recovery to prevent data loss in case of failures.

**3-Tier Architecture**:

The 3-tier architecture, also known as the three-tier architecture, is a software design and deployment pattern commonly used in web applications and other distributed systems. It separates the application into three distinct layers, each with its specific responsibilities. The three tiers are as follows:

**Presentation Tier (Client Tier)**:

The presentation tier is the topmost layer and is responsible for user interaction and presentation. It includes user interfaces (UIs) such as web browsers, mobile apps, or desktop applications.

The primary goal of this tier is to provide a user-friendly interface for users to interact with the application.

**Application Tier (Middle Tier)**:

The application tier, also known as the middle tier, contains the business logic of the application. It processes user requests, handles application-specific functionality, and communicates with the database.

This tier often includes web servers, application servers, and services that perform tasks such as data processing, authentication, and authorization.

**Data Tier (Database Tier)**:

The data tier, or database tier, is responsible for storing and managing data. It includes the database management system (DBMS) and the actual database where data is stored.

The data tier is responsible for data retrieval, storage, and management, ensuring data consistency and security.

The 3-tier architecture promotes modularity, scalability, and maintainability in software design. Each tier can be developed and scaled independently, making it easier to update or replace one tier without affecting the others. It also enables better separation of concerns, as the presentation tier focuses on the user interface, the application tier handles business logic, and the data tier manages data storage and retrieval. This separation of responsibilities enhances code reusability and overall system flexibility.

Q6 What is ER diagram? (RU BCA 2019)

**Answer:**

An Entity-Relationship (ER) diagram, also known as an ER model, is a visual representation used to design and describe the structure of a relational database. ER diagrams are a popular tool in database design and help in modeling the entities, attributes, and relationships within a database system. They provide a clear and intuitive way to represent the data schema.

Key components of an ER diagram include:

**Entities**: Entities represent real-world objects, concepts, or things for which data is stored in the database. Each entity is typically depicted as a rectangle with a name. Examples of entities might include "Customer," "Product," "Employee," and "Order."

**Attributes**: Attributes describe the properties or characteristics of entities. These properties are used to store specific information about each instance of an entity. Attributes are typically represented as ovals connected to their respective entities. Examples of attributes for the "Customer" entity might include "CustomerID," "Name," "Email," and "Phone."

**Relationships**: Relationships represent the associations or connections between entities. They describe how different entities are related to each other. Relationships are typically shown as diamond shapes connecting the related entities. Examples of relationships might include "Customer places Order," "Product is part of Order," and "Employee manages Department."

**Cardinality**: Cardinality indicates the number of instances of one entity that can be associated with the instances of another entity through a relationship. It helps define the nature of the relationship, such as one-to-one (1:1), one-to-many (1:N), or many-to-many (N:N).

ER diagrams are a valuable tool in the database design process for several reasons:

They provide a clear and visual representation of the database schema, making it easier for database designers, developers, and stakeholders to understand the data structure.

They help identify and define the entities, attributes, and relationships that need to be included in the database.

They assist in the normalization process, which helps in optimizing the database structure and minimizing data redundancy.

They serve as a communication tool between different parties involved in the database project, ensuring a common understanding of the data model.

Q7 Define Normalization. (RU BCA 2019)

**Answer:**

Normalization is a database design technique used to structure a relational database in a way that minimizes data redundancy and reduces the likelihood of data anomalies (such as insertion, update, and deletion anomalies). The primary goal of normalization is to create a database schema that is organized, efficient, and maintains data integrity while ensuring that data is stored in a structured and efficient manner. The process involves breaking down large tables into smaller, related tables and establishing relationships between them.

Key objectives of normalization include:

**Eliminating Data Redundancy**: Redundant data is data that is stored in multiple places in the database. It increases storage requirements and can lead to inconsistencies and data anomalies.

**Minimizing Update Anomalies**: An update anomaly occurs when updating data in one place requires updates in multiple places, potentially leading to inconsistencies if updates are not made consistently.

**Minimizing Insertion Anomalies**: An insertion anomaly occurs when data cannot be added to the database without related data. For example, if a customer's order cannot be entered without the customer's information, it creates a dependency.

**Minimizing Deletion Anomalies**: A deletion anomaly occurs when deleting data in one place leads to unintended data loss, such as deleting a customer's order also deleting their contact information.

Normalization is typically carried out in multiple stages, known as normal forms. The most commonly used normal forms include:

**First Normal Form (1NF)**: Ensures that each column contains atomic (indivisible) values and that there are no repeating groups or arrays.

**Second Normal Form (2NF)**: Builds on 1NF and eliminates partial dependencies by ensuring that non-key attributes are functionally dependent on the entire primary key.

**Third Normal Form (3NF)**: Builds on 2NF and eliminates transitive dependencies by ensuring that non-key attributes are not functionally dependent on other non-key attributes.

**Boyce-Codd Normal Form (BCNF)**: Builds on 3NF and ensures that for every non-trivial functional dependency ($X \rightarrow Y$), X is a superkey (a set of attributes that can uniquely identify a row).

**Fourth Normal Form (4NF)**: Addresses multi-valued dependencies, which are beyond the scope of BCNF.

Q8 Explain 3NF with example. (RU BCA 2019)

**Answer:**

Normalization is an iterative process, and not all databases need to reach the highest normal form. The choice of normal form depends on the specific requirements and trade-offs of the database design. While normalization reduces data redundancy and anomalies, it can sometimes complicate query performance, so it's essential to strike a balance based on the specific use cases and requirements of the database system.

The Third Normal Form (3NF) is a level of normalization in database design that builds on the concepts of the First Normal Form (1NF) and the Second Normal Form (2NF). 3NF eliminates transitive dependencies and further reduces data redundancy by ensuring that non-key attributes are not functionally dependent on other non-key attributes within a table. Here's an explanation of 3NF with an example in a tabular format:

Suppose we have a table named "EmployeeProject" that tracks the projects assigned to employees in a company. The table has the following attributes: EmployeeID, EmployeeName, EmployeeLocation, ProjectID, ProjectName, and ProjectManager.

**EmployeeProject Table**:

| EmployeeID | EmployeeName | EmployeeLocation | ProjectID | ProjectName | ProjectManager |
|---|---|---|---|---|---|
| 101 | Alice | New York | 501 | ProjectA | John |
| 101 | Alice | New York | 502 | ProjectB | Jane |
| 102 | Bob | Los Angeles | 501 | ProjectA | John |
| 103 | Carol | Chicago | 503 | ProjectC | Carol |
| 104 | David | Boston | 504 | ProjectD | Alice |

In this table, we have data redundancy. For example, "EmployeeName" and "EmployeeLocation" are repeated for each EmployeeID, and "ProjectName" and "ProjectManager" are repeated for each ProjectID. To bring the table to 3NF, we'll follow these steps:

**Step 1: Identify the Primary Key**: In this example, the primary key is a combination of "EmployeeID" and "ProjectID" because it uniquely identifies each assignment of an employee to a project.

**Step 2: Eliminate Partial Dependencies**: We need to ensure that non-key attributes are not functionally dependent on part of the primary key. In this case, "EmployeeName" and "EmployeeLocation" are functionally dependent only on "EmployeeID." Therefore, they need to be removed to another table.

**Employee Table**:

| EmployeeID | EmployeeName | EmployeeLocation |
|---|---|---|
| 101 | Alice | New York |
| 102 | Bob | Los Angeles |
| 103 | Carol | Chicago |
| 104 | David | Boston |

**Step 3: Create a New Table for Project Information**: Since "ProjectName" and "ProjectManager" are functionally dependent on "ProjectID," they should be moved to a new table.

**Project Table**:

| ProjectID | ProjectName | ProjectManager |
|---|---|---|
| 501 | ProjectA | John |
| 502 | ProjectB | Jane |
| 503 | ProjectC | Carol |
| 504 | ProjectD | Alice |

With the Employee and Project tables, we have achieved 3NF, as there are no transitive dependencies and non-key attributes are fully functionally dependent on their respective primary keys. This reduces data redundancy and ensures that each table stores information in a way that is more efficient, maintainable, and less prone to data anomalies.

Q9 What is Normalization? Explain INF, 2NF, 3NF with suitable example. (RU BCA 2019, 2017)

**Answer:**

Normalization is a database design technique used to organize a relational database in a structured and efficient manner while minimizing data redundancy and reducing the likelihood of data anomalies. It is typically carried out in multiple stages or normal forms. The most commonly used normal forms include the First Normal Form (1NF), Second Normal Form (2NF), and Third Normal Form (3NF). Let's explore each of these with suitable examples.

**First Normal Form (1NF)**: 1NF focuses on ensuring that each table in a database represents a flat, two-dimensional structure with atomic (indivisible) values in each cell. It eliminates repeating groups or arrays within the table.

*Example*: Consider a table named "Orders" with attributes "OrderID," "CustomerName," and "ProductList," where "ProductList" is a comma-separated list of products in each order. This violates 1NF due to the repeating group in "ProductList."

| OrderID | CustomerName | ProductList |
|---|---|---|
| 1 | Alice | Apples, Bananas |
| 2 | Bob | Oranges, Grapes |
| 3 | Carol | Strawberries, Kiwi |

To bring this table to 1NF, you'd split it into two tables: one for orders and one for products, like this:

**Orders Table**:

| OrderID | CustomerName |
|---|---|
| 1 | Alice |
| 2 | Bob |
| 3 | Carol |

**Products Table**:

| OrderID | ProductName |
|---|---|
| 1 | Apples |
| 1 | Bananas |
| 2 | Oranges |
| 2 | Grapes |
| 3 | Strawberries |
| 3 | Kiwi |

**Second Normal Form (2NF)**: 2NF builds on 1NF and addresses partial dependencies. It requires that non-key attributes are functionally dependent on the entire primary key. In other words, each non-key attribute should depend on the entire primary key, not just a part of it.

*Example*: Consider a "Sales" table with attributes "OrderID," "ProductID," "ProductName," and "ProductPrice," where "ProductName" and "ProductPrice" depend on "ProductID" but not on "OrderID."

| OrderID | ProductID | ProductName | ProductPrice |
|---|---|---|---|
| 1 | 101 | Apples | 1.00 |
| 1 | 102 | Bananas | 0.75 |
| 2 | 101 | Oranges | 1.20 |
| 2 | 103 | Grapes | 1.50 |
| 3 | 102 | Strawberries | 2.00 |
| 3 | 104 | Kiwi | 1.80 |

To bring this table to 2NF, you'd split it into two tables: one for orders and one for products, similar to the 1NF example, and you'd add a new table to represent the relationship between orders and products.

**Orders Table**:

| OrderID |
|---|
| 1 |
| 2 |
| 3 |

**Products Table**:

| ProductID | ProductName | ProductPrice |
|---|---|---|
| 101 | Apples | 1.00 |
| 102 | Bananas | 0.75 |
| 103 | Oranges | 1.20 |
| 104 | Grapes | 1.50 |
| 105 | Strawberries | 2.00 |
| 106 | Kiwi | 1.80 |

**OrderDetails Table**:

| OrderID | ProductID |
|---|---|
| 1 | 101 |
| 1 | 102 |
| 2 | 101 |
| 2 | 103 |
| 3 | 102 |
| 3 | 104 |

**Third Normal Form (3NF)**: 3NF builds on 2NF and addresses transitive dependencies. It ensures that non-key attributes are not functionally dependent on other non-key attributes within the same table.

*Example*: Consider a "Students" table with attributes "StudentID," "StudentName," "Course," "Instructor," and "InstructorEmail," where "Instructor" and "InstructorEmail" depend on "Course" but not on the primary key "StudentID."

| StudentID | StudentName | Course | Instructor | InstructorEmail |
|---|---|---|---|---|
| 1 | Alice | Math | Mr. Smith | smith@example.com |
| 2 | Bob | History | Ms. Davis | davis@example.com |
| 3 | Carol | English | Mr. Turner | turner@example.com |
| 4 | David | Math | Mr. Smith | smith@example.com |
| 5 | Eve | Chemistry | Dr. Brown | brown@example.com |

To bring this table to 3NF, you'd split it into three tables: one for students, one for courses, and one for instructors.

**Students Table**:

| StudentID | StudentName |
|---|---|
| 1 | Alice |
| 2 | Bob |

Q10 What is the difference between 3rd normal form and BCNF with example? (RU BCA 2016)

**Answer:**

**Third Normal Form (3NF):** 3NF eliminates transitive dependencies. In other words, it ensures that non-key attributes are not functionally dependent on other non-key attributes within the same table.

**Boyce-Codd Normal Form (BCNF):** BCNF is a stricter form of normalization that further refines the concept of functional dependency. It ensures that for every non-trivial functional dependency ($X \rightarrow Y$) in a table, X is a superkey. A superkey is a set of attributes that can uniquely identify a row in a table.

**Comparison with Example**:

Let's consider an example to illustrate the difference between 3NF and BCNF. Suppose we have a table called "Students" that records student information, including "StudentID" (the primary key), "StudentName," and "CourseCode." The "CourseCode" attribute represents the code of the course the student is enrolled in, and "CourseName" is the name of the course. Additionally, "InstructorName" is the name of the instructor teaching the course. We have the following data:

**Students Table**:

| StudentID | StudentName | CourseCode | CourseName | InstructorName |
|---|---|---|---|---|
| 1 | Alice | MATH101 | Mathematics | Mr. Smith |
| 2 | Bob | HIST201 | History | Ms. Davis |
| 3 | Carol | ENGL301 | English | Mr. Turner |
| 4 | David | MATH101 | Mathematics | Mr. Smith |

This table has a transitive dependency. "InstructorName" depends on "CourseCode," and "CourseCode" depends on "StudentID" (the primary key). Therefore, "InstructorName" is transitively dependent on "StudentID."

**3NF Transformation**: To bring this table to 3NF, we'd split it into three tables: "Students" (containing student information), "Courses" (containing course information), and "Instructors" (containing instructor information). This eliminates transitive dependencies but still maintains some redundancy in the "CourseCode" and "InstructorName" attributes.

**BCNF Transformation**: To achieve BCNF, we need to consider that "InstructorName" depends on "CourseCode." However, "CourseCode" is not a superkey of the "Courses" table. To address this, we create a new table, "Courses," with attributes "CourseCode" (as the primary key) and "InstructorName."

**Students Table**:

| StudentID | StudentName |
|---|---|
| 1 | Alice |
| 2 | Bob |
| 3 | Carol |
| 4 | David |

**Courses Table**:

| CourseCode | CourseName |
|---|---|
| MATH101 | Mathematics |
| HIST201 | History |
| ENGL301 | English |

**Instructors Table**:

| InstructorName | CourseCode |
|---|---|
| Mr. Smith | MATH101 |
| Ms. Davis | HIST201 |
| Mr. Turner | ENGL301 |

In the BCNF transformation, "InstructorName" is now directly dependent on the "CourseCode," which is a superkey of the "Courses" table. This eliminates the transitive dependency, and the table is in BCNF.

Q11 What is the need of normalization? Explain types of normal form. (RU BCA 2016)

**Answer:**

Normalization is a fundamental process in database design that serves several essential purposes in managing data efficiently and ensuring data integrity. The process of normalization is divided into different normal forms, each building upon the previous one to address specific types of data anomalies and dependencies. The most commonly used normal forms are:

**First Normal Form (1NF)**: Ensures that each table represents a two-dimensional structure with atomic (indivisible) values. It eliminates repeating groups or arrays within a table.

**Second Normal Form (2NF)**: Builds on 1NF and eliminates partial dependencies. It ensures that non-key attributes are functionally dependent on the entire primary key.

**Third Normal Form (3NF)**: Builds on 2NF and eliminates transitive dependencies. It ensures that non-key attributes are not functionally dependent on other non-key attributes within the same table.

**Boyce-Codd Normal Form (BCNF)**: BCNF is a stricter form of normalization that ensures that, for every non-trivial functional dependency ($X \rightarrow Y$) in a table, X is a superkey. A superkey is a set of attributes that can uniquely identify a row in a table.

**Fourth Normal Form (4NF)**: Addresses multi-valued dependencies, which are beyond the scope of BCNF. It ensures that a multi-valued attribute is represented in a separate table.

**Fifth Normal Form (5NF)**: Also known as Project-Join Normal Form (PJNF), this form addresses cases where a table can be decomposed into smaller tables, and the original table can be reconstructed through join operations. It is used in some advanced scenarios.

Each normal form has its specific goals and helps to further reduce redundancy, maintain data integrity, and optimize data storage. The choice of which normal forms to apply depends on the specific requirements of the database and the trade-offs between normalization and query performance.

Q12 What is mean by data independence. (RU BCA 2021)

**Answer:**

Data independence is a fundamental concept in database management systems (DBMS) that refers to the separation of the logical and physical aspects of data. It is a key principle in database design and management that allows for flexibility, adaptability, and ease of maintenance in a database system. Data independence comes in two main forms:

**Logical Data Independence**:

Logical data independence refers to the ability to change the logical schema or structure of the database without affecting the application programs that use the data.

It allows changes to be made to the organization of data, such as adding, modifying, or deleting tables, columns, or relationships, without impacting the functionality of applications.

The primary goal is to shield the logical view of the data from changes in the underlying physical storage.

For example, if you add a new table to the database to store additional information, the application programs that query the existing data in other tables should continue to function without modification. This is logical data independence in action.

**Physical Data Independence**:

Physical data independence refers to the ability to change the physical storage structures and methods without affecting the logical schema or application programs.

It allows changes to be made to the storage mechanisms, such as moving data to a different storage device, changing indexing methods, or altering the file structure, without impacting the way data is accessed or manipulated.

For example, you might decide to migrate data from one type of storage system (e.g., hard disk drive) to another (e.g., solid-state drive) for performance reasons. With physical data independence, applications and users would still interact with the data in the same way, despite the change in storage technology.

Data independence provides several benefits:

**Flexibility**: It allows for changes in the database schema and storage methods without causing widespread disruptions to applications and users.

**Security**: It can enhance data security by isolating the underlying storage details from unauthorized access.

**Performance**: It enables optimizations in data storage and access methods without requiring changes in the application layer.

Data independence is a core principle in DBMS design and contributes to the overall reliability, adaptability, and maintainability of a database system. It allows for a clear separation between the logical model of data and its physical representation, making it easier to evolve and adapt the database as needs change over time.

Q13 What is denormalization? (RU BCA 2022)

**Answer:**

Denormalization is a database design technique that intentionally introduces redundancy into a relational database in order to improve query performance or to simplify data retrieval. In a normalized database, data is organized to minimize redundancy and data anomalies, often following the rules of normal forms, such as the First, Second, and Third Normal Forms. Denormalization, on the other hand, reverses some of these normalization processes to achieve specific goals, which typically involve optimizing read-heavy operations at the expense of increased storage and update complexities.

Denormalization is often applied in situations where query performance is a top priority, such as in data warehousing, reporting systems, and analytical databases. Here are some common reasons for denormalizing a database:

**Improved Query Performance**: Denormalization can reduce the need for complex joins, which can significantly speed up query execution. This is particularly beneficial for systems with frequent and complex read operations.

**Aggregations and Reporting**: Data warehouses and reporting systems often require data in a format that is easy to aggregate, summarize, and present to users. Denormalization simplifies these processes.

**Reduction in Join Complexity**: Joining multiple normalized tables in complex queries can be computationally expensive. Denormalization can simplify query design by reducing the number of necessary joins.

**Reduced Disk I/O**: In a normalized database, data may be distributed across multiple tables, leading to more disk I/O operations during query execution. Denormalization can reduce the number of I/O operations by consolidating data.

**Caching**: In some cases, denormalization can make data caching more effective because it reduces the number of tables and relationships to cache.

Q14 Explain Codd's Relational database rules? (RU BCA 2022)

**Answer:**

Codd's 12 Rules for Relational Databases, proposed by Dr. E.F. Codd, are a set of principles and guidelines that a relational database management system (RDBMS) should adhere to in order to be considered a true relational database system. These rules, often referred to as Codd's Rules or Codd's Commandments, were introduced by Codd in his groundbreaking paper titled "A Relational Model of Data for Large Shared Data Banks" in 1970. Adherence to these rules ensures that a database system is truly relational, which means it follows the principles of the relational model for managing data. Here is a summary of Codd's 12 rules:

**Information Rule**:

All information in the database must be logically represented as values in a table. Each value must be accessible by specifying a table name, primary key value, and column name.

**Guaranteed Access Rule**:

Each data value must be accessible by specifying a precise primary key value.

**Systematic Treatment of Null Values**:

The DBMS must allow each field to remain null (or unknown) without requiring a default value. Null values are treated as a distinct concept, and computations involving null values must yield null results.

**Dynamic Online Catalog Based on The Relational Model**:

The database's structure (metadata) must be stored in the same format as regular data, accessible through a data manipulation language.

**Comprehensive Data Sublanguage Rule**:

The system must provide a comprehensive data sublanguage that is usable for defining, manipulating, and querying data.

**View Updating Rule**:

All views, which are virtual tables, must be updatable by the DBMS. This means that modifications to the data can be made through views.

**High-Level Insert, Update, and Delete Rule**:

The DBMS must support high-level insert, update, and delete operations, allowing users to work with data at a logical level without needing to specify physical data storage details.

**Physical Data Independence**:

Application programs and activities must not depend on the physical data storage characteristics of the database, which should be abstracted away.

**Logical Data Independence**:

Application programs and activities must not depend on the logical structure of the database, allowing changes in the logical schema without affecting application programs.

**Integrity Independence**:

Integrity constraints, such as referential integrity and check constraints, must be separate from the application programs and stored in the catalog.

**Distribution Independence**:

The distribution of data across multiple locations and systems should not affect the logical representation of data.

**The Nonsubversion Rule**:

If the system provides a low-level (record-at-a-time) interface, it must also provide a high-level (set-at-a-time) interface that is not subverted by users.

Q15 Explain Boycc Codd normal form with example. (RU BCA 2021)

**Answer:**

The Boyce-Codd Normal Form (BCNF) is a level of normalization in relational database design. It's a stricter form of normalization than the Third Normal Form (3NF) and aims to eliminate all types of functional dependencies in a table except for those based on candidate keys. A candidate key is a set of attributes that can uniquely identify each row in a table. BCNF helps ensure that the data is organized efficiently, reducing data anomalies and redundancy.

To understand BCNF, let's use an example:

Suppose we have a table called "Employees" that stores information about employees in a company. The table has the following attributes: "EmployeeID" (a unique identifier for each employee), "EmployeeName," "Department," and "Supervisor."

**Employees Table**:

| EmployeeID | EmployeeName | Department | Supervisor |
|---|---|---|---|
| 101 | Alice | HR | Bob |
| 102 | Bob | HR | Carol |
| 103 | Carol | Marketing | David |
| 104 | David | Marketing | Carol |
| 105 | Eve | Sales | David |

In this table, we can identify the following functional dependencies:

EmployeeID → EmployeeName (EmployeeID uniquely determines the employee's name)

EmployeeID → Department

Department → Supervisor (Department uniquely determines the supervisor)

However, there's an issue in this table. The "Department" attribute is not a superkey by itself, but it determines the "Supervisor" attribute. This creates a functional dependency where a non-key attribute ("Department") depends on another non-key attribute ("Supervisor"). This is a violation of BCNF because BCNF requires that for every non-trivial functional dependency X → Y, X must be a superkey.

To bring this table into BCNF, we need to decompose it into two separate tables: one for employee information and another for department and supervisor information.

**Employees Table**:

| EmployeeID | EmployeeName | Department |
|---|---|---|
| 101 | Alice | HR |
| 102 | Bob | HR |
| 103 | Carol | Marketing |
| 104 | David | Marketing |
| 105 | Eve | Sales |

**Supervisors Table**:

| Department | Supervisor |
|---|---|
| HR | Bob |
| Marketing | Carol |
| Sales | David |

Now, the "Supervisors" table contains only the department-supervisor relationship, and "Department" is a candidate key for this table. The "Employees" table contains the employee information, and "EmployeeID" is its primary key. With this decomposition, the "Supervisors" table satisfies BCNF because all non-trivial functional dependencies have a superkey on the left side of the arrow. This ensures data integrity and eliminates redundancy while adhering to the principles of BCNF.

Q16 CODD's rule. (RU BCA 2016)

**Answer:**

E.F. Codd's rules, often referred to as Codd's 12 rules, are a set of principles and guidelines for relational database management systems (RDBMS) that were introduced by Dr. Edgar F. Codd, a computer scientist and pioneer in the field of databases. These rules serve as a foundation for the design and implementation of relational database systems and are aimed at ensuring data consistency, integrity, and reliability. Here are Codd's 12 rules:

**Information Rule:** All information in the database, including metadata, is to be represented in one and only one way – as values in a table.

**Guaranteed Access Rule:** Each data value in the database should be accessible by specifying a table, primary key value, and column name.

**Systematic Treatment of Null Values:** The DBMS must allow each field to remain null, i.e., it must support missing information.

**Dynamic Online Catalog Based on the Relational Model:** The database schema, including the description of the schema itself, is stored in the database as metadata. This allows the schema to evolve without requiring system downtime.

**Comprehensive Data Sublanguage Rule:** The DBMS must support a comprehensive and non-procedural language for defining, querying, and manipulating data.

**View Updating Rule:** All views that are theoretically updatable must be updatable by the system.

**High-Level Insert, Update, and Delete Rule:** The DBMS must support high-level insert, update, and delete operations, rather than just individual record operations.

**Physical Data Independence:** Changes in physical storage structures should not require changes to the application's view of the data.

**Logical Data Independence:** Changes to the logical schema (e.g., adding or modifying tables) should not affect existing applications or their views of the data.

**Integrity Independence:** The DBMS should provide mechanisms to ensure the integrity of the database, and application programs should not be responsible for enforcing integrity constraints.

**Distribution Independence:** The DBMS should be able to distribute data across multiple locations, and this distribution should be transparent to the applications.

**Non-Subversion Rule:** If a relational system has a low-level language, then that language cannot be used to subvert or bypass the integrity rules and constraints of the relational model.

Q17 Discuss the architecture of DBMS. (RU BCA 2018)

**Answer:**

A Database Management System (DBMS) is a software system that provides an organized and efficient way to store, retrieve, manage, and manipulate data. The architecture of a DBMS describes its overall structure, components, and the way these components interact to manage databases. The architecture of a DBMS typically consists of several layers or components, each with its specific responsibilities. Here is an overview of the typical architecture of a DBMS:

**User Interface**:

The user interface is the top layer of the DBMS architecture, where users interact with the database system.

It includes tools, applications, and interfaces for performing various operations such as data entry, querying, reporting, and administration.

Users interact with the DBMS through query languages (e.g., SQL), graphical user interfaces, or application programming interfaces (APIs).

**Query Processor**:

The query processor is responsible for interpreting and executing user queries and commands.

It includes a query parser that validates query syntax, a query optimizer that generates efficient execution plans, and a query executor that carries out the execution of queries.

**Transaction Manager**:

The transaction manager ensures the ACID properties of transactions (Atomicity, Consistency, Isolation, Durability) in a multi-user environment.

It manages concurrent access to the database, handles locking and concurrency control, and ensures data consistency.

**Data Access Layer**:

The data access layer interfaces with the underlying storage systems.

It includes the Database Engine, which communicates with the storage subsystem and is responsible for data retrieval and storage.

The data access layer manages data retrieval, indexing, caching, and data distribution across different storage devices.

**Storage Subsystem**:

The storage subsystem is responsible for physically storing the data.

It includes the database files, data files, transaction logs, and other structures that hold the data.

The storage subsystem ensures data persistence and durability, and it manages physical data organization on storage devices.

**Database Engine**:

The database engine interacts with the storage subsystem to read and write data.

It includes the query execution engine, which processes queries, and the data manipulation engine, which handles insert, update, and delete operations.

The database engine also manages query optimization and query processing.

**Catalog Manager**:

The catalog manager stores metadata about the database schema, such as tables, columns, indexes, constraints, and relationships.

It provides data dictionary services and maintains information about the structure of the database.

**Security and Authorization**:

The security and authorization component enforces access control policies, ensuring that only authorized users can perform specific operations on the data.

It includes authentication, authorization, and auditing mechanisms to protect the data and maintain data security.

**Backup and Recovery**:

The backup and recovery module is responsible for creating and managing data backups and restoring the database in case of failures or data corruption.

It includes tools and processes for disaster recovery, backup scheduling, and data restoration.

**Utilities**:

Utilities are auxiliary tools and services that aid in database administration and maintenance.

These utilities include backup utilities, data loading tools, performance tuning tools, and database monitoring tools.

Q18 Explain the rules defined by CODD that are necessary for any DBMs to be considered as a RDBMS. (RU BCA 2017)

**Answer:**

Dr. Edgar F. Codd, a computer scientist and mathematician, defined a set of rules that any database management system (DBMS) must adhere to in order to be considered a true Relational Database Management System (RDBMS). These rules are designed to ensure that a DBMS fully implements the principles of the relational model, providing data consistency, integrity, and reliability. Here are the rules defined by Codd for RDBMS:

**Information Rule**:

All information in the database is to be represented in one and only one way: as values in a table.

This rule emphasizes the use of tables to represent data, where each value is stored at the intersection of a row and a column.

**Guaranteed Access Rule**:

Each data value in the database must be accessible by specifying a table name, primary key value, and column name.

This rule ensures that users can retrieve specific data values with precision using the appropriate table and keys.

**Systematic Treatment of Null Values**:

The DBMS must allow each field to remain null, meaning it should support missing or unknown information.

Null values are treated in a systematic and consistent manner, allowing for the representation of missing data.

**Dynamic Online Catalog Based on the Relational Model**:

The database schema, including the schema's description, is stored in the database itself, and users can query this schema using the same query language used for data.

This rule supports data independence and enables the dynamic modification of the schema without requiring system downtime.

**Comprehensive Data Sublanguage Rule**:

The DBMS must provide a comprehensive and non-procedural query language for defining, querying, and manipulating data.

The query language should be expressive enough to handle all types of data operations.

**View Updating Rule**:

All views that are theoretically updatable must be updatable by the system.

Views represent virtual tables based on the underlying data, and this rule ensures that updates through views are supported when possible.

**High-Level Insert, Update, and Delete Rule**:

The DBMS must support high-level insert, update, and delete operations for sets of data, rather than just individual record operations.

This rule simplifies data manipulation and ensures that data changes can be performed efficiently.

**Physical Data Independence**:

Changes in physical storage structures and access paths should not affect the user's view of the data.

Users should be shielded from the physical storage details, allowing for modifications without impacting the application.

**Logical Data Independence**:

Changes to the logical schema (e.g., adding or modifying tables) should not require changes to existing application programs.

Logical data independence separates the application's logical view of the data from the physical storage structure.

**Integrity Independence**:

The DBMS should provide mechanisms to ensure the integrity of the database, including integrity constraints and business rules.

Application programs should not be responsible for enforcing integrity constraints.

Q19. What do you mean by functional dependency? (RU BCA 2016)

**Answer:**

Functional dependency is a fundamental concept in the theory of relational databases. It defines a relationship between attributes (columns) in a relational database table. A functional dependency occurs when the value of one attribute uniquely determines the value of another attribute within the same table. In other words, if you know the value of one attribute, you can predict the value of another attribute based on a specific rule or condition.

Functional dependency is denoted as X -> Y, where X and Y represent sets of attributes. The arrow (->) indicates that the attributes in set X determine the attributes in set Y. Here are some key points about functional dependency:

**Determinant and Dependent Attributes**: In X -> Y, X is called the determinant, and Y is the dependent attribute. The value(s) in X determine the value(s) in Y.

**Full Functional Dependency**: X -> Y is a full functional dependency if removing any attribute from X would break the dependency. In other words, no proper subset of X can determine Y.

**Partial Functional Dependency**: A functional dependency X -> Y is partial if removing one or more attributes from X still allows it to determine Y. This typically indicates a violation of the Second Normal Form (2NF).

**Transitive Dependency**: A functional dependency is transitive if X -> Y, and Y -> Z, where X, Y, and Z are sets of attributes. This implies that X -> Z is also a valid functional dependency.

**Multivalued Dependency**: A multivalued dependency occurs when one attribute (or set of attributes) determines another set of attributes. It's a more complex form of dependency.

Functional dependencies play a crucial role in the process of database normalization, where the goal is to eliminate or minimize data redundancy and potential anomalies. Ensuring that data is organized based on functional dependencies helps maintain data integrity and consistency. The rules of normalization, such as the Third Normal Form (3NF) and Boyce-Codd Normal Form (BCNF), are designed to eliminate certain types of functional dependencies to improve the overall structure of a relational database.

Q20What do you mean by data independence? (RU BCA 2016)

**Answer:**

Data independence is a fundamental concept in database management systems (DBMS) that refers to the separation of the physical and logical aspects of data storage and retrieval. It allows for changes to be made to the physical storage structures of data without affecting the way data is accessed, manipulated, or perceived at the logical or application level. Data independence is a key characteristic of DBMS that offers several important advantages:

There are two main types of data independence:

**Physical Data Independence**:

Physical data independence allows changes to be made in the physical storage structures, such as storage devices, file organization, indexing methods, and data access methods, without impacting the logical schema or the way data is viewed by applications.

In other words, alterations to how data is stored do not require changes to the application programs or queries that access that data.

This type of data independence is particularly valuable for system administrators and database architects who can optimize the physical storage for performance, scalability, and cost considerations without disrupting application functionality.

**Logical Data Independence**:

Logical data independence allows changes to be made to the logical schema of the database, such as adding or modifying tables, columns, relationships, constraints, and views, without affecting the application programs.

It enables the database schema to evolve and adapt to changing business requirements without breaking existing applications that rely on the data.

Application developers benefit from this type of data independence as they can focus on application logic without being concerned about the underlying changes to the database schema.

Data independence is a critical aspect of DBMS design because it simplifies data management, promotes flexibility, and ensures that changes to the database can be made without causing widespread disruptions. It also helps in maintaining data consistency, integrity, and security by separating the physical and logical aspects of data.

Q21. Define Functional Dependency. [Marks: 2] (RTU MCA 2022)

**Answer:**

Functional dependency is a key concept in the normalization of databases in relational database management systems (RDBMS). It describes a relationship between two attributes, typically between the primary key and non-key attributes within a table.

For a given relation R, a functional dependency between two sets of attributes A and B in R is denoted as A -> B, which means 'B is functionally dependent on A'. This implies that for each value of A, there is precisely one corresponding value of B. In other words, if two rows of data in the table have the same value for A, they must also have the same value for B.

Functional dependency plays a crucial role in understanding the relational structure of a database and is fundamental in the process of normalization, which aims to minimize redundancy and dependency by organizing fields and tables of a database. The ultimate goal of defining functional dependencies is to ensure the database is in a normal form, which helps in maintaining data integrity and reducing anomalies in data manipulation operations (insertion, deletion, and update).

Examples of functional dependency include:

EmployeeID -> EmployeeName: Here, EmployeeName is functionally dependent on EmployeeID because each EmployeeID is associated with a unique EmployeeName.

StudentID -> (StudentName, CourseRegistered): In this case, both StudentName and CourseRegistered are functionally dependent on StudentID.

Identifying and applying functional dependencies are essential steps in database design that help in achieving a well-structured and efficient database system.

Q22. What do you mean by Normalization? [Marks: 2] (RTU MCA 2022)

**Answer:**

Normalization in the context of database systems is a process aimed at designing the schema of a database in a way that reduces redundancy and improves data integrity. It involves organizing the fields (attributes) and tables of a database to minimize duplication of information and to prevent data anomalies that can occur when adding, deleting, or updating records. This process is achieved by dividing large tables into smaller, more manageable ones and defining relationships between them according to rules designed to safeguard the data and make the database more efficient.

The normalization process is typically carried out in several steps, each of which corresponds to a "normal form," a condition that a database schema must meet. The most commonly used normal forms are:

**First Normal Form (1NF):** Ensures that the values in each column of a table are atomic, meaning each column must hold only individual (not group or set) values, and each row is unique.

**Second Normal Form (2NF):** Based on the concept of fully functional dependency. A table is in 2NF if it is in 1NF and all non-key attributes are fully functionally dependent on the primary key. This eliminates partial dependency, improving database efficiency.

**Third Normal Form (3NF):** A table is in 3NF if it is in 2NF and all its attributes are not only fully functionally dependent on the primary key but also non-transitively dependent. In other words, no non-key attribute depends on another non-key attribute.

**Boyce-Codd Normal Form (BCNF):** A stronger version of the 3NF. A table is in BCNF if, for every one of its non-trivial functional dependencies X → Y, X is a superkey—a set of attributes that uniquely identifies a row in a table.

Further normal forms exist (4NF and 5NF, related to multi-valued dependencies and join dependencies, respectively), but achieving 3NF or BCNF is often sufficient for most practical database designs. Normalization helps in reducing data redundancy, ensures data consistency, and simplifies the structure of the database, making it easier to maintain and update. However, over-normalization can lead to excessive table fragmentation, which can adversely affect query performance. Therefore, a balance must be struck between normalization for integrity and denormalization for performance.

Q23. The Schema S = (A, B, C, D, E). The F of functional dependencies is

{A —Y B, BC E, ED A)

Is S in BCNF? Why? [Marks: 4](RTU MCA 2022)

**Answer**

To determine if the schema S=(A,B,C,D,E) with the set of functional dependencies F={A→B,BC→E,ED→A} is in Boyce-Codd Normal Form (BCNF), we need to examine each functional dependency and ensure that for every dependency X→Y, X is a superkey of the schema. A superkey is a set of attributes that uniquely identifies a row in a table.

Let's analyze each functional dependency in F:

**A→B:** For this dependency to satisfy BCNF, A must be a superkey. This means A alone should be able to uniquely identify every row in the schema. Without more information (like additional functional dependencies or knowing that A is part of a candidate key), we can't automatically assume A is a superkey. However, this analysis typically requires considering the full set of functional dependencies and candidate keys, which are not fully provided here.

**BC→E:** For this dependency, BC should be a superkey. Since BC determines E, and if we assume that BC can uniquely identify a row (this assumption needs validation through candidate key analysis), this dependency could satisfy BCNF.

**ED→A:** Similarly, for ED to satisfy BCNF, ED must be a superkey. ED determines A, indicating that if ED is unique for each row, this dependency could meet BCNF requirements.

**Determining BCNF Compliance:**

**Without explicit candidate keys:** We cannot definitively conclude if S is in BCNF without knowing all the candidate keys of the schema because the status of A, BC, and ED as superkeys depends on the complete set of functional dependencies and the identification of all candidate keys.

**General Criterion for BCNF:** A schema is in BCNF if, for every one of its functional dependencies X→Y, X is a superkey.

Given the functional dependencies:

If A, BC, and ED are all superkeys, then S would be in BCNF.

If any of A, BC, or ED is not a superkey, then S is not in BCNF.

**Conclusion:**

To conclusively determine if S is in BCNF, we would need a comprehensive analysis including the identification of all candidate keys for the schema based on the provided functional dependencies and any others that might exist. Given the provided dependencies and without additional information about candidate keys, we can't definitively say whether S is in BCNF. The determination hinges on whether A, BC, and ED are superkeys, which requires further analysis beyond the given dependencies.

## ONLINE RESOURCES

**Practice Paper Link** : https://forms.gle/UCE3tkhwTNcDUAr39

**QR Code:**

**Video Content:** https://www.youtube.com/playlist?list=PLzlh_31VWEFrMmNTIGE7i4E0mcqQOaiY7

**QR Code:**

# Chapter 4:Database Administration

## Role of a Database Administrator (DBA)

The role of a Database Administrator (DBA) is crucial in managing, maintaining, and optimizing a database environment. DBAs play a pivotal role in ensuring the availability, security, and performance of databases, which are at the core of many organizations' data infrastructure. Here's a detailed overview of the role and responsibilities of a DBA:

**Database Installation and Configuration:**

DBAs are responsible for installing and configuring database management systems (DBMS) software. They ensure that the database software is correctly set up, optimized for performance, and aligned with organizational needs.

**Database Design:**

DBAs participate in database design and schema development. They work closely with application developers and data analysts to create efficient and well-structured databases that meet business requirements.

**Security Management:**

Database security is a top priority. DBAs implement security measures, including user access control, authentication, and encryption, to protect sensitive data from unauthorized access or breaches.

**User Management:**

DBAs manage user accounts and permissions within the database. They grant appropriate access rights to users and ensure compliance with data security policies.

**Backup and Recovery:**

Regular data backups are essential to safeguard against data loss due to hardware failures, human errors, or disasters. DBAs design and maintain backup and recovery strategies, ensuring data can be restored quickly when needed.

**Performance Tuning:**

Optimizing database performance is a critical aspect of the DBA role. DBAs monitor database performance, identify bottlenecks, and implement optimizations, such as indexing and query tuning, to ensure efficient data retrieval.

**Monitoring and Alerts:**

DBAs use monitoring tools to keep a watchful eye on the database environment. They set up alerts and notifications to proactively identify and address potential issues before they impact system performance.

**Patch Management:**

DBAs apply patches, updates, and software upgrades to keep the database software secure and up to date. They ensure that these changes do not disrupt ongoing operations.

**Capacity Planning:**

DBAs plan for future database growth by monitoring resource usage and predicting capacity requirements. They may recommend hardware upgrades or the addition of new database servers to accommodate increased data volumes.

**Disaster Recovery Planning:**

In collaboration with IT teams, DBAs develop and maintain disaster recovery plans. These plans outline procedures for data recovery in case of catastrophic events.

**Documentation:**

DBAs maintain comprehensive documentation of database configurations, security policies, and procedures. This documentation is essential for troubleshooting, auditing, and compliance purposes.

**Troubleshooting and Support:**

When database issues arise, DBAs are the first responders. They diagnose and resolve problems, working closely with application developers and system administrators to ensure minimal downtime.

**Compliance and Auditing:**

DBAs ensure that the database environment complies with regulatory requirements and industry standards. They may participate in compliance audits and assist in preparing audit reports.

Automation and Scripting:

DBAs often use automation scripts and tools to streamline routine tasks, such as data backups, performance monitoring, and user provisioning.

**Training and Knowledge Sharing:**

DBAs stay updated on the latest database technologies and best practices. They may provide training to other team members and share knowledge within the organization.

In summary, the role of a Database Administrator is multifaceted, encompassing database design, security, performance optimization, backup and recovery, and proactive monitoring. DBAs are instrumental in maintaining the integrity and availability of an organization's data, ensuring that databases operate efficiently and securely to support critical business functions.

## 4.2 Database Security and Authorization

Database security and authorization are critical aspects of Database Management Systems (DBMS) to protect sensitive data from unauthorized access, breaches, and data manipulation. Here's an in-depth overview of database security and authorization in DBMS:

**Authentication:**

Authentication is the process of verifying the identity of users or applications attempting to access the database. Common authentication methods include username and password, multi-factor authentication (MFA), and integration with identity providers like Active Directory.

**Authorization:**

Authorization determines what actions or operations users or applications are allowed to perform within the database. It involves defining roles, privileges, and permissions. Authorization controls can be categorized as follows:

Role-Based Access Control (RBAC): RBAC assigns roles to users, and each role is associated with specific privileges. Users inherit the permissions of the roles they are assigned.

Discretionary Access Control (DAC): DAC allows the owner of an object (e.g., a table) to specify who can access or modify it. Owners have full control over access permissions.

Mandatory Access Control (MAC): MAC enforces data access based on security labels and classifications. It is commonly used in government and military environments.

**Access Control Lists (ACLs):**

ACLs are lists of permissions associated with a database object. They specify which users or roles have read, write, execute, or other types of access to the object. ACLs are common in DAC-based authorization systems.

**Database Roles:**

Roles are used to group users and manage permissions more efficiently. Instead of assigning permissions to individual users, permissions can be assigned to roles, and users are then assigned to those roles. This simplifies user management and ensures consistency in access control.

**Privileges:**

Privileges define the specific actions or operations that users or roles can perform on database objects. Common privileges include SELECT, INSERT, UPDATE, DELETE, CREATE, and DROP.

**Encryption:**

Encryption ensures that data, both at rest and in transit, is protected from unauthorized access. Data encryption methods include Transparent Data Encryption (TDE) for data at rest and Secure Sockets Layer (SSL) for data in transit.

**Auditing and Logging:**

Database systems can log access and modification activities. Auditing helps detect and investigate security breaches, compliance violations, and suspicious activities. Auditing logs can include information about who accessed the data, what they did, and when it occurred.

**Security Policies and Procedures:**

Organizations should establish and enforce security policies and procedures to govern database access, user account management, password policies, and data classification. Regular security audits and compliance checks help ensure policy adherence.

**Database Firewalls:**

Firewalls specifically designed for databases monitor and filter incoming and outgoing database traffic, helping to block unauthorized access and SQL injection attacks.

**Vulnerability Assessment:**

Regular vulnerability assessments and security scans can identify potential weaknesses in the database system, allowing administrators to patch vulnerabilities before they are exploited.

**Database Activity Monitoring (DAM):**

DAM tools continuously monitor database activities in real-time, generating alerts for suspicious or unauthorized actions. They help detect and respond to security incidents promptly.

Effective database security and authorization practices are essential to protect sensitive data, comply with regulations (such as GDPR and HIPAA), and maintain the trust of customers and stakeholders. Database administrators and security teams should work together to implement robust security measures and stay vigilant against evolving threats.

**Authorization Matrix**

An authorization matrix, often referred to as an access control matrix or permission matrix, is a fundamental component of database security and authorization. It provides a structured representation of the permissions and access rights that users or entities have within a database management system (DBMS). This matrix is essential for controlling and managing who can perform specific actions on the database objects (e.g., tables, views, procedures) and the type of actions they can perform (e.g., read, write, execute).

Here's a more detailed explanation of an authorization matrix in the context of database security and authorization:

Rows and Columns: An authorization matrix typically consists of rows and columns. Rows represent individual users, roles, or entities, while columns represent specific actions or privileges associated with database objects.

Users/Entities: Each row in the matrix corresponds to a user or entity that interacts with the database. This can include database administrators, application users, or various roles defined within the DBMS.

Actions/Privileges: Each column in the matrix represents a specific action or privilege that can be applied to a database object. Common privileges include SELECT (read), INSERT (write), UPDATE (modify), DELETE (remove), and EXECUTE (execute stored procedures).

Permissions: The intersections of rows and columns in the matrix contain information about the permissions or access rights granted to a particular user or entity for a specific action or privilege. These permissions are typically represented as binary values (e.g., 1 for granted, 0 for denied).

Granularity: The granularity of the matrix can vary, depending on the complexity of the authorization requirements. In some cases, it may be fine-grained, specifying permissions for individual tables or even columns within tables. In other cases, it may be coarse-grained, defining permissions at a higher level (e.g., read access to an entire schema).

Dynamic vs. Static: Authorization matrices can be either static or dynamic. In a static matrix, permissions are predefined and rarely change. In a dynamic matrix, permissions may change more frequently based on user roles, organizational changes, or security policies.

Role-Based Access Control (RBAC): Many authorization matrices incorporate role-based access control, where permissions are assigned to roles, and users are assigned to roles. This simplifies access control management by associating permissions with roles rather than individual users.

Access Control Lists (ACLs): Some DBMSs use access control lists (ACLs) to manage permissions. An ACL is a list of permissions attached to an object, specifying who can access it and what actions they can perform.

The authorization matrix plays a crucial role in maintaining data security and integrity within a database system. It ensures that users and entities have the appropriate level of access while preventing unauthorized or malicious activities. Regular auditing and review of the matrix are essential to ensure that access rights remain aligned with organizational security policies.

To create an authorization matrix for two users, "Student" and "Administrator," for the given relations "student" and "marks," we'll make some assumptions about the permissions these users should have. Here's a simplified authorization matrix based on common access requirements:

Assumptions:

"Student" users can only view their own data (d name and address) in the "student" relation.

"Administrator" users have full access to both relations for management purposes.

Authorization Matrix:

For the "student" relation:

| | SELECT | INSERT | UPDATE | DELETE |
|---|---|---|---|---|
| **Student** | Yes | No | No | No |
| **Admin** | Yes | Yes | Yes | Yes |

For the "marks" relation:

| | SELECT | INSERT | UPDATE | DELETE |
|---|---|---|---|---|
| **Student** | Yes | No | No | No |
| **Admin** | Yes | Yes | Yes | Yes |

Explanation:

"Student" users have SELECT permissions on both the "student" and "marks" relations, allowing them to view data.

"Student" users do not have INSERT, UPDATE, or DELETE permissions for either relation, as they are only allowed to view their own data and not modify it.

"Administrator" users have full permissions (SELECT, INSERT, UPDATE, DELETE) for both relations. This allows them to manage and manipulate the data in both "student" and "marks" as needed.

These permissions are based on the assumption that "Student" users should have read-only access to their data, while "Administrator" users have complete control over both relations. Depending on your specific security and access control requirements, you can further refine these permissions or implement role-based access control (RBAC) for more complex scenarios.

## 4.3 Backup and Recovery

Backup and recovery are critical components of Database Management Systems (DBMS) to ensure data availability, business continuity, and disaster preparedness. Here's a detailed explanation of backup and recovery in DBMS:

**Backup:**

Backup is the process of creating copies of a database to safeguard against data loss due to various reasons, such as hardware failures, software errors, human mistakes, or disasters. Database backups serve as a point-in-time snapshot of the database, allowing data to be restored to a previous state if needed.

**Types of Backups:**

Full Backup: A full backup captures the entire database, including all its data and schema objects. It provides a complete restoration point but can be resource-intensive and time-consuming.

Differential Backup: A differential backup captures changes made since the last full backup. It reduces backup time and storage requirements compared to full backups but may require additional differential backups to maintain a complete restoration point.

Incremental Backup: An incremental backup captures changes made since the last backup (either full or incremental). It is the most space-efficient backup type but requires a full backup and all subsequent incremental backups for complete restoration.

**Backup Methods:**

**Physical Backup:** Physical backups create exact copies of database files, such as data files, log files, and configuration files. This method is faster but requires more storage space.

**Logical Backup:** Logical backups export database data in a human-readable format (e.g., SQL statements or CSV files). While they are less space-efficient, they offer greater flexibility when restoring specific data or objects.

**Recovery:**

Recovery involves restoring the database to a consistent and usable state after a failure or data loss incident. The recovery process aims to minimize downtime and data loss while ensuring data consistency.

**Recovery Techniques:**

Rollback: If a transaction encounters an error or fails, the database system can perform a rollback to undo any changes made by the transaction, ensuring data consistency.

Point-in-Time Recovery: This technique restores the database to a specific point in time, allowing data to be recovered up to that moment. It's useful for recovering from logical errors or human mistakes.

Media Recovery: In the event of hardware failure or data corruption, media recovery involves restoring the database from backups and applying transaction log files to bring it to a consistent state.

**Recovery Models:**

Full Recovery Model: This model provides complete data recoverability. It requires regular full and transaction log backups. It is suitable for mission-critical databases.

Simple Recovery Model: In this model, only full backups and minimal transaction log backups are required. It is suitable for less critical databases where some data loss is acceptable.

Bulk-Logged Recovery Model: It balances the need for data recoverability with reduced log space requirements for bulk data operations. It is used for large-scale data loading.

Best Practices

Regularly schedule backups and test their restore processes to ensure they work as expected.

Store backups in secure, offsite locations to protect against disasters like fires or floods.

Monitor database health and set up alerts for potential issues.

Maintain a disaster recovery plan that outlines procedures for different types of failures.

Train database administrators and staff on backup and recovery procedures.

Effective backup and recovery strategies are essential to minimize downtime, protect data integrity, and ensure business continuity in the event of database failures or data loss incidents. Organizations should tailor their backup and recovery plans to their specific needs and risk tolerance.

**Backward Recovery:**

Backward recovery, also known as roll-back recovery or compensating transactions, is a recovery technique that involves undoing the effects of a set of transactions to bring the database back to a consistent state.

Usage: It is typically used in situations where a failure has occurred during the execution of a transaction or a set of transactions. The goal is to reverse the changes made by the failed transaction(s) to ensure data consistency.

Process: When a failure is detected, backward recovery identifies the transactions that were in progress or had completed but had not yet been committed at the time of the failure. These transactions are rolled back, meaning their changes are undone.

Example: If a database transaction was transferring money from one account to another and the system crashed before the transaction was committed, backward recovery would reverse the transfer to maintain data consistency.

**Forward Recovery:**

Forward recovery, also known as roll-forward recovery, involves reapplying or re-executing transactions from a consistent state to bring the database up to the point just before the failure occurred.

Usage: It is used when a system failure has occurred, and the goal is to bring the database up to date with all the committed transactions and changes that were made before the failure.

Process: Forward recovery identifies the last consistent state of the database before the failure and then replays or reapplies transactions from that point onwards. This process brings the database back to its most recent consistent state.

Example: If a system failure occurred after several transactions were successfully committed, forward recovery would replay those transactions to ensure that the database reflects all the committed changes.

**Key Differences:**

The primary difference lies in the direction of recovery. Backward recovery undoes changes made by uncommitted transactions, while forward recovery reprocesses committed transactions.

Goal: Backward recovery's goal is to revert to a previous state, often to maintain consistency after a failure, whereas forward recovery's goal is to catch up to the latest consistent state before the failure.

Usage: Backward recovery is typically used for failures within transactions, while forward recovery is used for system failures that affect multiple transactions.

Transaction Handling: Backward recovery focuses on rolling back transactions, while forward recovery involves reapplying transactions.

Data Loss: Backward recovery may result in data loss for uncommitted changes, while forward recovery aims to minimize data loss by applying all committed changes.

Backward Recovery and Forward Recovery are two different approaches to database recovery in the context of a system failure or crash. They focus on different aspects of ensuring data consistency and bringing the database back to a valid state. Both backward and forward recovery are important techniques for ensuring data consistency and system resilience in database management systems. The choice between them depends on the specific requirements and circumstances of the recovery process.

**Checkpoint Mechanism**

The checkpoint mechanism in data recovery is a critical component of a database management system (DBMS) that helps ensure the consistency and durability of data in the event of a system failure or crash. It is a process that periodically records a snapshot or checkpoint of the database's state at a particular moment in time.

**How the Checkpoint Mechanism Works:**

Snapshot Creation: At regular intervals or predefined points in time, the DBMS creates a snapshot of the database's current state. This snapshot typically includes information about the current state of transactions, committed changes, and other relevant metadata.

Logging: Before the snapshot is created, the DBMS ensures that all changes made by transactions are written to a transaction log or a similar mechanism. This log records details of each transaction's activities, such as data modifications (inserts, updates, deletes), transaction start and commit times, and other relevant information.

Checkpoint Record: Along with the snapshot, the DBMS records a checkpoint record in the transaction log. This record serves as a marker or point of reference, indicating the point in time up to which all transactions have been safely written to the log and committed to the database.

Storage: Both the snapshot and the checkpoint record are stored in a safe and persistent location, typically on non-volatile storage devices like hard drives or solid-state drives (SSDs). This ensures that they survive system crashes or failures.

**Significance of the Checkpoint Mechanism in Data Recovery:**

Recovery Point: The checkpoint record establishes a known recovery point. In the event of a system failure, the DBMS can start the recovery process from this checkpoint, ensuring that all transactions up to that point are considered committed, while any uncommitted changes can be rolled back.

Efficiency: By periodically creating checkpoints and storing them, the DBMS reduces the amount of data that needs to be processed during recovery. Without checkpoints, the system would have to replay all transactions from the beginning, which could be time-consuming and resource-intensive.

Data Consistency: The checkpoint mechanism helps maintain data consistency. It ensures that only committed changes are considered permanent, reducing the risk of data corruption or inconsistency in the event of a failure.

Reduced Downtime: When a failure occurs, the DBMS can quickly recover to a consistent state using the most recent checkpoint, minimizing system downtime and data loss.

Log Management: The checkpoint mechanism also facilitates efficient log management. Once a checkpoint is created, the DBMS can truncate or archive older log entries, freeing up storage space for new transactions.

The checkpoint mechanism is a fundamental component of data recovery in a DBMS. It provides a well-defined recovery point, reduces recovery time and resource overhead, and helps maintain data consistency and durability in the face of system failures or crashes. It is an essential feature for ensuring the reliability of database systems.

**Log-based recovery**

Log-based recovery is a technique used in database management systems to ensure data consistency and recover from system failures or crashes. It relies on maintaining a log, also known as the transaction log or redo log, that records all changes made to the database. This log allows the system to reapply or undo transactions in the event of a failure, ensuring that the database remains in a consistent state.

Here's how log-based recovery works with an example of concurrent transactions:

Example Scenario:

Consider a database with a simple "bank_account" table that stores customer account balances. Two concurrent transactions, T1 and T2, are being executed:

Transaction T1: Transfer $100 from Account A to Account B.

Transaction T2: Withdraw $50 from Account B.

**Log Entries:**

The log records changes made by each transaction, including the type of operation (INSERT, UPDATE, DELETE), the affected table and rows, and the values before and after the change. Here's what the log might look like:

T1: Update bank_account set balance=balance-100 where account_id=A

T1: Update bank_account set balance=balance+100 where account_id=B

T2: Update bank_account set balance=balance-50 where account_id=B

**Recovery Process:**

Now, let's consider a system failure that occurs after transaction T1 has completed (but before T2) due to a power outage. When the system is restored, log-based recovery ensures data consistency:

During recovery, the system scans the transaction log to identify the last committed transactions, which is T1 in this case.

It then reverts any uncommitted transactions (incomplete transactions) like T2 by undoing their changes. In this example, T2's withdrawal of $50 from Account B is undone.

After the undo phase, the system reapplies the changes made by the committed transactions. In this case, T1's transfer of $100 from Account A to Account B is reapplied.

**Drawbacks of Log-Based Recovery:**

Performance Overhead: Maintaining detailed logs for every transaction can introduce performance overhead. Writing log entries for every database operation can slow down system performance.

Storage Requirements: Logs can consume significant storage space, especially in large databases with high transaction rates. Managing log storage and ensuring its integrity are crucial.

Complexity: Implementing log-based recovery mechanisms can be complex and may require careful design to ensure correctness and efficiency.

Recovery Time: The recovery process, particularly for large databases, can be time-consuming. The time taken to analyse and apply logs can result in database downtime during recovery.

Limited Granularity: Log-based recovery typically operates at the transaction level. It may not be suitable for scenarios where finer-grained recovery is required, such as recovering specific rows or individual changes

Despite these drawbacks, log-based recovery is widely used because it provides a robust and reliable method for database systems to recover from various types of failures while maintaining data consistency and integrity.

## 4.4 Performance Tuning

Performance tuning in Database Management Systems (DBMS) is the process of optimizing a database system's performance to ensure it operates efficiently and meets the required performance standards. Efficient database performance is critical for applications and organizations that rely on quick access to data. Here are key aspects and techniques of performance tuning in DBMS:

**Profiling and Monitoring:**

Start by profiling and monitoring the database system to identify performance bottlenecks. Tools and techniques like database profiling, query profiling, and performance monitoring tools can help pinpoint areas that require optimization.

**Query Optimization:**

One of the most effective ways to improve performance is by optimizing database queries. Ensure that SQL queries are well-written and efficient. This includes using appropriate indexes, reducing unnecessary data retrieval, and avoiding complex joins.

**Indexing**:

Proper indexing is crucial for efficient data retrieval. Identify and create indexes on columns frequently used in WHERE clauses or joins. However, be mindful of over-indexing, which can impact write performance.

**Data Modelling:**

A well-designed database schema can significantly impact performance. Normalize the schema to eliminate data redundancy but denormalize when necessary for read-heavy operations. Carefully select data types to minimize storage and improve query speed.

**Database Configuration:**

Adjust database configuration settings to match system resources and workload. Parameters such as buffer pool size, memory allocation, and thread settings can have a significant impact on performance.

**Hardware Upgrades:**

Consider hardware upgrades when dealing with performance bottlenecks. Increasing CPU power, adding more RAM, or using faster storage devices can boost database performance.

**Caching Strategies**:

Implement caching mechanisms at various levels, including query caching and application-level caching. Caching reduces the need to access the database for frequently requested data.

**Connection Pooling**:

Use connection pooling to manage database connections efficiently. Creating and destroying connections for each request can impose a significant overhead on the database.

**Partitioning:**

If you have large tables, consider partitioning them into smaller, more manageable pieces. This can improve query performance and maintenance tasks.

**Compression:**

Implement data compression techniques to reduce storage requirements and improve I/O performance. Many DBMSs offer built-in compression options.

**Regular Maintenance:**

Schedule regular database maintenance tasks, such as index rebuilding, statistics updating, and garbage collection. These tasks help maintain database performance over time.

**Load Balancing:**

In a multi-server setup, implement load balancing to evenly distribute queries and transactions across database servers. This can improve response times and scalability.

**Benchmarking and Testing:**

Continuously benchmark and test the database system to measure performance improvements accurately. Use performance testing tools and scenarios that simulate real-world usage.

**Historical Data Archiving:**

Archive and store historical data separately to reduce the size of active databases. This can improve query performance for current data.

**Query and Report Optimization:**

For reporting databases, optimize queries and reports separately. Aggregating data, using summary tables, or precomputing complex reports can significantly enhance performance.

**Database Sharding:**

In large-scale systems, consider database sharding, which partitions data across multiple databases or servers based on specific criteria. This approach can distribute the workload and improve scalability.

Performance tuning in DBMS is an ongoing process that requires constant monitoring and adjustment as the database and workload evolve. By implementing these techniques and regularly assessing database performance, organizations can ensure their database systems meet user expectations and deliver optimal performance.

**Exercise**

**Exercise 1 – MCQ**

Q 1. What is the primary role of a Database Administrator (DBA) in a database management system?

A) Writing application code

B) Optimizing SQL queries

C) Managing and maintaining the database

D) Designing database schemas

Q 2. Which aspect of database administration is concerned with protecting the database from data loss and ensuring data can be recovered in case of failures?

A) Performance tuning

B) Backup and recovery

C) Database design

D) Data modelling

**Exercise 2 – True/ False**

Q 1. The role of a Database Administrator (DBA) primarily involves designing application software.

Q 2. Database Security and Authorization are important only for large organizations and are not a concern for small businesses.

**Exercise 3 – Fill in the blanks**

Q 1. The primary responsibility of a Database Administrator (DBA) is to ensure the ____________ of the database system.

Q 2. Database ____________ involves creating copies of the database to safeguard against data loss.

**Exercise 4 – One word answer**

Q 1. What is the process of restoring data after a loss or corruption incident?

Q 2. What determines who can access and manipulate database data?

**Exercise 5 – Small answer**

Q 1. What is the primary responsibility of a Database Administrator (DBA) in an organization?

Q 2. Why is database security important, and what are some common security measures that a DBA can implement to protect sensitive data?

**Exercise 6 – Long answer**

Q 1. Explain Role of a Database Administrator (DBA)

Q 2. Explain Database Security and Authorization

**Answer**

**Exercise 1**

Answer 1:C), 2: B)

**Exercise 2**

Answer 1: False, 2: False

**Exercise 3**

Answer 1: integrity, 2: backup

**Exercise 4**

Answer 1: Recovery, 2: Authorization

**Previous Years Questions**

Q1. Consider the relations:

student (d name, address)

marks (id, course, marks). (IGNOU MCA 2010)

Create an authorization matrix for two users Viz. Student and Administrator. Make and state suitable assumptions.

Q2. What is log based recovery? Explain by taking an example of concurrent transactions. What are its drawback. (IGNOU MCA 2010)

Q3. Explain log-based recovery scheme with the help of an example. (IGNOU MCA 2011)

Q4. With the help of suitable example discuss the utility of check points in Database recovery. (IGNOU MCA 2011)

Q5. List any four responsibilities of DBA. (IGNOU MCA 2011)

Q6. What are the functions of a Database Administrator? (IGNOU MCA 2012)

Q7. Explain the purpose of check points in database recovery (IGNOU MCA 2012)

Q8. What is database recovery? Explain with an example, how system log is used for database recovery. (IGNOU MCA 2014)

Q9. Explain the Log-based recovery scheme with the help of an example. (IGNOU MCA 2015)

Q10. Differentiate between the following: Backward recovery and Forward recovery (IGNOU MCA 2016)

Q11. Discuss the role of a Database Administrator. (IGNOU MCA 2016)

Q12. How does a checkpoint mechanism help in database recovery? Explain through an example. (IGNOU MCA 2019)

**Previous Years Questions with Answers**

Q1 What is database and database management and explain the advantage? (RU BCA 2022)

**Answer:**

**Database**: A database is a structured collection of data that is organized, stored, and managed in a way that enables efficient retrieval, updating, and processing of information. Databases are used to store a wide range of data, including text, numbers, multimedia, and more, and they serve as a foundation for various applications, from simple address books to complex enterprise systems. Databases are designed to facilitate data management, accessibility, and security.

**Database Management**: Database management refers to the set of activities and processes involved in creating, organizing, maintaining, and using a database. Database management encompasses various tasks, including defining the database structure (schema design), data entry, data retrieval, data updates, data integrity maintenance, security, and database optimization. Database management is typically carried out using a Database Management System (DBMS), which is specialized software designed to assist in these tasks.

**Advantages of Database Management**:

**Data Centralization**: Databases consolidate data into a single, organized repository, reducing data duplication and redundancy. This centralization simplifies data management and ensures data consistency.

**Data Integrity**: A well-designed database enforces data integrity constraints and validation rules, reducing the risk of data errors, inconsistencies, and inaccuracies.

**Efficient Data Retrieval**: Databases allow for efficient data retrieval through query languages like SQL. This enables users to extract specific information quickly.

**Data Security**: DBMSs provide robust security features, including user authentication, access control, and encryption, to protect sensitive data from unauthorized access.

**Scalability**: Databases can grow to accommodate increasing data volumes and user loads. They offer scalability options such as partitioning and clustering.

**Concurrent Access**: DBMSs support concurrent access by multiple users or applications while ensuring data consistency through mechanisms like locking and transactions.

**Data Backup and Recovery**: Databases offer backup and recovery mechanisms to protect data from loss or corruption, helping with disaster recovery.

**Data Organization**: Databases provide data organization capabilities, allowing data to be structured logically in tables and related through relationships, which simplifies data management.

**Data Abstraction**: DBMSs provide data abstraction, allowing users and applications to work with high-level, user-friendly views of the data, hiding the complexity of physical storage.

**Ad Hoc Reporting**: Databases support ad hoc reporting and data analysis, enabling users to generate custom reports and perform complex queries.

**Data Consistency**: With databases, data remains consistent and free from anomalies (e.g., insertion, update, and deletion anomalies) when properly designed and normalized.

**Data Redundancy Reduction**: Database normalization minimizes data redundancy, reducing storage requirements and making data maintenance more efficient.

**Structured Query Language (SQL)**: Databases use SQL, a standardized query language, to interact with data. SQL provides a powerful and flexible means to retrieve and manipulate data.

**Historical Data Management**: Some databases can store and manage historical data, making it possible to analyze changes over time.

**Data Sharing and Collaboration**: Databases facilitate data sharing and collaboration among users and applications, improving information access and communication.

**Business Intelligence**: Databases support business intelligence and decision-making through data analysis and reporting tools.

Q2 Explain the role and duties of database administrator (DBA) in DBMS. (RU BCA 2022)

**Answer:**

A Database Administrator (DBA) plays a critical role in the management of a database management system (DBMS) and the data it contains. The DBA is responsible for overseeing and maintaining the database, ensuring its integrity, performance, and security. The role and duties of a DBA in a DBMS include:

**Database Design and Planning**:

Collaborate with application developers and business analysts to design and plan the database schema.

Define tables, columns, relationships, constraints, and data types to ensure an efficient and structured database.

**Database Installation and Configuration**:

Install, configure, and set up the DBMS software on servers and network environments.

Optimize database settings for performance, scalability, and security.

**Security Management**:

Implement and manage user authentication and authorization.

Assign roles and permissions to control access to the database and its objects.

Monitor and audit user activities to ensure data security and compliance with privacy regulations.

**Data Backup and Recovery**:

Plan and execute regular data backup and recovery procedures to prevent data loss and support disaster recovery.

Test backup and recovery strategies to ensure their reliability in case of system failures.

**Performance Tuning**:

Monitor database performance and identify and resolve bottlenecks or issues.

Optimize SQL queries, indexing, and database configurations to improve system responsiveness.

**Data Maintenance**:

Ensure data quality and consistency by enforcing data integrity constraints and validation rules.

Manage data archiving and purging to keep the database efficient and free from clutter.

**Data Migration and ETL**:

Oversee data migration between different database systems or versions.

Manage Extract, Transform, Load (ETL) processes to transfer and transform data from various sources into the database.

**Database Monitoring and Health**:

Continuously monitor the health of the database system, including disk space, memory, and CPU usage.

Set up alerts and triggers to detect and respond to issues in real-time.

**Capacity Planning**:

Analyze database growth trends and plan for future capacity needs.

Scale the database system as necessary to accommodate data and user expansion.

**Disaster Recovery and Business Continuity**:

Develop and maintain disaster recovery plans to ensure data availability in case of unforeseen events.

Test and document recovery procedures.

**Documentation**:

Create and maintain documentation related to the database schema, configurations, security policies, and standard operating procedures.

**Patch Management and Upgrades**:

Stay informed about DBMS updates, patches, and security fixes.

Plan and perform DBMS upgrades and patch installations.

**Collaboration and Support**:

Collaborate with developers, system administrators, and network administrators to resolve issues and optimize the overall system performance.

Provide support to users and application developers in database-related matters.

**Compliance and Regulations**:

Ensure that the database complies with legal and industry-specific regulations, such as GDPR, HIPAA, or PCI DSS, where applicable.

**Training and Knowledge Sharing**:

Stay up-to-date with the latest DBMS technologies, best practices, and security threats.

Share knowledge and provide training to other team members as needed.

Q3 Write notes on: (RU BCA 2019)

Role of Database Administrator.

Role of File Manager

Physical and logical independence

**Answer:**

**Role of Database Administrator**:

A Database Administrator (DBA) is responsible for the management, maintenance, and optimization of a database management system (DBMS) and the databases it contains. The DBA plays a crucial role in ensuring the reliability, performance, and security of the database. Here are some key responsibilities of a DBA:

**Database Design**: Collaborate with application developers and business analysts to design the database schema, including defining tables, relationships, constraints, and data types.

**Database Installation and Configuration**: Install, configure, and set up the DBMS software, optimizing settings for performance and security.

**Security Management**: Implement user authentication and authorization, assign roles and permissions, and monitor user activities to maintain data security.

**Data Backup and Recovery**: Plan and execute regular data backup and recovery procedures to prevent data loss and support disaster recovery.

**Performance Tuning**: Monitor database performance, identify and resolve bottlenecks, and optimize SQL queries and configurations.

**Data Maintenance**: Ensure data integrity by enforcing constraints and validation rules, and manage data archiving and purging.

**Data Migration and ETL**: Oversee data migration and Extract, Transform, Load (ETL) processes to transfer and transform data from various sources.

**Database Monitoring**: Continuously monitor the health of the database system, set up alerts, and respond to issues in real-time.

**Capacity Planning**: Analyze database growth trends and plan for future capacity needs, scaling the system as necessary.

**Disaster Recovery**: Develop and maintain disaster recovery plans, including testing and documentation.

**Patch Management and Upgrades**: Stay informed about DBMS updates, plan and perform upgrades and patch installations.

**Collaboration and Support**: Collaborate with IT teams to resolve issues and provide support to users and developers.

**Compliance and Regulations**: Ensure the database complies with legal and industry-specific regulations.

**Training and Knowledge Sharing**: Stay up-to-date with the latest technologies and share knowledge with team members.

**Role of File Manager**:

A File Manager is responsible for managing files and data stored on a computer system. In the context of a database system, a File Manager typically handles data at a lower level than a Database Administrator. Here are some key roles and responsibilities of a File Manager:

**File Organization**: Determine how data is stored on physical storage devices, including file structures, directories, and access methods.

**Data Storage and Retrieval**: Manage the storage and retrieval of files, records, and data blocks.

**Access Control**: Implement access controls to ensure data security and prevent unauthorized access to files.

**File Backup and Recovery**: Establish backup and recovery procedures for files and data to prevent data loss and support disaster recovery.

**File Compression and Encryption**: Implement file compression and encryption to optimize storage and protect data.

**Data Migration**: Manage data migration between different storage devices or systems.

**File Versioning**: Maintain different versions of files and ensure the ability to roll back to previous versions when needed.

**Storage Device Management**: Monitor and manage storage devices, including disk space, and ensure they are functioning efficiently.

**Physical and Logical Independence**:

**Physical Independence**: Physical independence in the context of a database system refers to the separation of the physical storage details from the logical data structure. It means that changes in the physical storage mechanisms, such as moving data to a different storage device, changing file organization, or altering indexing methods, do not affect the logical schema or the way data is accessed and manipulated by applications. This separation allows for flexibility and adaptability in managing the physical aspects of data storage without impacting the logical representation of data.

**Logical Independence**: Logical independence refers to the ability to modify the logical schema of the database without affecting the applications or programs that access the data. Changes to the logical schema, such as adding or modifying tables, columns, constraints, or relationships, can be made without requiring changes to the application layer. This separation between the logical view of data and the physical storage structure simplifies the process of evolving and adapting the database to changing business requirements.

Q4 Describe backup and recovery mechanism available in DBMS. (RU BCA 2017)

**Answer:**

Backup and recovery mechanisms are essential components of a database management system (DBMS) that ensure data durability, availability, and resilience in the face of data loss, corruption, or system failures. These mechanisms are crucial for maintaining data integrity and minimizing downtime. Here's an overview of backup and recovery processes in a DBMS:

**Backup Mechanisms**: Backup refers to the process of creating a copy of the database or its components to safeguard against data loss. There are several backup types and strategies, including:

**Full Backup**:

A full backup captures a complete copy of the entire database at a specific point in time.

It provides a comprehensive and up-to-date snapshot of the database but can be time-consuming and resource-intensive.

**Differential Backup**:

A differential backup captures changes made to the database since the last full backup.

It is faster than a full backup and requires less storage space, making it a practical choice for regular backups.

**Incremental Backup**:

An incremental backup captures changes made since the last backup, which can be a full or incremental backup.

It is efficient in terms of storage space and backup duration.

**Transaction Log Backup**:

Transaction log backups capture changes recorded in the transaction log files since the last log backup.

They are critical for point-in-time recovery and maintaining data consistency.

**Remote and Offsite Backups**:

Backup copies are often stored offsite or in remote locations to protect against disasters, theft, or on-site system failures.

**Recovery Mechanisms**: Recovery involves restoring the database to a consistent and usable state in the event of data loss or system failure. The primary recovery methods include:

**Rollback**:

Rollback is the process of undoing recent transactions to restore the database to its previous state.

It is typically used for reverting changes initiated by a specific transaction.

**Recovery from Backup**:

When data is lost or corrupted, it can be restored from the most recent backup.

A full or differential backup is used to restore the database to its state at the time of the backup.

**Point-in-Time Recovery**:

Point-in-time recovery allows for restoring the database to a specific moment in time, which is crucial for recovering from errors or data corruption.

Transaction log backups are used to replay transactions up to the desired point in time.

**Database Replication**:

Database replication involves maintaining multiple copies (replicas) of the database in different locations.

In the event of a failure, one of the replicas can be promoted to become the primary database.

**High Availability and Failover**:

Systems with high availability configurations use redundancy and failover mechanisms to minimize downtime.

If a system or server fails, traffic is directed to a standby system to ensure continuous service.

**Disaster Recovery Plan**:

A comprehensive disaster recovery plan outlines procedures and actions to recover from catastrophic events, such as natural disasters.

**Data Validation and Integrity Checks**:

Regular data validation and integrity checks help identify and correct data inconsistencies and errors.

Q5 What is the purpose of the database management system? (RU BCA 2016)

**Answer:**

The purpose of a Database Management System (DBMS) is to provide a structured and organized method for efficiently storing, retrieving, managing, and manipulating data. DBMSs serve as essential software tools that facilitate the management of databases, which are repositories of data used by individuals, businesses, and organizations. The key purposes of a DBMS include:

**Data Organization**: A DBMS organizes data into structured formats, such as tables, records, and fields, making it easier to store, access, and manage data. This structure improves data integrity and consistency.

**Data Retrieval**: DBMSs offer robust query and retrieval mechanisms, allowing users to extract specific information from large datasets quickly and accurately.

**Data Manipulation**: DBMSs support various data manipulation operations, such as inserting, updating, and deleting data, to maintain the accuracy and relevance of stored information.

**Data Integrity**: DBMSs enforce data integrity by implementing constraints, validation rules, and referential integrity to ensure the reliability and consistency of data.

**Data Security**: DBMSs provide security mechanisms, including user authentication, authorization, and encryption, to protect data from unauthorized access and data breaches.

**Concurrency Control**: In multi-user environments, DBMSs manage concurrent access to the database to prevent conflicts and ensure data consistency.

**Data Backup and Recovery**: DBMSs include features for data backup and recovery to safeguard data against loss, corruption, and system failures.

**Scalability**: DBMSs can handle data growth by offering scalability options, such as partitioning, clustering, and distributed databases.

**Data Redundancy Reduction**: DBMSs minimize data redundancy through normalization techniques, reducing storage requirements and improving data maintenance.

**Data Independence**: DBMSs provide logical and physical data independence, allowing changes to the database schema and storage mechanisms without impacting applications.

**Ad Hoc Reporting and Analysis**: DBMSs support ad hoc reporting and data analysis through query languages, reporting tools, and analytics capabilities.

**Business Intelligence**: DBMSs play a critical role in business intelligence by providing historical and real-time data for decision-making, trend analysis, and reporting.

**Data Sharing and Collaboration**: DBMSs enable data sharing and collaboration among users and applications, improving information access and communication.

**Data Validation and Constraints**: DBMSs enforce data validation rules and constraints to prevent errors and inconsistencies.

**Historical Data Management**: Some DBMSs offer features for managing historical data, allowing organizations to track changes over time.

**Compliance and Regulations**: DBMSs assist in meeting compliance requirements and industry-specific regulations, such as GDPR, HIPAA, or PCI DSS.

In summary, a DBMS serves as a central platform for data management, ensuring data accuracy, accessibility, security, and reliability. It empowers organizations to efficiently use data for decision-making, reporting, and application development, ultimately supporting their business objectives and processes.

Q6 What are five main functions of a database administrator? (RU BCA 2016)

**Answer:**

Database Administrators (DBAs) play a critical role in the management of database systems. Their responsibilities encompass a wide range of functions to ensure the integrity, security, and performance of a database. Here are five main functions of a Database Administrator:

**Database Design and Planning**:

DBAs collaborate with application developers and business analysts to design and plan the database schema. This involves defining tables, columns, relationships, constraints, and data types to ensure that the database structure aligns with business requirements.

They consider factors like data volume, access patterns, and growth projections to design an efficient and scalable database.

**Database Installation and Configuration**:

DBAs are responsible for the installation and configuration of database management systems (DBMS) on servers and network environments.

They optimize the database settings, including memory allocation, file storage, indexing methods, and security configurations to ensure optimal performance and security.

**Data Security and Access Control**:

DBAs implement and manage data security measures, including user authentication, authorization, and encryption.

They assign user roles and permissions, controlling who can access, modify, or delete data. Monitoring and auditing user activities is part of this function to ensure data security and compliance.

**Backup and Recovery**:

Ensuring data availability and recoverability is a crucial function of DBAs. They plan and execute regular data backup and recovery procedures to prevent data loss and support disaster recovery.

They create and manage backup and recovery strategies, often involving full backups, differential backups, and transaction log backups.

**Performance Tuning and Monitoring**:

DBAs are responsible for monitoring database performance and identifying and resolving bottlenecks and issues.

They optimize SQL queries, indexing, and configurations to improve the system's responsiveness and ensure efficient data retrieval.

Q7 What is data recovery. (RU BCA 2021)

**Answer:**

**Data recovery** is the process of retrieving and restoring data that has been lost, deleted, corrupted, or made inaccessible due to various reasons, such as hardware or software failures, accidental deletion, human error, viruses, or physical damage to storage media. Data recovery aims to recover as much of the lost data as possible, ensuring that valuable information is not permanently lost.

Here are some key points about data recovery:

**Data Loss Scenarios**: Data loss can occur in various scenarios, including hard drive failures, accidental deletion, formatting errors, file system corruption, virus attacks, and physical damage to storage devices.

**Data Recovery Methods**:

**Software-Based Data Recovery**: Software tools are available to recover deleted files or restore data from corrupted or formatted storage media. These tools scan the storage device for recoverable data and may be effective in many cases.

**Hardware-Based Data Recovery**: In cases of physical damage to storage media, specialized hardware and equipment may be used by professional data recovery services to retrieve data from damaged drives.

**Backups**: Regular data backups are a fundamental form of data recovery. If data is lost, it can be restored from backup copies.

**Data Recovery Services**: Professional data recovery services are available for complex data loss scenarios, especially when data is critical and standard software tools cannot recover it. These services have specialized expertise and equipment to recover data from damaged or failed storage devices.

**Prevention and Preparedness**: While data recovery is essential, it's equally important to prevent data loss in the first place. Regular data backups, data redundancy, and maintaining the health of storage devices can minimize the need for data recovery.

**Data Recovery Time**: The time required for data recovery depends on the nature and severity of data loss. Simple recovery tasks may be quick, while complex cases may take longer. For businesses and organizations, minimizing downtime is critical in data recovery.

**Data Recovery Tools**: There are many data recovery tools and software solutions available, both free and commercial, that can help individuals and organizations recover lost data. These tools are often user-friendly and can be used for common data recovery tasks.

**Data Integrity**: Data recovery may not always guarantee 100% recovery, especially in cases of severe data corruption or overwriting. The success of data recovery depends on the condition of the lost data and the extent of damage or loss.

Q8 What is Backup and Recovery in DBMS? Explain with suitable examples. (RU BCA 2019)

**Answer:**

Backup and recovery in a Database Management System (DBMS) is a crucial process that involves creating copies of a database and implementing strategies to ensure data durability, availability, and resilience in the face of data loss, corruption, or system failures. These processes are essential for maintaining data integrity, minimizing downtime, and ensuring that data is recoverable in the event of unexpected incidents. Here's an overview of backup and recovery in a DBMS:

**Backup**:

**Purpose**: The primary purpose of backup is to create copies of the database to safeguard against data loss. It provides a means to restore the database to a known state in case of data corruption, accidental deletion, hardware failures, or other issues.

**Backup Types**: There are several types of backups, including:

**Full Backup**: A complete copy of the entire database is created. It provides a comprehensive snapshot of the database at a specific point in time.

**Differential Backup**: Captures changes made to the database since the last full backup. It is faster and requires less storage space than a full backup.

**Incremental Backup**: Captures changes since the last backup, which can be a full or incremental backup.

**Transaction Log Backup**: Captures changes recorded in the transaction log files since the last log backup.

**Remote and Offsite Backups**: Backup copies are stored offsite or in remote locations to protect against disasters and theft.

**Recovery**:

**Purpose**: The primary purpose of recovery is to restore the database to a consistent and usable state in case of data loss or system failures.

**Recovery Methods**: There are various recovery methods, including:

**Rollback**: Undoing recent transactions to revert the database to a previous state, typically used for errors initiated by a specific transaction.

**Recovery from Backup**: Restoring data from the most recent backup to recover the database.

**Point-in-Time Recovery**: Restoring the database to a specific moment in time, essential for recovering from errors or data corruption.

**Database Replication**: Maintaining multiple copies (replicas) of the database in different locations, where one can be promoted to the primary database in case of failure.

**High Availability and Failover**: Systems with high availability configurations use redundancy and failover mechanisms to minimize downtime.

**Disaster Recovery Plan**: Comprehensive plans outline procedures and actions to recover from catastrophic events like natural disasters.

Q9 What is mean by Backup and Recovery? (RU BCA 2018)

**Answer:**

**Backup and Recovery** are critical processes in information technology and data management that involve safeguarding and restoring data in the event of data loss, corruption, hardware or software failures, or other unexpected incidents. These processes are essential for ensuring data integrity, availability, and business continuity. Here's what each term means:

**Backup**:

**Purpose**: The primary purpose of backup is to create copies of data, files, or entire systems to prevent data loss and enable data recovery in the event of data-related incidents.

**Types of Backup**:

**Full Backup**: This involves creating a complete copy of all data at a specific point in time. It provides a comprehensive snapshot of the data but can be resource-intensive.

**Differential Backup**: A differential backup captures changes made to the data since the last full backup. It is more efficient in terms of storage space and backup duration.

**Incremental Backup**: Incremental backups capture changes made since the last backup, which can be a full or incremental backup. They are storage-efficient.

**Regular Backups**: Data is backed up at regular intervals, such as daily, weekly, or monthly, to maintain up-to-date copies.

**Offsite and Remote Backups**: Copies of data are stored in remote or offsite locations to protect against disasters, theft, or on-site system failures.

**Recovery**:

**Purpose**: Recovery refers to the process of restoring data or systems to a consistent and usable state after data loss, corruption, or system failures.

**Recovery Methods**:

**Data Recovery**: Data is recovered from backups or replicas, and lost or corrupted data is restored to its original state.

**System Recovery**: The entire system, including operating systems and applications, is restored to a working state.

**Point-in-Time Recovery**: Data is recovered to a specific moment in time, which is crucial for maintaining data consistency and integrity.

**Disaster Recovery**: Comprehensive plans and strategies are employed to recover from catastrophic events such as natural disasters, ensuring business continuity.

Q10 Define DBMS? What are the advantages of DBMS over conventional file system? What are the functions of a database administrator? (RU BCA 2017)

**Answer:**

**DBMS (Database Management System)**: A Database Management System (DBMS) is software that provides a systematic and organized way to create, manage, store, retrieve, and manipulate data in a database. It serves as an intermediary between users or applications and the underlying database, ensuring data integrity, security, and efficient data operations. Key components of a DBMS include the database itself (consisting of tables, records, and fields), the DBMS software, and a query language (e.g., SQL) for data manipulation.

**Advantages of DBMS over Conventional File Systems**:

**Data Integrity**: DBMS enforces data integrity constraints, ensuring that data remains accurate and consistent.

**Data Security**: DBMS provides authentication and authorization mechanisms to control who can access and modify data.

**Data Independence**: Changes to the database structure don't affect applications, offering both logical and physical data independence.

**Data Redundancy Reduction**: Normalization techniques minimize data redundancy, reducing storage requirements and improving data maintenance.

**Data Sharing and Collaboration**: Multiple users and applications can access the data simultaneously, enabling data sharing and collaboration.

**Efficient Data Retrieval**: Query languages and indexing mechanisms optimize data retrieval, making it faster and more efficient.

**Concurrent Access**: DBMS handles concurrent access by multiple users while maintaining data consistency.

**Data Backup and Recovery**: DBMS includes backup and recovery mechanisms to prevent data loss and support disaster recovery.

**Scalability**: Databases can grow to accommodate increasing data volumes and user loads.

**Ad Hoc Reporting and Analysis**: DBMS supports ad hoc reporting and data analysis, enabling users to generate custom reports and perform complex queries.

**Functions of a Database Administrator (DBA):**

A Database Administrator (DBA) is responsible for the management of the DBMS and the database. The functions of a DBA include:

**Database Design and Planning**:

Collaborating with stakeholders to design and plan the database schema.

**Database Installation and Configuration**:

Installing, configuring, and optimizing the DBMS software.

**Data Security and Access Control**:

Implementing security measures, user authentication, and access control.

**Backup and Recovery**:

Planning and executing data backup and recovery procedures.

**Performance Tuning and Monitoring**:

Monitoring database performance and optimizing SQL queries and configurations.

**Data Maintenance**:

Enforcing data integrity constraints, managing data archiving, and ensuring data consistency.

**Data Migration and ETL**:

Overseeing data migration and Extract, Transform, Load (ETL) processes.

**Capacity Planning**:

Analyzing database growth trends and planning for future capacity needs.

**Disaster Recovery and Business Continuity**:

Developing and maintaining disaster recovery plans.

**Documentation**:

Creating and maintaining documentation related to the database and operations.

**Patch Management and Upgrades**:

Staying informed about DBMS updates and performing upgrades.

**Collaboration and Support**:

Collaborating with IT teams and providing support to users and developers.

**Compliance and Regulations**:

Ensuring the database complies with legal and industry-specific regulations.

**Training and Knowledge Sharing**:

Staying up-to-date with technologies and sharing knowledge with team members.

Q11 What is database security? Why is it important? Also discuss the various security issues. (RU BCA 2016)

**Answer:**

**Database security** refers to the practices, mechanisms, and policies designed to protect a database from unauthorized access, data breaches, corruption, and other security threats. It is a crucial aspect of information security, as databases often store sensitive and valuable data, making them a prime target for malicious actors. The importance of database security is evident in several key aspects:

**Importance of Database Security**:

**Data Protection**: Database security ensures the confidentiality, integrity, and availability of data, safeguarding it from unauthorized access, disclosure, or alteration.

**Compliance**: Many industries and organizations are subject to legal and regulatory requirements related to data security. Failure to comply can result in severe penalties.

**Business Continuity**: Ensuring database security helps maintain business continuity by preventing data loss, which can disrupt operations and harm an organization's reputation.

**Reputation**: Data breaches and security incidents can tarnish an organization's reputation and erode trust with customers, partners, and stakeholders.

**Financial Impact**: Security breaches can result in financial losses due to data theft, legal costs, regulatory fines, and the cost of recovery and remediation.

**Various Security Issues in Database Security**:

**Unauthorized Access**:

**Issue**: Unauthorized users gaining access to sensitive data can lead to data breaches and misuse.

**Mitigation**: Strong authentication and access control mechanisms are essential to limit access to authorized personnel.

**Data Theft**:

**Issue**: Malicious actors may steal sensitive data, including customer information, trade secrets, or financial records.

**Mitigation**: Encryption, intrusion detection systems, and data loss prevention (DLP) tools can help protect against data theft.

**SQL Injection**:

**Issue**: Attackers inject malicious SQL queries into input fields, potentially gaining unauthorized access to the database.

**Mitigation**: Input validation, parameterized queries, and web application firewalls can help prevent SQL injection attacks.

**Data Manipulation**:

**Issue**: Unauthorized changes to data, such as inserting, updating, or deleting records, can compromise data integrity.

**Mitigation**: Implementing access controls, monitoring for suspicious activities, and maintaining audit logs can help prevent data manipulation.

**Malware and Ransomware**:

**Issue**: Malware and ransomware can infect database systems, leading to data encryption, data loss, or unauthorized access.

**Mitigation**: Regular system and antivirus updates, along with user training, can reduce the risk of malware infections.

**Insider Threats**:

**Issue**: Employees or trusted individuals may intentionally or accidentally misuse their access privileges to compromise data.

**Mitigation**: Monitoring user activities, enforcing the principle of least privilege, and conducting security awareness training are crucial.

**Weak or Default Passwords**:

**Issue**: Weak, easily guessable, or default passwords can make it easier for attackers to gain unauthorized access.

**Mitigation**: Enforcing password policies, implementing two-factor authentication, and regularly changing default passwords can improve security.

**Data Encryption**:

**Issue**: Data stored in databases may not be encrypted, making it vulnerable if the physical storage is compromised.

**Mitigation**: Implementing encryption at rest and in transit helps protect data from unauthorized access.

**Data Backup and Recovery**:

**Issue**: Lack of robust backup and recovery processes can result in data loss and hinder recovery efforts in the event of incidents.

**Mitigation**: Regularly backing up data and testing recovery processes are essential for resilience.

**Compliance Violations**:

**Issue**: Failure to comply with data protection regulations can result in legal consequences and fines.

**Mitigation**: Staying informed about and adhering to relevant data protection laws and regulations is essential.

Q12. Write short notes on

Log-Based recovery

Multimedia database [Marks: 10](RTU MCA 2022)

**Answer:**

**Log-Based Recovery**

Log-based recovery is a fundamental technique used in database management systems (DBMS) to ensure data integrity and consistency, especially after system failures. This method involves keeping a log (or journal) of all the transactions and their changes to the database. The log records contain enough information to either redo or undo the actions of a transaction, making it possible to recover the database to a consistent state in the event of a crash or other system failure.

Key Concepts:

**Redo:** Applying the changes of a transaction again to ensure that committed transactions are reflected in the database, even if the changes were not fully written to disk before a failure.

**Undo:**Reverting the changes of a transaction to ensure that the effects of uncommitted transactions are not present in the database, maintaining data integrity.

Types of Log-Based Recovery:

**Undo Logging (Undo/No-Redo):** This approach ensures that for any transaction that had not committed before a crash, its actions are undone using the log to maintain consistency.

**Redo Logging (Redo/No-Undo):** In this approach, the system ensures that all actions of committed transactions are redone to reflect their changes in the database, based on the assumption that changes are written to the log before they are applied to the database.

**Undo/Redo Logging:** This more comprehensive approach combines undo and redo operations. It ensures that the effects of uncommitted transactions are undone, and the effects of committed transactions are redone, providing robust recovery from failures.

Process:

The recovery process involves two main phases: the analysis phase, where the system scans the log to identify which transactions were active at the time of the failure, and which have committed; and the redo/undo phase, where the system redoes the actions of committed transactions and undoes the actions of uncommitted transactions, based on the log records.

Log-based recovery is critical for maintaining the ACID properties of transactions, particularly durability and atomicity, ensuring that databases can recover from failures without losing data or leaving the database in an inconsistent state.

**Multimedia Database**

A multimedia database is a database that efficiently stores, retrieves, and manages multimedia data types such as text, images, audio, video, and animation files, in addition to traditional structured data. Unlike conventional databases designed primarily for handling structured numerical and text data, multimedia databases are optimized to manage the complexities associated with large multimedia files, including their storage, indexing, searching, and retrieval requirements.

Key Features:

**Rich Data Types:** Support for a diverse range of data types, from simple text and numeric data to complex images, audio, and video.

**Content-Based Retrieval:** Enables searching and retrieving multimedia content based on its content rather than just metadata or file names. For example, searching for images based on visual features like color or shape, or searching for videos based on audio content.

**Efficient Storage:** Multimedia databases implement efficient storage mechanisms to handle the large size of multimedia files, often involving compression techniques and large-scale storage systems.

**Indexing and Categorization:** Advanced indexing techniques are used to facilitate quick searching and retrieval of multimedia content. This may involve creating indexes based on features extracted from the multimedia content itself.

**Streaming Support:** For audio and video data, multimedia databases often support streaming, allowing for the playback of content directly from the database without requiring a complete file download.

Applications:

Multimedia databases are widely used in various applications, including digital libraries, online galleries, media streaming services, digital asset management systems, and content delivery networks. They play a crucial role in industries such as entertainment, education, surveillance, and healthcare, where there is a need to manage and deliver rich multimedia content efficiently.

In summary, log-based recovery is essential for ensuring the reliability and consistency of database operations, especially in the face of system failures. Multimedia databases address the unique requirements of storing and managing diverse and large-scale multimedia content, providing efficient access and retrieval mechanisms tailored to the nature of multimedia data.

## ONLINE RESOURCES

**Practice Paper Link:** https://forms.gle/Vjhb2u2nTTkJUQyn9

**QR Code :**

**Video Content:**https://www.youtube.com/playlist?list=PLzlh_31VWEFqPevKzR_1UgioCBDHVSTnA

**QR Code :**

# Chapter 5: Data Modelling

## Data Models

Data models in database management systems (DBMS) provide a way to represent and organize data in a structured manner. There are several types of data models, including the hierarchical, network, relational, and object-oriented models. The relational data model is one of the most widely used in modern databases. Here's an overview of the relational data model with a simple diagram:

**Relational Data Model:**

The relational data model represents data as tables with rows and columns, also known as relations. Each table represents an entity, and each row represents a record or tuple, while each column represents an attribute or field.

Example of Relational Data Model:

Student Table:

| ID | Name | Age | ... |
|---|---|---|---|
| 1 | John | 22 | ... |
| 2 | Alice | 20 | ... |
| 3 | Bob | 23 | ... |

Course Table:

| ID | Title | Credits | ... |
|---|---|---|---|
| 101 | Math | 3 | ... |
| 102 | History | 4 | ... |
| 103 | Science | 3 | ... |

In the Example:

We have two tables: "Student" and "Course."

Each table has columns (attributes) representing specific information about the entities (students and courses).

Rows in each table represent individual records or instances of the entity, with unique IDs.

Relationships between tables can be established using keys, such as student IDs and course IDs, as foreign keys in related tables.

The relational data model's simplicity and flexibility make it suitable for organizing and managing structured data efficiently. Queries are performed using SQL (Structured Query Language) to retrieve, insert, update, or delete data while maintaining data integrity through keys and constraints.

Please note that this is a simplified example, and real-world database schemas can be much more complex, with multiple tables and relationships

## Relational Model

The relational model is a fundamental concept in database management systems (DBMS). It provides a structured way to organize and represent data in tabular form, where data is organized into tables with rows and columns. Here's a detailed explanation of the relational model in DBMS:

Key Concepts of the Relational Model:

**Tables**: In the relational model, data is organized into tables, also known as relations. Each table represents a specific entity or concept. For example, in a university database, you might have tables for students, courses, and professors.

**Attributes (Columns):** Each table consists of attributes (columns) that define the type of data that can be stored. For instance, a "Student" table might have attributes like "StudentID," "FirstName," "LastName," and "DOB" (Date of Birth).

**Tuples (Rows):** Rows in a table are called tuples. Each tuple represents a single record or instance of the entity being modeled. In the "Student" table, each row corresponds to a unique student.

**Primary Key**: Each table typically has one or more attributes that uniquely identify each tuple within the table. This attribute is known as the primary key. For the "Student" table, "StudentID" could be the primary key.

**Foreign Key:** Tables can be related to each other using foreign keys. A foreign key in one table refers to the primary key in another table, establishing a relationship between the two tables. For example, a "Course" table might have a foreign key that links to the "Student" table to indicate which students are enrolled in each course.

**Data Integrity**: The relational model enforces data integrity rules, such as uniqueness constraints for primary keys and referential integrity constraints for foreign keys. These rules help maintain data accuracy and consistency.

**SQL (Structured Query Language):** The relational model is closely associated with SQL, a language used for querying and manipulating relational databases. SQL provides a standardized way to interact with relational databases.

**Example:**

Consider a simplified "Student" table and a "Course" table:

Student Table:

| StudentID | FirstName | LastName | DOB |
|---|---|---|---|
| 1 | John | Smith | 1998-05-15 |
| 2 | Alice | Johnson | 1999-08-22 |
| 3 | Bob | Brown | 1997-03-10 |

Course Table:

| CourseID | CourseName | Credits |
|---|---|---|
| 101 | Math | 3 |
| 102 | History | 4 |
| 103 | Science | 3 |

In this example, "Student" and "Course" are two separate tables in a relational database. The attributes represent information about students and courses, and the primary keys (e.g., StudentID and CourseID) uniquely identify each record within their respective tables. Relationships between these tables can be established using foreign keys, allowing you to query and retrieve meaningful information about students' enrollment in courses, grades, and more.

The relational model provides a flexible and efficient way to store and manage structured data, making it a cornerstone of modern database systems.

## Conceptual, Logical, and Physical Data Models

In database modelling, there are three key levels of abstraction: conceptual, logical, and physical data models. Each level serves a distinct purpose in the database design and development process. Here, we'll delve into each of these models in detail:

**Conceptual Data Model:**

The conceptual data model represents the highest level of abstraction and focuses on the overall understanding of the data and its relationships within the organization. It does not concern itself with technical details but rather aims to capture business concepts and entities.

**Components:**

Entities: Represent real-world objects or concepts such as customers, products, orders, etc.

Attributes: Describe properties or characteristics of entities.

Relationships: Define how entities are related to one another.

Notation: Entity-Relationship Diagrams (ERDs) are commonly used to visualize conceptual data models. In ERDs, entities are depicted as rectangles, attributes as ovals, and relationships as lines connecting entities.

**Example**:

Conceptual Data Model: Library System

Entities:

Book: Represents books in the library.

Attributes: ISBN (Primary Key), Title, Author, Genre, Publication Year

| ISBN | Title | Author | Genre | Publication Year |
|---|---|---|---|---|
| **978-12345678** | "To Kill a Mockingbird" | Harper Lee | Fiction | 1960 |
| **978-23456789** | "1984" | George Orwell | Dystopian | 1949 |
| **978-34567890** | "Pride and Prejudice" | Jane Austen | Romance | 1813 |
| ... | ... | ... | ... | ... |

Member: Represents library members.

Attributes: MemberID (Primary Key), Name, Address, Phone Number, Email

| MemberID | Name | Address | Phone Number | Email |
|---|---|---|---|---|
| **1001** | John Smith | 123 Main St, Anytown | 555-123-4567 | john@example.com |
| **1002** | Jane Doe | 456 Elm St, AnotherTown | 555-987-6543 | jane@example.com |
| **1003** | Michael Brown | 789 Oak St, SomeCity | 555-555-5555 | michael@example.com |
| ... | ... | ... | ... | ... |

Checkout: Represents book checkouts by members.

Attributes: CheckoutID (Primary Key), MemberID (Foreign Key), ISBN (Foreign Key), Checkout Date, Due Date

| CheckoutID | MemberID | ISBN | Checkout Date | Due Date |
|---|---|---|---|---|
| **2001** | 1001 | 978-12345678 | 2023-08-15 | 2023-09-15 |
| **2002** | 1002 | 978-23456789 | 2023-08-20 | 2023-09-20 |
| **2003** | 1001 | 978-34567890 | 2023-08-25 | 2023-09-25 |
| ... | ... | ... | ... | ... |

Library Branch: Represents different branches of the library.

Attributes: BranchID (Primary Key), Branch Name, Location

| BranchID | Branch Name | Location |
|---|---|---|
| **3001** | Main Library | 123 Library St |
| **3002** | Downtown Branch | 456 Elm Ave |
| **3003** | Westside Branch | 789 Oak Rd |
| ... | ... | ... |

Relationships:

Each member can check out multiple books (one-to-many relationship between Member and Checkout).

Each book can be checked out by multiple members (one-to-many relationship between Book and Checkout).

Each library branch can have multiple books (one-to-many relationship between Library Branch and Book).

This conceptual data model provides an abstract view of the library system, showing the main entities (Book, Member, Checkout, and Library Branch) and their attributes. It also outlines the relationships between these entities. This model serves as a foundation for creating more detailed logical and physical data models that define how the data will be structured and stored in a database management system.

**Logical Data Model:**

The logical data model builds upon the conceptual model and provides a more structured representation of the data, independent of the specific database management system. It focuses on defining data elements, their relationships, and constraints.

**Components:**

Tables: Logical data models use tables to represent entities, each with its set of attributes.

Columns: Correspond to attributes of entities and have data types.

Keys: Define unique identifiers (primary keys) and relationships between tables (foreign keys).

Constraints: Enforce rules and relationships within the data.

Notation: Entity-Relationship Diagrams or Unified Modelling Language (UML) class diagrams can be used to create logical data models.

**Example:**

Creating a full logical data model for a database system typically involves defining tables, their attributes, primary keys, foreign keys, and relationships. It can be quite extensive, so I'll provide a simplified example of a logical data model for a library database system with a few tables:

Book Table:

| Column Name | Data Type | Primary Key | Description |
|---|---|---|---|
| ISBN | VARCHAR(13) | Yes | International Standard Book Number |
| Title | VARCHAR(255) | No | Title of the book |
| AuthorID | INT | No | Foreign key to Author table |
| GenreID | INT | No | Foreign key to Genre table |
| Publication_Year | INT | No | Year of publication |
| Copies_Available | INT | No | Number of copies available |
| Shelf_Location | VARCHAR(50) | No | Location on the library shelf |

Author Table:

| Column Name | Data Type | Primary Key | Description |
|---|---|---|---|
| AuthorID | INT | Yes | Unique author identifier |
| Author_Name | VARCHAR(100) | No | Name of the author |
| Birth_Year | INT | No | Year of birth |
| Nationality | VARCHAR(50) | No | Author's nationality |

Genre Table:

| Column Name | Data Type | Primary Key | Description |
|---|---|---|---|
| GenreID | INT | Yes | Unique genre identifier |
| Genre_Name | VARCHAR(50) | No | Name of the genre |

Member Table:

| Column Name | Data Type | Primary Key | Description |
|---|---|---|---|
| MemberID | INT | Yes | Unique member identifier |
| Member_Name | VARCHAR(100) | No | Name of the library member |
| Address | VARCHAR(255) | No | Member's address |
| Phone_Num | VARCHAR(15) | No | Member's phone number |
| Email | VARCHAR(100) | No | Member's email address |

Checkout Table:

| Column Name | Data Type | Primary Key | Description |
|---|---|---|---|
| CheckoutID | INT | Yes | Unique checkout identifier |
| MemberID | INT | No | Foreign key to Member table |
| ISBN | VARCHAR(13) | No | Foreign key to Book table |
| Checkout_Date | DATE | No | Date when the book was checked out |
| Due_Date | DATE | No | Date when the book is due |

This logical data model outlines the tables, their attributes, primary keys, and some relationships in a library database system. It's a simplified representation, and a real-world library system would likely have more tables and relationships, but this gives you an idea of how to structure a logical data model.

**Physical Data Model:**

The physical data model represents the actual implementation of the database on a specific database management system (DBMS). It addresses technical details such as storage, indexing, and optimization.

**Components:**

Tables: Reflect the tables defined in the logical model but with considerations for DBMS-specific optimizations.

Indexes: Specify which columns are indexed for faster data retrieval.

Partitions: Split large tables into smaller, more manageable pieces.

Storage Structures: Define where and how data is stored on disks.

**Notation:** While notations like ERDs or UML class diagrams can be used, the focus of a physical data model is often on SQL statements that create and define database objects.

**Example:**

Creating a complete physical data model for a database system can be quite extensive, so I'll provide a simplified example with a few tables. In a real-world scenario, a physical data model would include additional details like data types, indexes, and constraints.

Let's consider a database for a fictional online bookstore. Here are some tables in a simplified physical data model:

Book Table:

| Column Name | Data Type | Length | Constraints |
|---|---|---|---|
| ISBN (Primary Key) | VARCHAR | 13 | NOT NULL, UNIQUE |
| Title | VARCHAR | 255 | NOT NULL |
| Author | VARCHAR | 100 | NOT NULL |
| Genre | VARCHAR | 50 | |
| Publication Year | INT | | CHECK (YEAR >= 0) |
| Price | DECIMAL(10,2) | | CHECK (Price >= 0.00) |

Customer Table:

| Column Name | Data Type | Length | Constraints |
|---|---|---|---|
| CustomerID (PK) | INT | | NOT NULL, AUTO_INCREMENT |
| FirstName | VARCHAR | 50 | NOT NULL |
| LastName | VARCHAR | 50 | NOT NULL |
| Email | VARCHAR | 100 | NOT NULL, UNIQUE |
| Phone | VARCHAR | 20 | |

Order Table:

| Column Name | Data Type | Length | Constraints |
|---|---|---|---|
| OrderID (PK) | INT | | NOT NULL, AUTO_INCREMENT |
| CustomerID | INT | | NOT NULL, FOREIGN KEY |
| OrderDate | DATE | | NOT NULL |
| TotalAmount | DECIMAL(10,2) | | CHECK (TotalAmount >= 0) |

OrderItem Table:

| Column Name | Data Type | Length | Constraints |
|---|---|---|---|
| OrderItemID (PK) | INT | | NOT NULL, AUTO_INCREMENT |
| OrderID | INT | | NOT NULL, FOREIGN KEY |
| ISBN | VARCHAR | 13 | NOT NULL, FOREIGN KEY |
| Quantity | INT | | CHECK (Quantity > 0) |
| ItemPrice | DECIMAL(10,2) | | CHECK (ItemPrice >= 0.00) |

This simplified physical data model includes tables for books, customers, orders, and order items. Each table has columns with specified data types, lengths, and constraints. The primary keys, foreign keys, and uniqueness constraints help maintain data integrity and relationships between tables.

In a real-world scenario, this model would be more extensive, including additional tables, indexes, and optimizations for performance and security.

**Relationship Between the Models:**

The conceptual model provides a high-level view, which is refined into the logical model to define the data structure. The logical model serves as a bridge between the conceptual and physical models, ensuring that the database implementation aligns with the initial business requirements.

Changes made at the logical model level can propagate to the physical model, reflecting optimizations and configurations specific to the chosen DBMS.

Effective data modelling involves creating and maintaining these three models, ensuring that the database accurately represents the organization's data and provides efficient data storage and retrieval.

## Data Model Notations (ERD, UML, etc.)

Data model notations are visual representations used to design and communicate various aspects of a database structure and relationships. Different notations serve different purposes and are commonly used in database design and modeling. Here are some of the most popular data model notations:

**Entity-Relationship Diagrams (ERD):**

ERDs are widely used to visualize the structure of a database, focusing on entities, their attributes, and the relationships between them.

Components: Entities (represented as rectangles), attributes (represented as ovals), relationships (represented as lines connecting entities), primary keys (underlined attributes), and cardinality notation (e.g., 1:1, 1:N, N:M).

Use Cases: ERDs are used for conceptual and logical data modelling to depict the entities and relationships within a database.

**Unified Modelling Language (UML):**

UML is a comprehensive modelling language used not only for databases but also for software systems in general. It includes various diagram types, some of which are relevant to database modelling.

Components: Class diagrams (for representing entities and their attributes), association relationships, multiplicity notation, and generalization/specialization relationships.

Use Cases: UML diagrams, particularly class diagrams, can be used for conceptual and logical data modelling when a more comprehensive modelling approach is required.

**IDEF (Integration Definition for Function Modelling):**

IDEF is a family of modelling languages used for data modelling and process modelling. IDEF1X is the most common notation for data modelling.

Components: IDEF1X diagrams use boxes for entities, diamonds for relationships, lines with crow's feet notation for cardinality, and ellipses for attributes.

Use Cases: IDEF1X is suitable for both conceptual and logical data modelling, emphasizing semantic accuracy and integrity constraints.

**Barker's Notation:**

Barker's Notation is a variation of the Entity-Relationship Diagram (ERD) notation developed by Richard Barker. It is used for data modelling.

Components: Barker's Notation is similar to ERDs but uses different symbols for entities (outlined rectangles), attributes (ovals), relationships (lines connecting entities), and cardinality notation.

Use Cases: It can be used for conceptual and logical data modelling, providing an alternative to standard ERDs.

**Bachman Diagrams:**

Developed by Charles Bachman, these diagrams are used for data modelling, particularly in network and hierarchical databases.

Components: Blocks represent data structures, lines indicate relationships, and crows-foot notation is used for cardinality.

Use Cases: Bachman diagrams are suitable for logical data modelling, especially when dealing with network or hierarchical data structures.

**Chen Notation:**

Developed by Peter Chen, this notation is an alternative to standard ERDs for data modelling.

Components: Entities (represented as rectangles), attributes (represented as ovals), relationships (represented as diamonds connecting entities), and cardinality notation.

Use Cases: Chen notation is used for conceptual and logical data modelling, providing an alternative visual representation to traditional ERDs.

The choice of data model notation depends on the specific project requirements, the complexity of the database, and the preference of the database designers. In practice, many professionals use a combination of notations to effectively communicate the various aspects of database design and modelling.

## Translating Data Models to Database Schemas

Translating data models into database schemas is a critical step in the database design process. Data models, such as Entity-Relationship Diagrams (ERDs) or UML class diagrams, provide a high-level view of the database structure, entities, relationships, and attributes. To create a functional database, you must map these abstract representations into concrete database schemas, typically using SQL (Structured Query Language). Here's how the translation process works:

**Entity Mapping:**

Entities in your data model become tables in your database schema. Each table represents a distinct entity from the data model.

**Attribute Mapping:**

Attributes from your data model become columns in the corresponding tables. The data type of each column should be selected to match the attribute's data type and constraints.

**Relationship Mapping:**

Relationships between entities are translated into foreign key constraints. In most relational database management systems (RDBMS), foreign keys enforce referential integrity, ensuring that the relationships between tables are maintained.

**Cardinality Mapping:**

The cardinality and multiplicity of relationships (e.g., one-to-one, one-to-many, many-to-many) are translated into the appropriate foreign key constraints. For example, a one-to-many relationship would involve a foreign key in the "many" side table referencing the primary key in the "one" side table.

**Primary Keys:**

The primary keys in your data model become the primary key constraints in your database schema. Primary keys uniquely identify each record in a table.

**Indexes:**

Indexes are created to speed up data retrieval. You can map high-selectivity attributes (attributes with distinct values) or frequently used columns to database indexes.

**Data Types:**

Ensure that the data types of the attributes in your database schema match those specified in the data model. Most databases support a wide range of data types, including numeric, string, date/time, and more.

**Constraints:**

If your data model includes constraints (e.g., uniqueness, check constraints), translate them into the corresponding database constraints to ensure data integrity.

**Inheritance and Specialization:**

If your data model includes inheritance or specialization hierarchies (e.g., subtypes), decide how to implement them in your database schema. Common approaches include single-table inheritance, class-table inheritance, or shared-primary-key inheritance.

**Normalization:**

Depending on the complexity of your data model, you may need to apply normalization rules to optimize your database schema. Normalization reduces data redundancy and improves data integrity.

**Triggers and Stored Procedures**:

If your data model includes complex business logic or behaviours, you may need to implement them using triggers, stored procedures, or functions in your database schema.

**Views:**

Create views if your data model requires users to access data in a specific way. Views are virtual tables based on the underlying schema tables and can provide simplified access to complex data structures.

**Testing and Validation:**

After creating the database schema, thoroughly test it to ensure that it accurately reflects the data model and meets the functional and performance requirements of your application.

**Documentation:**

Document the database schema, including tables, columns, relationships, constraints, and indexes, for future reference and maintenance.

The translation process may require adjustments and refinements to align the data model with the specific capabilities and constraints of the chosen database management system (DBMS). Effective translation ensures that the resulting database schema efficiently stores and retrieves data while maintaining data integrity and adherence to the initial data model.

**Exercise**

**Exercise 1 – MCQ**

Q 1. What is the primary purpose of a Conceptual Data Model in the data modelling process?

A) To define database schema and table structures

B) To represent the high-level view of data entities and their relationships

C) To specify data types for attributes

D) To optimize query performance

Q 2. Which notation is commonly used for visualizing data models like Entity-Relationship Diagrams (ERD)?

A) XML

B) JSON

C) UML (Unified Modelling Language)

D) SQL (Structured Query Language)

**Exercise 2 – True/ False**

Q 1. In data modelling, the conceptual model focuses on the physical implementation details of the database schema.

Q 2. Data Model Notations such as ERD (Entity-Relationship Diagrams) and UML (Unified Modelling Language) are used primarily for logical data modelling.

**Exercise 3 – Fill in the blanks**

Q 1. In data modelling, the three main levels of data models are ________________________, ________________________, and ________________________.

Q 2. Data model notations, such as ERD (Entity-Relationship Diagrams) and UML (Unified Modelling Language), help visualize and represent the structure and relationships within ________________________.

**Exercise 4 – One word answer**

Q 1.What are the three main types of data models?

Q 2. What does ERD stand for in data modelling?

**Exercise 5 – Small answer**

Q 1. What are the main types of data models in the data modelling process?

Q 2. What is the purpose of data model notations like ERD and UML in data modelling?

**Exercise 6 – Long answer**

Q 1. Explain the Conceptual, Logical, and Physical Data Models and Their Significance in Data Modelling.

Q 2. Explain the Importance of Data Model Notations, Such as ERD and UML, in Data Modelling.

**Answer**

**Exercise 1**

Answer 1:B), 2: C)

**Exercise 2**

Answer 1: False, 2: True

**Exercise 3**

Answer 1: Conceptual, Logical, and Physical., 2: data models.

**Exercise 4**

Answer 1: Conceptual, Logical, Physical, 2: Entity-Relationship Diagram

**Previous Years Questions**

Q1. Explain the data models, used to structure the data in the database systems. (IGNOU MCA 2015)

Q2. Compare the shadow-paging recovery scheme with the log-based recovery scheme in respect to ease of implementation and overhead cost. (IGNOU MCA 2016)

**Previous Years Questions with Answers**

Q1 What do you understand by data model? (RU BCA 2022)

**Answer**

A **data model** is a conceptual representation or framework for organizing and structuring data in a database or information system. It defines the structure, relationships, constraints, and rules that govern how data is stored, retrieved, and manipulated within a database. Data models serve as a bridge between the real world (where data originates) and the physical database (where data is stored), providing a structured and abstract view of the data.

Key aspects of data models include:

**Entities**: Data models define the entities, which are objects, concepts, or things in the real world that are represented in the database. Each entity corresponds to a category of data, such as customers, products, employees, or orders.

**Attributes**: Attributes represent the characteristics or properties of entities. For example, in an "Employee" entity, attributes might include "EmployeeID," "FirstName," "LastName," "Salary," and "HireDate."

**Relationships**: Data models specify how entities are related or connected to each other. Relationships define the associations between entities. For instance, in a sales database, there might be a relationship between the "Customer" and "Order" entities.

**Constraints**: Data models include constraints that dictate rules and conditions for data, ensuring data integrity and quality. Constraints can define rules like unique keys, primary keys, foreign keys, and referential integrity.

**Data Types**: Data models define the types of data that can be stored in each attribute. Common data types include text, numbers, dates, and binary data.

**Cardinality**: Cardinality describes the number of instances of one entity that are associated with a single instance of another entity in a relationship. For example, a "one-to-many" relationship specifies that one entity is related to multiple instances of another entity.

Data models are used in the process of database design and development, helping database designers and administrators create databases that accurately represent the real-world data and meet the requirements of the applications that will use the database. They provide a blueprint for constructing the physical database schema, which includes tables, fields, keys, and indexes.

There are several types of data models, including:

**Conceptual Data Models**: These models provide a high-level, abstract view of the data and its relationships, focusing on business concepts rather than technical implementation details.

**Logical Data Models**: Logical models define the structure and relationships of data in a technology-agnostic way. They serve as a bridge between the conceptual model and the physical implementation.

**Physical Data Models**: Physical models specify how data is actually stored in a database system, taking into account details like data storage formats, indexing, and optimization.

Q2 Write short note: (RU BCA 2021)

Object oriented data model

Object relational database

**Answer**

**Object-Oriented Data Model**: The Object-Oriented Data Model (OODM) is a data model that extends the capabilities of traditional relational databases to handle complex data structures and relationships. In an OODM, data is organized into objects, much like in object-oriented programming. Each object combines both data and behavior (methods) and is classified into classes, which define the structure and behavior of the objects.

Key features of the Object-Oriented Data Model include:

**Encapsulation**: Objects encapsulate data and methods, allowing for data hiding and promoting information hiding.

**Inheritance**: Objects can inherit attributes and behaviors from other objects, promoting code reusability.

**Polymorphism**: Objects can have multiple forms and behaviors, allowing for flexibility and extensibility.

**Complex Relationships**: OODMs support complex relationships between objects, making them suitable for modeling real-world scenarios where entities have intricate interactions.

Object-Oriented Databases (OODBs) are built on OODMs and provide a platform for storing and managing data in an object-oriented manner. OODBs are particularly useful for applications that deal with complex data structures, such as computer-aided design (CAD), geographical information systems (GIS), and multimedia databases.

**Object-Relational Database (ORDB)**: An Object-Relational Database (ORDB) combines features of both relational databases and object-oriented databases. It extends the relational model to support the storage and retrieval of complex data types, user-defined data structures, and object-oriented concepts while maintaining the data integrity and query capabilities of relational databases.

Key characteristics of Object-Relational Databases include:

**User-Defined Types (UDTs)**: ORDBs allow users to define custom data types, such as arrays, lists, or geometric shapes, which can be stored in database tables.

**Inheritance**: ORDBs support object-oriented inheritance, where one object or type can inherit attributes and behaviors from another.

**Methods**: ORDBs enable the definition of methods associated with database objects, providing a way to encapsulate behavior with data.

**Complex Data Structures**: They can handle complex data structures and nested objects, making them suitable for scenarios that involve intricate relationships between entities.

Q3 Define Data Modeling. (RU BCA 2019)

**Answer**

**Data modeling** is the process of creating an abstract representation (a model) of data and its relationships within a domain or system. It is a fundamental step in database design, software engineering, and information systems development. Data modeling serves to clarify and organize complex data structures, making it easier to understand, design, and implement data storage and management systems.

Key aspects of data modeling include:

**Entities**: Identifying and defining the main objects, concepts, or entities in the domain, such as customers, products, employees, or orders.

**Attributes**: Describing the characteristics or properties of each entity. Attributes represent the data that needs to be stored for each entity, such as names, IDs, dates, and values.

**Relationships**: Specifying how entities are related to each other. Relationships describe the associations and connections between entities and often involve cardinality (e.g., one-to-one, one-to-many) and constraints.

**Constraints**: Setting rules and constraints on the data to ensure data integrity. Constraints include primary keys, foreign keys, unique constraints, and business rules.

Data modeling can be performed at different levels of abstraction:

**Conceptual Data Modeling**: This level focuses on high-level abstractions and is often independent of specific technologies. It helps stakeholders understand the core concepts and relationships within a system.

**Logical Data Modeling**: At this level, data modeling becomes more detailed, with a focus on defining the data structures, entities, attributes, relationships, and constraints. It is often technology-independent and serves as a bridge between the conceptual and physical levels.

**Physical Data Modeling**: This level is specific to the technology and database management system being used. It defines how the data is physically stored, including table structures, data types, indexing, and storage considerations.

Data modeling is typically facilitated by using various tools and notations, such as Entity-Relationship Diagrams (ERD), UML (Unified Modeling Language), and data modeling languages like SQL (for physical modeling). The resulting data model becomes a critical reference for designing and implementing databases, software systems, and applications.

Q4 Explain Data Abstractions Model. (RU BCA 2019)

**Answer**

A **Data Abstraction Model** is a conceptual framework that simplifies and abstracts the complexity of data structures, making it easier for designers and developers to work with data in software systems. It involves creating layers of abstraction that hide the implementation details of data structures and provide a clear and consistent interface for interacting with data. The main goal of data abstraction models is to promote modularity, encapsulation, and separation of concerns in software design.

Key components of a Data Abstraction Model include:

**Data Abstraction**: Data abstraction involves defining abstract data types (ADTs) or classes that encapsulate the data and the operations that can be performed on that data. It hides the internal details of data structures and exposes only relevant methods and properties.

**Encapsulation**: Encapsulation is the practice of bundling data and the methods that operate on that data into a single unit (an ADT or class). This unit enforces access control, protecting the data from unauthorized modification and ensuring data consistency.

**Modularity**: Data abstraction promotes modularity in software design by breaking down complex systems into smaller, manageable components. Each component is responsible for a specific set of data and operations, making the system more maintainable and extensible.

**Abstraction Layers**: A Data Abstraction Model often includes multiple layers of abstraction. The lower layers deal with low-level data management, while the upper layers provide a higher-level view of data that is closer to the needs of the application.

**Data Independence**: Data abstraction allows for data independence, separating the logical view of data from its physical representation. This separation is especially important in the context of databases and data management systems.

**Consistent Interfaces**: Data abstraction ensures that data access and manipulation are performed through consistent interfaces, making it easier for developers to work with data and understand how to use data structures.

Data Abstraction Models are commonly used in software development and data management, and they have several advantages:

**Simplicity**: They simplify complex data structures and operations, making software easier to design, understand, and maintain.

**Reusability**: Abstraction models promote the reuse of data structures and code, as encapsulated data and operations can be used in various parts of an application.

**Security**: By encapsulating data and controlling access through well-defined interfaces, data abstraction models enhance security and protect data integrity.

**Scalability**: Data abstraction allows for flexible data structures and operations that can scale with changing requirements.

**Collaboration**: Multiple developers can work on different parts of an application, focusing on specific abstractions, without needing to understand the entire system's complexity.

Q5Discuss Entity Relational Model with example. (RU BCA 2018)

**Answer**

The Entity-Relationship Model (ER Model) is a conceptual framework used to represent and describe the relationships and structure of data in a database. It is widely used in database design and serves as the foundation for creating database schemas. The ER Model uses a set of symbols and concepts to represent entities, attributes, and relationships between entities.

Key components of the Entity-Relationship Model include:

**Entity**: An entity represents a real-world object, concept, or thing that is distinguishable and can be uniquely identified. For example, in a database for a university, entities might include "Student," "Course," "Professor," and "Department."

**Attributes**: Attributes are the properties or characteristics of entities that describe them. For a "Student" entity, attributes could include "StudentID," "Name," "Date of Birth," and "Major."

**Relationship**: A relationship represents an association or connection between two or more entities. For example, in a university database, a "Student" entity may have a relationship with a "Course" entity, representing the fact that students enroll in courses.

**Cardinality**: Cardinality defines the number of instances of one entity that are related to a single instance of another entity in a specific relationship. Common cardinalities include "one-to-one," "one-to-many," and "many-to-many."

**Primary Key**: A primary key is an attribute (or set of attributes) that uniquely identifies each instance of an entity. It ensures data integrity and enables efficient data retrieval.

**Foreign Key**: A foreign key is an attribute that links an entity to another entity by referencing the primary key of the related entity. It enforces referential integrity in the database.

**Weak Entity**: A weak entity is an entity that cannot be uniquely identified by its attributes alone. It relies on a related strong entity for identification.

**Supertype and Subtype**: Supertype and subtype relationships allow for hierarchical organization of entities. The supertype represents a general entity, while subtypes represent specific types of that entity.

Here's a simple example of an Entity-Relationship Model for a library database:

**Entities**:

**Book**: Attributes include "ISBN" (primary key), "Title," "Author," and "Publication Year."

**Author**: Attributes include "AuthorID" (primary key), "Name," and "Nationality."

**Member**: Attributes include "MemberID" (primary key), "Name," "Address," and "Phone."

**Relationships**:

**Borrowed By** (between "Book" and "Member"): Represents the fact that members borrow books. Cardinality is "one-to-many" (one book can be borrowed by many members).

**Primary Keys**:

"ISBN" for the "Book" entity.

"AuthorID" for the "Author" entity.

"MemberID" for the "Member" entity.

**Foreign Keys**:

"MemberID" (in "Book" entity) references "Member" entity to track who borrowed a book.

In this example, the ER Model represents the structure and relationships of entities in a library database, allowing for the organization of data and the efficient retrieval of information about books, authors, and library members.
The ER Model serves as the foundation for creating the actual database schema, typically using a Database Management System (DBMS) and the SQL language for implementing and querying the database.

Q6 Differentiate between logical and physical, data independence? (RU BCA 2017)

**Answer**

**Logical Data Independence** and **Physical Data Independence** are two key concepts in database management that relate to how changes to a database's structure or storage mechanisms affect applications and the overall database system. Here's a differentiation between the two:

**Logical Data Independence**:

**Definition**: Logical Data Independence refers to the capacity to change the logical schema or structure of the database without affecting the application programs or the external view of the data.

**Focus**: It is primarily concerned with the organization of data at the conceptual or logical level, including the structure of tables, relationships, and attributes.

**Example**: If you add a new table, modify an existing table's structure, or define new relationships between tables, applications using the database shouldn't need to be rewritten or modified. They can continue to interact with the data as before.

**Benefits**: Logical data independence allows for changes in the database schema to accommodate new requirements or business rules without impacting the applications that rely on the database.

**Physical Data Independence**:

**Definition**: Physical Data Independence refers to the capacity to change the physical storage and access mechanisms of the database without affecting the logical schema or the application programs.

**Focus**: It deals with the storage and access methods used to store and retrieve data, including details like file structures, indexing methods, storage devices, or data distribution.

**Example**: If you decide to move the database from one storage system to another (e.g., from traditional hard drives to solid-state drives) or change the indexing strategy used for a particular table, these changes should not require modifications to the logical schema or application programs.

**Benefits**: Physical data independence allows for adaptations to changing storage technology or performance optimization without disturbing the logical structure of the database or the applications that depend on it.

In summary, the key difference between the two is in the level of abstraction and focus:

**Logical Data Independence** deals with changes at the logical or conceptual level of the database schema and ensures that modifications to the schema don't require changes to applications. It protects the external view of data.

**Physical Data Independence** deals with changes at the physical level, specifically in how data is stored and accessed. It ensures that changes in storage mechanisms or structures do not affect the logical schema or application programs.

Both forms of data independence are essential for maintaining flexibility, adaptability, and data stability in complex database systems, particularly in situations where databases need to evolve, scale, or integrate with various technologies without causing disruptions to existing applications.

Q7 Differentiate between hierarchical, network and relational model. (RU BCA 2016)

**Answer**

The **Hierarchical Model**, **Network Model**, and **Relational Model** are three different approaches to organizing and structuring data in a database management system. Each model has its own strengths and weaknesses. Here's a differentiation between these models:

**Hierarchical Model**:

**Structure**: In the hierarchical model, data is organized in a tree-like structure with a top-down hierarchy. Each record (or entity) is connected to one or more child records, forming parent-child relationships.

**Relationships**: Relationships are one-to-many, meaning one parent record can have multiple child records, but a child record can have only one parent.

**Flexibility**: The hierarchical model is rigid and less flexible. It is suitable for representing structured data with well-defined relationships, but it can be challenging to adapt to changing data requirements.

**Example**: An organization's employee structure can be represented using a hierarchical model, with the organization as the root, departments as branches, and employees as leaves.

**Network Model**:

**Structure**: The network model extends the hierarchical model by allowing many-to-many relationships. It uses sets and records to represent data, with each record connected to multiple sets.

**Relationships**: Relationships in the network model are more flexible and can be many-to-many, many-to-one, or one-to-one.

**Flexibility**: It provides more flexibility than the hierarchical model and can handle complex, interconnected data. However, it is still less flexible than the relational model in some respects.

**Example**: A university database can be represented in a network model, with students, courses, and instructors interconnected in various ways.

**Relational Model**:

**Structure**: In the relational model, data is organized into tables (relations) with rows (tuples) and columns (attributes). It does not use hierarchical or network-like structures.

**Relationships**: Relationships are represented by defining keys and foreign keys between tables. It supports one-to-many, many-to-many, and one-to-one relationships.

**Flexibility**: The relational model is highly flexible and adaptable. It allows data to be queried and manipulated without defining complex structures in advance. It is the most widely used model in modern database systems.

**Example**: In a relational database, customer data can be stored in one table, orders in another, and a relationship between them can be established using keys.

**Key Differences**:

**Structure**: Hierarchical and network models use hierarchical or interconnected structures, while the relational model uses tabular structures.

**Relationships**: The hierarchical model primarily supports one-to-many relationships, while the network model allows for more complex relationships. The relational model is highly flexible in handling various types of relationships.

**Flexibility**: The hierarchical and network models are less flexible and more rigid, making them suitable for specific use cases. The relational model offers greater flexibility and adaptability, making it suitable for a wide range of applications.

**Popularity**: The relational model is the most widely used and accepted model in modern database management systems. Hierarchical and network models have become less common but are still used in specific applications where they fit well.

In summary, the choice between these models depends on the nature of the data, the complexity of the relationships, and the flexibility required in the database system. The relational model is the most versatile and widely applicable, but the hierarchical and network models can still be relevant for certain specialized scenarios.

Q8 What is specialization and generalization? Explain with suitable example. (RU BCA 2016)

**Answer**

**Specialization and Generalization** are concepts in database modeling and design that are used to represent hierarchies and inheritance in entity-relationship modeling. These concepts allow you to create a more structured and organized database schema, particularly when dealing with entities that have common attributes and shared characteristics.

**Specialization**: Specialization is the process of defining subtypes or subclasses of an entity based on specific characteristics or attributes that are unique to that subtype. It involves taking a more general entity and breaking it down into more specific categories.

**Generalization**: Generalization is the reverse of specialization. It is the process of combining several subtypes or subclasses with common attributes and features into a more general, overarching entity.

Here's an example to illustrate these concepts:

Let's consider a database for a transportation company, which includes entities for "Vehicles." Vehicles can be of different types, such as "Cars," "Trucks," and "Motorcycles." Each of these types has certain unique attributes and behaviors.

**Specialization**:

*Specializing "Vehicles" into "Cars," "Trucks," and "Motorcycles"*:

"Cars" may have attributes like "Model," "Color," and "Number of Doors."

"Trucks" may have attributes like "Load Capacity," "Number of Wheels," and "Truck Bed Size."

"Motorcycles" may have attributes like "Engine Capacity," "Type of Motorcycle," and "Number of Seats."

In this case, "Vehicles" is specialized into subtypes based on the specific attributes and characteristics of each vehicle type.

**Generalization**:

*Generalizing "Cars," "Trucks," and "Motorcycles" into "Vehicles"*:

"Vehicles" would be a more general entity that includes attributes shared by all types, such as "License Plate Number," "Manufacturing Year," and "Owner."

In this scenario, "Cars," "Trucks," and "Motorcycles" are subtypes of "Vehicles," and they share common attributes and behaviors.

The key point to note is that specialization and generalization help create a structured and organized database schema. Specialization identifies the unique characteristics of subtypes, while generalization groups common attributes to avoid redundancy and improve data integrity.

These concepts are valuable in scenarios where entities exhibit hierarchical or inheritance relationships. They allow for the efficient representation of data and support the development of more specific and relevant queries and reports in the database system.

## ONLINE RESOURCES

**Practice Paper Link:** https://forms.gle/nk8PNaLkiPW4yhkRA

**QR Code:**

**Video Content:** https://www.youtube.com/playlist?list=PLzlh_31VWEFoFVGYleZ8kkXloq2XqaRWk

**QR Code:**

# Chapter 6: Transactions

## Transactions Concepts

A transaction is a fundamental concept in database management systems (DBMS). A transaction is a sequence of one or more SQL statements that are executed as a single, indivisible unit of work. The primary goal of transactions is to ensure the consistency and integrity of the database, even in the presence of failures. Here are some key transaction concepts:

**ACID Properties:**

Atomicity: A transaction is atomic, which means it is treated as a single, indivisible unit. It is either fully completed (commit) or fully undone (rollback) in case of failure.

Consistency: A transaction takes the database from one consistent state to another. It ensures that the integrity constraints and business rules are not violated during the transaction.

Isolation: Transactions are isolated from each other. The operations of one transaction are not visible to other transactions until the first transaction is complete.

Durability: Once a transaction is committed, its effects are permanent and survive any subsequent system failures.

**Schedules:**

A schedule is an arrangement of transactions in time. It defines the order in which transactions are executed.

Serializable schedules are schedules that produce the same result as if the transactions were executed one after the other.

**Serializability:**

Serializability is a property of schedules in which the transactions appear to be executed serially, one after the other. It ensures that the outcome of a set of concurrent transactions is equivalent to the outcome if they were executed serially.

**Concurrency Control:**

Concurrency control mechanisms manage the execution of transactions in a multi-user environment to ensure isolation and consistency.

Techniques like two-phase locking, timestamp ordering, and optimistic concurrency control are used to achieve this.

**Transaction Support in SQL:**

SQL provides keywords like BEGIN TRANSACTION, COMMIT, and ROLLBACK to define and manage transactions.

Transactions can be explicitly started, committed, or rolled back using these SQL commands.

**Need for Concurrency:**

Concurrency allows multiple transactions to execute simultaneously, improving system throughput and responsiveness.

However, it introduces the potential for conflicts and anomalies that need to be managed.

**Deadlock Handling:**

Deadlock occurs when two or more transactions are unable to proceed because each is waiting for a resource that the other holds.

Deadlock detection and resolution mechanisms are employed to resolve such situations.

**Recovery Concepts:**

Recovery mechanisms ensure that the database can be restored to a consistent state in case of system failures. Techniques like deferred and immediate update, shadow paging, and the ARIES algorithm are used for recovery.

In summary, transactions are essential for maintaining data consistency and integrity in a DBMS. They follow the ACID properties, and concurrency control mechanisms ensure that multiple transactions can run concurrently without compromising data integrity. Recovery mechanisms help in restoring the database to a consistent state after system failures.

**Global Transactions and Local Transactions:**

Global transactions and local transactions are concepts in the context of database systems, particularly in the context of distributed databases. They refer to the scope and extent of a transaction's operations within a database environment. Here's an explanation of each:

**Global Transactions:**

Scope: Global transactions span multiple databases or multiple sites within a distributed database system. They involve operations on data that are distributed across different locations or nodes.

Dependency: Global transactions may involve multiple local transactions at different sites. These local transactions are coordinated as part of the global transaction. Global transactions ensure that all participating local transactions either commit or abort together to maintain data consistency.

Coordination: Global transactions require coordination mechanisms to ensure that all distributed sites agree on the outcome (commit or abort) of the transaction. Two-phase commit (2PC) is a common coordination protocol for global transactions.

Atomicity: Global transactions follow the ACID properties (Atomicity, Consistency, Isolation, Durability) and ensure that all participating local transactions are atomic, meaning they either all succeed (commit) or all fail (abort) to maintain data consistency.

Data Distribution: Global transactions are used when data is distributed across multiple sites for reasons such as load balancing, fault tolerance, or data replication. They ensure that changes to distributed data are synchronized.

Complexity: Implementing and managing global transactions can be more complex due to the need for coordination, distributed data management, and ensuring the consistency of data across sites.

**Local Transactions:**

Scope: Local transactions operate on data within a single database or at a single site. They involve operations on data that are confined to a specific database or location.

Dependency: Local transactions are independent of each other and do not depend on transactions at other sites. They are confined to the local database and are not aware of transactions occurring at remote sites.

Coordination: Local transactions do not require coordination with other sites since they operate within the boundaries of a single database. They are managed using conventional transaction management mechanisms.

Atomicity: Local transactions also follow the ACID properties but only within the context of the local database. They are atomic with respect to the local data but do not necessarily involve coordination with other sites.

Data Distribution: Local transactions are appropriate when data operations are limited to a single database or site and do not involve distributed data.

Complexity: Local transactions are simpler to manage because they involve only one database or site and do not require coordination with other sites.

The key difference between global and local transactions is their scope. Global transactions span multiple databases or sites and involve coordination, while local transactions are confined to a single database or site and do not involve distributed data management

**Distributed Transaction:**

A distributed transaction is a database transaction in which two or more distinct computer systems or databases are involved. These systems, often referred to as distributed databases, can be geographically dispersed and may use different database management systems (DBMS). Distributed transactions ensure that a series of database operations across multiple systems are treated as a single, indivisible unit of work, just like in a local (single-system) transaction.

## ACID Properties

ACID properties are a set of fundamental principles that guarantee the reliability and consistency of database transactions in a Database Management System (DBMS). These properties are essential for ensuring data integrity and reliability, especially in environments where multiple transactions can occur simultaneously. The acronym ACID stands for:

**Atomicity:**

Atomicity ensures that a transaction is treated as a single, indivisible unit of work. It follows the "all or nothing" principle.

If a transaction is successful and completes all its operations, the changes are committed to the database as a whole.

If any part of the transaction fails (e.g., due to an error or a violation of constraints), the entire transaction is rolled back, and no changes are applied to the database.

Example: Consider a funds transfer operation between two bank accounts. Atomicity ensures that if the debit from one account succeeds, the corresponding credit to the other account will also succeed. If either operation fails, the entire transaction is rolled back.

**Consistency:**

Consistency ensures that a transaction takes the database from one consistent state to another.

It enforces the integrity constraints and business rules defined for the database.

Transactions should not violate any constraints, ensuring that the database remains in a valid state.

Example: In a database of student records, consistency ensures that if a student's grade is updated, it remains within a valid range (e.g., between A and F).

**Isolation:**

Isolation ensures that the operations of one transaction are isolated from the operations of other concurrent transactions.

Transactions should not interfere with each other, and the database should behave as if transactions are executed serially.

Example: If two users concurrently update the same record in a database, isolation ensures that one user's changes do not affect the other user's transaction until they are committed.

**Durability:**

Durability guarantees that once a transaction is committed, its effects are permanent and will survive any subsequent system failures (e.g., power outage or crash).

Committed changes are stored in non-volatile storage, typically on disk, to ensure their persistence.

Example: After a customer submits an online order and receives a confirmation, the order information is durable, even if the web server crashes immediately afterward.

ACID properties collectively ensure the reliability and integrity of transactions in a DBMS, making it suitable for applications that require data consistency and durability, such as banking systems, healthcare records, and e-commerce platforms. These properties provide a robust foundation for handling complex data operations in a multi-user and multi-threaded environment.

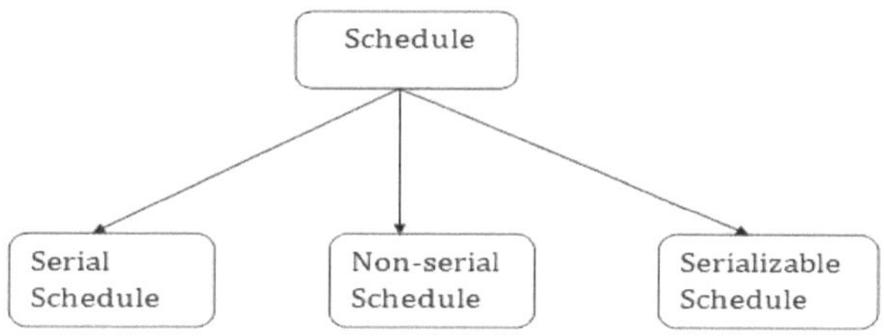


## Schedules

A series of operation from one transaction to another transaction is known as schedule. It is used to preserve the order of the operation in each of the individual transaction.

**Serial Schedule**

The serial schedule is a type of schedule where one transaction is executed completely before starting another transaction. In the serial schedule, when the first transaction completes its cycle, then the next transaction is executed.

For example: Suppose there are two transactions T1 and T2 which have some operations. If it has no interleaving of operations, then there are the following two possible outcomes:

Execute all the operations of T1 which was followed by all the operations of T2.

Execute all the operations of T1 which was followed by all the operations of T2.

In the given (a) figure, Schedule A shows the serial schedule where T1 followed by T2.

In the given (b) figure, Schedule B shows the serial schedule where T2 followed by T1.

(a)

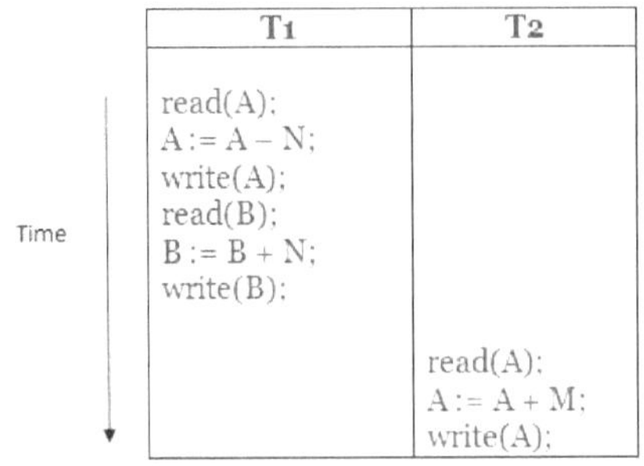


Schedule A

(d)

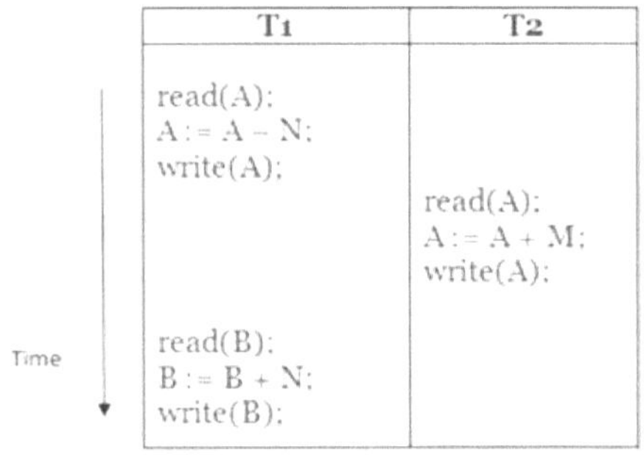


Schedule D

(c)

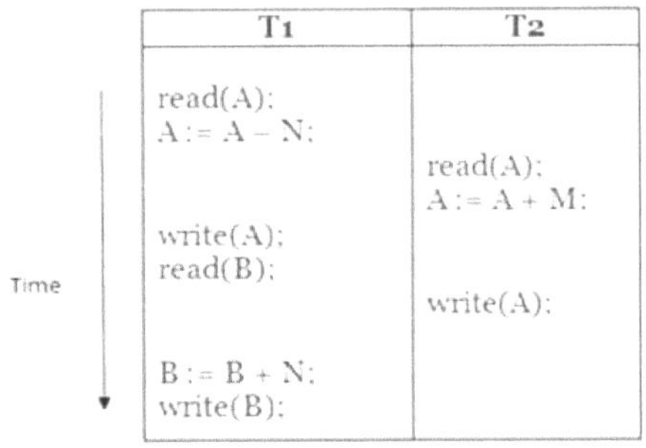


Schedule C

(b)

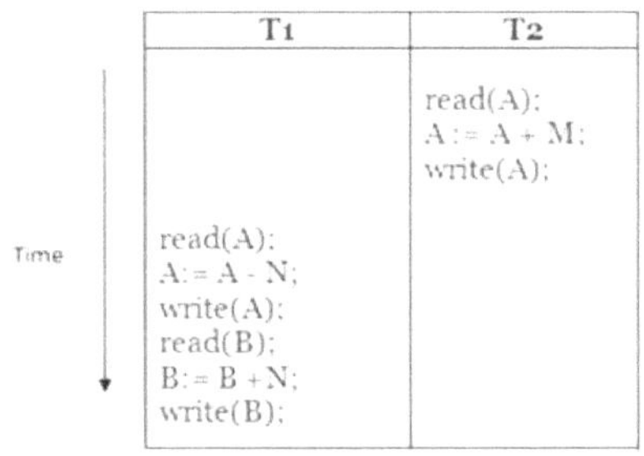


Schedule B

**Non-serial Schedule**

If interleaving of operations is allowed, then there will be non-serial schedule.

It contains many possible orders in which the system can execute the individual operations of the transactions.

In the given figure (c) and (d), Schedule C and Schedule D are the non-serial schedules. It has interleaving of operations.

**Serializable schedule**

The serializability of schedules is used to find non-serial schedules that allow the transaction to execute concurrently without interfering with one another.

It identifies which schedules are correct when executions of the transaction have interleaving of their operations.

A non-serial schedule will be serializable if its result is equal to the result of its transactions executed serially.

Here,

Schedule A and Schedule B are serial schedule.

Schedule C and Schedule D are non-serial schedule.

**Optimistic Scheduling:**

Optimistic scheduling, often referred to as optimistic concurrency control, is a strategy used in database management systems and transaction processing to handle concurrency and ensure data consistency. It is based on the optimistic assumption that conflicts between transactions are rare, and it allows transactions to proceed without locking data resources excessively. Here's a description of optimistic scheduling:

**Principle:**

Optimistic scheduling operates on the principle that conflicts or contention for data resources among transactions are infrequent. Instead of locking data resources immediately, transactions are allowed to proceed concurrently without blocking.

**Key Characteristics:**

No Immediate Locking: In optimistic scheduling, transactions do not acquire locks on data resources at the beginning. This means that multiple transactions can access and modify the same data simultaneously.

Validation Phase: Each transaction performs its operations independently and keeps track of the changes it intends to make. These changes are recorded in a tentative or private workspace.

Validation Check: After a transaction has completed its operations and is ready to commit, it undergoes a validation check. During this phase, the DBMS examines whether the changes made by the transaction conflict with changes made by other concurrent transactions. If there are no conflicts, the transaction is allowed to commit.

Commit or Rollback: If the validation check reveals no conflicts, the transaction is allowed to commit, and its changes are applied to the shared database. However, if conflicts are detected, the transaction is rolled back, and the changes are discarded.

**Benefits:**

Optimistic scheduling is beneficial when conflicts are indeed rare, as it minimizes the overhead of locking and waiting for resources. This can lead to improved system throughput and reduced contention.

It is particularly useful in scenarios where most transactions do not interfere with each other, such as read-heavy workloads or scenarios where the probability of conflicts is low.

**Drawbacks:**

In cases where conflicts are frequent, optimistic scheduling can result in a high rate of transaction rollbacks. This can lead to wasted computational resources and decreased performance.

The effectiveness of optimistic scheduling depends on the nature of the workload and the specific application. It may not be suitable for all types of applications, especially those with high contention for resources.

Implementing optimistic scheduling requires additional mechanisms for recording and checking changes, which can introduce complexity into the system.

Optimistic scheduling is a concurrency control strategy that assumes conflicts are rare and allows transactions to proceed without immediate locking. It offers benefits in scenarios with low contention but may not be suitable for all types of applications. Its success depends on the characteristics of the workload and the system's ability to detect and handle conflicts during the validation phase.

## Serializability

Serializability is a fundamental concept in database management systems (DBMS) that ensures the correctness and consistency of transactions executed in a multi-user environment. It defines a set of rules and criteria for the execution of transactions to maintain the illusion that they are executed one at a time, even when they are running concurrently. This concept is closely related to the ACID (Atomicity, Consistency, Isolation, Durability) properties of database transactions. Here are the details of serializability in DBMS:

**Serial Execution Illusion:**

Serializability ensures that even though multiple transactions may be executing concurrently, the outcome is equivalent to a situation where transactions are executed one after the other in some order.

This illusion is crucial for maintaining data consistency and correctness in a multi-user environment.

**Transaction Schedules:**

A transaction schedule represents the order of execution of transactions and the sequence of their individual operations (reads and writes) on the database.

In concurrent environments, schedules can be interleaved, where operations from different transactions may overlap in time.

**Conflict Operations:**

Serializability focuses on conflict operations that involve reading and writing shared data items.

There are two primary types of conflicts:

Read-Write Conflict: When one transaction reads a data item that another transaction is currently writing to.

Write-Write Conflict: When two transactions attempt to write to the same data item simultaneously.

**Serializable Schedules:**

A schedule is considered serializable if it is equivalent to some serial (non-concurrent) execution of the transactions.

Serializable schedules ensure that the overall state of the database remains consistent, regardless of the order in which transactions are executed.

**Testing for Serializability:**

There are various techniques for testing if a given schedule is serializable:

Conflict Graph: One common approach involves constructing a conflict graph, where nodes represent transactions, and edges represent conflicts.

Precedence Graph: Another method uses a precedence graph to represent the order of operations and detect cycles, which indicate non-serializability.

**Conflict-Serializable Schedules:**

A schedule is conflict-serializable if its conflict graph (or precedence graph) is acyclic.

Conflict-serializability ensures that conflicting operations are serialized in such a way that the final state of the database is consistent.

**Serializable vs. Serializable Schedules:**

While conflict-serializability is a subset of serializability, not all serializable schedules are conflict-serializable.

Serializable schedules may involve non-conflicting operations, such as independent reads, which do not affect the serializability of the schedule.

**Concurrency Control:**

DBMSs employ concurrency control mechanisms, such as locking, timestamp ordering, and two-phase locking, to ensure serializability.

These mechanisms prevent conflicts and enforce the order of execution to maintain data integrity.

In summary, serializability is a critical concept in DBMS that ensures that concurrent transactions produce results equivalent to those of serial (non-concurrent) executions, maintaining the ACID properties of database transactions. It allows multiple transactions to operate on a database concurrently while preserving data consistency and correctness. Conflict-serializability, which focuses on conflict operations, is a practical way to test for serializability in complex schedules.

## Transaction Support in SQL

Transaction support in SQL (Structured Query Language) is a crucial aspect of database management systems (DBMS) that ensures the integrity and reliability of database operations. Transactions are sequences of one or more SQL statements that are treated as a single, indivisible unit of work. The primary goal of transaction support is to maintain the ACID (Atomicity, Consistency, Isolation, Durability) properties of database transactions. Here's a detailed explanation of transaction support in SQL:

**Atomicity (A):**

Atomicity ensures that a transaction is treated as an all-or-nothing operation. Either all its SQL statements are executed successfully, or none are.

If any part of a transaction fails (e.g., due to a system crash, constraint violation, or error), the entire transaction is rolled back to its previous state, and no changes are applied to the database.

**Consistency (C):**

Consistency guarantees that a transaction takes the database from one consistent state to another. It enforces data integrity and ensures that all integrity constraints are satisfied.

Before and after a transaction, the database must adhere to a set of predefined rules and constraints (e.g., primary keys, foreign keys, check constraints).

**Isolation (I):**

Isolation ensures that concurrent transactions do not interfere with each other. Each transaction operates in isolation and appears to be the only transaction executing on the database.

Isolation levels, such as Read Uncommitted, Read Committed, Repeatable Read, and Serializable, define the degree of isolation between transactions. Higher isolation levels provide stronger guarantees but may impact performance.

**Durability (D):**

Durability guarantees that once a transaction is committed, its changes are permanent and will survive system failures (e.g., crashes, power outages).

DBMSs achieve durability by writing transaction logs and data changes to non-volatile storage (e.g., disk) before confirming the transaction's success to the user.

**Transaction Commands in SQL:**

SQL provides commands to manage transactions:

BEGIN TRANSACTION or BEGIN WORK: Initiates a new transaction.

COMMIT: Marks the successful completion of a transaction and applies its changes to the database.

ROLLBACK: Undoes all changes made by a transaction, returning the database to its state before the transaction started.

SAVEPOINT and ROLLBACK TO SAVEPOINT: Allow for finer-grained control within a transaction by creating savepoints that can be used to roll back to specific points in the transaction.

**Implicit vs. Explicit Transactions:**

In SQL, transactions can be explicitly defined by the programmer using BEGIN TRANSACTION and COMMIT/ROLLBACK, or they can be implicitly managed by the DBMS.

Implicit transactions are often used for single SQL statements, which are automatically treated as transactions by the DBMS.

**Transaction Control Statements:**

SQL also provides control statements for specifying transaction behaviour:

SET TRANSACTION: Allows you to set properties like isolation level and access mode for a transaction.

SET AUTOCOMMIT: Specifies whether each statement is treated as a separate transaction.

**Concurrency Control:**

To ensure isolation, DBMSs employ concurrency control mechanisms like locking (e.g., row-level or table-level locks) and multiversion concurrency control (MVCC), depending on the isolation level selected.

**Error Handling:**

SQL includes mechanisms for handling errors within transactions, such as BEGIN TRY...END TRY and BEGIN CATCH...END CATCH blocks in T-SQL (Transact-SQL), the SQL dialect used in Microsoft SQL Server.

**Logging and Recovery:**

DBMSs maintain logs of all transactions to support recovery in case of system failures. The logs record both the before and after states of the database.

In summary, transaction support in SQL is essential for maintaining data integrity, consistency, and reliability in database systems. SQL provides commands and features to define, control, and manage transactions, ensuring that database operations follow the ACID properties and can withstand system failures and concurrent access by multiple users.

## 6.6 Need for Concurrency

Concurrency control in a database management system (DBMS) is essential to manage simultaneous access to a database by multiple users or transactions. Here are the detailed reasons explaining the need for concurrency control in a DBMS:

**Simultaneous Access:** In a multi-user environment, multiple users or transactions may need to access the same data simultaneously. Without concurrency control, conflicts can arise when two or more transactions attempt to modify the same data concurrently.

**Data Integrity**: One of the primary goals of a DBMS is to maintain data integrity. Data integrity ensures that the data stored in the database remains accurate, consistent, and valid. Concurrent access can introduce anomalies, such as lost updates, uncommitted data, and inconsistent reads, which can compromise data integrity.

**Isolation of Transactions**: Concurrency control ensures that transactions are isolated from each other, meaning that the changes made by one transaction are not visible to other transactions until the first transaction is complete. This isolation prevents transactions from interfering with each other and provides a sense of consistency.

**Efficiency:** Concurrency control mechanisms aim to strike a balance between ensuring data integrity and maximizing system efficiency. Allowing multiple transactions to execute concurrently can lead to better system utilization and response times. However, it must be done while preserving data consistency.

**Improved Throughput**: By enabling multiple transactions to run in parallel, concurrency control can increase the overall throughput of the DBMS. This is especially important in systems with a high volume of concurrent users or transactions.

Concurrency Anomalies: Without proper concurrency control, several anomalies can occur:

**Lost Update**: When two transactions attempt to update the same data concurrently, one transaction's update may be lost or overwritten by the other.

**Dirty Read**: A transaction reads data that has been modified by another transaction but not yet committed. If the other transaction is later rolled back, the data read becomes invalid.

Non-repeatable Read: A transaction reads the same data multiple times, but the data changes between reads due to updates by other transactions.

**Phantom Read:** A transaction retrieves a set of rows that satisfy a condition, but between subsequent reads, other transactions insert, update, or delete rows that meet the same condition, causing the result set to change.

Conflict Resolution: Concurrency control mechanisms provide methods for resolving conflicts that arise when multiple transactions try to access or modify the same data concurrently. Common techniques include locking (e.g., row-level or table-level locks) and optimistic concurrency control (e.g., using timestamps or version numbers).

**Consistency Levels:** Concurrency control allows for different levels of isolation, depending on the specific requirements of the application. Isolation levels, such as Read Uncommitted, Read Committed, Repeatable Read, and Serializable, provide varying degrees of data consistency and isolation.

**Data Safety**: Concurrency control ensures that even in cases of system failures (e.g., crashes or power outages), the database remains in a consistent state. Transactions can be rolled back or replayed from the transaction logs to recover from failures.

In summary, concurrency control in a DBMS is essential to enable multiple users or transactions to work with a shared database while maintaining data integrity, consistency, and isolation. It helps prevent conflicts, anomalies, and data corruption, ensuring that the database remains reliable and safe in a multi-user environment.

### 6.7 Concurrency Control

Executing a single transaction at a time will increase the waiting time of the other transactions which may result in delay in the overall execution. Hence for increasing the overall throughput and efficiency of the system, several transactions are executed.

Concurrently control is a very important concept of DBMS which ensures the simultaneous execution or manipulation of data by several processes or user without resulting in data inconsistency.

Concurrency control provides a procedure that is able to control concurrent execution of the operations in the database.

**Concurrency Control Problems**

There are several problems that arise when numerous transactions are executed simultaneously in a random manner. The database transaction consist of two major operations "Read" and "Write". It is very important to manage these operations in the concurrent execution of the transactions in order to maintain the consistency of the data.

**Dirty Read Problem(Write-Read conflict)**

Dirty read problem occurs when one transaction updates an item but due to some unconditional events that transaction fails but before the transaction performs rollback, some other transaction reads the updated value. Thus creates an inconsistency in the database. Dirty read problem comes under the scenario of Write-Read conflict between the transactions in the database

The lost update problem can be illustrated with the below scenario between two transactions T1 and T2.

Transaction T1 modifies a database record without committing the changes.

T2 reads the uncommitted data changed by T1

T1 performs rollback

T2 has already read the uncommitted data of T1 which is no longer valid, thus creating inconsistency in the database.

**Lost Update Problem**

Lost update problem occurs when two or more transactions modify the same data, resulting in the update being overwritten or lost by another transaction. The lost update problem can be illustrated with the below scenario between two transactions T1 and T2.

T1 reads the value of an item from the database.

T2 starts and reads the same database item.

T1 updates the value of that data and performs a commit.

T2 updates the same data item based on its initial read and performs commit.

This results in the modification of T1 gets lost by the T2's write which causes a lost update problem in the database.

**Concurrency Control Protocols**

Concurrency control protocols are the set of rules which are maintained in order to solve the concurrency control problems in the database. It ensures that the concurrent transactions can execute properly while maintaining the database consistency. The concurrent execution of a transaction is provided with atomicity, consistency, isolation, durability, and serializability via the concurrency control protocols.

Locked based concurrency control protocol

Timestamp based concurrency control protocol

**Locked based Protocol**

In locked based protocol, each transaction needs to acquire locks before they start accessing or modifying the data items. There are two types of locks used in databases.

Shared Lock : Shared lock is also known as read lock which allows multiple transactions to read the data simultaneously. The transaction which is holding a shared lock can only read the data item but it can not modify the data item.

Exclusive Lock : Exclusive lock is also known as the write lock. Exclusive lock allows a transaction to update a data item. Only one transaction can hold the exclusive lock on a data item at a time. While a transaction is holding an exclusive lock on a data item, no other transaction is allowed to acquire a shared/exclusive lock on the same data item.

There are two kind of lock based protocol mostly used in database:

Two Phase Locking Protocol : Two phase locking is a widely used technique which ensures strict ordering of lock acquisition and release. Two phase locking protocol works in two phases.

Growing Phase : In this phase, the transaction starts acquiring locks before performing any modification on the data items. Once a transaction acquires a lock, that lock can not be released until the transaction reaches the end of the execution.

Shrinking Phase : In this phase, the transaction releases all the acquired locks once it performs all the modifications on the data item. Once the transaction starts releasing the locks, it can not acquire any locks further.

Strict Two Phase Locking Protocol : It is almost similar to the two phase locking protocol the only difference is that in two phase locking the transaction can release its locks before it commits, but in case of strict two phase locking the transactions are only allowed to release the locks only when they performs commits.

**Timestamp based Protocol**

In this protocol each transaction has a timestamp attached to it. Timestamp is nothing but the time in which a transaction enters into the system.

The conflicting pairs of operations can be resolved by the timestamp ordering protocol through the utilization of the timestamp values of the transactions. Therefore, guaranteeing that the transactions take place in the correct order.

**Advantages of Concurrency**

In general, concurrency means, that more than one transaction can work on a system. The advantages of a concurrent system are:

Waiting Time: It means if a process is in a ready state but still the process does not get the system to get execute is called waiting time. So, concurrency leads to less waiting time.

Response Time: The time wasted in getting the response from the cpu for the first time, is called response time. So, concurrency leads to less Response Time.

Resource Utilization: The amount of Resource utilization in a particular system is called Resource Utilization. Multiple transactions can run parallel in a system. So, concurrency leads to more Resource Utilization.

Efficiency: The amount of output produced in comparison to given input is called efficiency. So, Concurrency leads to more Efficiency.

**Disadvantages of Concurrency**

Overhead: Implementing concurrency control requires additional overhead, such as acquiring and releasing locks on database objects. This overhead can lead to slower performance and increased resource consumption, particularly in systems with high levels of concurrency.

Deadlocks: Deadlocks can occur when two or more transactions are waiting for each other to release resources, causing a circular dependency that can prevent any of the transactions from completing. Deadlocks can be difficult to detect and resolve, and can result in reduced throughput and increased latency.

Reduced concurrency: Concurrency control can limit the number of users or applications that can access the database simultaneously. This can lead to reduced concurrency and slower performance in systems with high levels of concurrency.

Complexity: Implementing concurrency control can be complex, particularly in distributed systems or in systems with complex transactional logic. This complexity can lead to increased development and maintenance costs.

Inconsistency: In some cases, concurrency control can lead to inconsistencies in the database. For example, a transaction that is rolled back may leave the database in an inconsistent state, or a long-running transaction may cause other transactions to wait for extended periods, leading to data staleness and reduced accuracy.

### Two-Phase Locking

The two-phase locking protocol divides the execution phase of the transaction into three parts.

In the first part, when the execution of the transaction starts, it seeks permission for the lock it requires.

In the second part, the transaction acquires all the locks. The third phase is started as soon as the transaction releases

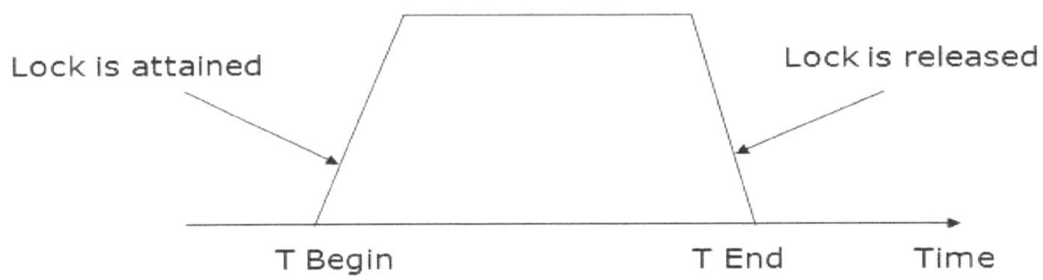


its first lock.

In the third phase, the transaction cannot demand any new locks. It only releases the acquired locks.

There are two phases of 2PL:

**Growing phase**: In the growing phase, a new lock on the data item may be acquired by the transaction, but none can be released.

**Shrinking phase**: In the shrinking phase, existing lock held by the transaction may be released, but no new locks can be acquired.

In the below example, if lock conversion is allowed then the following phase can happen:

Upgrading of lock (from S(a) to X (a)) is allowed in growing phase.

Downgrading of lock (from X(a) to S(a)) must be done in shrinking phase.

Example:

|  | T1 | T2 |
|---|---|---|
| 0 | LOCK-S(A) |  |
| 1 |  | LOCK-S(A) |
| 2 | LOCK-X(B) |  |
| 3 | ----- | ----- |
| 4 | UNLOCK(A) |  |
| 5 |  | LOCK-X(C) |
| 6 | UNLOCK(B) |  |
| 7 |  | UNLOCK(A) |
| 8 |  | UNLOCK(C) |
| 9 | ----- | ----- |

The following way shows how unlocking and locking work with 2-PL.

Transaction T1:

Growing phase: from step 1-3

Shrinking phase: from step 5-7

Lock point: at 3

Transaction T2:

Growing phase: from step 2-6

Shrinking phase: from step 8-9

Lock point: at 6

**Two-Phase Commit (2PC) Protocol:**

The Two-Phase Commit Protocol is a distributed algorithm used to ensure the consistency and reliability of distributed transactions involving multiple participants (often referred to as nodes or resources) in a distributed database system. It follows the ACID properties (Atomicity, Consistency, Isolation, Durability) and plays a crucial role in managing distributed transactions. Here's a short note on the 2PC protocol:

Phases of 2PC:

Prepare Phase: In this phase, the transaction coordinator (often referred to as the coordinator node) sends a "prepare" request to all participating nodes. Each participating node examines the local transaction to ensure it can be executed successfully without violating any constraints or integrity rules. If everything is in order, each participating node responds with an acknowledgment (vote) to the coordinator, indicating that it is ready to commit the transaction.

Commit Phase: After receiving "prepare" responses from all participating nodes, the coordinator decides whether to commit or abort the transaction. If all nodes voted "yes" during the prepare phase, the coordinator sends a "commit" request to all nodes, instructing them to make the changes permanent. If any node voted "no" during the prepare phase or if the coordinator detects a failure in the process, it sends an "abort" request to all nodes, instructing them to roll back the transaction.

Key Features:

Atomicity: The 2PC protocol ensures atomicity by making sure that either all participating nodes commit the transaction or all of them abort it. There is no partial commitment.

Blocking: The protocol may block if any participating node fails to respond during the prepare phase. This ensures that a decision is made only when there is a clear consensus among all participants.

Blocking vs. Deadlock: While blocking can occur in 2PC, it's generally considered more acceptable than the possibility of distributed deadlocks that might arise in other protocols.

Reliability: 2PC is a reliable protocol, and it can handle various failure scenarios, including node failures and network partitions.

Drawbacks:

Blocking: The blocking nature of the 2PC protocol can lead to performance issues and, in some cases, a complete halt of transaction processing if a node is unresponsive.

Lack of Flexibility: The protocol assumes that participants can always make a definite decision during the prepare phase. In reality, a participant might not be able to determine its vote without performing the actual transaction, especially if the transaction involves external services or resources.

Stalemate: In certain situations, a scenario called "distributed stalemate" can occur, where multiple transactions are blocked because they are waiting for one another to release locks.

Despite its limitations, the Two-Phase Commit Protocol is widely used in distributed database systems where strong consistency and reliability are paramount. It provides a structured approach to managing distributed transactions and ensuring that they meet the requirements of atomicity and consistency. However, in scenarios where lower latency and greater flexibility are needed, alternative protocols like Three-Phase Commit or heuristic approaches might be considered.

## Timestamp and Multiversion

Timestamp-based concurrency control and multiversion concurrency control (MVCC) are techniques used in database management systems (DBMS) to handle concurrent access to data.

### Timestamp-Based Concurrency Control:

Timestamp-based concurrency control assigns a unique timestamp to each transaction when it starts. These timestamps are used to determine the order of transactions and resolve conflicts. A transaction with a lower timestamp must wait if a conflicting transaction with a higher timestamp is already executing.

Example:

Suppose we have two transactions, T1 and T2, accessing a bank account:

T1 (timestamp 1): T1 wants to withdraw $100.

T2 (timestamp 2): T2 wants to deposit $50.

Here's how timestamp-based concurrency control works:

T1 starts first, so it gets timestamp 1.

T2 starts later, so it gets timestamp 2.

Now, let's consider two scenarios:

Scenario 1:

T1 reads the account balance, which is $500.

T2 reads the account balance.

T1 subtracts $100 and updates the balance to $400.

T2 adds $50 and updates the balance to $550.

In this case, there is no conflict, and both transactions can commit successfully.

Scenario 2:

T1 reads the account balance, which is $500.

T2 reads the account balance.

T2 adds $50 and updates the balance to $550.

T1 subtracts $100 and attempts to update the balance to $400.

In this scenario, T1 conflicts with T2 because T2 modified the balance before T1. The DBMS would detect this conflict based on timestamps and prevent T1 from updating the balance. T1 would need to be rolled back or retried.

**Multiversion Concurrency Control (MVCC):**

MVCC is a concurrency control method that maintains multiple versions of each data item in the database. Each version is associated with a timestamp range representing when it was valid. Transactions read from the version of the data item that matches their timestamp.

**Example:**

Consider a simple database table for customer transactions:

| CustomerID | Transaction | Timestamp |
|---|---|---|
| 1 | Purchase | 100 |
| 2 | Refund | 150 |
| 1 | Purchase | 200 |

Here's how MVCC works:

Transaction T1 with timestamp 120 reads the table. It sees only the "Purchase" with timestamp 100 for Customer 1.

Transaction T2 with timestamp 175 reads the table. It sees both the "Purchase" with timestamp 100 for Customer 1 and the "Refund" with timestamp 150 for Customer 2.

Transaction T3 with timestamp 180 reads the table. It sees all three records.

Now, suppose T1 wants to update the "Purchase" record for Customer 1:

T1 creates a new version with its timestamp 120 and updates the "Purchase" record.

The table now looks like this:

| CustomerID | Transaction | Timestamp |
|---|---|---|
| 1 | Purchase | 100 |
| 2 | Refund | 150 |
| 1 | Purchase | 120 |

In MVCC, concurrent transactions can read and modify different versions of data, allowing for high concurrency without conflicts.

Diagrams illustrating timestamp-based and MVCC-based concurrency control are more complex and typically involve timelines and data versioning. If you need diagrams, you may consider using dedicated database modeling tools to create visual representations of these concepts.

## Validation and Snapshot Isolation

Validation and Snapshot Isolation are two concurrency control techniques used in database management systems (DBMS) to ensure data consistency and isolation among concurrent transactions.

**Validation:**

Validation-based concurrency control uses the concept of timestamps or version numbers associated with each data item.

When a transaction wants to update a data item, it first reads the timestamp or version number of that item.

During validation, the DBMS checks if the transaction's read timestamps are consistent with the write timestamps of the data items it intends to modify. If there is a conflict (i.e., if another transaction has modified the same data item after the current transaction read it), validation fails, and the transaction must be rolled back and retried.

Validation prevents the "lost update" problem by ensuring that a transaction only commits if its read data is still valid when it attempts to write.

**Snapshot Isolation:**

Snapshot Isolation is a concurrency control technique that ensures that transactions see a consistent snapshot of the database as of their start time.

Transactions run in isolation and can't see the changes made by other transactions running concurrently.

If two transactions attempt to modify the same data, one of them will be chosen as the winner, and the other will be rolled back.

Snapshot Isolation prevents the "dirty read" problem by allowing transactions to read a consistent snapshot of the database.

**Example:**

Consider a simple bank account table with columns for account number, balance, and timestamps:

| Account Number | Balance | Timestamp |
|---|---|---|
| 101 | $500 | 1 |
| 102 | $750 | 2 |
| 103 | $300 | 3 |

Two transactions, T1 and T2, want to update account balances:

**Validation Example**

Transaction T1:

T1 starts at timestamp 4 and reads the balance of account 101, which is $500.

T1 subtracts $100 and intends to update the balance to $400.

During validation, T1 checks if the timestamp of account 101 (timestamp 1) matches its read timestamp (timestamp 4). It doesn't match, indicating that someone else updated the account after T1 read it.

Validation fails for T1, and it is rolled back.

Transaction T2:

T2 starts at timestamp 5 and reads the balance of account 101, which is $500.

T2 adds $50 and intends to update the balance to $550.

During validation, T2 checks if the timestamp of account 101 (timestamp 1) matches its read timestamp (timestamp 5). It doesn't match.

Validation fails for T2, and it is rolled back.

In this case, both T1 and T2 attempted to update the same account, but validation ensured that only one of them could commit while the other was rolled back.

**Snapshot Isolation Example**

Using the same bank account table, consider the following transactions:

Transaction T1:

T1 starts at timestamp 6 and reads the balance of account 102, which is $750.

T1 subtracts $200 and intends to update the balance to $550.

Transaction T2:

T2 starts at timestamp 7 and reads the balance of account 102, which is still $750 (as of its start time).

T2 adds $100 and intends to update the balance to $850.

**In Snapshot Isolation:**

Both T1 and T2 run concurrently without seeing each other's changes.

When they attempt to commit, one of them (let's say T2) succeeds and updates the balance to $850, while the other (T1) is rolled back because it attempted to modify a data item that has been changed by another transaction.

Snapshot Isolation ensures that each transaction sees a consistent snapshot of the database as of its start time, preventing conflicts between concurrent transactions.

## Multiple Granularity Locking

Multiple Granularity Locking (MGL) is a locking technique used in database management systems to improve concurrency control by allowing different levels of locks on data items, also known as granularity levels. This technique helps balance the trade-off between fine-grained locking, which can lead to excessive contention, and coarse-grained locking, which can reduce concurrency.

In MGL, locks can be acquired at various levels of granularity:

Database Level: This is the coarsest level, where a single lock covers the entire database.

Table Level: Locks are acquired at the table level, allowing exclusive access to a specific table.

Page Level: Locks are acquired at the page level, typically representing a fixed-size block of data storage. Pages are part of a table.

Row Level: The finest level of granularity, where locks are acquired at the row level. This allows locking individual rows within a table.

Example of Multiple Granularity Locking:

Consider a simplified database for an online store with two tables: Products and Orders.

At the database level, a lock is acquired by a transaction that intends to perform a global operation affecting multiple tables, such as a backup or a database schema change.

At the table level, a lock is acquired when a transaction needs exclusive access to a specific table, like Products or Orders. For example, during a table rebuild operation, a transaction can acquire an exclusive lock on the Products table to prevent other transactions from accessing it.

At the page level, a lock is acquired when a transaction intends to modify a page of data within a table. Suppose the Products table contains pages with product information. A transaction can acquire a lock on a specific page of the Products table while updating the products on that page.

At the row level, a lock is acquired when a transaction needs to modify or read a specific row in a table. For instance, when a customer places an order, a transaction might acquire a lock on the specific rows in the Products table corresponding to the ordered items to ensure that the available quantity is updated correctly.

MGL allows transactions to lock data at an appropriate level of granularity, reducing contention and improving concurrency. It's essential for maintaining data consistency while enabling multiple transactions to work concurrently on different parts of the database. However, it also requires careful management to avoid deadlocks and ensure that locks are released appropriately to prevent blocking other transactions.

## Deadlock Handling and Recovery Concepts

In a database management system (DBMS), a deadlock occurs when two or more transactions are waiting for each other to release resources, such as locks on database objects, that they need to complete their operations. As a result, none of the transactions can proceed, leading to a situation where they are stuck or "deadlocked."

Deadlocks can happen in multi-user environments when two or more transactions are running concurrently and try to access the same data in a different order. When this happens, one transaction may hold a lock on a resource that another transaction needs, while the second transaction may hold a lock on a resource that the first transaction needs. Both transactions are then blocked, waiting for the other to release the resource they need.

DBMSs often use various techniques to detect and resolve deadlocks automatically. These techniques include timeout mechanisms, where a transaction is forced to release its locks after a certain period of time, and deadlock detection algorithms, which periodically scan the transaction log for deadlock cycles and then choose a transaction to abort to resolve the deadlock.

It is also possible to prevent deadlocks by careful design of transactions, such as always acquiring locks in the same order or releasing locks as soon as possible. Proper design of the database schema and application can also help to

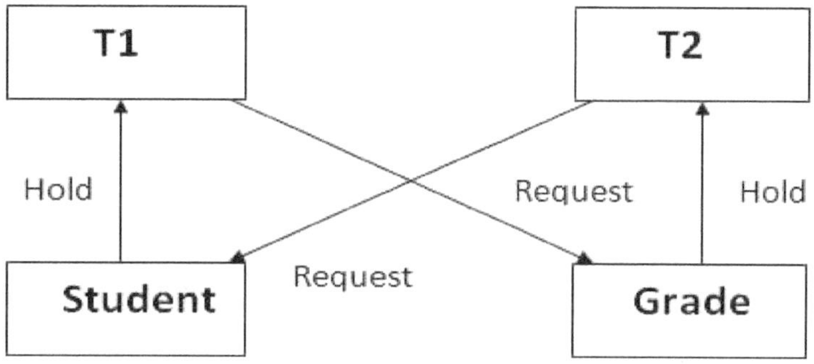


minimize the likelihood of deadlocks

**Deadlock Avoidance**

When a database is stuck in a deadlock state, then it is better to avoid the database rather than aborting or restating the database. This is a waste of time and resource. Deadlock avoidance mechanism is used to detect any deadlock situation in advance. A method like "wait for graph" is used for detecting the deadlock situation but this method is suitable only for the smaller database. For the larger database, deadlock prevention method can be used.

**Deadlock Detection**

When a transaction waits indefinitely to obtain a lock, The database management system should detect whether the transaction is involved in a deadlock or not.

**Wait-for-graph**

One of the methods for detecting the deadlock situation. This method is suitable for smaller databases. In this method, a graph is drawn based on the transaction and its lock on the resource. If the graph created has a closed loop or a cycle, then there is a deadlock.

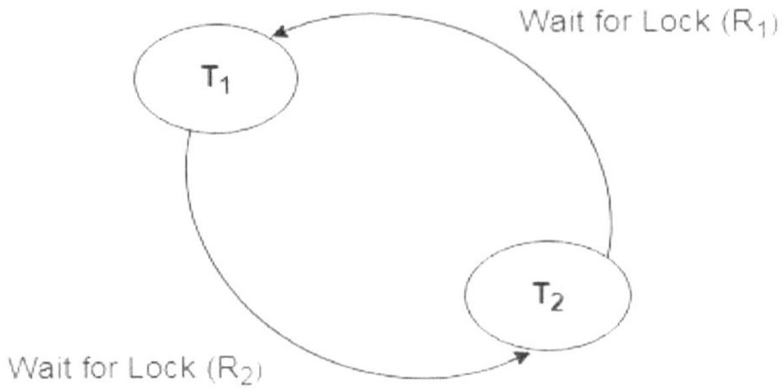


For the above-mentioned scenario, the Wait-For graph is drawn below:

**Deadlock Prevention**

Deadlock prevention method is suitable for a large database. If the resources are allocated in such a way that deadlock never occurs, then the deadlock can be prevented. The Database management system analyzes the operations of the transaction whether they can create a deadlock situation or not. If they do, then the DBMS never allowed that transaction to be executed.

**Wait-Die scheme**

In this scheme, if a transaction requests for a resource which is already held with a conflicting lock by another transaction then the DBMS simply checks the timestamp of both transactions. It allows the older transaction to wait until the resource is available for execution.

Let's assume there are two transactions Ti and Tj and let TS(T) is a timestamp of any transaction T. If T2 holds a lock by some other transaction and T1 is requesting for resources held by T2 then the following actions are performed by DBMS:

Check if TS(Ti) < TS(Tj) - If Ti is the older transaction and Tj has held some resource, then Ti is allowed to wait until the data-item is available for execution. That means if the older transaction is waiting for a resource which is locked by the younger transaction, then the older transaction is allowed to wait for resource until it is available.

Check if TS(Ti) < TS(Tj) - If Ti is older transaction and has held some resource and if Tj is waiting for it, then Tj is killed and restarted later with the random delay but with the same timestamp.

**Wound Wait Scheme:** In this scheme, if an older transaction requests for a resource held by a younger transaction, then an older transaction forces a younger transaction to kill the transaction and release the resource. The younger transaction is restarted with a minute delay but with the same timestamp. If the younger transaction is requesting a resource that is held by an older one, then the younger transaction is asked to wait till the older one releases it.

## Recovery Based on Deferred and Immediate Update

**Deferred Update:**

It is a technique for the maintenance of the transaction log files of the DBMS. It is also called NO-UNDO/REDO technique. It is used for the recovery of transaction failures that occur due to power, memory, or OS failures. Whenever any transaction is executed, the updates are not made immediately to the database. They are first recorded on the log file and then those changes are applied once the commit is done. This is called the "Re-doing" process. Once the rollback is done none of the changes are applied to the database and the changes in the log file are also discarded. If the commit is done before crashing the system, then after restarting the system the changes that have been recorded in the log file are thus applied to the database.

**Immediate Update:**

It is a technique for the maintenance of the transaction log files of the DBMS. It is also called UNDO/REDO technique. It is used for the recovery of transaction failures that occur due to power, memory, or OS failures. Whenever any transaction is executed, the updates are made directly to the database and the log file is also maintained which contains both old and new values. Once the commit is done, all the changes get stored permanently in the database, and records in the log file are thus discarded. Once rollback is done the old values get restored in the database and all the changes made to the database are also discarded. This is called the "Un-doing" process. If the commit is done before crashing the system, then after restarting the system the changes are stored permanently in the database.

## Shadow Paging and ARIES Algorithm

**Shadow Paging**isrecovery technique that is used to recover database. In this recovery technique, database is considered as made up of fixed size of logical units of storage which are referred as pages. pages are mapped into physical blocks of storage, with help of the page table which allow one entry for each logical page of database. This method uses two-page tables named current page table and shadow page table. The entries which are present in current page table are used to point to most recent database pages on disk. Another table i.e., Shadow page table is used when the transaction starts which is copying current page table. After this, shadow page table gets saved on disk and current page table is going to be used for transaction. Entries present in current page table may be changed during execution but in shadow page table it never gets changed. After transaction, both tables become identical. This technique is also known as Cut-of-Place updating.

To understand concept, consider above figure. In this 2 write operations are performed on page 3 and 5. Before start of write operation on page 3, current page table points to old page 3. When write operation starts following steps are performed:

Firstly, search start for available free block in disk blocks.

After finding free block, it copies page 3 to free block which is represented by Page 3 (New).

Now current page table points to Page 3 (New) on disk but shadow page table points to old page 3 because it is not modified.

The changes are now propagated to Page 3 (New) which is pointed by current page table.

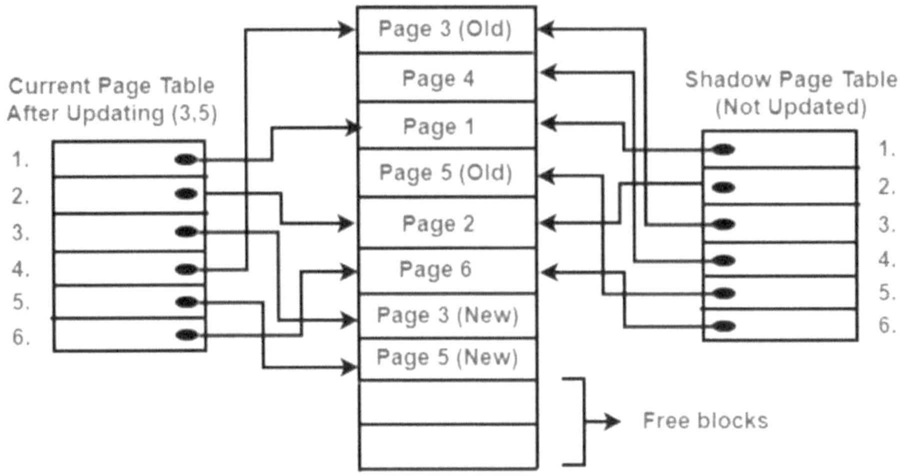


**Database disk blocks**

**Failure**: If system crashes during execution of transaction but before commit operation, With this, it is sufficient only to free modified database pages and discard current page table. Before execution of transaction, state of database get recovered by reinstalling shadow page table. If the crash of system occur after last write operation then it does not affect propagation of changes that are made by transaction. These changes are preserved and there is no need to perform redo operation. **Advantages:**

This method requires fewer disk accesses to perform operation.

In this method, recovery from crash is inexpensive and quite fast.

There is no need of operations like- Undo and Redo.

Recovery using this method will be faster.

Improved fault tolerance: Shadow paging provides improved fault tolerance since it isolates transactions from each other. This means that if one transaction fails, it does not affect the other transactions that are currently executing.

Increased concurrency: Since modifications made during a transaction are written to the shadow copy instead of the actual database, multiple transactions can be executed concurrently without interfering with each other. This leads to increased concurrency and better performance.

Simplicity: Shadow paging is a relatively simple technique to implement. It requires minimal modifications to the existing database system, making it easier to integrate into existing systems.

No need for log files: In traditional database systems, log files are used to maintain a record of all changes made to the database. Shadow paging eliminates the need for log files since all changes are made to the shadow copy. This reduces the overhead associated with maintaining log files and makes the system more efficient.

**Disadvantages:**

Due to location change on disk due to update database it is quite difficult to keep related pages in database closer on disk.

During commit operation, changed blocks are going to be pointed by shadow page table which have to be returned to collection of free blocks otherwise they become accessible.

The commit of single transaction requires multiple blocks which decreases execution speed.

To allow this technique to multiple transactions concurrently it is difficult.

Data fragmentation: The main disadvantage of this technique is the updated Data will suffer from fragmentation as the data is divided up into pages that may or not be in linear order for large sets of related hence, complex storage management strategies.

Garbage collection: Garbage will accumulate in the pages on the disk as data is updated and pages lose any references. For example if i have a page that contains a data item X that is replaced with a new value then a new page will be created. Once the shadow page table is updated nothing will reference the old value of X. The operation to migrate between current and shadow directories must be implemented as an atomic mode.

Performance overhead: Since modifications made during a transaction are written to the shadow copy, there is a performance overhead associated with copying the changes back to the actual database once the transaction is committed. This can impact the overall performance of the system.

Limited concurrency control: Shadow paging does not provide strong concurrency control mechanisms. While it allows for multiple transactions to execute concurrently, it does not prevent conflicts between transactions. This means that transactions can interfere with each other, leading to inconsistencies in the database.

Difficult to implement for some systems: Shadow paging can be difficult to implement for some systems that have complex data structures or use a lot of shared memory. In these cases, it may not be possible to maintain a shadow copy of the entire database.

Limited fault tolerance: While shadow paging does provide improved fault tolerance in some cases, it does not provide complete fault tolerance. In the event of a crash, there is still a risk of data loss if the changes made during a transaction are not properly copied to the actual database.

**Algorithm for Recovery and Isolation Exploiting Semantics (ARIES)** is based on the Write Ahead Log (WAL) protocol. Every update operation writes a log record which is one of the following:

Undo-only log record: Only the before image is logged. Thus, an undo operation can be done to retrieve the old data.

Redo-only log record: Only the after image is logged. Thus, a redo operation can be attempted.

Undo-redo log record: Both before images and after images are logged.

In it, every log record is assigned a unique and monotonically increasing log sequence number (LSN). Every data page has a page LSN field that is set to the LSN of the log record corresponding to the last update on the page. WAL requires that the log record corresponding to an update make it to stable storage before the data page corresponding to that update is written to disk. For performance reasons, each log write is not immediately forced to disk. A log tail is maintained in main memory to buffer log writes. The log tail is flushed to disk when it gets full. A transaction cannot be declared committed until the commit log record makes it to disk.

Once in a while the recovery subsystem writes a checkpoint record to the log. The checkpoint record contains the transaction table and the dirty page table. A master log record is maintained separately, in stable storage, to store the LSN of the latest checkpoint record that made it to disk. On restart, the recovery subsystem reads the master log record to find the checkpoint's LSN, reads the checkpoint record, and starts recovery from there on.

The recovery process actually consists of 3 phases:

Analysis: The recovery subsystem determines the earliest log record from which the next pass must start. It also scans the log forward from the checkpoint record to construct a snapshot of what the system looked like at the instant of the crash.

Redo: Starting at the earliest LSN, the log is read forward and each update redone.

Undo: The log is scanned backward and updates corresponding to loser transactions are undone.

**Exercise**

**Exercise 1 – MCQ**

Q 1. Which of the following is a primary goal of Transactions and Concurrency Control in a database management system?

A) Maximizing data redundancy

B) Ensuring data integrity

C) Minimizing query performance

D) Reducing the number of indexes

Q 2. In a database, what is the primary purpose of query optimization?

A) Increasing data redundancy

B) Enhancing data security

C) Improving query performance

D) Simplifying data modelling

**Exercise 2 – True/ False**

Q 1. In a distributed database system, data is stored in a single location for easy management and reduced latency.

Q 2. In-memory databases primarily store data on traditional hard drives to ensure data durability.

**Exercise 3 – Match case**

A. Transactions and Concurrency Control

B. Indexing and Query Optimization

C. Distributed Databases

D. In-Memory Databases

Descriptions:

1. Ensures that multiple users can access and modify the database simultaneously without data inconsistencies.
2. Techniques and strategies to improve the efficiency and speed of database queries.
3. Involves storing and managing data primarily in the computer's RAM for faster data access.
4. Involves managing data across multiple physical locations or nodes, often in a networked environment.

**Exercise 4 – One word answer**

Q 1. What is the primary goal of Transactions in a database system?

Q 2. What is the purpose of Indexing in a database system?

**Exercise 5 – Small answer**

Q 1. What is the purpose of transactions in a database, and how does the ACID (Atomicity, Consistency, Isolation, Durability) property ensure data integrity?

Q 2. Explain the role of indexing in a database and how it improves query performance.

**Exercise 6 – Long answer**

Q 1. Explain the concepts of transactions and concurrency control in a database system. How do transactions ensure data consistency, and what are some common concurrency control mechanisms? Provide examples to illustrate your points.

Q 2. Discuss the importance of indexing and query optimization in a database system. Explain how indexing works, different types of indexes, and strategies for query optimization. Provide examples to illustrate your points.

**Answer**

**Exercise 1**

Answer 1: B), 2: B)

**Exercise 2**

Answer 1: False, 2: False.

**Exercise 3**

Answer A)1, B)2, C)4, D)3.

**Exercise 4**

Answer 1: Consistency., 2: Efficiency.

**Previous Years Questions**

Q1. What is a transaction? Describe the ACID properties of transaction.(IGNOU MCA 2010)

Q2. What is a deadlock. Explain the schemes of deadlock prevention. (IGNOU MCA 2010)

Q3. Differentiate between the followings: Global and local transaction (IGNOU MCA 2010)

Q4. Explain the following with the help of an example / diagram wherever needed:

Conditions of occurrence of deadlocks

Two phase locking (IGNOU MCA 2010)

Q5. A concurrent schedule of transactions T1 and T2 acting on "SUM" is given below :

| Schedule | T1 | T2 | Sum |
|---|---|---|---|
| - | - | - | 100 |
| Read1(Sum) | Read1(Sum) | | |
| Sum = Sum +10 | Sum = Sum + 10 | | |
| Read2(Sum) | | Read2(Sum) | |
| Write1(Sum) | Write1(Sum) | | |
| Sum =Sum - 10 | | Sum = Sum - 10 | |
| Write2(Sum) | | Write2(Sum) | |

Analysing the given concurrent schedule performing following tasks.

What is the final value of "SUM"?

Verify that the given schedule is serializable or not. Explain. (IGNOU MCA 2011)

Q6. Explain 2 phase locking protocol. (IGNOU MCA 2011)

Q7. What is a transaction? Briefly describe the properties of the transactions. (IGNOU MCA 2011)

Q8. Describe the following: Optimistic scheduling (IGNOU MCA 2011)

Q9. Justify the following statements: Two phase locking leads to serializability schedules. (IGNOU MCA 2012)

Q10. Discuss the problems associated with concurrent transactions. (IGNOU MCA 2012)

Q11. What are the problems caused by deadlock? Give a Mechanism to detect deadlock. (IGNOU MCA 2012)

Q12. Discuss the different states of a Transaction with the help of a diagram (IGNOU MCA 2012)

Q13. Discuss the two-phase locking protocol in concurrency controls? (IGNOU MCA 2013)

Q14. Explain the ACID properties of transactions in Database system. (IGNOU MCA 2013)

Q15.Explain distributed transaction with the help of an example. (IGNOU MCA 2014)

Q16. Explain ANSI SPARC 3 - Level Architecture of DBMS, with the details of languages associated at different levels and the type of data independence involved in between different levels (IGNOU MCA 2014)

Write short note on the following: Concurrency Control and Database Views (IGNOU MCA 2014)

Q17. Discuss the 3-level architecture of DBMS. Explain how it leads to data independence. (IGNOU MCA 2015)

Q18. Discuss briefly about Sparse and Dense Indexes with the help of an example. (IGNOU MCA 2015)

Q19. Explain 2-phase locking protocol. (IGNOU MCA 2015)

Q20. List and explain the 4 basic properties of a Transaction with the help of appropriate examples. (IGNOU MCA 2015)

Q21. Differentiate between the following: Serial Schedule and Serializable Schedule. (IGNOU MCA 2016)

Q22. Discuss the different possible states of a transaction with the help of a diagram. (IGNOU MCA 2016)

Q23.What do you understand by the term 'Transaction' in a database? Discuss the properties of the transactions and explain the states through which a transaction passes during execution. (IGNOU MCA 2017)

Q24. For what reasons is 2-phase locking protocol required? Explain. Discuss the disadvantages of basic 2-phase locking protocol. List the ways and means that can be used to overcome the disadvantages. (IGNOU MCA 2017)

Q25. Write short notes on any four of the following: Optimistic Scheduling and 2-Phase Commit Protocol. (IGNOU MCA 2017)

Q26. Write short notes on any four of the following: Serializable Scheduling. (IGNOU MCA 2017)

Q27. What is a serializable schedule in concurrent transaction? How does serializable schedule differ from serial schedule? Give suitable example in support of your discussion. The problems of deadlock and starvation are addressed by which schedules respectively? Justify. (IGNOU MCA 2018)

Q28. Discuss the term wait-for graph. What is the utility of wait-for graph in describing deadlocks? Give suitable example in support of your discussion. (IGNOU MCA 2018)

Q29. Differentiate between the following: 10 (i) Two-phase locking vs Two-phase commit protocol (ii) Wait-wound vs Wait-die protocol. (IGNOU MCA 2018)

Q30.Discuss the term optimistic scheduling. How is this technique used to manage concurrent transactions in databases? What is the difference between timestamping and optimistic scheduling? Give suitable examples in support of your discussion. (IGNOU MCA 2018)

Q31. Write short notes on the following: Shadow Paging. (IGNOU MCA 2018)

Q32. Explain wound-wait scheme for deadlock prevention with the help of an example. (IGNOU MCA 2019)

Q33. Differentiate between the Basic 2PL and Strict 2PL with respect to atomicity, concurrency and deadlock. (IGNOU MCA 2019)

Q34.How do we recover from a transaction failure using "log"? Illustrate through an example. (IGNOU MCA 2019)

Q35. Explain any two problems of concurrent transactions with the help of an example. (IGNOU MCA 2019)

Q36. Discuss the optimistic concurrency control with the help of an example. (IGNOU MCA 2019)

Q37. What are concurrent transactions? Briefly discuss the problems encountered by concurrent transactions. (IGNOU MCA 2020)

Q38. Write short notes on the following: (i) 2-Phase locking protocol (ii) 2-Phase commit protocol (iii) Time-stamping protocol (iv) Checkpoints. (IGNOU MCA 2020)

Q39. Differentiate the following: Deadlock avoidance and Deadlock prevention protocols, 2 Phase locking and 2 Phase commit. (IGNOU MCA 2021)

Q40. Differentiate the terms UNDO and REDO process during the transaction processing. (ANNA University M.Sc 2013)

Q41. What are ACID properties of a transaction? (ANNA University M.Sc 2013)

**Previous Years Questions with Answers**

Q1 What is meant by ACID properties in DBMS? (RU BCA 2022)

**Answer:**

**ACID** is an acronym that stands for **Atomicity, Consistency, Isolation, and Durability**. These are a set of properties that ensure the reliability and integrity of transactions in a database management system (DBMS). ACID properties are fundamental to maintaining the accuracy and consistency of data in a database, especially in multi-user and concurrent access scenarios. Let's dive into each property:

**Atomicity**:

**Definition**: Atomicity ensures that a transaction is treated as a single, indivisible unit of work. It means that all the operations within a transaction are executed completely or not at all. If any part of the transaction fails, the entire transaction is rolled back, and the database returns to its original state.

**Example**: Consider a funds transfer transaction between two bank accounts. If the debit operation (subtracting funds from one account) succeeds but the credit operation (adding funds to the other account) fails, atomicity ensures that both operations are undone to maintain the database's integrity.

**Consistency**:

**Definition**: Consistency ensures that a transaction takes the database from one consistent state to another consistent state. It enforces integrity constraints and business rules to guarantee that the database is always in a valid state.

**Example**: In an e-commerce system, when a customer places an order, the consistency property ensures that the total order amount matches the sum of the individual item prices and that the items are deducted from the available inventory.

**Isolation**:

**Definition**: Isolation ensures that concurrent transactions do not interfere with each other. It means that one transaction is isolated from the effects of other concurrently executing transactions until it's completed. Isolation levels, such as "Read Uncommitted," "Read Committed," "Repeatable Read," and "Serializable," control the level of isolation.

**Example**: In a multi-user database system, when two users concurrently attempt to update the same set of data, isolation ensures that their changes do not overlap and that each user sees a consistent snapshot of the data.

**Durability**:

**Definition**: Durability ensures that once a transaction is committed (successfully completed), its effects are permanent and will survive system failures, such as power outages or crashes. This property is typically achieved by writing transaction data to non-volatile storage like disk.

**Example**: After a user completes an online banking transaction and receives a confirmation, the durability property ensures that the transaction details are securely stored and can be retrieved even if the database server crashes.

ACID properties provide a strong guarantee of data integrity and are essential in database systems where data accuracy and reliability are critical, such as banking, e-commerce, healthcare, and many other domains. However, enforcing all ACID properties can come at the cost of performance, particularly in distributed systems, so there are scenarios where eventual consistency models, such as BASE (Basically Available, Soft state, Eventually consistent), may be considered as an alternative.

Q2 Explain different type of lock with example. (RU BCA 2022)

**Answer:**

In database management systems, **locks** are used to control access to data in a way that ensures data consistency and integrity, particularly in multi-user or multi-transaction environments. Locks prevent multiple transactions from concurrently modifying the same data, which could lead to issues like data corruption or inconsistent results. There are several types of locks used in database systems. Here are some of the most common ones:

**Shared Lock (S-Lock)**:

**Purpose**: A shared lock allows multiple transactions to read the same data simultaneously. It is used to provide read consistency and ensures that data is not modified while being read.

**Example**: Consider a database of library books. Multiple users can simultaneously read the information about a book (e.g., title, author) without interfering with each other. In this case, shared locks are used to allow concurrent reading.

**Exclusive Lock (X-Lock)**:

**Purpose**: An exclusive lock ensures that only one transaction can modify the data, and all other transactions are blocked from reading or writing until the lock is released. It is used to provide write consistency.

**Example**: In the library database, when a user checks out a book, an exclusive lock is acquired to prevent other users from checking out or modifying the book's status until the transaction is complete.

**Intent Lock**:

**Purpose**: Intent locks are high-level locks that indicate the intention to acquire a lower-level lock on a resource. They are used to coordinate and manage locks on different levels of granularity.

**Example**: If a transaction intends to acquire shared locks on multiple pages within a file, it can first acquire an intent shared lock on the file to signal its intention to other transactions. This allows other transactions to know that there is concurrent access to the file.

**Update Lock (U-Lock)**:

**Purpose**: Update locks are a combination of shared and exclusive locks. They are used to indicate the intention to read a resource and later update it. These locks are compatible with shared locks but not with other update or exclusive locks.

**Example**: In an e-commerce system, when a customer adds an item to their shopping cart, an update lock is acquired on the product to allow concurrent reads but prevent other updates. Later, when the customer proceeds to purchase, an exclusive lock is acquired for finalizing the transaction.

**Schema Modification Lock**:

**Purpose**: These locks are used to prevent concurrent schema changes, such as adding or dropping tables or columns, while other transactions are accessing the schema.

**Example**: If one transaction is adding a new column to a database table, schema modification locks prevent other transactions from attempting to read or modify the table until the schema change is complete.

**Row-Level Lock**:

**Purpose**: Row-level locks allow fine-grained control over data access by locking individual rows within a table. This is often used in situations where concurrent access to specific rows is necessary.

**Example**: In an online forum, when two users are posting comments to different threads, row-level locks can be used to ensure that they can simultaneously post their comments to different threads without contention.

These are just a few examples of the types of locks used in database systems. The choice of lock type and strategy depends on the specific requirements and concurrency control mechanisms of the database management system being used. Lock management is a critical aspect of ensuring data integrity and consistency in multi-user database environments.

Q3 Explain concurrency control with locking method with example. (RU BCA 2022)

**Answer:**

**Concurrency control** in a database management system (DBMS) is the process of managing and coordinating access to shared data by multiple transactions or users to ensure that data integrity and consistency are maintained. One of the common methods for implementing concurrency control is through **locking**. Locking involves acquiring and releasing locks on data items to control access. Here's an explanation of concurrency control using locking with an example:

**Example Scenario**: Consider a simple banking database with a single table called "Accounts." Transactions in this database include withdrawals and deposits to different bank accounts. Two transactions, T1 and T2, are simultaneously accessing and modifying the same account.

**Concurrency Control with Locking**:

**Shared Locks (S-Locks) and Exclusive Locks (X-Locks)**:

In this example, when Transaction T1 begins, it first requests a shared lock (S-Lock) on the account it intends to read. This shared lock allows other transactions to also read the account simultaneously.

Transaction T2 starts and requests an exclusive lock (X-Lock) on the same account it intends to modify. An X-Lock prevents other transactions from acquiring shared or exclusive locks on the same data item.

Transaction T1 is reading the account balance, and it is allowed because it holds a shared lock. T2 is waiting to acquire an exclusive lock on the same account.

**Lock-Based Concurrency Control**:

In a lock-based concurrency control system, each transaction must follow a protocol to request and release locks. Common protocols include Two-Phase Locking (2PL) and Strict Two-Phase Locking.

Transaction T1, having read the balance, decides to proceed with a withdrawal. It requests an exclusive lock (X-Lock) on the account.

Since T1 has acquired the X-Lock, it is allowed to proceed with the modification of the account balance.

**Release of Locks**:

After Transaction T1 has completed its work (in this case, the withdrawal), it releases the X-Lock on the account, making it available for other transactions.

Transaction T2, which was waiting for the X-Lock, is now granted access to the account. It can proceed with its deposit operation.

**Ensuring Data Consistency**:

Locking ensures that data consistency and integrity are maintained. T1 and T2 cannot concurrently modify the same account balance, preventing potential issues like overdrawn accounts or data corruption.

**Completion of Transactions**:

Each transaction must be completed in a timely manner. If a transaction encounters an issue or cannot proceed, it should release its locks promptly to avoid blocking other transactions indefinitely.

Concurrency control with locking is essential in multi-user database systems to prevent data anomalies, such as lost updates and uncommitted data. Properly managed locks ensure that transactions operate on a consistent view of the data and that their operations do not interfere with each other. However, it is important to design locking protocols carefully to avoid issues like deadlock, where transactions block each other indefinitely. Deadlock detection and resolution mechanisms are typically employed to handle such situations.

Q4 Define transaction. (RU BCA 2021, 2017)

**Answer:**

A **transaction** in the context of a database management system (DBMS) is a sequence of one or more operations or commands that are treated as a single, indivisible unit of work. Transactions are fundamental to database systems and play a critical role in ensuring data integrity, consistency, and reliability. They follow the principles of the ACID properties (Atomicity, Consistency, Isolation, and Durability) to guarantee the reliability of database operations. Here's a breakdown of these properties in the context of a transaction:

**Atomicity**:

Atomicity ensures that a transaction is treated as a single, indivisible unit. It means that all the operations within a transaction are executed completely or not at all. If any part of the transaction fails, the entire transaction is rolled back, and the database returns to its original state.

**Consistency**:

Consistency ensures that a transaction takes the database from one consistent state to another consistent state. It enforces integrity constraints and business rules to guarantee that the database is always in a valid state.

**Isolation**:

Isolation ensures that concurrent transactions do not interfere with each other. It means that one transaction is isolated from the effects of other concurrently executing transactions until it's completed. Isolation levels, such as "Read Uncommitted," "Read Committed," "Repeatable Read," and "Serializable," control the level of isolation.

**Durability**:

Durability ensures that once a transaction is committed (successfully completed), its effects are permanent and will survive system failures, such as power outages or crashes. This property is typically achieved by writing transaction data to non-volatile storage like disk.

Common operations in a transaction include read operations (e.g., querying data), write operations (e.g., inserting, updating, or deleting data), and control operations (e.g., managing the transaction's start and end). A transaction is typically initiated by a "BEGIN TRANSACTION" command and concluded with a "COMMIT" to make its changes permanent or a "ROLLBACK" to undo any changes made during the transaction.

Transactions are crucial in various applications, such as banking (where funds transfers need to be atomic), e-commerce (where inventory and order processing require consistency), and many other scenarios where data integrity and reliability are paramount. The concept of transactions provides a reliable way to ensure data accuracy and consistency in the face of concurrent access and system failures.

Q5 What is access control? (RU BCA 2019, 2017)

**Answer:**

**Access control** in the context of computer security and database management refers to the process of regulating and managing access to information systems, resources, or data. It involves defining, enforcing, and monitoring policies and rules that determine who is allowed to access what, when, and under what conditions. Access control mechanisms are implemented to protect the confidentiality, integrity, and availability of data and to prevent unauthorized access or misuse.

Key components of access control include:

**Identification**: The process of identifying individuals or entities, typically through usernames, account IDs, or other identifiers.

**Authentication**: Verifying the claimed identity of a user or system, often through a combination of something the user knows (e.g., a password), something the user has (e.g., a smart card), or something the user is (e.g., biometric information like a fingerprint).

**Authorization**: Determining what actions or resources a user or system is allowed to access after they have been authenticated. Authorization is based on roles, permissions, and access rights associated with the user or system.

**Access Control Lists (ACLs)**: Lists or tables that specify which users or system components have access to specific resources or data and the type of access they are allowed (e.g., read, write, execute).

**Role-Based Access Control (RBAC)**: Access control based on the roles of users or systems within an organization. Users are assigned roles, and access permissions are associated with those roles.

**Mandatory Access Control (MAC)**: A security model where access is determined by system policies and labels, often used in government and military systems.

**Discretionary Access Control (DAC)**: A model where users have discretion over who can access their data, and access control decisions are based on the user's own decisions or choices.

**Access Control Policies**: Formalized rules and policies that govern access to data and resources. These policies are typically configured and enforced through access control mechanisms.

**Access Control Mechanisms**: The software and hardware tools used to enforce access control policies. This includes firewalls, security software, directory services, and database management systems.

Access control is a fundamental aspect of information security and is essential in various domains, including:

**Database Management**: Controlling access to database systems, tables, and records to ensure data confidentiality and integrity.

**Network Security**: Managing access to network resources, such as routers, switches, and servers.

**Operating Systems**: Regulating access to files, directories, and system resources.

**Physical Security**: Controlling access to physical locations and facilities.

**Cloud Computing**: Managing access to cloud-based resources and services.

Effective access control is essential for protecting sensitive information, ensuring data privacy, and complying with various regulatory requirements, such as the General Data Protection Regulation (GDPR) and the Health Insurance Portability and Accountability Act (HIPAA). It is a critical component of a comprehensive security strategy.

Q6 What is concurrency control? (RU BCA 2019)

**Answer:**

**Concurrency control** is a fundamental concept in database management systems (DBMS) and computer science that deals with managing simultaneous access and modification of data by multiple transactions or users in a way that ensures data consistency, integrity, and isolation. The primary goal of concurrency control is to allow multiple transactions to run concurrently without causing conflicts or data anomalies.

Key aspects of concurrency control include:

**Transaction Isolation**: Ensuring that transactions run in isolation from each other, meaning that one transaction's changes are not visible to other transactions until the first transaction is completed.

**Conflict Resolution**: Detecting and resolving conflicts that can arise when multiple transactions access and modify the same data concurrently.

**Deadlock Prevention and Resolution**: Preventing or resolving deadlocks, which are situations where two or more transactions are unable to proceed because they are each waiting for a resource held by the other.

**Concurrency Control Mechanisms**: Implementing various techniques and algorithms to manage locks, timestamps, and other mechanisms to control access to data and enforce isolation and consistency.

Concurrency control is critical in multi-user database systems and multi-threaded applications where data is accessed and modified simultaneously by multiple entities. Without effective concurrency control, issues like data corruption, lost updates, inconsistent query results, and race conditions can occur.

Common methods and mechanisms used in concurrency control include:

**Lock-Based Concurrency Control**: Transactions acquire locks (e.g., shared locks, exclusive locks) on data items to control access. This prevents multiple transactions from modifying the same data simultaneously.

**Timestamp-Based Concurrency Control**: Each transaction is assigned a unique timestamp, and transactions are ordered and executed based on these timestamps to ensure a consistent view of the data.

**Isolation Levels**: Defining and enforcing isolation levels (e.g., Read Uncommitted, Read Committed, Repeatable Read, Serializable) to control the degree of isolation between transactions.

**Two-Phase Locking (2PL)**: Enforcing a protocol where transactions acquire locks in two phases (growing phase and shrinking phase) to ensure consistency and avoid conflicts.

**Optimistic Concurrency Control**: Allowing transactions to proceed without locking data initially and checking for conflicts only when committing the changes.

Q7 How transaction is committed in a distributed system? (RU BCA 2017)

**Answer:**

Committing a transaction in a distributed system involves ensuring that all the changes made by the transaction are made permanent, and the transaction is successfully concluded. Committing a transaction in a distributed system is a complex process due to the inherent challenges of coordinating multiple nodes or sites. Here's a high-level overview of how transactions are committed in a distributed system:

**Prepare Phase**:

Before a transaction can be committed, the distributed system enters the "prepare phase." During this phase, the transaction coordinator (a component responsible for managing transactions in a distributed system) ensures that all the participating nodes or sites are ready to commit the transaction.

The transaction coordinator sends a "prepare to commit" message to each participating node or site, requesting confirmation that they are ready to commit the transaction.

Each participating node performs a series of checks to ensure that it can safely commit the transaction. These checks include verifying that all resource managers (e.g., databases) associated with the transaction are in a state to commit, and any necessary locks and resources are available.

If a participating node encounters an issue during the prepare phase and cannot commit the transaction, it sends an "abort" message to the coordinator, indicating the reason for the failure.

**Voting Phase**:

After receiving responses from all participating nodes, the coordinator enters the "voting phase." During this phase, the coordinator collects the votes from all participants.

If all participants confirm that they are ready to commit (i.e., they reply with a "vote to commit"), the coordinator proceeds to the next step. If any participant votes to abort, the coordinator will initiate the abort process.

**Commit Phase**:

In the "commit phase," the coordinator sends a "commit" message to all participants, instructing them to make the transaction's changes permanent.

Upon receiving the "commit" message, each participant applies the transaction's changes to its local resources, updates its state, and acknowledges the coordinator.

After all participants have successfully committed the transaction, the coordinator acknowledges the transaction's global commit to the application or user.

**Durability and Recovery**:

After a transaction is committed, the distributed system ensures that the changes made by the transaction are durable. This typically involves writing the changes to non-volatile storage, such as disks, to guarantee that they survive system failures.

Additionally, the system maintains records of committed transactions to support recovery mechanisms in case of failures. These records are essential for ensuring that the system can recover to a consistent state after a crash or other failures.

It's important to note that distributed systems use different protocols and algorithms for two-phase commit and three-phase commit to handle the transaction commitment process. The choice between these protocols depends on factors such as fault tolerance requirements and the desired level of coordination. The main goal is to ensure that transactions in a distributed system are committed consistently and reliably, even in the presence of failures or network issues.

Q8 What do you mean by concurrency control? (RU BCA 2017)

**Answer:**

**Concurrency control** is a fundamental concept in the field of computer science and database management. It refers to the techniques and mechanisms used to manage and coordinate concurrent access to shared resources, such as data or databases, by multiple users or processes in a way that ensures data integrity, consistency, and isolation. The primary goal of concurrency control is to allow multiple operations or transactions to run concurrently without causing conflicts, data anomalies, or corruption.

Key aspects and objectives of concurrency control include:

**Isolation**: Ensuring that transactions run in isolation from each other, meaning that one transaction's changes are not visible to other transactions until the first transaction is completed. This provides a consistent view of the data to each transaction.

**Conflict Resolution**: Detecting and resolving conflicts that can arise when multiple transactions access and modify the same data concurrently. Conflicts can occur when one transaction reads data while another transaction is modifying it, potentially leading to inconsistencies.

**Deadlock Prevention and Resolution**: Preventing or resolving deadlocks, which are situations where two or more transactions are unable to proceed because they are each waiting for a resource held by the other. Deadlocks can lead to system gridlock and must be handled appropriately.

**Concurrency Control Mechanisms**: Implementing various techniques and algorithms to manage locks, timestamps, and other mechanisms to control access to data and enforce isolation and consistency.

Concurrency control is particularly important in multi-user database systems, multi-threaded applications, and distributed systems where data is accessed and modified simultaneously by multiple users or processes. Without effective concurrency control, issues like data corruption, lost updates, inconsistent query results, and race conditions can occur.

Common methods and mechanisms used in concurrency control include:

**Lock-Based Concurrency Control**: Transactions acquire locks (e.g., shared locks, exclusive locks) on data items to control access. This prevents multiple transactions from modifying the same data simultaneously.

**Timestamp-Based Concurrency Control**: Each transaction is assigned a unique timestamp, and transactions are ordered and executed based on these timestamps to ensure a consistent view of the data.

**Isolation Levels**: Defining and enforcing isolation levels (e.g., Read Uncommitted, Read Committed, Repeatable Read, Serializable) to control the degree of isolation between transactions.

**Two-Phase Locking (2PL)**: Enforcing a protocol where transactions acquire locks in two phases (growing phase and shrinking phase) to ensure consistency and avoid conflicts.

**Optimistic Concurrency Control**: Allowing transactions to proceed without locking data initially and checking for conflicts only when committing the changes.

Concurrency control is a complex and essential aspect of database management and software design, as it impacts the reliability, performance, and data integrity of systems that support multiple users or concurrent operations.

Q9 What are the properties of transaction? Explain. (RU BCA 2016)

**Answer:**

Transactions in the context of a database management system (DBMS) are governed by a set of properties known as the ACID properties. ACID is an acronym that stands for **Atomicity, Consistency, Isolation, and Durability**. These properties ensure the reliability and integrity of database transactions. Here's an explanation of each of these properties:

**Atomicity**:

**Definition**: Atomicity ensures that a transaction is treated as a single, indivisible unit of work. It means that all the operations within a transaction are executed completely or not at all. If any part of the transaction fails, the entire transaction is rolled back, and the database is returned to its original state.

**Example**: In a fund transfer transaction, atomicity ensures that both the debit and credit operations occur together, and if either one fails, both are undone to maintain the database's integrity.

**Consistency**:

**Definition**: Consistency ensures that a transaction takes the database from one consistent state to another consistent state. It enforces integrity constraints and business rules to guarantee that the database is always in a valid state.

**Example**: In an e-commerce system, when a customer places an order, the consistency property ensures that the total order amount matches the sum of the individual item prices, and that the items are deducted from the available inventory.

**Isolation**:

**Definition**: Isolation ensures that concurrent transactions do not interfere with each other. It means that one transaction is isolated from the effects of other concurrently executing transactions until it's completed. Isolation levels, such as "Read Uncommitted," "Read Committed," "Repeatable Read," and "Serializable," control the level of isolation.

**Example**: In a multi-user database system, when two users concurrently attempt to update the same set of data, isolation ensures that their changes do not overlap, and each user sees a consistent snapshot of the data.

**Durability**:

**Definition**: Durability ensures that once a transaction is committed (successfully completed), its effects are permanent and will survive system failures, such as power outages or crashes. This property is typically achieved by writing transaction data to non-volatile storage like disk.

**Example**: After a user completes an online banking transaction and receives a confirmation, the durability property ensures that the transaction details are securely stored and can be retrieved even if the database server crashes.

These ACID properties provide a strong guarantee of data integrity and are essential in database systems where data accuracy and reliability are critical, such as banking, e-commerce, healthcare, and many other domains. The properties ensure that database transactions are reliable and maintain the integrity and consistency of data even in the face of system failures or concurrent access.

Q10 Explain state transition. Explain when a transaction is said to be failed. (RU BCA 2016)

**Answer:**

A **state transition** refers to the different states that a transaction can go through during its lifecycle, from initiation to completion or failure. Understanding these states is crucial for managing and controlling transactions effectively. The typical states that a transaction can go through include:

**Active State**: The transaction begins in the active state when it is initiated. In this state, the transaction is executing a series of operations (read, write, etc.) on the database.

**Partially Committed State**: After the transaction has executed its operations successfully and is ready to make its changes permanent, it enters the partially committed state. At this point, it awaits confirmation from the DBMS to proceed with the final commit.

**Committed State**: When the DBMS confirms the transaction's request to commit, it enters the committed state. In this state, all the changes made by the transaction are made permanent and are reflected in the database. The transaction is considered successful and concluded.

**Failed State**: A transaction is said to be **failed** when it cannot complete its execution due to some error or exceptional condition. Failures can occur for various reasons, such as constraint violations, system errors, or conflicts with other transactions. When a transaction fails, it must be rolled back to its previous state (typically the active state), and any changes it made to the database are undone to maintain data integrity.

**Aborted State**: After a transaction fails, it enters the aborted state. In this state, the transaction is rolled back, and any changes made by the transaction are reversed. The database returns to its previous consistent state.

**Terminated State**: The transaction enters the terminated state after it has been successfully committed or after it has been aborted. In this state, the transaction is no longer active and cannot be rolled back or committed.

A transaction can transition from the active state to the partially committed state and then to the committed state if everything proceeds without errors. However, if any issues or errors occur during execution, it transitions from the active state to the failed state and then to the aborted state.

Transactions can also be explicitly rolled back by the application or the DBMS in cases where the application decides to cancel the transaction for some reason.

The concept of transaction states is essential for ensuring data integrity, reliability, and consistency in database management systems. Proper management of transaction states helps maintain the integrity of the data and ensures that the database remains in a consistent state even in the presence of failures or errors.

Q11 What are the conditions to occur deadlock in database? (RU BCA 2016)

**Answer:**

Deadlocks in a database occur when two or more transactions or processes are unable to proceed because each of them is waiting for a resource (e.g., locks) that is held by one of the other transactions involved. To have a deadlock situation, the following conditions, known as the **four necessary conditions for deadlock**, must all be true simultaneously:

**Mutual Exclusion**:

Transactions must be able to request exclusive access to resources. In other words, a resource can only be used by one transaction at a time. This condition is inherent in most locking systems, where only one transaction can hold an exclusive lock on a resource.

**Hold and Wait**:

Transactions must hold one or more resources while waiting for additional resources. In other words, a transaction that holds at least one resource can request additional resources without releasing the ones it already holds. This condition allows transactions to get stuck waiting for more resources to be released.

**No Preemption**:

Resources cannot be forcibly taken away from a transaction. In other words, a transaction that is holding a resource cannot have that resource forcibly removed and given to another transaction. This condition is important for data integrity but can contribute to deadlocks.

**Circular Wait**:

Transactions must be in a circular chain of waiting, where each transaction is waiting for a resource held by the next transaction in the chain. For example, Transaction A is waiting for a resource held by Transaction B, which is waiting for a resource held by Transaction C, and so on, until Transaction Z is waiting for a resource held by Transaction A. This circular wait condition creates a deadlock.

To avoid deadlocks, at least one of these necessary conditions must not hold. This can be achieved through various methods and techniques, including deadlock prevention, detection, and resolution strategies. Some common approaches to deal with deadlocks include:

**Deadlock Prevention**: Adjusting the system's rules to ensure that one or more of the necessary conditions is never true. For example, ensuring transactions request and release resources in a specific order.

**Deadlock Detection and Resolution**: Periodically checking for deadlocks and, if detected, taking action to break the deadlock by aborting one or more transactions involved.

**Timeouts**: If a transaction waits for a resource for too long, it can be aborted to release the resource and prevent a deadlock.

**Wait-Die and Wound-Wait Schemes**: These are strategies for handling deadlocks based on the ages of transactions. In the Wait-Die scheme, older transactions wait for younger ones, while in the Wound-Wait scheme, older transactions preempt younger ones.

**Resource Allocation Graphs**: Visual representations of resources and transactions, used to detect and resolve deadlocks.

Proper management of resources, careful design of transaction logic, and the use of deadlock prevention and detection mechanisms are essential in minimizing the occurrence and impact of deadlocks in database systems.

Q12. Define Shadow paging. [Marks: 2]

**Answer:**

Shadow paging is a technique used in database management systems and file systems to ensure atomic and durable transactions, which are crucial properties for maintaining data consistency and reliability. This technique provides a way of recovering from system crashes or failures by maintaining two sets of pointers: one for the current page table (or database state) and one for the shadow page table, which reflects the state before the transaction began.

Here's how shadow paging works:

**Initial State:** At the start of a transaction, the system creates a copy of the current page table, known as the shadow page table. This shadow page table remains unchanged throughout the transaction and acts as a backup that reflects the state of the database before any changes are made.

**Transaction Processing:** During the transaction, all changes are made to a new copy of the affected pages rather than the original pages. This means the system writes updates to a temporary set of pages, keeping the original data intact. The current page table is updated to point to these new pages as changes are made, while the shadow page table still points to the original pages.

**Committing the Transaction:** If the transaction successfully completes, the changes become permanent. The system then atomically switches the root of the page table from pointing to the shadow page table to the current page table, reflecting all the updates. This atomic switch ensures that the database transitions from the old state to the new state instantly, without any intermediate states being visible.

**Recovery:** In case of a system failure before the transaction is committed, recovery is straightforward. Since the shadow page table still points to the database state before the transaction began, the system can simply discard the changes by reverting to the shadow page table, effectively rolling back the transaction. This ensures that the database remains consistent and no partial updates are applied.

Shadow paging is advantageous because it provides a simple and effective mechanism for ensuring data integrity without requiring complex logging and undo operations. However, it can be expensive in terms of storage and performance because it requires copying entire pages even if only small parts of them are changed. Despite its benefits, shadow paging is less commonly used than other techniques such as write-ahead logging (WAL), especially in large databases, due to these overheads and scalability issues.

Q13. What are two problems of lock-based protocols? [Marks: 2] (RTU MCA 2022)

**Answer:**

Lock-based protocols are widely used in database management systems to control access to data by concurrent transactions, ensuring data consistency and integrity. However, despite their advantages, these protocols come with several challenges and limitations, of which two notable problems are:

**Deadlocks**

Deadlock occurs when two or more transactions hold locks on resources and each transaction is waiting for the other to release its lock before it can proceed. This situation creates a cycle of dependencies with no transaction able to move forward, effectively halting their progress. For example, if Transaction 1 holds a lock on Resource A and needs a lock on Resource B to continue, but Transaction 2 holds a lock on Resource B and is waiting for a lock on Resource A, both transactions are stuck waiting indefinitely. Detecting and resolving deadlocks can be complex and resource-intensive, often requiring the DBMS to implement deadlock detection algorithms and to choose and abort one of the transactions to break the deadlock, leading to performance overheads and the need for transaction rollback and restart.

**Concurrency Control Overhead**

Implementing lock-based protocols introduces significant overhead in terms of managing locks and ensuring data integrity. Each time a transaction needs to access a database resource, it must acquire the appropriate lock(s), which involves checking the current lock status, possibly waiting for other locks to be released, and then maintaining lock information as the transaction proceeds. This process increases the complexity of the database management system and can significantly impact performance, particularly in high-concurrency environments. The overhead includes the time and resources needed to manage locks, the potential for increased waiting times for transactions, and the overall impact on system throughput.

Lock-based protocols must carefully balance the need for strict data consistency with the performance implications of locking. While essential for preventing anomalies like lost updates, uncommitted data visibility, and inconsistent retrievals, these protocols require careful design and tuning to mitigate problems like deadlocks and concurrency control overhead. Alternatives and enhancements, such as optimistic concurrency control, time-stamp ordering, and multiversion concurrency control, are sometimes used to address these challenges in different scenarios.

Q14. What are the ACID properties? [Marks: 2] (RTU MCA 2022)

**Answer:**

The ACID properties are a set of principles that guarantee that database transactions are processed reliably and ensure the integrity of the database even in the event of errors, power failures, and other mishaps. ACID stands for Atomicity, Consistency, Isolation, and Durability. These properties are essential for the management of transaction processing systems, such as relational databases.

**Atomicity:** This property ensures that each transaction is treated as a single unit, which either completely succeeds or completely fails. If any part of the transaction fails, the entire transaction is rolled back, and the database state is left unchanged. Atomicity guarantees that partial transactions (i.e., transactions that are only partially completed) do not affect the database.

**Consistency:** Consistency ensures that a transaction can only bring the database from one valid state to another, maintaining all predefined rules, such as constraints, cascades, and triggers. This means that any transaction will leave the database in a consistent state at its completion, preserving the correctness of the database according to all defined rules.

**Isolation:** The isolation property ensures that transactions are securely and independently processed simultaneously without interference, giving each transaction the illusion of being the only system operation. Different levels of isolation offer a balance between performance and the degree of visibility of one transaction's changes to others. Isolation prevents concurrency problems, such as dirty reads, non-repeatable reads, and phantom reads.

**Durability:** Durability guarantees that once a transaction has been committed, it will remain so, even in the event of power loss, crashes, or errors. This means the changes made by the transaction are permanently recorded in the database's storage system, ensuring that the committed transactions are not lost.

The ACID properties are foundational to the reliability and robustness of a database system, ensuring that despite system failures or attempts to make simultaneous data updates, the data integrity and consistency of the database are maintained.

Q15. What is deadlock in DBMS? Give two deadlock prevention schemes. [Marks: 4] (RTU MCA 2022)

**Answer**

Deadlock in a Database Management System (DBMS) refers to a situation where two or more transactions are waiting indefinitely for one another to release locks on resources. Each transaction in the deadlock situation holds a lock on a resource that another transaction needs to continue its execution. As a result, none of the transactions can proceed, leading to a standstill in the system. Deadlocks prevent the normal execution of transactions, impacting the database system's throughput and efficiency.

Deadlocks occur due to the concurrent execution of transactions that compete for the same resources. The four necessary conditions for a deadlock are mutual exclusion (only one transaction can hold a lock on a resource at a time), hold and wait (a transaction holds at least one resource and waits for additional resources), no preemption (resources cannot be forcibly removed from transactions that are holding them), and circular wait (a circular chain of transactions exists where each transaction holds a resource that the next transaction in the chain needs).

**Deadlock Prevention Schemes**

To avoid deadlocks, DBMSs implement various deadlock prevention schemes. Two common schemes are:

**Lock Ordering:**

This scheme involves imposing a total ordering on all locks and ensuring that transactions acquire locks in this predefined order. By doing so, it prevents the circular wait condition, effectively eliminating deadlocks. For example, if there are resources A, B, and C, a global order might be A < B < C. A transaction would have to acquire a lock on A before it could acquire a lock on B or C, and similarly, it would have to lock B before C. This method prevents transactions from acquiring locks in a circular manner that could lead to deadlocks.

**Timeouts:**

In the timeout approach, transactions are allowed a specified amount of time to complete their execution and release any locks they hold. If a transaction exceeds this time limit, it is assumed to be in a deadlock and is aborted, releasing all resources it holds. The transaction may then be restarted. Timeouts can prevent deadlocks by ensuring that no transaction holds onto resources indefinitely. However, this approach may lead to the unnecessary abortion of transactions that are not actually deadlocked, potentially reducing system efficiency due to repeated restarts.

Both of these schemes aim to mitigate the risk of deadlocks by either structuring the way locks are acquired to prevent circular wait conditions or by aborting transactions that might be involved in a deadlock. While effective in preventing deadlocks, these schemes must be carefully implemented to avoid unnecessary transaction aborts and to maintain system performance.

Q16. Explain the properties of a transaction with example. [Marks: 4] (RTU MCA 2022)

**Answer**

Transactions in database management systems (DBMS) are sequences of operations performed as a single logical unit of work that must either be completed in its entirety or not executed at all. To ensure the reliability and integrity of data within a database, transactions are designed to adhere to four key properties, collectively known as the ACID properties: Atomicity, Consistency, Isolation, and Durability.

**Atomicity**

**Definition:** AtomiciQty guarantees that a transaction is treated as a single unit, which is either fully completed or not executed at all. If any part of the transaction fails, the entire transaction is rolled back, and the database state is reverted to its state before the transaction started.

**Example:** Consider a banking system where a fund transfer from Account A to Account B involves two steps: debiting Account A and crediting Account B. Under atomicity, if either the debit or credit fails (e.g., due to a technical glitch), the entire transaction is aborted, ensuring that money isn't incorrectly deducted without the corresponding credit.

**Consistency**

**Definition:** Consistency ensures that a transaction transforms the database from one valid state to another valid state, maintaining all database rules, such as integrity constraints. It means the transaction does not violate any predefined rules set on the database.

**Example:** In the banking system, if the fund transfer transaction is successful, it must also ensure that the total amount before and after the transaction remains constant (assuming no interest or charges), thus preserving the integrity of the database.

**Isolation**

**Definition:** Isolation ensures that transactions are executed in isolation from each other, meaning the intermediate states produced by a transaction are invisible to other transactions until that transaction is completed. Isolation is crucial for preventing transactions from interfering with each other.

**Example:** If two transactions are simultaneously transferring funds between two accounts, isolation ensures that each transaction sees a consistent view of the accounts' balances, preventing them from acting on intermediate states that could lead to errors like lost updates.

**Durability**

**Definition:** Durability guarantees that once a transaction has been committed, its effects are permanently recorded in the database. This property ensures that the committed changes persist even in the event of a system failure.

**Example:** After the banking transaction is successfully committed, the changes to Account A and Account B's balances are written to disk. Even if the system crashes immediately after, the updated balances will be retained and restored when the system restarts.

These ACID properties are fundamental to the design and operation of reliable transaction processing systems in databases, ensuring data integrity and consistency across all transactions.

Q17. What do you mean by Serializability? Discuss the conflict and view Serializability with suitable example. [Marks: 10] (RTU MCA 2022)

**Answer:**

Serializability in the context of database management systems (DBMS) is a concept that ensures the consistency of the database by making sure that concurrent transactions result in the same state as if the transactions were executed serially, i.e., one after the other, without overlapping in time. Serializability is the gold standard for transaction scheduling and concurrency control because it preserves the consistency of the database while allowing for concurrency.

There are two main types of serializability:

**Conflict Serializability**

Conflict serializability is a subset of serializability where the schedule (order of execution of operations) of transactions can be re-ordered without changing the final result, as long as non-conflicting operations are preserved in their original order. Two operations are considered to be in conflict if they are from different transactions, operate on the same data item, and at least one of these operations is a write.

**Example of Conflict Serializability:**

Consider two transactions, T1 and T2:

T1: R(A) → W(A) → R(B) → W(B)

T2: R(B) → W(B) → R(A) → W(A)

Here, R(A) and W(A) denote read and write operations on data item A, respectively.

These transactions are conflict-serializable because we can find a serial order of transactions (e.g., T1 followed by T2 or T2 followed by T1) that preserves the order of conflicting operations. The conflicts are between W(A) in T1 and R(A) in T2, and between W(B) in T1 and R(B) in T2. By executing T1 and T2 serially in either order, we avoid these conflicts, ensuring data consistency.

**View Serializability**

View serializability is a broader concept than conflict serializability. A schedule is view serializable if it is view equivalent to a serial schedule. Two schedules are view equivalent if:

They read the same initial values for each data item.

The final value written by each data item is the same.

Each read operation of a data item in one schedule reads the value written by the same write operation as in the other schedule.

View serializability does not require conflict serializability, but every conflict-serializable schedule is also view serializable.

**Example of View Serializability:**

Consider two transactions, T1 and T2:

T1: R(A) → W(A) → R(B) → W(B)

T2: R(B) → R(A)

These transactions are view serializable if the final write operations on A and B by T1 are the only write operations, and T2's reads of A and B do not conflict with T1's writes. There's no need for T2 to write anything, so as long as T2 reads the values of A and B before T1 writes to them (or reads the final values written by T1, depending on the scheduling), the schedule can be considered view serializable.

**Conclusion**

Serializability, especially conflict serializability, is crucial for maintaining the consistency and integrity of databases in concurrent environments. It ensures that even though transactions are executed concurrently, the outcome is as if the transactions were executed one after the other, in some order. This is essential for the correctness of database operations and for preventing anomalies such as dirty reads, non-repeatable reads, and phantom reads.

Q18. What is 'lock' in DBMS? What is the difference between lock-based, time-stamp base and validation-based protocol for concurrency control? [Marks: 10](RTU MCA 2022)

**Answer:**

A "lock" in a Database Management System (DBMS) is a mechanism to control access to database resources by concurrent transactions. Locks help ensure data integrity and consistency by preventing multiple transactions from simultaneously modifying the same data item (e.g., a row or table) or preventing a transaction from reading data that is being modified by another transaction. The locking mechanism is a fundamental part of implementing concurrency control in databases, ensuring that transactions adhere to the ACID properties (Atomicity, Consistency, Isolation, Durability).

**Types of Locks**

**Exclusive Locks (X-Locks):** Used when a transaction wants to write to a resource. No other locks can be placed on a resource that has an exclusive lock, ensuring that no other transaction can read or write to the resource until the lock is released.

**Shared Locks (S-Locks):** Used when a transaction wants to read a resource. Other transactions can also place shared locks and read the resource, but no transaction can write to the resource until all shared locks are released.

**Lock-Based Protocols**

Lock-based protocols use locks to manage access to data by transactions. The protocol ensures that locks are acquired before a transaction can access the data and released when the transaction is done. The main challenge with lock-based protocols is dealing with deadlocks, which occur when two or more transactions are waiting for each other to release locks, causing a standstill.

**Time-Stamp Based Protocols**

Time-stamp based protocols order transactions using time-stamps to ensure serializability. Each transaction is assigned a unique time-stamp when it starts. When a transaction wants to read or write a data item, its time-stamp is compared with the time-stamps of the last transactions that read and wrote the data item. This comparison determines whether the transaction can proceed, ensuring that transactions execute in time-stamp order and preventing the need for locks. This method avoids deadlocks but can lead to more transaction rollbacks if the time-stamp ordering is violated.

**Validation-Based Protocols (Optimistic Concurrency Control)**

Validation-based protocols, also known as optimistic concurrency control, assume that conflicts among transactions are rare and allow transactions to execute without acquiring locks on data. Instead, transactions are validated before commit to ensure that they have not interfered with other transactions. This validation typically occurs in three phases: read phase, validation phase, and write phase. If a transaction passes validation, it can commit; otherwise, it is rolled back. This approach reduces the overhead and contention associated with locks but can result in a higher rate of transaction rollbacks under high contention scenarios.

**Differences Between Protocols**

**Lock-Based vs. Time-Stamp Based:** Lock-based protocols manage access through explicit locking, which can lead to deadlocks but allows for flexibility in transaction processing. Time-stamp based protocols avoid deadlocks by strictly ordering transactions based on their time-stamps, potentially leading to more transaction aborts if the time-stamp order is violated.

**Lock-Based vs. Validation-Based:** Lock-based protocols control access to data through locks, potentially causing delays and deadlocks. Validation-based (optimistic) protocols allow transactions to proceed without locks, with a validation step at the end to ensure consistency, potentially leading to higher rollback rates but lower lock contention.

**Time-Stamp Based vs. Validation-Based:** Both avoid explicit locking, but time-stamp based protocols pre-emptively abort transactions based on time-stamp ordering rules, while validation-based protocols allow transactions to complete and validate at commit time, which can lead to rollbacks if the validation fails.

Each concurrency control protocol has its advantages and trade-offs, and the choice between them depends on the specific requirements of the database system, including the expected transaction load, the nature of the transactions, and the priority of minimizing deadlocks versus minimizing rollbacks.

## ONLINE RESOURCES

**Practice Paper Link:** https://forms.gle/sYcZLE5P5meB6xRP9

**QR Code:**

**Video Content:** https://www.youtube.com/playlist?list=PLzlh_31VWEFr7Vqg60ws_vmGVa1a6PE9-

**QR Code:**

# Chapter 7: Implementation Techniques

## RAID

RAID refers to redundancy array of the independent disk. It is a technology which is used to connect multiple secondary storage devices for increased performance, data redundancy or both. It gives you the ability to survive one or more drive failure depending upon the RAID level used.

It consists of an array of disks in which multiple disks are connected to achieve different goals.

**Why Data Redundancy?**

Data redundancy, although taking up extra space, adds to disk reliability. This means, in case of disk failure, if the same data is also backed up onto another disk, we can retrieve the data and go on with the operation. On the other hand, if the data is spread across just multiple disks without the RAID technique, the loss of a single disk can affect the entire data.

**RAID technology**

There are 7 levels of RAID schemes. These schemas are as RAID 0, RAID 1, ...., RAID 6.

These levels contain the following characteristics:

It contains a set of physical disk drives.

In this technology, the operating system views these separate disks as a single logical disk.

In this technology, data is distributed across the physical drives of the array.

Redundancy disk capacity is used to store parity information.

In case of disk failure, the parity information can be helped to recover the data.

RAID is very transparent to the underlying system. This means, to the host system, it appears as a single big disk presenting itself as a linear array of blocks. This allows older technologies to be replaced by RAID without making too many changes to the existing code.

**Different RAID Levels**

RAID-0 (Stripping)

RAID-1 (Mirroring)

RAID-2 (Bit-Level Stripping with Dedicated Parity)

RAID-3 (Byte-Level Stripping with Dedicated Parity)

RAID-4 (Block-Level Stripping with Dedicated Parity)

RAID-5 (Block-Level Stripping with Distributed Parity)

RAID-6 (Block-Level Stripping with two Parity Bits)

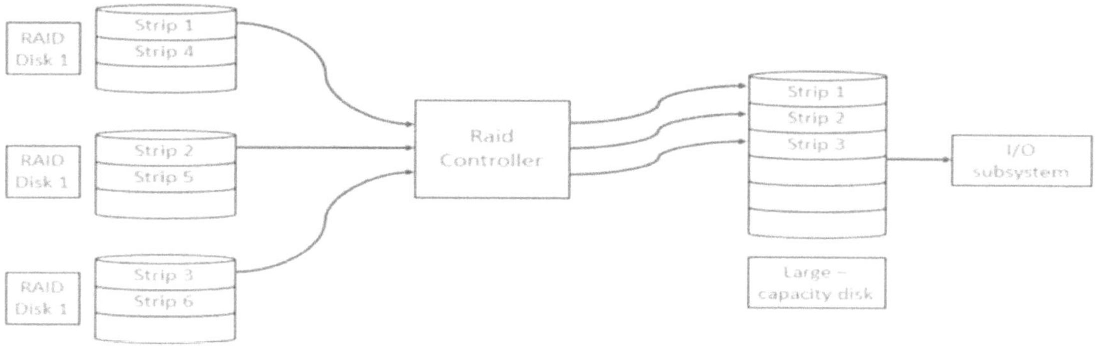


RAID-10 (Combination of RAID 1 and RAID 0)

**RAID 0**

RAID level 0 provides data stripping, i.e., a data can place across multiple disks. It is based on stripping that means if one disk fails then all data in the array is lost.

This level doesn't provide fault tolerance but increases the system performance.

| **Disk 0** | **Disk 1** | **Disk 2** | **Disk 3** |
|---|---|---|---|
| **20** | 21 | 22 | 23 |
| **24** | 25 | 26 | 27 |
| **28** | 29 | 30 | 31 |
| **32** | 33 | 34 | 35 |

In this table, block 0, 1, 2, 3 form a stripe.

In this level, instead of placing just one block into a disk at a time, we can work with two or more blocks placed it into a disk before moving on to the next one.

| **Disk 0** | **Disk 1** | **Disk 2** | **Disk 3** |
|---|---|---|---|
| **20** | 22 | 24 | 26 |
| **21** | 23 | 25 | 27 |
| **28** | 30 | 32 | 34 |
| **29** | 31 | 33 | 35 |

In this above Table, there is no duplication of data. Hence, a block once lost cannot be recovered.

Pros of RAID 0:

In this level, throughput is increased because multiple data requests probably not on the same disk.

This level full utilizes the disk space and provides high performance.

It requires minimum 2 drives.

Cons of RAID 0:

It doesn't contain any error detection mechanism.

The RAID 0 is not a true RAID because it is not fault-tolerance.

In this level, failure of either disk results in complete data loss in respective array.

**RAID-1 (Mirroring)**

More than one copy of each block is stored in a separate disk. Thus, every block has two (or more) copies, lying on different disks.

| Disk 0 | Disk 1 | Disk 2 | Disk 3 |
|---|---|---|---|
| 0 | 0 | 1 | 1 |
| 2 | 2 | 3 | 3 |
| 4 | 4 | 5 | 5 |
| 6 | 6 | 7 | 7 |

The above table shows a RAID-1 system with mirroring level 2.

RAID 0 was unable to tolerate any disk failure. But RAID 1 is capable of reliability.

Pros of RAID 1:

It covers complete redundancy.

It can increase data security and speed.

Cons of RAID 1:

It is highly expensive.

Storage capacity is less.

**RAID 2**

RAID 2 consists of bit-level striping using hamming code parity. In this level, each data bit in a word is recorded on a separate disk and ECC code of data words is stored on different set disks.

Due to its high cost and complex structure, this level is not commercially used. This same performance can be achieved by RAID 3 at a lower cost.

Pros of RAID 2:

This level uses one designated drive to store parity.

It uses the hamming code for error detection.

Cons of RAID 2:

It requires an additional drive for error detection.

**RAID 3**

RAID 3 consists of byte-level striping with dedicated parity. In this level, the parity information is stored for each disk section and written to a dedicated parity drive.

In case of drive failure, the parity drive is accessed, and data is reconstructed from the remaining devices. Once the failed drive is replaced, the missing data can be restored on the new drive.

In this level, data can be transferred in bulk. Thus, high-speed data transmission is possible.

| Disk 0 | Disk 1 | Disk 2 | Disk 3 |
|---|---|---|---|
| A | B | C | P (A, B, C) |
| D | E | F | P (D, E, F) |
| G | H | I | P (G, H, I) |
| J | K | L | P (J, K, L) |

Pros of RAID 3:

In this level, data is regenerated using parity drive.

It contains high data transfer rates.

In this level, data is accessed in parallel.

Cons of RAID 3:

It required an additional drive for parity.

It gives a slow performance for operating on small sized files.

**RAID-4**

Instead of duplicating data, this adopts a parity-based approach.

| Disk 0 | Disk 1 | Disk 2 | Disk 3 | Disk 4 |
|---|---|---|---|---|
| 0 | 1 | 2 | 3 | P0 |
| 4 | 5 | 6 | 7 | P1 |
| 8 | 9 | 10 | 11 | P2 |
| **12** | 13 | 14 | 15 | P3 |

In the table, we can observe one column (disk) dedicated to parity.

Parity is calculated using a simple XOR function. If the data bits are 0,0,0,1 the parity bit is XOR(0,0,0,1) = 1. If the data bits are 0,1,1,0 the parity bit is XOR(0,1,1,0) = 0. A simple approach is that an even number of ones results in parity 0, and an odd number of ones results in parity 1.

| C1 | C2 | C3 | C4 | Parity |
|---|---|---|---|---|
| 0 | 0 | 0 | 1 | 1 |
| 0 | 1 | 1 | 0 | 0 |

Assume that in the above figure, C3 is lost due to some disk failure. Then, we can recompute the data bit stored in C3 by looking at the values of all the other columns and the parity bit. This allows us to recover lost data.

Pros of RAID 4:

It helps in reconstructing the data if at most one data is lost.

Cons of RAID 4:

It can't help in reconstructing when more than one data is lost.

**RAID-5**

This is a slight modification of the RAID-4 system where the only difference is that the parity rotates among the drives.

| Disk 0 | Disk 1 | Disk 2 | Disk 3 | Disk 4 |
|---|---|---|---|---|
| 0 | 1 | 2 | 3 | P0 |
| 5 | 6 | 7 | P1 | 4 |
| **10** | 11 | P2 | 8 | 9 |
| **15** | P3 | 12 | 13 | 14 |
| **P4** | 16 | 17 | 18 | 19 |

In the table, we can notice how the parity bit "rotates".

This was introduced to make the random write performance better.

Pros of RAID 5:

Data can be reconstructed using parity bits.

It makes the performance better.

Cons of RAID 5:

Its technology is complex and extra space is required.

If both discs get damaged, data will be lost forever.

**RAID-6**

Raid-6 helps when there is more than one disk failure. A pair of independent parities are generated and stored on multiple disks at this level. Ideally, you need four disk drives for this level.

There are also hybrid RAIDs, which make use of more than one RAID level nested one after the other, to fulfill specific requirements.

| Disk 1 | Disk 2 | Disk 3 | Disk 4 |
|---|---|---|---|
| **A1** | B1 | P (B1) | P (B1) |
| **A2** | P (B2) | P (B2) | B2 |
| **P (B3)** | P (B3) | A3 | B3 |
| **P (B4)** | A4 | A4 | P (B4) |

Pros of RAID 6:

Very high data Accessibility.

Fast read data transactions.

Cons of RAID 6:

Due to double parity, it has slowed written data transactions.

Extra space is required.

**RAID 10 (Combination of RAID 1 and RAID 0):**

Data Mirroring and Striping: Data is mirrored and then striped across multiple disks.

Performance: Offers excellent read/write performance and high fault tolerance.

Fault Tolerance: Can tolerate the failure of multiple drives, depending on the configuration.

Use Cases: Suitable for high-performance database systems and mission-critical applications.

Pros of RAID 10:

High fault tolerance

Excellent read/write performance

Redundancy and data integrity

Well-suited for mission-critical applications and databases

**Advantages of RAID**

Increased data reliability: RAID provides redundancy, which means that if one disk fails, the data can be recovered from the remaining disks in the array. This makes RAID a reliable storage solution for critical data.

Improved performance: RAID can improve performance by spreading data across multiple disks. This allows multiple read/write operations to co-occur, which can speed up data access.

Scalability: RAID can be scaled by adding more disks to the array. This means that storage capacity can be increased without having to replace the entire storage system.

Cost-effective: Some RAID configurations, such as RAID 0, can be implemented with low-cost hardware. This makes RAID a cost-effective solution for small businesses or home users.

**Disadvantages of RAID**

Cost: Some RAID configurations, such as RAID 5 or RAID 6, can be expensive to implement. This is because they require additional hardware or software to provide redundancy.

Performance limitations: Some RAID configurations, such as RAID 1 or RAID 5, can have performance limitations. For example, RAID 1 can only read data as fast as a single drive, while RAID 5 can have slower write speeds due to the parity calculations required.

Complexity: RAID can be complex to set up and maintain. This is especially true for more advanced configurations, such as RAID 5 or RAID 6.

Increased risk of data loss: While RAID provides redundancy, it is not a substitute for proper backups. If multiple drives fail simultaneously, data loss can still occur.

## File Organization

A database consists of a huge amount of data. The data is grouped within a table in RDBMS, and each table has related records. A user can see that the data is stored in the form of tables, but in actuality, this huge amount of data is stored in physical memory in the form of files.

**What is File?**

A file is named a collection of related information that is recorded on secondary storage such as magnetic disks, magnetic tapes, and optical disks.

**What is File Organization?**

File Organization refers to the logical relationships among various records that constitute the file, particularly with respect to the means of identification and access to any specific record. In simple terms, Storing the files in a certain order is called File Organization. File Structure refers to the format of the label and data blocks and of any logical control record.

The Objective of File Organization

It helps in the faster selection of records i.e. it makes the process faster.

Different Operations like inserting, deleting, and update on different records are faster and easier.

It prevents us from inserting duplicate records via various operations.

It helps in storing the records or the data very efficiently at a minimal cost

Types of File Organizations

Various methods have been introduced to Organize files. These particular methods have advantages and disadvantages on the basis of access or selection. Thus it is all upon the programmer to decide the best-suited file Organization method according to his requirements.

Some types of File Organizations are :

Sequential File Organization

Heap File Organization

Hash File Organization

B+ Tree File Organization

Clustered File Organization

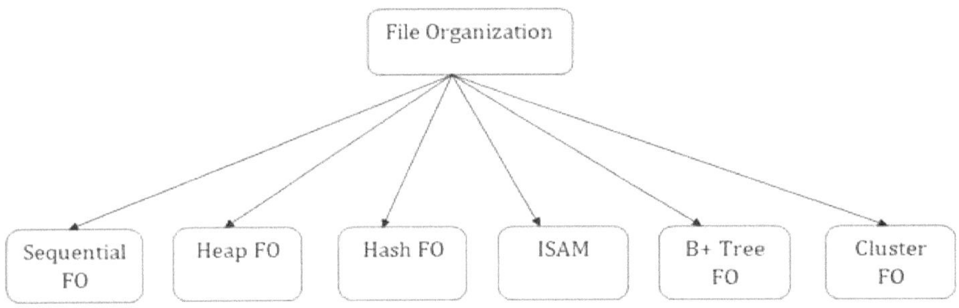


ISAM (Indexed Sequential Access Method)

**Sequential File Organization**

This method is the easiest method for file organization. In this method, files are stored sequentially. This method can be implemented in two ways:

**Pile File Method:**

It is a quite simple method. In this method, we store the record in a sequence, i.e., one after another. Here, the record will be inserted in the order in which they are inserted into tables.

In case of updating or deleting of any record, the record will be searched in the memory blocks. When it is found, then it will be marked for deleting, and the new record is inserted.

**Insertion of the new record**:

Suppose we have four records R1, R3 and so on upto R9 and R8 in a sequence. Hence, records are nothing but a row in the table. Suppose we want to insert a new record R2 in the sequence, then it will be placed at the end of the file. Here, records are nothing but a row in any table.

**Sorted File Method:**

In this method, the new record is always inserted at the file's end, and then it will sort the sequence in ascending or descending order. Sorting of records is based on any primary key or any other key.

In the case of modification of any record, it will update the record and then sort the file, and lastly, the updated record is placed in the right place.

**Insertion of the new record:**

Suppose there is a preexisting sorted sequence of four records R1, R3 and so on upto R6 and R7. Suppose a new record R2 has to be inserted in the sequence, then it will be inserted at the end of the file, and then it will sort the sequence.

Pros of sequential file organization

It contains a fast and efficient method for the huge amount of data.

In this method, files can be easily stored in cheaper storage mechanism like magnetic tapes.

It is simple in design. It requires no much effort to store the data.

This method is used when most of the records have to be accessed like grade calculation of a student, generating the salary slip, etc.

This method is used for report generation or statistical calculations.

Cons of sequential file organization

It will waste time as we cannot jump on a particular record that is required but we have to move sequentially which takes our time.

Sorted file method takes more time and space for sorting the records.

**Heap file organization**

It is the simplest and most basic type of organization. It works with data blocks. In heap file organization, the records are inserted at the file's end. When the records are inserted, it doesn't require the sorting and ordering of records.

When the data block is full, the new record is stored in some other block. This new data block need not to be the very next data block, but it can select any data block in the memory to store new records. The heap file is also known as an unordered file.

In the file, every record has a unique id, and every page in a file is of the same size. It is the DBMS responsibility to store and manage the new records.

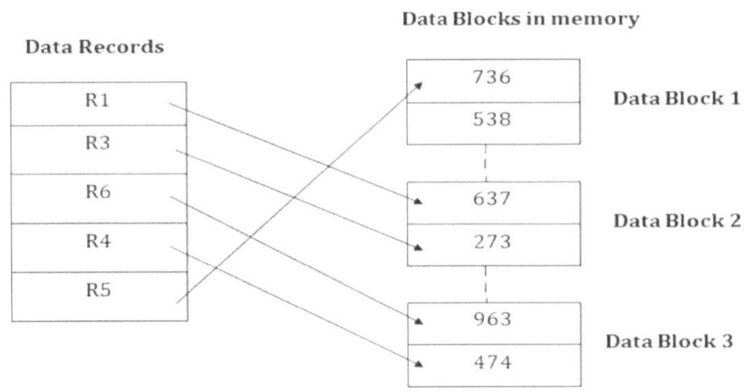


**Insertion of a new record**

Suppose we have five records R1, R3, R6, R4 and R5 in a heap and suppose we want to insert a new record R2 in a heap. If the data block 3 is full then it will be inserted in any of the database selected by the DBMS, let's say data block 1.

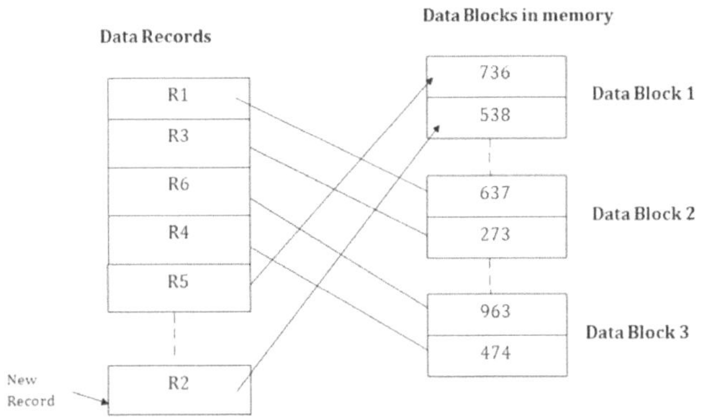


If we want to search, update or delete the data in heap file organization, then we need to traverse the data from staring of the file till we get the requested record. If the database is very large then searching, updating or deleting of record will be time-consuming because there is no sorting or ordering of records. In the heap file organization, we need to check all the data until we get the requested record.

Pros of Heap file organization

It is a very good method of file organization for bulk insertion. If there is a large number of data which needs to load into the database at a time, then this method is best suited.

In case of a small database, fetching and retrieving of records is faster than the sequential record.

Cons of Heap file organization

This method is inefficient for the large database because it takes time to search or modify the record.

This method is inefficient for large databases.

**Hash File Organization**

Hash File Organization uses the computation of hash function on some fields of the records. The hash function's output determines the location of disk block where the records are to be placed.

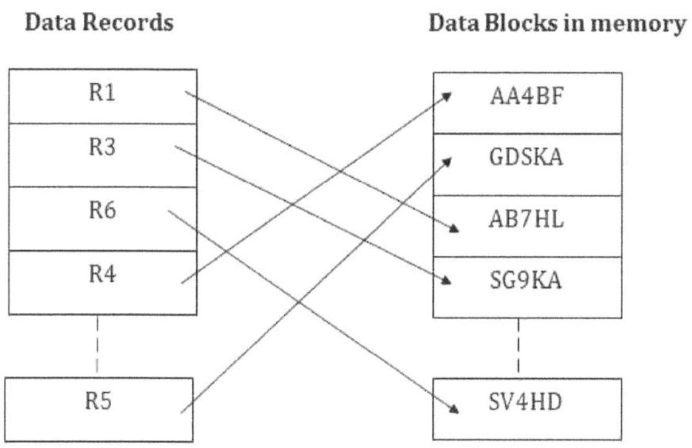


When a record has to be received using the hash key columns, then the address is generated, and the whole record is retrieved using that address. In the same way, when a new record has to be inserted, then the address is generated using the hash key and record is directly inserted. The same process is applied in the case of delete and update. In this method, there is no effort for searching and sorting the entire file. In this method, each record will be stored randomly in the memory.

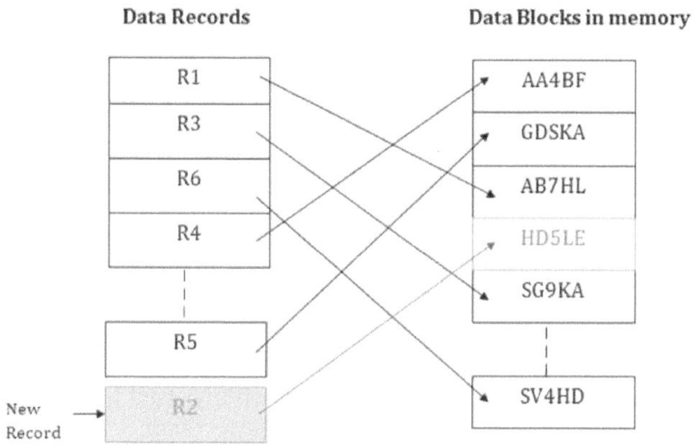


## B+ File Organization

B+ tree file organization is the advanced method of an indexed sequential access method. It uses a tree-like structure to store records in File.

It uses the same concept of key-index where the primary key is used to sort the records. For each primary key, the value of the index is generated and mapped with the record.

The B+ tree is similar to a binary search tree (BST), but it can have more than two children. In this method, all the records are stored only at the leaf node. Intermediate nodes act as a pointer to the leaf nodes. They do not contain any records.

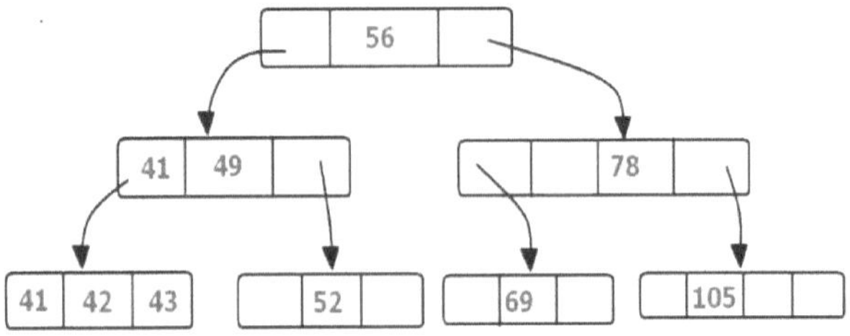


In the above diagram, 56 is the root node which is also called the main node of the tree.

The intermediate nodes here, just consist of the address of leaf nodes. They do not contain any actual records. Leaf nodes consist of the actual record. All leaf nodes are balanced.

Advantages of B+ Tree File Organization

Tree traversal is easier and faster.

Searching becomes easy as all records are stored only in leaf nodes and are sorted in sequentially linked lists.

There is no restriction on B+ tree size. It may grow/shrink as the size of the data increases/decreases.

Disadvantages of B+ Tree File Organization

Inefficient for static tables.

**Cluster File Organization**

In Cluster file organization, two or more related tables/records are stored within the same file known as clusters. These files will have two or more tables in the same data block and the key attributes which are used to map these tables together are stored only once.

Thus, it lowers the cost of searching and retrieving various records in different files as they are now combined and kept in a single cluster. For example, we have two tables or relation Employee and Department. These tables are related to each other.

Clustered file organization is a method of file organization where records with similar characteristics are stored physically close to each other for efficient retrieval. Here's an example of a clustered file organization for a library database where books are clustered by genre:

Library Book Database - Clustered by Genre

| Genre | Title | Author | ISBN |
|---|---|---|---|
| **Science Fiction** | Dune | Frank Herbert | 978-0441172719 |
| **Science Fiction** | Ender's Game | Orson Scott Card | 978-0812550702 |
| **Science Fiction** | Foundation | Isaac Asimov | 978-0553293357 |
| **Mystery** | The Da Vinci Code | Dan Brown | 978-0307474278 |
| **Mystery** | Gone Girl | Gillian Flynn | 978-0307588371 |
| **Mystery** | The Girl with... | Stieg Larsson | 978-0307454546 |

In this example, books of the same genre are physically stored together in the file. This clustering allows for more efficient retrieval when searching for books within a specific genre. For instance, if you're interested in science fiction books, the system can quickly locate and retrieve them without scanning the entire file.

Types of Cluster file organization:

Cluster file organization is of two types:

Indexed Clusters:

In indexed cluster, records are grouped based on the cluster key and stored together. The above EMPLOYEE and DEPARTMENT relationship is an example of an indexed cluster. Here, all the records are grouped based on the cluster key- DEP_ID and all the records are grouped.

Hash Clusters:

It is similar to the indexed cluster. In hash cluster, instead of storing the records based on the cluster key, we generate the value of the hash key for the cluster key and store the records with the same hash key value.

Pros of Cluster file organization

The cluster file organization is used when there is a frequent request for joining the tables with same joining condition.

It provides the efficient result when there is a 1:M mapping between the tables.

Cons of Cluster file organization

This method has the low performance for the very large database.

If there is any change in joining condition, then this method cannot use. If we change the condition of joining then traversing the file takes a lot of time.

This method is not suitable for a table with a 1:1 condition.

**Indexed sequential access method (ISAM)**

ISAM method is an advanced sequential file organization. In this method, records are stored in the file using the primary key. An index value is generated for each primary key and mapped with the record. This index contains the address of the record in the file.

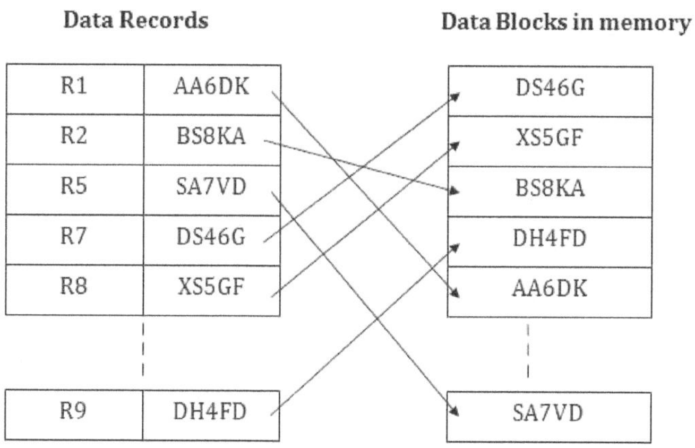

If any record has to be retrieved based on its index value, then the address of the data block is fetched and the record is retrieved from the memory.

Pros of ISAM:

In this method, each record has the address of its data block, searching a record in a huge database is quick and easy.

This method supports range retrieval and partial retrieval of records. Since the index is based on the primary key values, we can retrieve the data for the given range of value. In the same way, the partial value can also be easily searched, i.e., the student's name starting with 'JA' can be easily searched.

Cons of ISAM:

This method requires extra space in the disk to store the index value.

When the new records are inserted, then these files have to be reconstructed to maintain the sequence.

When the record is deleted, then the space used by it needs to be released. Otherwise, the performance of the database will slow down.

**Database Systems vs. File-Based Systems:**

**Database Systems:**

Data Structure:

Structured: Database systems use structured data models like the relational model, which organize data into tables with rows and columns.

Data Independence: They provide data independence, separating the logical schema from the physical storage schema.

Data Integrity:

Enforced: Database systems enforce data integrity using constraints and rules defined in the schema.

Consistency: ACID properties (Atomicity, Consistency, Isolation, Durability) ensure data consistency even in the presence of failures.

Data Redundancy:

Minimized: Data redundancy is minimized through normalization techniques, reducing the risk of inconsistent data.

Data Retrieval:

Query Language: They use a query language (e.g., SQL) for complex and flexible data retrieval, supporting various operations like filtering, sorting, and joining.

Concurrency Control:

Sophisticated: Database systems have sophisticated concurrency control mechanisms to manage multiple users accessing and modifying data simultaneously.

Scalability:

Horizontal and Vertical: They can scale both horizontally (adding more machines) and vertically (upgrading hardware) to handle growing data and user demands.

**File-Based Systems:**

Data Structure:

Unstructured or Semi-Structured: File-based systems manage data in unstructured or semi-structured formats, such as text, CSV, or XML files.

Data Format: The data format is often application-specific, leading to inconsistency.

Data Integrity:

Limited: Ensuring data integrity is the responsibility of individual applications, making it prone to errors and inconsistencies.

Data Redundancy:

Common: Data redundancy is common, as each application may duplicate data, leading to potential inconsistencies.

Data Retrieval:

Custom Code: Data retrieval typically involves custom code within each application, making it less flexible and harder to maintain.

Concurrency Control:

Basic or Manual: File-based systems often lack built-in concurrency control, requiring manual synchronization of access to files.

Scalability:

Limited: Scaling a file-based system can be challenging, as it often involves duplicating entire file structures, which can lead to data synchronization issues.

**Key Differences:**

Data Structure: Database systems use structured models, while file-based systems work with unstructured or semi-structured data.

Data Integrity: Database systems enforce data integrity through constraints and ACID properties, while file-based systems rely on individual application logic.

Data Redundancy: Database systems minimize redundancy through normalization, while file-based systems often have duplicated data.

Data Retrieval: Database systems provide query languages for flexible data retrieval, while file-based systems require custom code for each application.

Concurrency Control: Database systems have sophisticated concurrency control mechanisms, while file-based systems may lack built-in control.

Scalability: Database systems are more scalable, supporting both horizontal and vertical scaling, whereas file-based systems have limited scalability.

## 7.3 Organization of Records in Files

In a database management system (DBMS), the organization of records in files plays a crucial role in data storage and retrieval efficiency. There are various methods of organizing records in files, each with its own advantages and use cases. Here are some common methods:

**Sequential File Organization:**

Records are stored in a sequential order, one after the other.

Suitable for applications where data access is primarily in a sequential manner, such as batch processing.

Inefficient for random access and updates.

Example:

```
Record 1
Record 2
Record 3
```

**Indexed File Organization:**

Records are stored sequentially, and an index table is maintained separately.

The index table contains key values and pointers to the corresponding record in the data file.

Enables faster access to records based on indexed fields.

Example:

```
Index Table:
Key    Pointer
101    1
205    2
309    3

Data File:
Record 1
Record 2
Record 3
```

**Hashed File Organization:**

Records are distributed across multiple buckets based on a hash function applied to a key field.

Suitable for applications with high-speed retrieval requirements.

Efficient for direct access to records if the hash function is well-designed.

Example:

```
Bucket 1:
Record 1
Record 4

Bucket 2:
Record 2
Record 5

Bucket 3:
Record 3
```

**Clustered (Clustered Index) File Organization:**

Records are physically stored together based on one or more key fields.

Typically used in conjunction with a B-tree index on the key field(s).

Allows for efficient retrieval based on the clustered key(s).

Example:

```
Clustered Index (sorted by ID):
Record 1 (ID: 101)
Record 2 (ID: 205)
Record 3 (ID: 309)

Other Records:
Record 4 (ID: 112)
Record 5 (ID: 250)
```

**Heap File Organization:**

Records are inserted without a specific order, and no indexing is used.

Suitable for scenarios where records are constantly inserted, and the order of retrieval is not important.

Retrieving specific records may require a full scan of the file.

Example:

```
Record 1
Record 2
Record 3
```

The choice of file organization method depends on the specific requirements of the application, including data access patterns, performance needs, and data volume. In practice, a combination of these methods may be used within a DBMS to optimize data storage and retrieval.

## Data Dictionary Storage

In a database management system (DBMS), a data dictionary, also known as a system catalog or metadata repository, is a critical component that stores metadata about the database. This metadata includes information about the database's structure, schema, constraints, relationships, data types, and more. Here are details about data dictionary storage along with an example:

**Data Dictionary Storage Components:**

**Table Information:**

The data dictionary stores details about tables in the database, such as table names, column names, data types, default values, constraints, and more.

It maintains information about primary keys, foreign keys, unique constraints, and check constraints associated with tables.

**Index Information:**

Information about indexes created on tables is stored in the data dictionary.

This includes the names of indexes, the columns they are based on, and whether they are unique or non-unique.

**User and Privilege Information:**

The data dictionary maintains data about users and their privileges.

It tracks who has access to the database, what permissions they have, and which objects they can manipulate.

**Data Types and Domains:**

Information about data types and domains used in the database is stored.

This includes data type names, size constraints, and descriptions.

**Views and Procedures:**

The data dictionary keeps records of views and stored procedures, including their definitions and dependencies.

**System Parameters:**

Details about system-wide parameters and configuration settings are maintained.

These parameters control the behavior of the DBMS.

**Example of Data Dictionary Storage:**

Consider a simplified example of a data dictionary for a relational database that tracks employee information:

**Table Information:**

Table Name: Employees

Columns:

EmployeeID (INT)

FirstName (VARCHAR)

LastName (VARCHAR)

DepartmentID (INT)

**Index Information:**

Index Name: Employees_PK

Columns: EmployeeID (Unique Index)

**User and Privilege Information:**

User: HR_Manager

Privileges: SELECT, INSERT, UPDATE on Employees table

**Data Types and Domains:**

Data Type: INT

Description: Integer data type.

Data Type: VARCHAR

Description: Variable-length character data type.

**Views and Procedures:**

View: EmployeeSummary

Definition: SELECT FirstName, LastName, DepartmentID FROM Employees

Procedure: UpdateEmployeeSalary

Definition: UPDATE Employees SET Salary = Salary + 5000 WHERE EmployeeID = @EmployeeID

**System Parameters:**

Parameter: MaxConnections

Value: 100

Description: Maximum allowed concurrent database connections.

The data dictionary provides a central repository of metadata that helps database administrators, developers, and the DBMS itself manage and maintain the database effectively. It ensures data integrity, enforces constraints, and supports various operations, such as query optimization and access control.

## Column-Oriented Storage

Column-oriented storage, also known as columnar storage, is a database storage format that organizes and stores data in a column-wise fashion, as opposed to the traditional row-wise storage used in relational databases. This storage method offers several advantages for specific types of queries and workloads. Here's a detailed explanation of column-oriented storage in DBMS:

**Key Characteristics of Column-Oriented Storage:**

**Columnar Data Organization**:

In a column-oriented database, each column of a table is stored separately from others.

All values within a column are of the same data type, allowing for efficient compression and encoding techniques.

**Compression and Encoding**:

Columnar storage often employs various compression and encoding techniques to reduce storage space.

Since columns usually contain similar or repeating values, compression can be more effective compared to row-based storage.

**Selective Column Retrieval:**

Column-oriented storage excels at queries that involve selecting specific columns from a table.

It retrieves only the necessary columns, reducing I/O and improving query performance.

**Aggregation Queries:**

For aggregation queries (e.g., SUM, COUNT, AVG), columnar storage can process data more efficiently.

It can read and process only the required columns, minimizing disk I/O and CPU usage.

**Data Warehousing and Analytics**:

Columnar databases are commonly used in data warehousing and analytical databases.

They can handle large datasets and complex analytical queries with better performance than row-based databases.

**Insert and Update Performance**:

Columnar databases may not perform as well for individual record inserts or updates compared to row-based databases.

However, they are optimized for batch processing and analytical workloads.

**Advantages of Column-Oriented Storage:**

Query Performance: Columnar databases excel in analytical queries that involve scanning and aggregating large volumes of data. They minimize disk I/O and improve query speed.

Compression Efficiency: Similar data values in a column can be compressed effectively, reducing storage costs.

Analytics and Data Warehousing: Columnar storage is well-suited for data warehousing and analytics applications, where complex queries are common.

Parallel Processing: Columnar databases can take advantage of parallel processing capabilities in modern hardware architectures, further enhancing performance.

**Disadvantages of Column-Oriented Storage:**

Insert and Update Performance: Individual record inserts and updates can be slower in columnar databases due to the need to write or update data across multiple columns.

Transactional Workloads: Columnar databases may not be the best choice for transactional workloads with frequent updates and inserts.

Complexity: Implementing and maintaining a columnar database system can be more complex than row-based databases.

Example:

Consider a table called "Sales" in a columnar database:

| OrderID | Product | Quantity | Price |
|---|---|---|---|
| 1 | Laptop | 2 | 800 |
| 2 | Smartphone | 3 | 400 |
| 3 | Tablet | 1 | 600 |

In columnar storage, this table would be stored as follows:

**OrderID Column:**

1

2

3

**Product Column:**

Laptop

Smartphone

Tablet

**Quantity Column:**

2

3

1

**Price Column:**

800

400

600

This format allows the database to read and process specific columns efficiently, which is beneficial for queries that involve aggregation or selecting specific attributes.

## Indexing and Hashing

**Indexing:**

Indexing, as name suggests, is a technique or mechanism generally used to speed up access of data. Index is basically a type of data structure that is used to locate and access data in database table quickly. Indexes can easily be developed or created using one or more columns of database table.

**Hashing:**

Hashing, as name suggests, is a technique or mechanism that uses hash functions with search keys as parameters to generate address of data record. It calculates direct location of data record on disk without using index structure. A good hash functions only uses one-way hashing algorithm and hash cannot be converted back into original key. In simple words, it is a process of converting given key into another value known as hash value or simply hash.

**Example of Indexing:**

Consider a database table "Employees" with columns like "EmployeeID," "FirstName," "LastName," and "Department." An index is created on the "EmployeeID" column. When a query searches for an employee by their ID, the DBMS uses the index to quickly locate the corresponding record.

**Example of Hashing:**

In a hash-based system, consider a dictionary where words are hashed based on their first letter. To find the definition of the word "apple," the hash function determines the location of words starting with 'A.' It quickly directs you to the "apple" entry without searching the entire dictionary.

In summary, indexing and hashing are crucial techniques in DBMS to optimize data retrieval. Indexing provides efficient retrieval of data based on sorted columns, while hashing enables fast direct access to data based on known keys. The choice between them depends on the specific use case and query patterns of the database system.

## Ordered Indices

Ordered indices are a type of database index that arranges data in a specific order, usually ascending or descending, based on the values of one or more columns in a table. These indices improve the efficiency of data retrieval operations like searching and sorting. Here's a detailed explanation of ordered indices with an example:

**Key Points about Ordered Indices:**

Sorting Order: Ordered indices maintain the data in a sorted order, either in ascending (smallest to largest) or descending (largest to smallest) based on the indexed column(s).

Binary Search: Ordered indices enable efficient binary search operations, allowing the DBMS to quickly locate specific values within the index.

Duplicate Values: Ordered indices can handle duplicate values in the indexed column(s) by associating each value with a list of corresponding row pointers.

Balanced Trees: Common data structures used for ordered indices include balanced search trees like B-trees and B+ trees. These structures ensure logarithmic search times.

Types of Ordered Indices: There are different types of ordered indices, including single-level indices (for a single column) and multi-level indices (for multiple columns or composite keys).

Example of Ordered Indices:

Consider a database table "Students" with the following columns:

StudentID (Primary Key)

FirstName

LastName

Age

Suppose we want to create an ordered index on the "LastName" column in ascending order.

**Initial Data:**

| StudentID | FirstName | FirstName | Age |
|---|---|---|---|
| 1 | Alice | Smith | 20 |
| 2 | Bob | Johnson | 22 |
| 3 | Charlie | Brown | 21 |
| 4 | Charlie | Smith | 23 |

**Creating the Ordered Index:**

The ordered index on the "LastName" column will arrange the data alphabetically by last name.

| LastName | StudentID | (Pointer) |
|---|---|---|
| **Brown** | 3 | |
| **Johnson** | 2 | |
| **Smith** | 1,4 | |

**Searching with the Index:**

If we want to find all students with the last name "Smith," the DBMS can perform a binary search within the index to quickly locate the associated StudentIDs (pointers).

Search for "Smith" in the index.

The index points to StudentIDs 1 and 4.

Retrieve the corresponding records from the table.

**Efficiency:**

Ordered indices significantly improve the efficiency of searching for specific values or ranges of values in the indexed column. They also facilitate sorting operations on the indexed column.

Ordered indices are essential for databases with large datasets, as they help reduce the time required for data retrieval and improve overall query performance. However, they come with the cost of increased storage space and the need to maintain the index when data is inserted, updated, or deleted in the table.

## B+ Tree Index Files and B-Tree Index Files

B+ tree and B-tree index files are two common types of index structures used in database management systems (DBMS) to improve the efficiency of data retrieval operations. They are particularly useful for large datasets and support rapid searching and sorting. Below, you'll find detailed explanations of B+ tree and B-tree index files:

**B-Tree Index Files:**

Structure: B-trees are balanced tree structures consisting of nodes. Each node contains a set of keys and pointers to child nodes. The number of keys in a node is limited by a factor called the "order" of the B-tree.

Balanced: B-trees are balanced, ensuring that all leaf nodes are at the same level. This balance is maintained by redistributing keys between nodes during insertions and deletions.

Sorting Order: B-trees maintain keys in sorted order, making them efficient for range queries and equality searches.

Search Efficiency: B-trees provide efficient search operations with a time complexity of O(log n), where n is the number of keys. They are suitable for both point queries and range queries.

Use Cases: B-tree index files are commonly used in DBMS for indexing columns with high cardinality, such as primary keys and unique constraints.

Example:

Suppose we have a database table that stores employee records with the employee ID as the primary key. Here's a simplified B-tree index structure for the employee ID:

```
      10
     / | \
   5   15   20
  / \  / \  / \
 2   7 12  18 17  25
```

In this B-tree:

The root node has keys [10] and pointers to three child nodes.

Node 10 has keys [5, 15, 20] and pointers to four child nodes.

Nodes 5, 15, and 20 have their respective keys and pointers to child nodes or data.

When searching for an employee ID, the B-tree allows for efficient lookups with a time complexity of O(log n).

**B+ Tree Index Files:**

Structure: B+ trees are similar to B-trees but with some key differences. In B+ trees, data entries are stored only in leaf nodes, while internal nodes contain keys and pointers to child nodes. Additionally, B+ trees have a fanout that is greater than or equal to the B-tree fanout.

Balanced: B+ trees are balanced like B-trees, ensuring that leaf nodes are at the same level. However, they have fewer internal nodes, resulting in a flatter structure.

Sorting Order: B+ trees also maintain keys in sorted order, facilitating range queries and equality searches.

Search Efficiency: B+ trees offer efficient search operations with a time complexity of O(log n), similar to B-trees. They are well-suited for point queries, range queries, and range scans.

Use Cases: B+ tree index files are commonly used in DBMS for indexing columns where range queries are frequent or when you need to retrieve multiple consecutive rows efficiently.

Example:

Let's consider the same employee records database with an employee ID index, but this time, we'll use a B+ tree structure:

```
      10
     / | \
   5  12  17
  /\  |  | \
 2  7 15 18 25
```

In this B+ tree:

All data entries (employee IDs) are stored in the leaf nodes.

The leaf nodes are linked together, allowing for efficient range scans.

Internal nodes contain keys and pointers to child nodes.

When searching for an employee ID or performing range queries, the B+ tree provides efficient access with a time complexity of O(log n). Additionally, the B+ tree's leaf node structure simplifies range scans because they are sequential.

**Comparison:**

B+ trees are preferred for DBMS index files when range queries and range scans are crucial because they have fewer levels and better cache locality.

B-trees are used when point queries and equality searches are more common and the dataset is not as large.

Both B-trees and B+ trees maintain balance, ensuring efficient insertions and deletions.

Both B-tree and B+ tree structures offer efficient index management, but the B+ tree is often preferred for databases with range query requirements due to its leaf node structure, which simplifies sequential access.

In summary, B+ tree and B-tree index files are valuable tools in DBMS for optimizing data retrieval operations. The choice between them depends on the specific requirements of the database and the types of queries it needs to support.

## Static Hashing and Dynamic Hashing

### Static Hashing

In static hashing, the resultant data bucket address will always be the same. That means if we generate an address for EMP_ID =103 using the hash function mod (5) then it will always result in same bucket address 3. Here, there will be no change in the bucket address.

Hence in this static hashing, the number of data buckets in memory remains constant throughout. In this example,

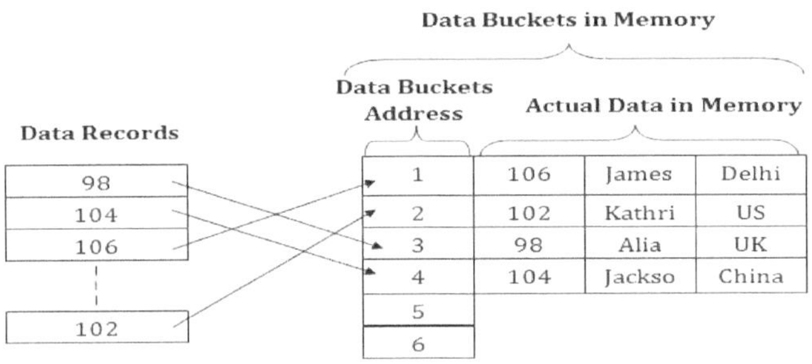


we will have five data buckets in the memory used to store the data.

### Operations of Static Hashing

**Searching a record**

When a record needs to be searched, then the same hash function retrieves the address of the bucket where the data is stored.

**Insert a Record**

When a new record is inserted into the table, then we will generate an address for a new record based on the hash key and record is stored in that location.

**Delete a Record**

To delete a record, we will first fetch the record which is supposed to be deleted. Then we will delete the records for that address in memory.

**Update a Record**

To update a record, we will first search it using a hash function, and then the data record is updated.

If we want to insert some new record into the file but the address of a data bucket generated by the hash function is not empty, or data already exists in that address. This situation in the static hashing is known as bucket overflow. This is a critical situation in this method.

To overcome this situation, there are various methods. Some commonly used methods are as follows:

**Open Hashing**

When a hash function generates an address at which data is already stored, then the next bucket will be allocated to it. This mechanism is called as Linear Probing.

For example: suppose R3 is a new address which needs to be inserted, the hash function generates address as 112 for

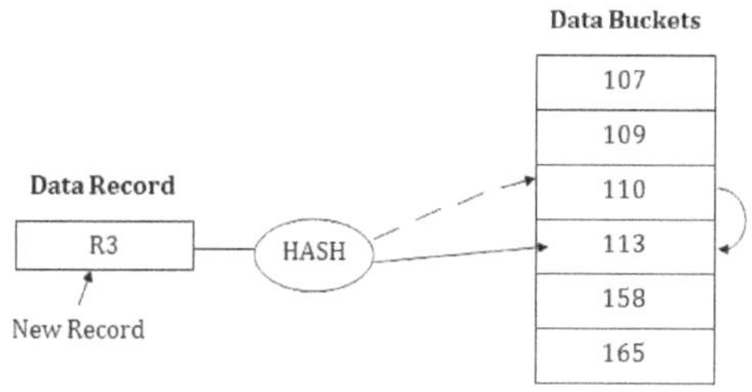


R3. But the generated address is already full. So, the system searches next available data bucket, 113 and assigns R3 to it.

**Close Hashing**

When buckets are full, then a new data bucket is allocated for the same hash result and is linked after the previous one. This mechanism is known as Overflow chaining.

For example: Suppose R3 is a new address which needs to be inserted into the table, the hash function generates address as 110 for it. But this bucket is full to store the new data. In this case, a new bucket is inserted at the end of

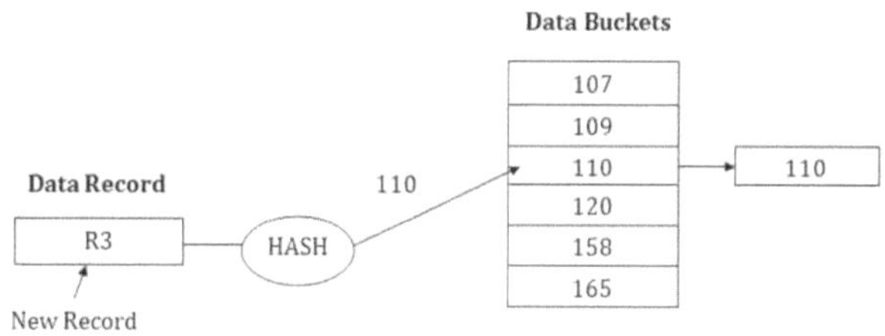


110 buckets and is linked to it.

**Dynamic Hashing**

The dynamic hashing method is used to overcome the problems of static hashing like bucket overflow.

In this method, data buckets grow or shrink as the records increases or decreases. This method is also known as Extendable hashing method.

This method makes hashing dynamic, i.e., it allows insertion or deletion without resulting in poor performance.

How to search a key

First, calculate the hash address of the key.

Check how many bits are used in the directory, and these bits are called as i.

Take the least significant i bits of the hash address. This gives an index of the directory.

Now using the index, go to the directory and find bucket address where the record might be.

How to insert a new record

Firstly, you have to follow the same procedure for retrieval, ending up in some bucket.

If there is still space in that bucket, then place the record in it.

If the bucket is full, then we will split the bucket and redistribute the records.

For example:

Consider the following grouping of keys into buckets, depending on the prefix of their hash address:

| Key | Hash address |
|---|---|
| 1 | 11010 |
| 2 | 00000 |
| 3 | 11110 |
| 4 | 00000 |
| 5 | 01001 |
| 6 | 10101 |
| 7 | 10111 |

The last two bits of 2 and 4 are 00. So it will go into bucket B0. The last two bits of 5 and 6 are 01, so it will go into

bucket B1. The last two bits of 1 and 3 are 10, so it will go into bucket B2. The last two bits of 7 are 11, so it will go into B3.

Insert key 9 with hash address 10001 into the above structure:

Since key 9 has hash address 10001, it must go into the first bucket. But bucket B1 is full, so it will get split.

The splitting will separate 5, 9 from 6 since last three bits of 5, 9 are 001, so it will go into bucket B1, and the last three bits of 6 are 101, so it will go into bucket B5.

Keys 2 and 4 are still in B0. The record in B0 pointed by the 000 and 100 entry because last two bits of both the entry are 00.

Keys 1 and 3 are still in B2. The record in B2 pointed by the 010 and 110 entry because last two bits of both the entry are 10.

Key 7 are still in B3. The record in B3 pointed by the 111 and 011 entry because last two bits of both the entry are

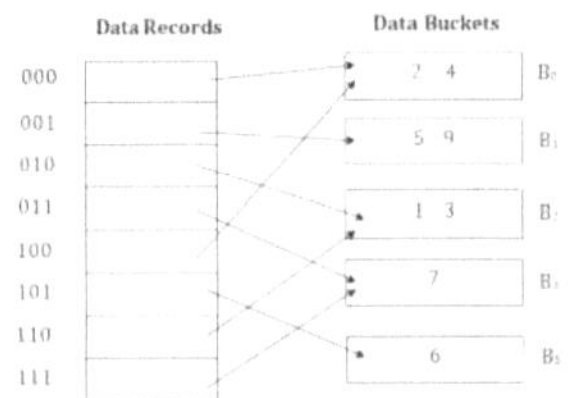


11.

Advantages of dynamic hashing

In this method, the performance does not decrease as the data grows in the system. It simply increases the size of memory to accommodate the data.

In this method, memory is well utilized as it grows and shrinks with the data. There will not be any unused memory lying.

This method is good for the dynamic database where data grows and shrinks frequently.

Disadvantages of dynamic hashing

In this method, if the data size increases then the bucket size is also increased. These addresses of data will be maintained in the bucket address table. This is because the data address will keep changing as buckets grow and shrink. If there is a huge increase in data, maintaining the bucket address table becomes tedious.

In this case, the bucket overflow situation will also occur. But it might take little time to reach this situation than static hashing.

## Query Processing Overview

Query processing is a fundamental aspect of database management systems (DBMS) that involves the execution of user queries on a database. It includes various stages like parsing, optimization, and execution. Let's explore the query processing overview in detail with an example:

**Query Processing Overview:**

Parsing: When a user submits a query to the DBMS, the first step is parsing. In this stage, the query is analyzed to ensure it's syntactically correct. The DBMS checks for proper SQL keywords, table and column names, and the overall structure of the query.

Semantic Analysis: After parsing, the DBMS performs semantic analysis to ensure the query's validity. This involves checking if the referenced tables and columns exist, if the user has the necessary permissions, and if the query adheres to constraints and data types.

Query Optimization: Once the query is validated, the DBMS proceeds to optimize it for efficient execution. The goal is to find the most efficient way to access and retrieve the requested data. The DBMS generates multiple execution plans and selects the one with the lowest cost, often using techniques like cost-based optimization.

Execution Plan: The selected execution plan outlines how the query will be executed. It specifies the order of table access, which indexes to use, and any join operations. The DBMS generates an execution plan that minimizes resource usage and maximizes query performance.

Execution: With the execution plan in place, the DBMS executes the query. It retrieves data from the database, performs any necessary calculations or transformations, and returns the result to the user.

**Example:**

Let's consider a simple example to illustrate query processing:

Suppose you have a relational database with two tables: "Employees" and "Departments." You want to retrieve the names of all employees in the "Sales" department.

```
SELECT Employees.EmployeeName
FROM Employees
INNER JOIN Departments ON Employees.DepartmentID = Departments.DepartmentID
```

WHERE Departments.DepartmentName = 'Sales';

**Query Processing Steps:**

Parsing: The DBMS parses the query to check its syntax and structure. It confirms that the query follows SQL conventions.

Semantic Analysis: The DBMS verifies that "Employees" and "Departments" tables exist, that the columns like "EmployeeName," "DepartmentID," and "DepartmentName" exist, and that the user has appropriate permissions.

Query Optimization: The DBMS considers multiple execution plans. It may choose to perform an inner join between the "Employees" and "Departments" tables using the "DepartmentID" column. It selects an index on the "DepartmentName" column for efficient filtering.

Execution Plan: The DBMS generates an execution plan that involves accessing the necessary rows in the "Departments" table using the index on "DepartmentName" and then performing an inner join with the "Employees" table based on "DepartmentID."

Execution: The query is executed, and the result is returned. You receive a list of employee names in the "Sales" department.

Query processing plays a crucial role in ensuring that database queries are executed efficiently, even for complex operations involving multiple tables and large datasets.

## Algorithms for Selection, Sorting, and Join Operations

In a database management system (DBMS), algorithms for selection, sorting, and join operations are essential for efficiently retrieving, organizing, and combining data. Let's explore these algorithms with examples:

**Selection Operation Algorithm:**

The selection operation filters rows from a table based on a specified condition. A common algorithm for selection is the "Linear Search" or "Sequential Search."

Example:

Suppose you have an "Employees" table with columns: "EmployeeID," "EmployeeName," "Salary," and you want to select all employees with a salary greater than $50,000.

SELECT EmployeeName

FROM Employees

WHERE Salary > 50000;

In this case, the DBMS performs a linear search through the table, examining each row's "Salary" column to identify rows that satisfy the condition (Salary > 50000).

**Sorting Operation Algorithm:**

Sorting arranges rows in a table in a specific order, such as ascending or descending based on one or more columns. A commonly used sorting algorithm in DBMS is "QuickSort."

Example:

Suppose you want to retrieve a sorted list of employees by their names in alphabetical order.

SELECT EmployeeName

```
FROM Employees
ORDER BY EmployeeName ASC;
```

Here, the DBMS uses the QuickSort algorithm to rearrange the rows in the "Employees" table based on the "EmployeeName" column in ascending order.

**Join Operation Algorithm:**

Join operations combine data from two or more tables based on a related column. A widely used algorithm for join operations is the "Nested Loop Join."

Example:

Consider two tables, "Employees" and "Departments," where "Employees" have a "DepartmentID" column and "Departments" have a "DepartmentID" column. You want to retrieve a list of employees along with their department names.

```
SELECT Employees.EmployeeName, Departments.DepartmentName
FROM Employees
INNER JOIN Departments ON Employees.DepartmentID = Departments.DepartmentID;
```

In this example, the DBMS performs a nested loop join. For each row in the "Employees" table, it looks up the corresponding "DepartmentID" in the "Departments" table to fetch the department name. These algorithms are just a few examples of how DBMS handles selection, sorting, and join operations efficiently. DBMS systems often use optimized algorithms and indexing techniques to improve performance, especially when dealing with large datasets.

## Query Optimization Using Heuristics

Query optimization is a crucial aspect of database management systems (DBMS) to enhance query performance. Heuristics-based optimization relies on rules and guidelines to make informed decisions about how to execute queries efficiently. Let's explore query optimization using heuristics with an example:

Example:

Consider a simplified database with two tables, "Orders" and "Customers," and you want to retrieve a list of customers who placed orders with a total order value exceeding $1,000. Here's the SQL query:

```
SELECT Customers.CustomerName
FROM Customers
INNER JOIN Orders ON Customers.CustomerID = Orders.CustomerID
WHERE Orders.TotalAmount > 1000;
```

Now, let's discuss some heuristics-based optimizations for this query:

Index Selection: If indexes exist on the relevant columns (e.g., "CustomerID" in both tables and "TotalAmount" in the "Orders" table), the optimizer may choose to use these indexes for efficient data retrieval.

Join Order: The order in which tables are joined can significantly impact query performance. Heuristics-based optimization can evaluate different join orders and select the most efficient one. In this case, joining "Customers" and "Orders" on "CustomerID" before filtering by "TotalAmount" might be more efficient.

Filter Pushdown: The optimizer may choose to push the filtering condition (WHERE clause) closer to the data source. In this example, it might apply the "TotalAmount" filter to the "Orders" table before joining with "Customers."

Parallelism: For large datasets, the optimizer may consider parallel execution of the query by splitting the work among multiple processors or threads, improving query speed.

Aggregation: If the query required aggregations (e.g., calculating the sum of "TotalAmount" for each customer), the optimizer would optimize the aggregation step, potentially using specialized algorithms like hash aggregation.

Cost-Based Optimization: Some DBMS systems employ cost-based optimization, which estimates the cost of different query execution plans and selects the one with the lowest estimated cost. It considers factors like data distribution, index statistics, and system resources.

Caching: The optimizer may recognize frequently executed queries and cache their execution plans for faster retrieval in subsequent runs.

Materialized Views: If precomputed materialized views exist that cover part or all of the query, the optimizer might use them to avoid recomputation.

The specific optimizations applied can vary depending on the DBMS, its configuration, and the database schema. Heuristic-based optimization helps the DBMS choose an execution plan that balances resource usage and query speed for optimal performance.

## Cost Estimation

Cost estimation in a database management system (DBMS) is a critical aspect of query optimization. It involves estimating the cost associated with different query execution plans to select the most efficient one. Let's consider an example to understand cost estimation:

Example:

Suppose you have a database with two tables, "Employees" and "Departments," and you want to retrieve a list of employees who work in the "Sales" department and have a salary greater than $50,000. Here's the SQL query:

```
SELECT Employees.EmployeeName
FROM Employees
INNER JOIN Departments ON Employees.DepartmentID = Departments.DepartmentID
WHERE Departments.DepartmentName = 'Sales'
 AND Employees.Salary > 50000;
```

Now, let's discuss how cost estimation works in optimizing this query:

Access Methods: The cost estimation starts by considering how data is accessed. It assesses whether there are indexes on the relevant columns, such as "DepartmentID" and "Salary." Accessing data through indexes is generally faster than full table scans.

Data Distribution: Cost estimation takes into account the distribution of data in the tables. For example, if the "Sales" department has a large number of employees, it might be more efficient to start the query by filtering the "Sales" department first.

Join Strategies: In this query, there's an inner join between the "Employees" and "Departments" tables. Cost estimation evaluates different join strategies (e.g., nested loop join, hash join) and estimates the cost associated with each.

Filtering Conditions: The cost estimation considers filtering conditions in the WHERE clause. It evaluates the selectivity of each condition (i.e., how many rows are expected to meet the condition) and estimates the cost accordingly.

Index Usage: If there are indexes on the columns used in filtering or joining, cost estimation assesses whether using those indexes is more efficient than full table scans.

Resource Usage: Cost estimation factors in the consumption of system resources such as CPU, memory, and disk I/O during query execution. It aims to minimize resource usage while maximizing query speed.

Parallelism: If the DBMS supports parallel processing, cost estimation evaluates whether parallel execution can reduce query execution time.

The optimizer assigns a cost to each potential query execution plan and selects the one with the lowest estimated cost. It's important to note that cost estimation is influenced by statistics and data distribution, and the accuracy of statistics plays a significant role in optimizing queries.

In practice, DBMS systems use a combination of heuristics and statistics to estimate costs accurately and optimize queries for efficient execution.

**Exercise**

**Exercise 1 – MCQ**

Q 1. Which of the following is a storage technique used in DBMS to improve query performance by storing frequently accessed data in a highly efficient, read-only format?

A) Normalization

B) Column-Oriented Storage

C) Data Mining

D) Indexing

Q 2. In a DBMS, which of the following is NOT an implementation technique for organizing records in files?

A) RAID

B) Static Hashing

C) Dynamic Hashing

D) B+ Tree Indexing

**Exercise 2 – True/ False**

Q 1. RAID (Redundant Array of Independent Disks) is an implementation technique commonly used to improve data storage reliability and performance in DBMS.

Q 2. B+ trees and B-trees are examples of file organization techniques used in DBMS for indexing and efficient data retrieval.

**Exercise 3 – One word answer**

Q 1. What does RAID stand for?

Q 2. What technique is used to speed up data retrieval in databases?

**Exercise 4 – Small answer**

Q 1. What is the purpose of indexing in a DBMS, and how does it improve query performance?

Q 2. Explain the concept of RAID in the context of DBMS implementation. What are the advantages of using RAID for data storage and reliability?

**Exercise 5 – Long answer**

Q 1. Explain the Role of Indexing and Hashing in Database Management Systems (DBMS).

Q 2. Compare and Contrast Different File Organization Techniques in Database Systems.

**Answer**

**Exercise 1**

Answer 1: B), 2: A)

**Exercise 2**

Answer 1: True, 2: True

**Exercise 3**

Answer 1: Redundant Array of Independent Disks., 2: Indexing.

**Previous Years Questions**

Q1. Explain the hash file - organisation with the help of a suitable diagram. What are its shortcomings.(IGNOU MCA 2010)

Q2. Explain the following with the help of an example / diagram wherever needed: Primary and Secondary indexes (IGNOU MCA 2010)

Q3. What are the advantages of using B tree as a structure for creating index? (IGNOU MCA 2011)

Q4. it always beneficial to work with database systems, or some times filebase system is a better option ? Comment on it with suitable arguments. (IGNOU MCA 2011)

Q5. An ordered employee file (ordering field is emp_id) has 20000 records, stored on a disk having block size 1k. Assume that each student record is of 100 bytes, the ordering field is of 8 bytes and block pointer is also of 8 bytes, find how many block accesses on average may be saved on using primary index. (IGNOU MCA 2011)

Q6. Why is a B tree a better structure than a binary search tree for implementation of an index? (IGNOU MCA 2012)

Q7. Discuss the difference between database systems and file Based systems. (IGNOU MCA 2013)

Q8. What are the differences between BST-Tree and B tree Indexes? (IGNOU MCA 2013)

Q9. Compare sequential file organisation with Heap files organisation. Discuss the advantages and disadvantages of sequential file organisation. (IGNOU MCA 2013)

Q10. What is the need of Indexing in DBMS ? Explain the significance of primary Index with the help of an example. (IGNOU MCA 2014)

Q11. Give the limitations of file based system. How can they be overcome using DBMS ? (IGNOU MCA 2015)

Q12. Discuss the use of B-Tree as a structure for creating index, with the help of an example in support. (IGNOU MCA 2015)

Q13. Discuss the importance of file organisation in databases. Mention the different types of file organisations available. Discuss any one of the mentioned file organisations in detail. (IGNOU MCA 2017)

Q14. Write short notes on any four of the following : Indexed Sequential File Organisation. (IGNOU MCA 2017)

Q15. Can we use Binary Search Tree (BST) for indexing ? Justify. (IGNOU MCA 2018 & 2021)

Q16. Write short notes on the following: Clustering Indexes and their Implementation. (IGNOU MCA 2018)

Q17. How do we implement "B-Trees" as an Index? Give an example to illustrate. What are its advantages ? (IGNOU MCA 2018)

Q18. Write difference between DBMS and File Processing System. (Pune University MCA 2013)

Q19. What is RAID? Explain it in detail. (ANNA University MCA 2010)

**Previous Years Questions with Answers**

Q1 What are the disadvantages of file processing system? (RU BCA 2022)

**Answer:**

File processing systems, while historically used for managing data and information, have several disadvantages compared to modern database management systems (DBMS). Some of the key disadvantages of file processing systems include:

**Data Redundancy**:

Data redundancy is common in file processing systems, as the same data may be stored in multiple files or locations. This redundancy can lead to data inconsistency and increase the risk of errors when data needs to be updated in multiple places.

**Data Inconsistency**:

Inconsistent data can result from redundancy, where changes made to data in one file are not reflected in other files. This can lead to discrepancies and inaccuracies in reports and operations.

**Data Isolation**:

In file processing systems, data is typically isolated within specific applications or departments. This isolation makes it challenging to share and access data across the organization, hindering collaboration and data integration.

**Lack of Data Integrity**:

File systems often lack built-in data integrity mechanisms. There is no standardized way to enforce data consistency, constraints, or validation rules, which can lead to errors and data quality issues.

**Limited Data Security**:

File systems may lack robust security features, making it difficult to control and restrict access to data. In a multi-user environment, sensitive data may be vulnerable to unauthorized access.

**Data Dependence**:

Changes to data structures or file formats can have a significant impact on applications. In file processing systems, data and applications are tightly coupled, making maintenance and updates more challenging.

**Data Isolation**:

Data is isolated within specific programs or applications. This makes it difficult to access and share data across different departments or applications, leading to data silos.

**Inefficient Data Retrieval**:

Retrieving specific information from files can be time-consuming and inefficient. Searching for data typically requires writing custom code for each retrieval, leading to duplicated efforts.

**Limited Concurrent Access**:

File processing systems may not support concurrent access to data by multiple users or applications. This can lead to bottlenecks and hinder collaboration.

**Scalability Challenges**:

Expanding or scaling the system to accommodate growing data volumes and user needs can be challenging and costly. File systems are not as adaptable to changes as modern DBMS.

**Maintenance Complexity**:

Maintaining file processing systems can be complex, especially as the number of files and applications grows. It often involves writing custom code to address specific data-related tasks.

**Lack of Data Independence**:

Changes to data structures or formats can impact the functionality of applications. Modern DBMS provide data independence, separating the logical and physical aspects of data storage.

**Difficulty in Data Backup and Recovery**:

Backing up and recovering data in a file processing system can be cumbersome and may not provide the level of data protection and disaster recovery capabilities offered by DBMS.

Modern database management systems, in contrast, address many of these disadvantages by providing centralized, structured, and secure data storage with mechanisms for data integrity, security, and efficient data retrieval. These advantages make DBMS a preferred choice for managing and processing data in a wide range of applications and organizations.

Q2 Explain advantages of DBMS over file system. (RU BCA 2019)

**Answer:**

Database Management Systems (DBMS) offer several advantages over traditional file processing systems. These advantages contribute to improved data management, efficiency, and overall data reliability. Here are the key advantages of DBMS over file systems:

**Data Integrity and Accuracy**:

DBMS enforces data integrity constraints and validation rules, ensuring that data is accurate and consistent. This reduces the risk of data anomalies and errors due to data redundancy.

**Data Security**:

DBMS provides robust security features, including user authentication, authorization, and access controls. This helps protect sensitive data from unauthorized access and ensures data privacy.

**Data Redundancy Reduction**:

DBMS minimizes data redundancy through normalization techniques, reducing the chances of data inconsistencies and making data storage more efficient.

**Concurrent Data Access**:

Multiple users and applications can access and modify data simultaneously without data corruption or conflicts. DBMS handles concurrent access through locking and isolation mechanisms.

**Data Consistency**:

DBMS maintains data consistency by enforcing ACID properties (Atomicity, Consistency, Isolation, Durability) for transactions. This ensures that data remains in a consistent state even in the presence of failures.

**Data Independence**:

DBMS separates the logical data structure from the physical data storage, providing data independence. Changes to the data structure (schema) do not affect application programs, offering flexibility and ease of maintenance.

**Centralized Data Management**:

All data is centralized in a database, making it accessible to various applications and users across the organization. This eliminates data silos and promotes data sharing.

**Efficient Data Retrieval**:

DBMS offers powerful query languages (e.g., SQL) and indexing mechanisms that enable efficient data retrieval. Complex queries can be executed with ease.

**Scalability**:

DBMS systems can handle large amounts of data and are scalable to accommodate data growth. This makes them suitable for organizations with evolving data needs.

**Data Recovery and Backup**:

DBMS systems provide mechanisms for data backup and recovery. Regular backups and transaction logs facilitate data restoration in the event of system failures or data loss.

**Concurrent Data Modification**:

Multiple users can modify data concurrently, and DBMS ensures that changes are applied in a controlled and coordinated manner, preserving data consistency.

**Query Optimization**:

DBMS optimizes query execution by using query optimization techniques, reducing query processing time and improving system performance.

**Data Validation and Constraints**:

DBMS allows the definition of data validation rules and constraints, helping maintain data quality and consistency.

**Data Reporting and Analysis**:

DBMS supports data reporting and analysis through tools and interfaces that simplify data exploration and decision-making.

**Data Versioning and History Tracking**:

Some DBMS systems offer features for versioning and history tracking, allowing organizations to track changes to data over time.

**Data Recovery and Rollback**:

In the event of a transaction failure, DBMS provides mechanisms to roll back the transaction and maintain data consistency.

**Data Compression and Storage Efficiency**:

Some DBMS systems support data compression techniques, reducing storage requirements and improving performance.

Overall, DBMS provides a structured, organized, and secure environment for data management, offering numerous benefits for organizations in terms of data reliability, efficiency, and adaptability to changing data requirements. These advantages make DBMS a superior choice for managing data compared to traditional file systems.

Q3 Give any four drawback of file System. (RU BCA 2018)

**Answer:**

File systems, which were widely used for data management in the past, have several drawbacks compared to modern database management systems (DBMS). Here are four significant drawbacks of file systems:

**Data Redundancy**:

In a file system, data redundancy is common. The same data can be stored in multiple files or locations, leading to the duplication of data. Data redundancy can result in inconsistencies and errors when updates are made to the same data in different locations.

**Data Isolation**:

Data in a file system is typically isolated within specific applications or departments. This isolation makes it challenging to share and access data across the organization. Different departments may maintain their own copies of the same data, leading to data silos and inefficiency.

**Limited Data Integrity and Validation**:

File systems lack built-in mechanisms for ensuring data integrity and enforcing data validation rules. There is no standardized way to maintain the consistency of data, validate data inputs, or enforce constraints, making data quality control difficult.

**Scalability Challenges**:

Expanding or scaling a file system to accommodate growing data volumes and user needs can be challenging and costly. File systems are not as adaptable to changes as modern DBMS, which are designed to handle increasing data loads more efficiently.

Q4. What are the disadvantages of File processing System? [Marks: 2](RTU MCA 2022)

**Answer:**

File Processing Systems, which were the precursors to modern database management systems (DBMS), involve the management of data using files in a file system. While they can be simple and straightforward for very small-scale applications, file processing systems have several disadvantages, especially when dealing with larger, more complex data requirements:

**Data Redundancy and Inconsistency:** Multiple copies of the same data may be stored in different files, leading to data redundancy. This redundancy not only consumes unnecessary storage space but can also lead to inconsistency, where updates, deletions, or additions to the data in one file are not replicated in other files containing the same data.

**Difficulty in Data Access:** Accessing data stored across various files can be cumbersome and inefficient, especially if complex queries involving multiple data items are required. Unlike DBMS, which offer sophisticated querying capabilities, file processing systems lack advanced data retrieval mechanisms.

**Concurrent Access Issues:** File processing systems do not inherently support the management of concurrent access by multiple users or applications. This can lead to issues such as data corruption, lost updates, and other anomalies when multiple entities try to read from and write to a file simultaneously without proper synchronization.

**Limited Data Sharing:** Sharing data among different applications or users is often difficult with file-based systems. Each application may have its own files, making it hard to coordinate data access or ensure consistency across applications.

**Lack of Security:** File processing systems typically do not provide built-in mechanisms to enforce data security. They rely on the underlying file system's permissions, which may not be granular enough for specific data access control requirements, such as differentiating read, write, or delete permissions at the data item level.

**Data Integrity Issues:** Ensuring data integrity (e.g., maintaining valid data relationships and constraints) is challenging in file processing systems. There's no built-in support for enforcing integrity rules, which means applications themselves must handle these concerns, leading to duplicated effort and potential for errors.

**Scalability and Maintenance Challenges:** As the volume of data and the number of applications grow, maintaining a file processing system becomes increasingly complex and challenging. Making changes to the data structure or format can require significant modifications to every application that accesses the data.

**Lack of Transaction Support:** File processing systems do not support transactions or the ACID properties (Atomicity, Consistency, Isolation, Durability) associated with database systems. This makes it difficult to ensure that data operations are completed successfully and reliably, particularly in the face of errors or system failures.

Due to these disadvantages, modern applications typically use relational or non-relational database management systems, which overcome many of the limitations of file processing systems by providing efficient, secure, and flexible data management solutions.

## ONLINE RESOURCES

**Practice Paper Link:**https://forms.gle/9LGy1nyjNd1QwDcj9

**QR Code :**

**Video Content:** https://www.youtube.com/playlist?list=PLzlh_31VWEFoXkU4ET9iBpaYefWMqpeHq

**QR Code :**

# Chapter 8: Advanced Topics

## Distributed Databases: Architecture, Data Storage, Transaction Processing, Query Processing, and Optimization

### Introduction

A distributed database is basically a database that is not limited to one system, it is spread over different sites, i.e, on multiple computers or over a network of computers. A distributed database system is located on various sites that don't share physical components. This may be required when a particular database needs to be accessed by various users globally. It needs to be managed such that for the users it looks like one single database.

Types:

Homogeneous Database:

In a homogeneous database, all different sites store database identically. The operating system, database management system, and the data structures used – all are the same at all sites. Hence, they're easy to manage.

Heterogeneous Database:

In a heterogeneous distributed database, different sites can use different schema and software that can lead to problems in query processing and transactions. Also, a particular site might be completely unaware of the other sites. Different computers may use a different operating system, different database application. They may even use different data models for the database. Hence, translations are required for different sites to communicate.

### Architecture

**Client-Server Architecture of DDBMS:**

This architecture is two level architecture where clients and servers are the points or levels where the main functionality is divided. There is various functionality provided by the server, like managing the transaction, managing the data, processing the queries, and optimization.

**Peer-to-peer Architecture of DDBMS:**

In this architecture, each node or peer is considered as a server as well as a client, and it performs its database services as both (server and client). The peers coordinate their efforts and share their resources with one another.

**Multi DBMS Architecture of DDBMS:**

This is an amalgam of two or more independent Database Systems that functions as a single integrated Database System.

Advantages of Distributed Database System:

There is fast data processing as several sites participate in request processing.

Reliability and availability of this system is high.

It possesses reduced operating cost.

It is easier to expand the system by adding more sites.

It has improved sharing ability and local autonomy.

Disadvantages of Distributed Database System:

The system becomes complex to manage and control.

The security issues must be carefully managed.

The system requires deadlock handling during the transaction processing otherwise the entire system may be in inconsistent state.

There is need of some standardization for processing of distributed database system.

**Distributed Data Storage:**

There are two methods by which we can store the data on different sites:

**Replication:**

This method involves redundantly storing the full relationship at two or more locations. Since a complete database can be accessed from each site, it becomes a redundant database. Systems preserve copies of the data as a result of replication.

This has advantages because it makes more data accessible at many locations. Additionally, query requests can now be handled in parallel.

However, there are some drawbacks as well. Data must be updated frequently. Any changes performed at one site must be documented at every site where that relation is stored in order to avoid inconsistent results. There is a tonne of overhead here. Additionally, since concurrent access must now be monitored across several sites, concurrency control becomes far more complicated.

**Fragmentation:**

According to this method, the relationships are divided (i.e., broken up into smaller pieces), and each fragment is stored at the many locations where it is needed. To ensure there is no data loss, the pieces must be created in a way that allows for the reconstruction of the original relation.

Since Fragmentation doesn't result in duplicate data, consistency is not a concern.

Fragmentation of relations can be done in two ways:

**Horizontal fragmentation – Splitting by rows –**

The relation is fragmented into groups of tuples so that each tuple is assigned to at least one fragment.

**Vertical fragmentation – Splitting by columns –**

The schema of the relation is divided into smaller schemas. Each fragment must contain a common candidate key so as to ensure a lossless join.

In certain cases, an approach that is hybrid of fragmentation and replication is used.

Applications of Distributed Database:

It is used in Corporate Management Information System.

It is used in multimedia applications.

Used in Military's control system, Hotel chains etc.

It is also used in manufacturing control system.

A distributed database system is a type of database management system that stores data across multiple computers or sites that are connected by a network. In a distributed database system, each site has its own database, and the databases are connected to each other to form a single, integrated system. The main advantage of a distributed database system is that it can provide higher availability and reliability than a centralized database system. Because the data is stored across multiple sites, the system can continue to function even if one or more sites fail. In addition, a distributed database system can provide better performance by distributing the data and processing load across multiple sites.

**Transaction Processing**

The transaction is a set of logically related operation. It contains a group of tasks.

A transaction is an action or series of actions. It is performed by a single user to perform operations for accessing the contents of the database.

Example: Suppose an employee of bank transfers Rs 800 from X's account to Y's account. This small transaction contains several low-level tasks:

X's Account

Open_Account(X)

Old_Balance = X.balance

New_Balance = Old_Balance - 800

X.balance = New_Balance

Close_Account(X)

Y's Account

Open_Account(Y)

Old_Balance = Y.balance

New_Balance = Old_Balance + 800

Y.balance = New_Balance

Close_Account(Y)

Operations of Transaction:

Following are the main operations of transaction:

Read(X): Read operation is used to read the value of X from the database and stores it in a buffer in main memory.

Write(X): Write operation is used to write the value back to the database from the buffer.

Let's take an example to debit transaction from an account which consists of following operations:

R(X);

X = X - 500;

W(X);

Let's assume the value of X before starting of the transaction is 4000.

The first operation reads X's value from database and stores it in a buffer.

The second operation will decrease the value of X by 500. So buffer will contain 3500.

The third operation will write the buffer's value to the database. So X's final value will be 3500.

But it may be possible that because of the failure of hardware, software or power, etc. that transaction may fail before finished all the operations in the set.

For example: If in the above transaction, the debit transaction fails after executing operation 2 then X's value will remain 4000 in the database which is not acceptable by the bank.

To solve this problem, we have two important operations:

Commit: It is used to save the work done permanently.

Rollback: It is used to undo the work done.

**Query Processing**

Query processing in a distributed database management system requires the transmission of data between the computers in a network. A distribution strategy for a query is the ordering of data transmissions and local data processing in a database system. Generally, a query in Distributed DBMS requires data from multiple sites, and this need for data from different sites is called the transmission of data that causes communication costs. Query processing in DBMS is different from query processing in centralized DBMS due to the communication cost of data transfer over the network. The transmission cost is low when sites are connected through high-speed Networks and is quite significant in other networks.

**Costs (Transfer of data) of Distributed Query processing:**

In Distributed Query processing, the data transfer cost of distributed query processing means the cost of transferring intermediate files to other sites for processing and therefore the cost of transferring the ultimate result files to the location where that result's required. Let's say that a user sends a query to site S1, which requires data from its own and also from another site S2. Now, there are three strategies to process this query which are given below:

We can transfer the data from S2 to S1 and then process the query

We can transfer the data from S1 to S2 and then process the query

We can transfer the data from S1 and S2 to S3 and then process the query. So the choice depends on various factors like, the size of relations and the results, the communication cost between different sites, and at which the site result will be utilized.

Commonly, the data transfer cost is calculated in terms of the size of the messages. By using the below formula, we can calculate the data transfer cost:

Data transfer cost = C * Size

Where C refers to the cost per byte of data transferring and Size is the no. of bytes transmitted.

Example: Consider the following table EMPLOYEE and DEPARTMENT.

Site1: EMPLOYEE

| EID | NAME | SALARY | DID |
|---|---|---|---|

EID- 10 bytes

SALARY- 20 bytes

DID- 10 bytes

Name- 20 bytes

Total records- 1000

Record Size- 60 bytes

Site2: DEPARTMENT

**DID DNAME**

DID- 10 bytes

DName- 20 bytes

Total records- 50

Record Size- 30 bytes

**Using Semi join in Distributed Query processing :**

The semi-join operation is used in distributed query processing to reduce the number of tuples in a table before transmitting it to another site. This reduction in the number of tuples reduces the number and the total size of the transmission ultimately reducing the total cost of data transfer. Let's say that we have two tables R1, R2 on Site S1, and S2. Now, we will forward the joining column of one table say R1 to the site where the other table say R2 is located. This column is joined with R2 at that site. The decision whether to reduce R1 or R2 can only be made after comparing the advantages of reducing R1 with that of reducing R2. Thus, semi-join is a well-organized solution to reduce the transfer of data in distributed query processing.

**Optimization**

Optimizing a distributed database involves several strategies and considerations to ensure efficient data access, minimize latency, and improve overall system performance. Here are key optimization techniques for distributed databases:

**Data Partitioning and Replication:**

Careful data partitioning: Divide data into smaller subsets or shards based on criteria such as customer, location, or time to distribute the load evenly.

Strategic data replication: Replicate frequently accessed or critical data across multiple nodes for redundancy and faster access.

**Load Balancing:**

Dynamic load balancing: Use load balancers to distribute incoming requests evenly among database nodes based on their current capacity and workload.

**Caching:**

Implement caching mechanisms like Redis or Memcached to store frequently accessed data in-memory, reducing the need to query the database for the same data repeatedly.

**Query Optimization:**

Distributed query optimization: Optimize queries to minimize data transfer between nodes, use distributed query processing techniques, and select appropriate join strategies.

Query rewriting: Rewrite queries to take advantage of parallel processing capabilities in distributed databases.

**Indexing and Data Structures:**

Use appropriate indexing techniques for distributed databases, such as distributed hash indexes or global secondary indexes, to speed up data retrieval.

Choose data structures that are efficient for distributed storage and access.

**Compression and Serialization:**

Implement data compression techniques to reduce storage and network bandwidth requirements.

Use efficient serialization formats to minimize data size when transmitting between nodes.

**Replication Strategies:**

Select replication strategies carefully, considering factors like consistency requirements (e.g., strong vs. eventual consistency) and the impact on read and write operations.

**Consistency Models:**

Choose the appropriate consistency model (e.g., eventual consistency, strong consistency) based on application requirements to balance data consistency and system performance.

**Network Optimization:**

Optimize network configurations to reduce latency, such as using Content Delivery Networks (CDNs), improving network infrastructure, or using dedicated network links between nodes.

**Monitoring and Profiling:**

Implement comprehensive monitoring and profiling tools to identify performance bottlenecks, resource utilization, and query performance.

Use metrics to make informed decisions about scaling or optimizing specific parts of the distributed database.

**Scaling Strategies**:

Plan for horizontal scaling by adding more nodes or partitions as data and user loads increase.

Implement auto-scaling mechanisms to dynamically adjust the cluster size based on demand.

**Failure Handling and Recovery:**

Develop robust failover and recovery mechanisms to handle node failures gracefully without compromising data integrity.

**Security:**

Implement strong security measures to protect data during transmission and at rest. Encryption and access control are essential.

**Distributed Transaction Management:**

Use distributed transaction protocols and strategies to ensure data consistency across distributed nodes while optimizing performance.

**Database Sharding:**

Consider sharding as a strategy for horizontally partitioning data across multiple databases or clusters to distribute the workload effectively.

Optimizing a distributed database is an ongoing process that requires continuous monitoring, testing, and adjustment as data volumes and usage patterns evolve. The specific optimization strategies employed will depend on the database technology, architecture, and the unique requirements of the application.

## NoSQL Databases: Introduction, CAP Theorem, Document-Based Systems, Key-Value Stores, Column-Based Systems, Graph Databases

### Introduction

NoSQL databases, often referred to as "Not Only SQL" databases, are a category of database management systems that provide flexible and scalable data storage solutions. They are designed to address the limitations of traditional relational databases, particularly in handling large volumes of unstructured or semi-structured data and providing support for distributed computing. Here's a detailed introduction to NoSQL databases:

**Key Characteristics of NoSQL Databases:**

Schema Flexibility: Unlike relational databases, NoSQL databases do not require a fixed schema. They can handle data with varying structures, making them suitable for applications with evolving or undefined data models.

Scalability: NoSQL databases are designed to scale horizontally, which means you can add more servers or nodes to the database to accommodate increased data and traffic. This makes them ideal for web applications and big data processing.

High Performance: NoSQL databases are optimized for read and write operations, often providing low-latency access to data. They excel in scenarios where rapid data retrieval and processing are essential.

Support for Unstructured Data: NoSQL databases can store a wide range of data types, including text, JSON, XML, binary, and more. This flexibility is particularly valuable for applications dealing with multimedia, sensor data, social media posts, and user-generated content.

Distribution and Replication: NoSQL databases are designed with distributed architectures in mind. They can replicate data across multiple nodes or data centers to ensure fault tolerance and high availability. This is critical for applications with global user bases.

**Types of NoSQL Databases:**

There are several types of NoSQL databases, each tailored to specific use cases and data models:

Document-Based Databases: These databases store data in flexible, semi-structured documents, such as JSON or BSON. Each document can have its own structure, making it easy to accommodate changes in data requirements. Examples include MongoDB, Couchbase, and RavenDB.

Key-Value Stores: Key-value stores are simple data stores that use unique keys to retrieve values. They are highly performant for read and write operations and are often used for caching and real-time applications. Examples include Redis, Riak, and Amazon DynamoDB.

Column-Based Databases: Column-based databases organize data into columns rather than rows, which is especially efficient for analytical queries and aggregations. They are used in data warehousing and analytics applications. Examples include Apache Cassandra, HBase, and Amazon Redshift.

Graph Databases: Graph databases are designed for managing and querying data in the form of graphs, consisting of nodes (entities) and edges (relationships). They excel in handling complex relationships and are used in social networks, recommendation engines, and knowledge graphs. Examples include Neo4j, Amazon Neptune, and OrientDB.

**Use Cases for NoSQL Databases:**

NoSQL databases are suitable for a wide range of applications and industries, including:

Web Applications: NoSQL databases are commonly used to store user profiles, session data, and real-time data in web applications.

Big Data Processing: They are integral to big data platforms for handling large volumes of unstructured data and real-time analytics.

IoT (Internet of Things): NoSQL databases can efficiently manage sensor data from IoT devices and support real-time monitoring and analysis.

Content Management: They are used to store and manage multimedia content, documents, and metadata in content management systems (CMS).

E-commerce: NoSQL databases help in managing product catalogs, user reviews, and recommendations in e-commerce platforms.

Gaming: They are used to store user profiles, game states, and leaderboards in online gaming applications.

Social Media: NoSQL databases are critical for social networking platforms to manage user-generated content, connections, and activity feeds.

In summary, NoSQL databases provide flexibility, scalability, and high performance for handling various types of data in modern applications. Their diverse data models cater to different use cases, making them a valuable addition to the database landscape alongside traditional SQL databases. The choice between SQL and NoSQL databases depends on the specific requirements of the application.

**CAP Theorem**

The CAP theorem, originally introduced as the CAP principle, can be used to explain some of the competing requirements in a distributed system with replication. It is a tool used to make system designers aware of the trade-offs while designing networked shared-data systems.

The three letters in CAP refer to three desirable properties of distributed systems with replicated data: consistency (among replicated copies), availability (of the system for read and write operations) and partition tolerance (in the face of the nodes in the system being partitioned by a network fault).

The CAP theorem states that it is not possible to guarantee all three of the desirable properties – consistency, availability, and partition tolerance at the same time in a distributed system with data replication.

The theorem states that networked shared-data systems can only strongly support two of the following three properties:

**Consistency**

Consistency means that the nodes will have the same copies of a replicated data item visible for various transactions. A guarantee that every node in a distributed cluster returns the same, most recent and a successful write. Consistency refers to every client having the same view of the data. There are various types of consistency models. Consistency in CAP refers to sequential consistency, a very strong form of consistency.

**Availability**

Availability means that each read or write request for a data item will either be processed successfully or will receive a message that the operation cannot be completed. Every non-failing node returns a response for all the read and write requests in a reasonable amount of time. The key word here is "every". In simple terms, every node (on either side of a network partition) must be able to respond in a reasonable amount of time.

**Partition Tolerance**

Partition tolerance means that the system can continue operating even if the network connecting the nodes has a fault that results in two or more partitions, where the nodes in each partition can only communicate among each other. That means, the system continues to function and upholds its consistency guarantees in spite of network partitions. Network partitions are a fact of life. Distributed systems guaranteeing partition tolerance can gracefully recover from partitions once the partition heals.

The use of the word consistency in CAP and its use in ACID do not refer to the same identical concept.

In CAP, the term consistency refers to the consistency of the values in different copies of the same data item in a replicated distributed system. In ACID, it refers to the fact that a transaction will not violate the integrity constraints specified on the database schema.

The CAP theorem states that distributed databases can have at most two of the three properties: consistency, availability, and partition tolerance. As a result, database systems prioritize only two properties at a time.

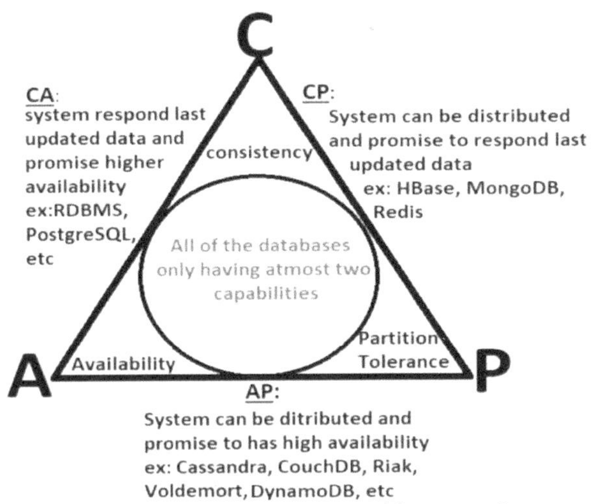


The following figure represents which database systems prioritize specific properties at a given time:

**CA (Consistency and Availability)**

The system prioritizes availability over consistency and can respond with possibly stale data.

Example databases: Cassandra, CouchDB, Riak, Voldemort.

**AP (Availability and Partition Tolerance)-**

The system prioritizes availability over consistency and can respond with possibly stale data.

The system can be distributed across multiple nodes and is designed to operate reliably even in the face of network partitions.

Example databases: Amazon DynamoDB, Google Cloud Spanner.

**CP (Consistency and Partition Tolerance)-**

The system prioritizes consistency over availability and responds with the latest updated data.

The system can be distributed across multiple nodes and is designed to operate reliably even in the face of network partitions.

Example databases: Apache HBase, MongoDB, Redis.

It's important to note that these database systems may have different configurations and settings that can change their behaviour with respect to consistency, availability, and partition tolerance. Therefore, the exact behaviour of a database system may depend on its configuration and usage.

for example, Neo4j, a graph database, the CAP theorem still applies. Neo4j prioritizes consistency and partition tolerance over availability, which means that in the event of a network partition or failure, Neo4j will sacrifice availability to maintain consistency.

**Document-Based Systems or Document Data Model**

A Document Data Model is a lot different than other data models because it stores data in JSON, BSON, or XML documents. in this data model, we can move documents under one document and apart from this, any particular elements can be indexed to run queries faster. Often documents are stored and retrieved in such a way that it becomes close to the data objects which are used in many applications which means very less translations are required to use data in applications. JSON is a native language that is often used to store and query data too.

So, in the document data model, each document has a key-value pair below is an example for the same.

```
{
"Name" : "Yashodhra",
"Address" : "Near Patel Nagar",
"Email" : "yahoo123@yahoo.com",
"Contact" : "12345"
}
```

**Working of Document Data Model:**

This is a data model which works as a semi-structured data model in which the records and data associated with them are stored in a single document which means this data model is not completely unstructured. The main thing is that data here is stored in a document.

**Features:**

Document Type Model: As we all know data is stored in documents rather than tables or graphs, so it becomes easy to map things in many programming languages.

Flexible Schema: Overall schema is very much flexible to support this statement one must know that not all documents in a collection need to have the same fields.

Distributed and Resilient: Document data models are very much dispersed which is the reason behind horizontal scaling and distribution of data.

Manageable Query Language: These data models are the ones in which query language allows the developers to perform CRUD (Create Read Update Destroy) operations on the data model.

**Examples of Document Data Models :**

Amazon DocumentDB

MongoDB

Cosmos DB

ArangoDB

Couchbase Server

CouchDB

**Advantages:**

Schema-less: These are very good in retaining existing data at massive volumes because there are absolutely no restrictions in the format and the structure of data storage.

Faster creation of document and maintenance: It is very simple to create a document and apart from this maintenance requires is almost nothing.

Open formats: It has a very simple build process that uses XML, JSON, and its other forms.

Built-in versioning: It has built-in versioning which means as the documents grow in size there might be a chance they can grow in complexity. Versioning decreases conflicts.

**Disadvantages:**

Weak Atomicity: It lacks in supporting multi-document ACID transactions. A change in the document data model involving two collections will require us to run two separate queries i.e. one for each collection. This is where it breaks atomicity requirements.

Consistency Check Limitations: One can search the collections and documents that are not connected to an author collection but doing this might create a problem in the performance of database performance.

Security: Nowadays many web applications lack security which in turn results in the leakage of sensitive data. So it becomes a point of concern, one must pay attention to web app vulnerabilities.

**Applications of Document Data Model:**

Content Management: These data models are very much used in creating various video streaming platforms, blogs, and similar services Because each is stored as a single document and the database here is much easier to maintain as the service evolves over time.

Book Database: These are very much useful in making book databases because as we know this data model lets us nest.

Catalog: When it comes to storing and reading catalog files these data models are very much used because it has a fast reading ability if incase Catalogs have thousands of attributes stored.

Analytics Platform: These data models are very much used in the Analytics Platform.

**Key-Value Stores**

Key-Value Stores are a type of NoSQL database that store data as a collection of key-value pairs. These databases are designed for simplicity, scalability, and high performance. Below, I'll explain the concept of Key-Value Stores in more detail:

**Key-Value Data Model**: In a Key-Value Store, data is organized as a set of unique keys and their associated values. Each key serves as a unique identifier for retrieving its corresponding value. This simplicity makes Key-Value Stores highly efficient for specific use cases.

**Characteristics and Features**:

Schemaless: Key-Value Stores are typically schemaless, meaning that each key-value pair can have a different structure or format. This flexibility allows you to store a wide variety of data without the constraints of a fixed schema.

High Performance: Key-Value Stores are optimized for high-speed read and write operations. They excel at simple data retrieval by key, making them ideal for caching and frequently accessed data.

Scalability: Most Key-Value Stores are designed to scale horizontally, allowing you to distribute data across multiple servers or nodes. This scalability makes them suitable for handling large amounts of data and high traffic loads.

Low Latency: Due to their efficient key-based lookup, Key-Value Stores offer low-latency data access. This makes them suitable for applications requiring real-time responsiveness.

Use Cases: Key-Value Stores are commonly used in various scenarios, including caching systems (e.g., Redis, Memcached), distributed session management, user profiles, configuration settings, and counters. They are also a fundamental building block for more complex NoSQL databases like document-oriented and column-family stores.

**Examples of Key-Value Stores:**

Redis: Redis is an in-memory Key-Value Store known for its blazing-fast performance. It supports various data types and offers features like caching, pub-sub messaging, and geospatial indexing.

Memcached: Memcached is another in-memory Key-Value Store used for caching frequently accessed data. It's simple and fast, but it lacks some of the advanced features of Redis.

Amazon DynamoDB: DynamoDB is a fully managed, highly available Key-Value Store offered by AWS. It provides seamless scalability and is suitable for a wide range of applications.

**Challenges:**

While Key-Value Stores offer many advantages, they also come with some challenges:

Limited Query Capabilities: Key-Value Stores are not well-suited for complex querying and analytics. Retrieving data based on criteria other than the key can be inefficient or impossible without additional indexing.

Data Integrity: Ensuring data consistency and integrity may require additional application-level logic because Key-Value Stores don't enforce referential integrity or complex relationships between data items.

Data Serialization: Since values in Key-Value Stores can be of various formats, proper serialization and deserialization of data are crucial.

In summary, Key-Value Stores are a type of NoSQL database that excels in simplicity, speed, and scalability. They are a valuable tool for applications that require fast and efficient data retrieval by key, but they may not be suitable for use cases that demand complex querying and transactional support.

**Column-Based Systems or Columnar Data Model**

The Columnar Data Model of NoSQL is important. NoSQL databases are different from SQL databases. This is because it uses a data model that has a different structure than the previously followed row-and-column table model used with relational database management systems (RDBMS). NoSQL databases are a flexible schema model which is designed to scale horizontally across many servers and is used in large volumes of data.

Working of Columnar Data Model:

In Columnar Data Model instead of organizing information into rows, it does in columns. This makes them function the same way that tables work in relational databases. This type of data model is much more flexible obviously because it is a type of NoSQL database. The below example will help in understanding the Columnar data model:

Row-Oriented Table:

| S.No | Name | Course | Branch | ID |
|---|---|---|---|---|
| 01 | Tanmay | B-Tech | Computer | 2 |
| 02 | Abhishek | B-Tech | Electronics | 5 |
| 03 | Samriddha | B-Tech | IT | 7 |
| 04 | Aditi | B-Tech | E & TC | 8 |

Column – Oriented Table:

| S.No | Name | ID |
|---|---|---|
| 01 | Tanmay | 2 |
| 02 | Abhishek | 5 |
| 03 | Samriddha | 7 |
| 04 | Aditi | 8 |

| S.No | Course | ID |
|---|---|---|
| 01 | B-Tech | 2 |
| 02 | B-Tech | 5 |
| 03 | B-Tech | 7 |
| 04 | B-Tech | 8 |

| S.No | Branch | ID |
|---|---|---|
| 01 | Computer | 2 |
| 02 | Electronics | 5 |
| 03 | IT | 7 |

Columnar Data Model uses the concept of keyspace, which is like a schema in relational models.

**Advantages of Columnar Data Model:**

Well structured: Since these data models are good at compression so these are very structured or well organized in terms of storage.

Flexibility: A large amount of flexibility as it is not necessary for the columns to look like each other, which means one can add new and different columns without disrupting the whole database

Aggregation queries are fast: The most important thing is aggregation queries are quite fast because a majority of the information is stored in a column. An example would be Adding up the total number of students enrolled in one year.

Scalability: It can be spread across large clusters of machines, even numbering in thousands.

Load Times: Since one can easily load a row table in a few seconds so load times are nearly excellent.

**Disadvantages of Columnar Data Model:**

Designing indexing Schema: To design an effective and working schema is too difficult and very time-consuming.

Suboptimal data loading: incremental data loading is suboptimal and must be avoided, but this might not be an issue for some users.

Security vulnerabilities: If security is one of the priorities then it must be known that the Columnar data model lacks inbuilt security features in this case, one must look into relational databases.

Online Transaction Processing (OLTP): Online Transaction Processing (OLTP) applications are also not compatible with columnar data models because of the way data is stored.

**Applications of Columnar Data Model:**

Columnar Data Model is very much used in various Blogging Platforms.

It is used in Content management systems like WordPress, Joomla, etc.

It is used in Systems that maintain counters.

It is used in Systems that require heavy write requests.

It is used in Services that have expiring usage.

**Graph Databases or Graph Data Model**

Graph databases are a specialized type of NoSQL database designed for managing and querying data that has complex relationships and connections. They are particularly well-suited for scenarios where the relationships between data points are as important as the data itself. Here's an in-depth look at graph databases:

Graph databases use a graph data model to represent and store data. In this model, data entities are represented as nodes, and the relationships between entities are represented as edges or links.

Nodes and edges can have properties or attributes associated with them, adding rich metadata to the data.

**Relationships:**

Graph databases excel in modeling and querying relationships between data entities. These relationships can be directional or bidirectional, and they can have labels or types to define their semantics.

Graph databases enable the traversal of relationships to discover patterns and insights in the data. This makes them ideal for applications involving social networks, recommendation engines, fraud detection, and more.

**Query Language:**

Graph databases typically use a specialized query language, such as Cypher (used by Neo4j) or Gremlin (used by Apache TinkerPop), designed specifically for graph operations.

These query languages allow for expressive queries that navigate the graph structure efficiently.

**Use Cases:**

Graph databases are well-suited for applications where the relationships between data elements are complex and need to be queried efficiently. Some common use cases include:

Social networks: Modeling users, friends, and interactions.

Recommendation engines: Finding connections between users and products.

Knowledge graphs: Representing and querying relationships in a knowledge base.

Fraud detection: Identifying suspicious patterns in financial transactions.

Network and IT operations: Analyzing network topology and dependencies.

**Performance and Scalability:**

Graph databases are optimized for relationship traversals and are highly performant for such operations.

They can handle large-scale graphs with millions or even billions of nodes and edges, making them suitable for both small and large datasets.

Some graph databases offer clustering and distribution capabilities to scale horizontally across multiple machines.

**Examples of Graph Databases:**

Neo4j: One of the most popular graph databases, known for its expressive query language (Cypher) and scalability.

Amazon Neptune: A managed graph database service by AWS that supports both property graph and RDF graph models.

JanusGraph: An open-source distributed graph database that supports the Apache TinkerPop query language.

**Challenges:**

While graph databases excel in handling complex relationships, they may not be the best choice for applications with primarily tabular or document-oriented data.

Storing and querying graph data can be more resource-intensive compared to other database models, especially for deep and complex traversals.

In summary, graph databases are a powerful tool for managing and querying data with intricate relationships. They provide a flexible and efficient way to model, store, and query data that involves networks, connections, and patterns.

## Database Security: Security Issues, Access Control Based on Privileges, Role-Based Access Control, SQL Injection, Statistical Database Security, Flow Control, Encryption, and Public Key Infrastructures.

### Security Issues

Database security is a critical aspect of database management systems (DBMS) to protect sensitive data from unauthorized access, tampering, or loss. Here are some key security issues in DBMS:

**Unauthorized Access:** Unauthorized users gaining access to the database can be a significant security threat. This can happen through various means, such as weak passwords, unpatched vulnerabilities, or insider threats.

**Data Breaches:** Data breaches involve the unauthorized disclosure of sensitive information. This can lead to significant financial losses, legal consequences, and damage to an organization's reputation.

**Data Tampering**: Unauthorized users may attempt to modify or delete data in the database. This can have severe consequences, especially in critical applications like financial systems or healthcare records.

**Data Theft:** Sensitive data, such as personal information, financial records, or intellectual property, can be stolen from the database and used for malicious purposes or sold on the black market.

**SQL Injection:** SQL injection attacks occur when malicious SQL statements are injected into input fields, manipulating the database query. Proper input validation and parameterized queries can help mitigate this risk.

**Inadequate Authentication and Authorization**: Weak user authentication and authorization mechanisms can allow unauthorized users to access or modify data. Role-based access control (RBAC) and strong authentication methods are essential.

**Inadequate Encryption:** Data should be encrypted both in transit and at rest. Without proper encryption, data may be vulnerable to interception or theft.

**Lack of Patch Management:** Failing to keep the DBMS software and underlying operating systems up to date with security patches can expose vulnerabilities that attackers can exploit.

**Insider Threats**: Employees or individuals with legitimate access to the database can misuse their privileges to steal data, engage in fraud, or damage the system. Monitoring and auditing can help detect insider threats.

**Data Redundancy and Backup:** Backup systems that are not secure can be compromised, leading to data loss or theft. Proper backup encryption and access controls are essential.

**Data Masking and Privacy:** Protecting sensitive data while still making it available for certain uses is a challenge. Techniques like data masking and anonymization can help strike a balance between data utility and privacy.

**Audit Logging and Monitoring:** Insufficient auditing and monitoring make it difficult to detect security incidents. Detailed audit logs and real-time monitoring are essential for identifying and responding to security threats.

**Compliance and Regulatory Requirements**: Many industries and regions have specific data security regulations (e.g., GDPR, HIPAA) that organizations must comply with. Failure to do so can result in legal consequences.

**Database Vulnerabilities:** Vulnerabilities in the database software itself can be exploited by attackers. Regular vulnerability assessments and patching are necessary to address these issues.

**Third-Party Access**: Integrations with third-party applications or services can introduce security risks. Proper authentication and authorization mechanisms should be in place for such access.

To address these security issues, organizations need to implement a comprehensive database security strategy. This includes robust access controls, encryption, regular security assessments, employee training, and a proactive incident response plan. Security should be a top priority to safeguard valuable data assets.

## Access Control Based on Privileges

Access control based on privileges is a fundamental component of database security in database management systems (DBMS). It involves defining and enforcing access rights and permissions for users and roles to ensure that they can only perform authorized actions on the database. Here's a detailed explanation of access control based on privileges:

**Users and Roles**: In a DBMS, users are individuals or entities that interact with the database. Roles are groups or categories that users can belong to. Access control is often defined at the role level to simplify management.

**Privileges:** Privileges are specific rights or permissions granted to users or roles. These privileges determine what actions users or roles can perform on database objects, such as tables, views, procedures, or schemas. Common privileges include SELECT (read), INSERT, UPDATE, DELETE, EXECUTE (for stored procedures), and CREATE (for creating objects).

**Objects**: Database objects are the structures or components within a database, such as tables, views, indexes, and stored procedures. Access control is often applied at the object level, specifying who can perform actions on each object.

**GRANT and REVOKE**: Database administrators (DBAs) use SQL commands like GRANT and REVOKE to manage privileges. GRANT assigns privileges to users or roles, while REVOKE revokes previously granted privileges. For example, a DBA can grant SELECT privileges on a specific table to a user or role.

**Ownership**: Each database object is associated with an owner, typically the user who created it. The owner automatically has full control over the object but can grant specific privileges to other users or roles. Ownership can be transferred to another user if needed.

**Access Levels**: Privileges can be granted with different levels of access control. For example, a user may have SELECT privilege on a table, but the level of access can vary, from read-only to read-write. This granularity allows fine-tuned control over data manipulation.

**Implicit vs. Explicit Privileges**: Some privileges are implicitly granted based on predefined roles or user groups. For example, a user in the "DBA" role might have administrative privileges. Explicit privileges are those specifically granted or revoked by administrators.

**Security Labels and Policies**: In some security-sensitive environments, databases use security labels and policies to control access. Data is classified based on sensitivity, and users or roles are granted access based on their security clearance and need-to-know.

**Auditing and Logging**: Access control activities, such as granting and revoking privileges, should be audited and logged. This ensures transparency and accountability in database security.

**Regular Review and Maintenance**: Access control configurations should be periodically reviewed and updated to reflect changes in user roles or security requirements. This includes removing unnecessary privileges and adjusting permissions as needed.

Access control based on privileges is crucial for protecting data integrity, confidentiality, and availability. It helps prevent unauthorized access, data breaches, and misuse of sensitive information. Properly configured access control ensures that users can only interact with the database in ways that align with their roles and responsibilities within an organization.

## Role-Based Access Control

Role-Based Access Control (RBAC) is a database security mechanism used to restrict access to database resources based on roles and privileges assigned to users. It is a vital component of database security, providing a structured and efficient way to manage access to data and functionalities within a database management system (DBMS). Here's an overview of RBAC in DBMS:

### Key Concepts in RBAC:

Roles: In RBAC, roles are defined to represent groups of users with similar responsibilities or job functions. Roles simplify user management by assigning permissions to roles rather than individual users.

Privileges: Privileges are the specific permissions or access rights granted to roles. These can include read, write, delete, execute, and other database operations.

Users: Users are individuals or entities with access to the DBMS. Users are assigned one or more roles, which determine their access to database objects.

### How RBAC Works:

Role Assignment: Users are assigned to one or more roles based on their job roles or responsibilities within the organization. For example, an employee may be assigned roles like "sales," "marketing," or "finance."

Privilege Assignment: Database administrators assign specific privileges to roles. These privileges define what actions or operations role members can perform on various database objects, such as tables, views, or stored procedures.

Role Activation: When a user logs into the DBMS, their associated roles are activated. This means that the user inherits the privileges associated with those roles during their session.

Access Control: The DBMS enforces access control based on the activated roles. Users can only perform actions and access data for which they have been granted privileges through their assigned roles. This ensures that users can only access the data and functionalities necessary for their job functions.

**Benefits of RBAC:**

Simplified Administration: RBAC simplifies user management by grouping users into roles and assigning privileges at the role level. This reduces the complexity of managing individual user permissions.

Granular Control: RBAC allows for granular control over access to database resources. Different roles can have different levels of access, ensuring that users have only the necessary permissions.

Security: RBAC enhances security by minimizing the risk of unauthorized access or data breaches. Users can't access resources beyond what is defined in their roles.

Scalability: As organizations grow, RBAC scales well because new users can be easily assigned to existing roles, and new roles can be created as needed.

**Example:**

Consider an e-commerce website's database:

Roles: Customer, Sales Representative, Database Administrator.

Privileges: Customers can view products and place orders. Sales Representatives can view and edit orders. Database Administrators have full access to all tables and functions.

A user's role assignment determines their actions within the system. A customer can browse and place orders, a sales representative can manage orders, and a database administrator has complete control over the database.

RBAC is a crucial component of maintaining data integrity and security in a DBMS, ensuring that users have appropriate access to data and functionalities while minimizing security risks.

**SQL Injection**

SQL injection is a common and dangerous database security vulnerability that occurs when an attacker is able to manipulate a web application's input to execute malicious SQL queries against the underlying database. This can lead to unauthorized access, data leakage, and even data manipulation. The SQL Injection is a code penetration technique that might cause loss to our database. It is one of the most practiced web hacking techniques to place malicious code in SQL statements, via webpage input. SQL injection can be used to manipulate the application's web server by malicious users.

SQL injection generally occurs when we ask a user to input their username/userID. Instead of a name or ID, the user gives us an SQL statement that we will unknowingly run on our database. For Example - we create a SELECT statement by adding a variable "demoUserID" to select a string. The variable will be fetched from user input (getRequestString).

demoUserI = getrequestString("UserId");

demoSQL = "SELECT * FROM users WHERE UserId =" +demoUserId;

**Types of SQL injection attacks**

SQL injections can do more harm other than passing the login algorithms. Some of the SQL injection attacks include:

Updating, deleting, and inserting the data: An attack can modify the cookies to poison a web application's database query.

It is executing commands on the server that can download and install malicious programs such as Trojans.

We are exporting valuable data such as credit card details, email, and passwords to the attacker's remote server.

Getting user login details: It is the simplest form of SQL injection. Web application typically accepts user input through a form, and the front end passes the user input to the back-end database for processing.

**Example of SQL Injection**

We have an application based on employee records. Any employee can view only their own records by entering a unique and private employee ID. We have a field like an Employee ID. And the employee enters the following in the input field:

236893238 or 1=1

It will translate to: SELECT * from EMPLOYEE where EMPLOYEE_ID == 236893238 or 1=1

The SQL code above is valid and will return EMPLOYEE_ID row from the EMPLOYEE table. The 1=1 will return all records for which this holds true. All the employee data is compromised; now, the malicious user can also similarly delete the employee records.

Example:

SELECT * from Employee where (Username == "" or 1=1) AND (Password="" or 1=1).

Now the malicious user can use the '=' operator sensibly to retrieve private and secure user information. So instead of the

query mentioned above, the following query, when exhausted, retrieve protected data, not intended to be shown to users.

SELECT * from EMPLOYEE where (Employee_name =" " or 1=1) AND (Password=" " or 1=1)

**SQL injection based on Batched SQL statements**

Several databases support batched SQL statements. It is a group of two or more SQL statements separated by semicolons.

The SQL statement given below will return all rows from the Employee table, then delete the Employee_Add table.

SELECT * From Employee; DROP Table Employee_Add

**How to detect SQL Injection attacks**

Creating a SQL Injection attack is not difficult, but even the best and good-intentioned developers make mistakes. The detection of SQL Injection is, therefore, an essential component of creating the risk of an SQL injection attack.

Web Application Firewall can detect and block basic SQL injection attacks, but we should depend on it as the sole preventive measure.

Intrusion Detection System (IDS) is both network-based and host-based. It can be tuned to detect SQL injection attacks. Network-based IDSec can monitor all connections to our database server, and flags suspicious activities. The host-based IDS can monitor web server logs and alert when something strange happens.

**Impact of SQL Injection**

The intruder can retrieve all the user-data present in the database, such as user details, credit card information, and social security numbers, and can also gain access to protected areas like the administrator portal. It is also possible to delete the user data from the tables. These days all the online shopping applications, bank transactions use back-end database servers. If the intruder can exploit SQL injection, the entire server is compromised.

**How to prevent SQL Injection attack**

We should use user authentication to validate input from the user by pre-defining length, input type, and the input field.

Restricting the access privileges of users and defining the amount of data any outsider can access from the database. Generally, the user cannot be granted permission to access everything in the database.

We should not use system administrator accounts.

**Statistical Database Security**

Statistical database security is a subfield of database security that focuses on protecting sensitive statistical information stored within a database while still allowing users to perform meaningful analyses and obtain aggregated results. The primary goal of statistical database security is to strike a balance between data privacy and data utility.

**Statistical Queries** : The queries which allow only aggregate functions such as COUNT, SUM, MIN, MAX, AVERAGE, and STANDARD DEVIATION are called statistical queries. Statistical queries are mainly used for knowing population statistics and in companies/industries to maintain their employees' database etc. Example – Consider the following examples of statistical queries where EMP_SALARY is confidential database that contains the income of each employee of company. Query-1:

```
SELECT COUNT(*)
FROM EMP_SALARY
WHERE Emp-department = '3';
```

Query-2:

```
SELECT AVG(income)
FROM EMP_SALARY
WHERE Emp-id = '2';
```

Here, the "Where" condition can be manipulated by attacker and there is chance to access income of individual employees or confidential data of employee if he knows id/name of particular employee. The possibility of accessing individual information from statistical queries is reduced by using the following measures –

Partitioning of Database – This means the records of database must be not be stored as bulk in single record. It must be divided into groups of some minimum size according to confidentiality of records. The advantage of Partitioning of database is queries can refer to any complete group or set of groups, but queries cannot access the subsets of records within a group. So, attacker can access at most one or two groups which are less private.

If no statistical queries are permitted whenever number of tuples in population specified by selection condition falls below some threshold.

Prohibit sequences of queries that refer repeatedly to same population of tuples.

**Flow Control**

Database Security means keeping sensitive information safe and prevent the loss of data. Security of data base is controlled by Database Administrator (DBA).

The following are the main control measures are used to provide security of data in databases:

Authentication

Access control

Inference control

Flow control

Database Security applying Statistical Method

Encryption

These are explained as following below.

**Authentication:**

Authentication is the process of confirmation that whether the user log in only according to the rights provided to him to perform the activities of data base. A particular user can login only up to his privilege but he can't access the other sensitive data. The privilege of accessing sensitive data is restricted by using Authentication.

By using these authentication tools for biometrics such as retina and figure prints can prevent the data base from unauthorized/malicious users.

**Access Control:**

The security mechanism of DBMS must include some provisions for restricting access to the data base by unauthorized users. Access control is done by creating user accounts and to control login process by the DBMS. So, that database access of sensitive data is possible only to those people (database users) who are allowed to access such data and to restrict access to unauthorized persons.

The database system must also keep the track of all operations performed by certain user throughout the entire login time.

**Inference Control:**

This method is known as the countermeasures to statistical database security problem. It is used to prevent the user from completing any inference channel. This method protect sensitive information from indirect disclosure.

Inferences are of two types, identity disclosure or attribute disclosure.

**Flow Control:**

This prevents information from flowing in a way that it reaches unauthorized users. Channels are the pathways for information to flow implicitly in ways that violate the privacy policy of a company are called convert channels.

**Database Security applying Statistical Method:**

Statistical database security focuses on the protection of confidential individual values stored in and used for statistical purposes and used to retrieve the summaries of values based on categories. They do not permit to retrieve the individual information.

This allows to access the database to get statistical information about the number of employees in the company but not to access the detailed confidential/personal information about the specific individual employee.

**Encryption:**

This method is mainly used to protect sensitive data (such as credit card numbers, OTP numbers) and other sensitive numbers. The data is encoded using some encoding algorithms.

An unauthorized user who tries to access this encoded data will face difficulty in decoding it, but authorized users are given decoding keys to decode data.

**Encryption**

Data Encryption is a method of preserving data confidentiality by transforming it into ciphertext, which can only be decoded using a unique decryption key produced at the time of the encryption or prior to it.Data encryption converts data into a different form (code) that can only be accessed by people who have a secret key (formally known as a decryption key) or password. Data that has not been encrypted is referred to as plaintext, and data that has been encrypted is referred to as ciphertext. Encryption is one of the most widely used and successful data protection technologies in today's corporate world.

Encryption is a critical tool for maintaining data integrity, and its importance cannot be overstated. Almost everything on the internet has been encrypted at some point.

**Importance of Data Encryption:**

The significance of encryption cannot be overstated in any way. Even though your data is stored in a standard infrastructure, it is still possible for it to be hacked. There's always the chance that data will be compromised, but with data encryption, your information will be much more secure.

Consider it this way for a moment. If your data is stored in a secure system, encrypting it before sending it out will keep it safe. Sanctioned systems do not provide the same level of protection.

So, how do you think this would play out in real life? Consider the case of a user of a company's data who has access to sensitive information while at work. The user may put the information on a portable disc and move it anywhere they choose without any encryption. If the encryptions are set in place ahead of time, the user can still copy the information, but the data will be unintelligible when they try to see it someplace else. These are the benefits of data encryption that demonstrate its genuine value.

**Types of Data Encryption:**

Symmetric Encryption

Asymmetric Encryption

Encryption is frequently used in one of two ways i.e. with a symmetric key or with an asymmetric key.

**Symmetric Key Encryption:**

There are a few strategies used in cryptography algorithms. For encryption and decryption processes, some algorithms employ a unique key. In such operations, the unique key must be secured since the system or person who knows the key has complete authentication to decode the message for reading. This approach is known as "symmetric encryption" in the field of network encryption.

**Asymmetric Key Encryption:**

Some cryptography methods employ one key for data encryption and another key for data decryption. As a result, anyone who has access to such a public communication will be unable to decode or read it. This type of cryptography, known as "public-key" encryption, is used in the majority of internet security protocols. The term "asymmetric encryption" is used to describe this type of encryption.

**States of Data Encryption:**

Data, whether it's being transferred between users or stored on a server, is valuable and must be protected at all times.

Data encryption in transit: Information that is actively traveling from one point to another, such as via the internet or over a private network, is referred to as data in transit. Data is deemed less safe when in transit due to the weaknesses of transfer techniques. End-to-end encryption encrypts data throughout transmission, guaranteeing that it remains private even if intercepted.

Encryption of data at rest: Data at rest refers to information that is not actively moving from one device to another or from one network to another, such as information stored on a hard drive, laptop, flash drive, or archived/stored in another way. Due to device security features restricting access, data at rest is often less vulnerable than data in transit, but it is still vulnerable. It also contains more valuable information, making it a more appealing target for criminals.

Data encryption at rest reduces the risk of data theft caused by lost or stolen devices, inadvertent password sharing, or accidental permission granting by increasing the time it takes to access information and providing the time required to discover data loss, ransomware attacks, remotely erased data, or changed credentials.

**Uses of Data Encryption:**

Using digital signatures, Encryption is used to prove the integrity and authenticity of the information. Digital-rights management and copy protection both require encryption.

Encryption can be used to erase data. But since data recovery tools can sometimes recover deleted data, if you encrypt the data first and then throw away the key, the only thing anyone can recover is the ciphertext, not the original data.

Data Migration is used when transferring data over a network to ensure that no one else on the network can read it.

PNs (Virtual Private Networks) uses encryption, and you should encrypt everything you store in the cloud. This can encrypt the entire hard drive as well as voice calls.

Given the importance of data security, many organizations, governments, and businesses require data to be encrypted in order to protect the company or user data. Employees will not have unauthorized access to user data as a result of this.

**Advantages of Data Encryption:**

Encryption is a low-cost solution.

Data encryption keeps information distinct from the security of the device on which it is stored. Encryption provides security by allowing administrators to store and send data via insecure channels.

Regulatory Fines Can Be Avoided With Encryption

Remote Workers Can Benefit from Encryption

If the password or key is lost, the user will be unable to open the encrypted file. Using simpler keys in data encryption, on the other hand, makes the data insecure, and anybody may access it at any time.

Encryption improves the security of our information.

Consumer Trust Can Be Boosted by Encryption

**Disadvantages of Data Encryption:**

If the password or key is lost, the user will be unable to open the encrypted file. Using simpler keys in data encryption, on the other hand, makes the data insecure, and anybody may access it at any time.

Data encryption is a valuable data security approach that necessitates a lot of resources, such as data processing, time consumption, and the use of numerous encryption and decryption algorithms. As a result, it is a somewhat costly approach.

Data protection solutions might be difficult to utilize when the user layers them for contemporary systems and applications. This might have a negative influence on the device's normal operations.

If a company fails to realize any of the restrictions imposed by encryption techniques, it is possible to set arbitrary expectations and requirements that might undermine data encryption protection.

**Examples of Data Encryption algorithms:**

Depending on the use case, there are a variety of data encryption algorithms to choose from, but the following are the most commonly used:

DES (Data Encryption Standard) is an old symmetric encryption algorithm that is no longer considered suitable for modern applications. As a result, DES has been superseded by other encryption algorithms.

Triple DES (3DES or TDES): Encrypts, decrypts, and encrypts again to create a longer key length by running the DES algorithm three times. It may be run with a single key, two keys, or three separate keys to increase security. 3DES is vulnerable to attacks such as block collisions since it uses a block cipher.

RSA is a one-way asymmetric encryption algorithm that was one of the first public-key algorithms. Because of its long key length, RSA is popular and widely used on the Internet. It is used by browsers to create secure connections over insecure networks and is part of many security protocols such as SSH, OpenPGP, S/MIME, and SSL/TLS.

Twofish is one of the fastest algorithms, with sizes of 128, 196, and 256 bits and a complex key structure for added security. It is available for free and is included in some of the best free software, including VeraCrypt, PeaZip, and KeePass, as well as the OpenPGP standard.

**Public Key Infrastructures**

Public key infrastructure or PKI is the governing body behind issuing digital certificates. It helps to protect confidential data and gives unique identities to users and systems. Thus, it ensures security in communications.

The public key infrastructure uses a pair of keys: the public key and the private key to achieve security. The public keys are prone to attacks and thus an intact infrastructure is needed to maintain them.

Managing Keys in the Cryptosystem:

The security of a cryptosystem relies on its keys. Thus, it is important that we have a solid key management system in place. The 3 main areas of key management are as follows:

A cryptographic key is a piece of data that must be managed by secure administration.

It involves managing the key life cycle which is as follows:

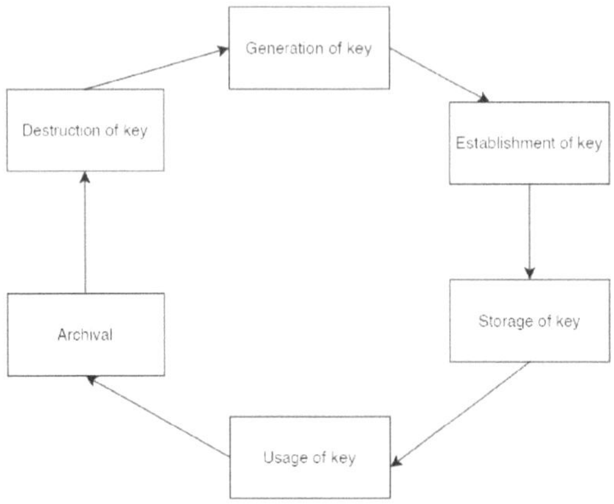


Public key management further requires:

Keeping the private key secret: Only the owner of a private key is authorized to use a private key. It should thus remain out of reach of any other person.

Assuring the public key: Public keys are in the open domain and can be publicly accessed. When this extent of public accessibility, it becomes hard to know if a key is correct and what it will be used for. The purpose of a public key must be explicitly defined.

PKI or public key infrastructure aims at achieving the assurance of public key.

**Public Key Infrastructure:**

Public key infrastructure affirms the usage of a public key. PKI identifies a public key along with its purpose. It usually consists of the following components:

A digital certificate also called a public key certificate

Private Key tokens

Registration authority

Certification authority

CMS or Certification management system

**Working on a PKI:**

Let us understand the working of PKI in steps.

PKI and Encryption: The root of PKI involves the use of cryptography and encryption techniques. Both symmetric and asymmetric encryption uses a public key. The challenge here is – "how do you know that the public key belongs to the right person or to the person you think it belongs to?". There is always a risk of MITM(Man in the middle).

This issue is resolved by a PKI using digital certificates. It gives identities to keys in order to make the verification of owners easy and accurate.

Public Key Certificate or Digital Certificate: Digital certificates are issued to people and electronic systems to uniquely identify them in the digital world. Here are a few noteworthy things about a digital certificate. Digital certificates are also called X.509 certificates. This is because they are based on the ITU standard X.509.

The Certification Authority (CA) stores the public key of a user along with other information about the client in the digital certificate. The information is signed and a digital signature is also included in the certificate.

The affirmation for the public key then thus be retrieved by validating the signature using the public key of the Certification Authority.

Certifying Authorities: A CA issues and verifies certificates. This authority makes sure that the information in a certificate is real and correct and it also digitally signs the certificate. A CA or Certifying Authority performs these basic roles:

Generates the key pairs – This key pair generated by the CA can be either independent or in collaboration with the client.

Issuing of the digital certificates – When the client successfully provides the right details about his identity, the CA issues a certificate to the client. Then CA further signs this certificate digitally so that no changes can be made to the information.

Publishing of certificates – The CA publishes the certificates so that the users can find them. They can do this by either publishing them in an electronic telephone directory or by sending them out to other people.

Verification of certificate – CA gives a public key that helps in verifying if the access attempt is authorized or not.

Revocation – In case of suspicious behavior of a client or loss of trust in them, the CA has the power to revoke the digital certificate.

**Classes of a Digital Certificate:**

A digital certificate can be divided into four broad categories. These are :

Class 1: These can be obtained by only providing the email address.

Class 2: These need more personal information.

Class 3: This first checks the identity of the person making a request.

Class 4: They are used by organizations and governments.

**Process of creation of certificate:**

The creation of a certificate takes place as follows:

Private and public keys are created.

CA requests identifying attributes of the owner of a private key.

Public key and attributes are encoded into a CSR or Certificate Signing Request.

Key owner signs that CSR to prove the possession of a private key.

CA signs the certificate after validation.

**Creation of Trust layers among CA Hierarchies:**

Each CA has its own certificate. Thus, trust is built hierarchically where one CA issues certificates to other CAs. Moreover, there is a root certificate that is self-signed. For a root CA, the issuer and the subject are not two separate parties but a single party.

**Security of Root CA:**

As you saw above, the ultimate authority is the root CA. Hence, the security of root CA is of huge importance. If the private key of a root CA is not taken care of, then it might turn into a catastrophe. This is because anyone disguised as the root CA can then issue certificates. To meet security standards, a root CA should be offline 99.9% of the time. However, it does need to come online to create public and private keys and to issue new certificates. Ideally, these activities should be performed 2-4 times a year.

**Use of PKI in Today's Digital Age:**

Today, there are an enormous number of applications that need require authentication. Certifications are needed at millions of places. This can not be done without a Public key infrastructure. The importance of PKI, depending on the use case and needs, has evolved over time. Here is a part of that track.

For the very first time during the period of 1995 to 2002, the use of PKI was limited to the most important and high-value certificates. This included the certificates of eCommerce websites that enabled them to display the lock icon in the search bar. The goal was to make consumers confident about the security and authenticity of various websites.

The second episode of PKI emerged around 2003 to 2010 when enterprises came into the picture. It was at this time that employees received laptops and the use of mobile phones was rising. Thus, employees needed access to the organization's assets even outside the office. That is when the use of PKI looked like the best way for authentication.

The third phase started in 2011 and is continuing to date. With the advent of new technologies like IoT(Internet of Things) and need the to scale PKI, the use, as well as the challenges in using PKI, have increased tremendously. Today, millions of certificates are issued to authenticate mobile workforces. However, managing this huge number of certificates is quite challenging.

S/MIME, Document Signing, code or app signing also uses PKI.

**Challenges that a PKI Solves:**

PKI owes its popularity to the various problems its solves. Some use cases of PKI are:

Securing web browsers and communicating networks by SSL/TLS certifications.

Maintaining Access Rights over Intranets and VPNs.

Data Encryption

Digitally Signed Software

Wi-fi Access Without Passwords

Other than these, one of the most important use cases of PKI is based around IoT(Internet of Things). Here are two industries that are using PKI for IoT devices:

Auto Manufacturers: Cars these days have features like GPS, call for services, assistants, etc. These require communication paths where a lot of data is passed. Making these connections secure is very important to avoid malicious parties hacking into the cars. This is where PKI comes in.

Medical device Manufacturers: Devices like surgical robots require high security. Also, FDA mandates that any next-generation medical device must be updatable so that bugs can be removed and security issues can be dealt with. PKI is used to issues certificates to such devices.

**Disadvantages of PKI:**

Speed: Since PKI uses super complex algorithms to create a secure key pair. So it eventually slows down the process and data transfer.

Private Key Compromise: Even though PKI can't be hacked very easily but a private key can be hacked by a professional hacker, since PKI uses Public and Private key to encrypt and decrypt data so with user's private key in hand and public key which is easily available the information can be decrypted easily.

## 8.4 Challenges in Modern Databases

Modern databases face several challenges due to evolving technology, data volume, and user demands. Here are some key challenges in modern databases:

**Big Data Handling:** The sheer volume, velocity, and variety of data generated today pose a significant challenge. Databases must efficiently store, process, and analyze large datasets to derive meaningful insights.

**Data Variety**: Data comes in various formats, including structured, semi-structured, and unstructured data. Modern databases need to handle this diversity and provide tools for processing different data types.

**Real-time Processing**: Users expect real-time or near-real-time data access and analysis. Databases need to support streaming data, event-driven architectures, and low-latency processing.

**Scalability:** Databases must scale horizontally to accommodate growing workloads and data volumes. Scalability often involves distributed architectures, load balancing, and sharding.

**Data Security**: With increasing cyber threats, data security is a paramount concern. Modern databases need robust authentication, authorization, encryption, and auditing mechanisms to protect sensitive data.

**Privacy Compliance**: Stringent data privacy regulations, such as GDPR and CCPA, require databases to implement features like data anonymization, consent management, and compliance reporting.

**Data Integration**: Many organizations have data stored in various databases, cloud platforms, and third-party systems. Ensuring seamless data integration and interoperability is a challenge.

**Data Quality**: Maintaining data quality and consistency is crucial. Databases need to provide tools for data cleansing, validation, and error handling.

**Complex Queries**: Users often require complex queries and analytics. Modern databases must support advanced querying capabilities, including joins, aggregations, and window functions.

**Machine Learning Integration**: Integrating machine learning models within databases for predictive analytics and recommendation systems is a challenge that many modern databases are addressing.

**Multi-cloud and Hybrid Environments**: Organizations are increasingly adopting multi-cloud and hybrid cloud strategies. Databases must support seamless data movement and management across these environments.

**Cost Management**: Cloud-based databases often involve variable costs based on usage. Managing costs while ensuring optimal performance can be challenging.

**Concurrency and Transactions**: Maintaining data consistency in distributed and concurrent environments is complex. Databases must implement effective concurrency control and transaction management.

**Database Administration**: With the proliferation of database instances, managing, monitoring, and maintaining databases at scale require automation and sophisticated management tools.

**Vendor Lock-In**: Organizations may face vendor lock-in when using cloud-based databases. Ensuring data portability and flexibility is crucial.

**Legacy Systems Integration**: Many organizations still rely on legacy databases and systems. Modern databases need to provide tools for integrating with these legacy systems.

**Energy Efficiency**: Green computing is gaining importance. Databases should be designed for energy efficiency and reduced environmental impact.

Addressing these challenges requires ongoing innovation and adaptation in the field of database management. Database vendors, open-source communities, and researchers are actively working to develop solutions that meet the evolving needs of modern applications and organizations.

## Cloud Databases: Cloud Database Services (AWS, Azure, GCP), Database as a Service (DBaaS), Scalability and High Availability in the Cloud

### Cloud Database Services (AWS, Azure, GCP)

Cloud databases are database management systems (DBMS) that are hosted and operated in a cloud computing environment. These databases offer several advantages over traditional on-premises databases, including scalability, flexibility, cost-efficiency, and ease of management. Here's a detailed overview of cloud databases:

**Types of Cloud Databases:**

Relational Databases: Cloud providers offer managed services for relational databases like MySQL, PostgreSQL, SQL Server, and Oracle. These services handle database administration tasks, such as provisioning, patching, backups, and scaling.

NoSQL Databases: Cloud platforms provide managed NoSQL database services that support various data models, including document-based (e.g., JSON or XML), key-value, column-family, and graph databases.

**Key Features and Benefits:**

Scalability: Cloud databases can easily scale up or down based on demand, ensuring optimal performance and cost-efficiency. Horizontal and vertical scaling options are available.

High Availability: Cloud database services often include built-in high availability and failover mechanisms, reducing downtime and ensuring data reliability.

Managed Services: Cloud providers handle routine database management tasks like software updates, security patches, backups, and monitoring, allowing businesses to focus on application development.

Global Reach: Cloud databases can be deployed in data centers worldwide, enabling low-latency access to data for users across different regions.

Security: Cloud providers offer robust security features, including encryption, identity and access management, and compliance certifications to protect data.

Cost Efficiency: Pay-as-you-go pricing models help organizations manage costs effectively, as they only pay for the resources they use.

Backup and Disaster Recovery: Cloud databases typically offer automated backup and disaster recovery solutions to safeguard data against unexpected events.

**Examples of Cloud Database Services:**

Amazon Web Services (AWS):

Amazon RDS (Relational Database Service): AWS RDS offers managed relational database engines like MySQL, PostgreSQL, MariaDB, Oracle, and Microsoft SQL Server. It handles routine database tasks such as patching, backups, and scaling while ensuring high availability.

Amazon Aurora: Aurora is a high-performance, MySQL and PostgreSQL-compatible relational database engine. It offers greater scalability and performance compared to traditional databases.

Amazon DynamoDB: DynamoDB is a NoSQL database service designed for fast and predictable performance at any scale. It is suitable for applications that require seamless scaling and low-latency data access.

Amazon Redshift: Redshift is a fully managed data warehousing service that allows you to run complex analytical queries on large datasets. It's optimized for high-performance data analytics.

Amazon Neptune: Neptune is a fully managed graph database service. It's designed for building applications that require highly connected datasets, such as social networks and recommendation engines.

Microsoft Azure:

Azure SQL Database: Azure SQL Database offers a fully managed relational database service compatible with SQL Server. It provides high availability, security, and scalability.

Azure Cosmos DB: Cosmos DB is a globally distributed NoSQL database service that supports multiple data models, including document, key-value, graph, and column-family.

Azure Synapse Analytics: Formerly known as SQL Data Warehouse, Azure Synapse Analytics is a data warehousing service for running analytics queries at scale.

Azure Database for MySQL and PostgreSQL: These services offer fully managed open-source relational database engines, providing high availability, security, and scalability.

Azure Cache for Redis: Azure Cache for Redis is an in-memory data store service that provides high-speed data access for applications.

Google Cloud Platform (GCP):

Google Cloud SQL: Cloud SQL offers managed relational database services for MySQL, PostgreSQL, and SQL Server. It includes automated backups, high availability, and security features.

Google Cloud Bigtable: Bigtable is a NoSQL, scalable database service designed for handling large analytical and operational workloads.

Google Cloud Firestore: Firestore is a serverless, NoSQL document database for building web, mobile, and server applications. It offers real-time data synchronization and offline support.

Google Cloud Spanner: Spanner is a globally distributed, horizontally scalable, and strongly consistent database service that combines the best of both relational and NoSQL databases.

Google Cloud Datastore: Datastore is a NoSQL database service designed for web and mobile applications. It provides automatic scaling and high availability.

**Use Cases:**

Web Applications: Cloud databases are commonly used for web applications due to their scalability and global reach. They can handle dynamic workloads and sudden traffic spikes.

Analytics: Data warehousing services in the cloud, such as Amazon Redshift and Azure Synapse Analytics, are ideal for running complex analytical queries on large datasets.

IoT and Big Data: Cloud databases can store and process vast amounts of data generated by IoT devices and big data applications.

Development and Testing: Developers often use cloud databases for development, testing, and staging environments, reducing the need for on-premises infrastructure.

Hybrid and Multi-Cloud: Organizations with hybrid or multi-cloud strategies can leverage cloud databases to centralize data management across environments.

**Challenges:**

Data Transfer Costs: Moving large volumes of data to and from the cloud can incur additional costs, especially when dealing with high-speed or low-latency requirements.

Data Lock-In: Organizations must consider data portability and potential lock-in when choosing a cloud database provider.

Security and Compliance: Ensuring data security and compliance with industry regulations is crucial when storing sensitive information in the cloud.

Cloud databases have become a fundamental component of modern application architectures, offering the flexibility and scalability needed to support today's dynamic and data-intensive applications. However, organizations should carefully evaluate their requirements and choose the right cloud database service that aligns with their needs and budget.

**Database as a Service (DBaaS)**

Database as a Service (DBaaS) is a cloud computing offering that provides database management and hosting as a fully managed service. In a DBaaS model, cloud service providers handle most, if not all, of the database-related tasks, including provisioning, configuration, maintenance, security, backups, and scaling. Users can access and use the database without worrying about the underlying infrastructure or administrative responsibilities.

**Key Characteristics and Features:**

Managed Service: DBaaS providers handle routine database administration tasks, such as patching, updates, backups, and performance optimization. This allows organizations to focus on their applications and data rather than database management.

Scalability: DBaaS solutions offer the flexibility to scale database resources up or down based on demand. This scalability is crucial for handling varying workloads and accommodating growth.

Multi-Tenancy: DBaaS platforms are typically designed to support multiple tenants or customers on shared infrastructure. Each tenant's data is logically isolated from others, ensuring data security and privacy.

Automated Backup and Recovery: DBaaS providers offer automated backup and disaster recovery solutions to protect data from loss or corruption. Users can easily restore data to a previous state.

Security: Security features, including encryption, access control, authentication, and compliance certifications, are integral to DBaaS offerings, ensuring the protection of sensitive data.

High Availability: Many DBaaS solutions include high availability features, such as failover and redundancy, to minimize downtime and ensure continuous access to data.

Cost-Efficiency: DBaaS models often use a pay-as-you-go pricing structure, allowing organizations to manage costs more effectively by paying only for the resources and services they use.

**How does DBaaS work?**

It is a service that is added to our databases which make our daily tasks easier. It eliminates tedious and time-consuming administration tasks and makes our tasks simpler and more flexible. Now most of the organizations are going for DBaaS as it helps organizations to accelerate their business performance by starting their working with database more easily and running the workloads without delay.

Once we move our database to the cloud, we have the option to add software deployment as a service. Doing so simplifies the processes required to make information available through Internet-based communications. Storage consolidation can also be useful for moving company databases to the cloud.

**Benefits of DBaaS:**

Reduced Administrative Overhead: Organizations can offload the burden of database administration to the DBaaS provider, freeing up IT resources for more strategic tasks.

Faster Time to Market: DBaaS accelerates the development and deployment of applications by eliminating the need to set up and configure database infrastructure manually.

Scalability: Organizations can easily scale their databases as their needs change, avoiding the upfront costs and complexity associated with traditional database scaling.

Global Reach: DBaaS providers often have data centers in multiple regions, enabling low-latency access to data for users worldwide.

Data Security: DBaaS providers invest in robust security measures, making it easier for organizations to comply with data protection regulations.

**Disadvantages of DBaaS:**

Traditional enterprises may have objections to cloud-based services generally.

In case of significant failure of the DBaaS server or network, the organization might lose its knowledge.

Companies already equipped with resources and IT-related human resources might not realize DBaaS solutions economically viable.

Intrinsic network connected problems with cloud can impact the performance of a DBaaS.

Features offered within the typical RDBMS might not perpetually be offered during a DBaaS system.

The use of DBaaS may result in revenue loss in alternative areas of code updates and hardware management.

**Common DBaaS Providers:**

Amazon Web Services (AWS): Amazon RDS, Amazon Aurora, Amazon DynamoDB.

Microsoft Azure: Azure SQL Database, Azure Cosmos DB, Azure Database for MySQL/PostgreSQL.

Google Cloud Platform (GCP): Google Cloud SQL, Google Cloud Firestore, Google Cloud Bigtable.

Oracle Cloud: Oracle Autonomous Database.

IBM Cloud: Db2 on Cloud.

**Use Cases:**

Web Applications: DBaaS is widely used for web applications and e-commerce platforms due to its scalability and ease of management.

Development and Testing: Developers can quickly provision database instances for testing and development, reducing lead times.

Analytics: DBaaS offerings include data warehousing solutions for running complex analytical queries.

IoT and Mobile Apps: DBaaS supports applications that handle large volumes of data generated by IoT devices and mobile apps.

Hybrid and Multi-Cloud: Organizations with hybrid or multi-cloud strategies can use DBaaS to centralize database management.

While DBaaS offers many benefits, organizations should carefully consider factors such as data sovereignty, compliance requirements, and vendor lock-in when adopting a DBaaS solution. Proper planning and due diligence are essential to ensure that a chosen DBaaS offering aligns with the organization's needs and goals.

## Scalability

Scalability in cloud databases refers to the ability of a database system to handle an increasing volume of data, workload, or users while maintaining acceptable performance levels. It is a critical aspect of cloud-based database solutions, as it allows organizations to adapt to changing demands without significant disruptions or performance degradation. Here are the key aspects of scalability in cloud databases:

**Vertical Scalability (Scaling Up):** Vertical scalability involves increasing the capacity of a single database server by adding more resources, such as CPU, RAM, or storage. In a cloud environment, this can be achieved by resizing the virtual machine or instance hosting the database. Vertical scaling is suitable for handling increased workloads up to a certain point but may have limitations regarding cost and scalability beyond a certain threshold.

**Horizontal Scalability (Scaling Out):** Horizontal scalability is achieved by distributing the database workload across multiple database servers or nodes. Each node operates independently, and data is partitioned or replicated across these nodes. This approach allows for virtually unlimited scalability and improved fault tolerance. Cloud databases are well-suited for horizontal scaling, as cloud providers offer services that support automatic load balancing and scaling based on demand.

**Data Sharding:** Data sharding is a technique used to horizontally partition data across multiple database instances or shards. Each shard stores a portion of the data, and a centralized management system routes queries to the appropriate shard. Data sharding is particularly effective for distributing large datasets and handling read and write operations in a distributed manner.

**Elasticity:** Elasticity refers to the ability to dynamically allocate or deallocate resources based on real-time demand. Cloud databases can automatically scale up or down in response to workload fluctuations. This ensures that organizations pay only for the resources they use and helps maintain optimal performance during peak usage.

**Read and Write Scaling:** Many cloud databases support separate read and write replicas. Read replicas allow for distributing read queries to multiple nodes, improving read performance and reducing the load on the primary database. Write scaling involves distributing write operations across multiple nodes or using techniques like write-ahead logging (WAL) to optimize write performance.

**Load Balancing:** Load balancers distribute incoming database requests evenly across multiple database instances or replicas. Cloud providers often offer load balancing services that can automatically route traffic to healthy database nodes. Load balancing helps ensure that no single database node becomes a performance bottleneck.

**Auto-Scaling Policies:** Cloud database services typically allow users to define auto-scaling policies based on various metrics, such as CPU utilization, query latency, or the number of active connections. When a specified threshold is reached, the system can automatically add or remove resources as needed.

**Global Distribution:** Some cloud databases offer global distribution capabilities, allowing data to be replicated across multiple regions or data centers. This ensures low-latency access to data for users worldwide and enhances fault tolerance.

**Caching and Content Delivery Networks (CDNs):** To further enhance performance, organizations can employ caching mechanisms and CDNs to reduce the load on the database. Frequently accessed data can be cached closer to end-users, reducing the need for database queries.

**Database as a Service (DBaaS):** Cloud-based database services, such as Amazon RDS, Azure SQL Database, or Google Cloud SQL, often include built-in scalability features, making it easier for organizations to manage and scale their databases without the need for extensive manual configuration.

Scalability is crucial for modern applications and services that need to handle variable workloads and growing data volumes. Cloud databases provide the flexibility and tools needed to achieve scalability efficiently, allowing organizations to scale their infrastructure in line with their evolving requirements. Proper planning, monitoring, and optimization are essential for effectively managing scalable cloud databases.

## High Availability in the Cloud

High availability (HA) in the cloud is a critical aspect of ensuring that databases and applications remain accessible and operational with minimal downtime. It is achieved through various strategies and technologies designed to eliminate single points of failure and maintain continuous service availability. Here are key considerations and methods for achieving high availability in the cloud for database management systems (DBMS):

**Redundancy**: Redundancy involves duplicating critical components of your database infrastructure to ensure that if one component fails, another can take over seamlessly. Cloud providers offer various redundancy options, such as:

Multi-Availability Zone Deployment: Deploying your database across multiple availability zones within a cloud region ensures that if one zone experiences an outage, the others can continue serving traffic.

Replication: Implementing database replication, where data is copied to multiple instances, can provide redundancy. Some databases support asynchronous replication, while others offer synchronous replication for higher consistency.

Auto-Failover: Leveraging cloud services that provide automatic failover, such as Amazon RDS Multi-AZ or Azure SQL Database auto-failover groups, can help ensure minimal downtime during a database instance failure.

**Load Balancing**: Load balancers distribute incoming traffic across multiple instances or replicas of your database. This helps in ensuring that no single database instance becomes overwhelmed, improving both availability and performance.

**Monitoring and Alerting**: Implement comprehensive monitoring and alerting systems to continuously assess the health and performance of your database. Cloud providers often offer monitoring services that can trigger alerts based on predefined thresholds or anomalies.

**Backup and Restore**: Regularly back up your database and store backups in a secure, off-site location. Cloud providers offer backup services with automated backup scheduling and retention policies. In case of a failure, you can quickly restore data from these backups.

**Database as a Service (DBaaS):** Consider using managed database services provided by cloud providers. These services often include built-in high availability features, such as automated failover, backup, and monitoring.

**Disaster Recovery**: Develop a disaster recovery plan that includes procedures for data recovery and service restoration in case of a major outage, data corruption, or catastrophic events. Implementing disaster recovery across multiple regions can provide additional resilience.

**Global Distribution**: For applications with a global user base, use cloud providers' global distribution capabilities to replicate data and services across multiple regions. This ensures that users can access resources from the nearest geographical location, reducing latency and improving availability.

**Failover Testing**: Regularly conduct failover testing to ensure that your high availability configurations work as expected. This helps identify and address any issues before they impact production environments.

**Scaling**: Be prepared to scale your database infrastructure horizontally or vertically as needed to handle increased workloads. Cloud environments provide the flexibility to scale resources dynamically based on demand.

**Security**: Implement robust security measures to protect your database from unauthorized access, data breaches, and other security threats. This includes strong authentication, encryption, and access controls.

**Service-Level Agreements (SLAs)**: Review the SLAs provided by your cloud provider for the services you use. Ensure that they align with your availability requirements and consider implementing additional redundancy if needed to meet your desired SLA.

**Continuous Improvement**: Continuously assess and refine your high availability strategies based on evolving business needs, changes in technology, and lessons learned from past incidents.

High availability in the cloud is a combination of proactive planning, redundancy, monitoring, and rapid response. By implementing these strategies and leveraging cloud provider services, organizations can maintain reliable and resilient database systems that minimize downtime and ensure uninterrupted access to data and applications.

**Exercise**

**Exercise 1 – MCQ**

Q 1. What is one of the main challenges in dealing with big data in modern databases?

A) Limited storage capacity

B) Slow network speeds

C) Data privacy concerns

D) Scalability and performance

Q 2. Which cloud service model provides the highest level of control and customization over the database environment?

A) Infrastructure as a Service (IaaS)

B) Platform as a Service (PaaS)

C) Software as a Service (SaaS)

D) Database as a Service (DBaaS)

**Exercise 2 – True/ False**

Q 1. Distributed databases are always faster and more reliable than centralized databases.

Q 2. Encryption is a security measure used in database security to protect data at rest, in transit, and during processing.

**Exercise 3 – One word answer**

Q 1. What is a common feature of distributed databases?

Q 2. In NoSQL databases, what does "CAP" refer to in the CAP theorem?

**Exercise 4 – Small answer**

Q 1. What is a key characteristic of a Distributed Database System?

Q 2. What is a benefit of using Cloud Databases for businesses?

**Exercise 5 – Long answer**

Q 1. Explain the Role of Indexing and Hashing in Database Management Systems (DBMS).

Q 2. Compare and Contrast Different File Organization Techniques in Database Systems.

**Answer**

**Exercise 1**

Answer 1: D), 2: A)

**Exercise 2**

Answer 1: False, 2: True

**Exercise 3**

Answer 1: Scalability., 2: Consistency, Availability, and Partition tolerance.

**Previous Years Questions**

Q1. How client server databases differ from Distributed Databases? Explain with the help of an example (IGNOU MCA 2011)

Q2. Explain the horizontal and vertical data fragmentation, with examples. (IGNOU MCA 2011)

Q3. Explain the following: Data Replication (IGNOU MCA 2011)

Q4. Write down the advantages and disadvantages of distributed DBMS. (IGNOU MCA 2012)

Q5. What is a fragment of a relation? What are the main types of fragments? Why is fragmentation used in distributed Database Design? (IGNOU MCA 2012)

Q6. Discuss the different types of fragmentation in distributed databases with the help of an example. (IGNOU MCA 2013)

Q7. Explain briefly advantages and disadvantages of Distributed Database Management Systems. (IGNOU MCA 2014)

Q8. What is Data Fragmentation ? Explain differences between Horizontal Fragmentation and vertical Fragmentation with the help of suitable example of each. (IGNOU MCA 2014 & 2021)

Q9. plain the need of Distributed DBMS over Centralized DBMS. Also give the structure of Distributed DBMS. (IGNOU MCA 2014)

Q10.Write short notes on the following: Data fragmentation in Distributed databases and Data Replication in Distributed Databases. (IGNOU MCA 2015)

Q11. With the help of an example, explain client server databases. How are they different from distributed databases? (IGNOU MCA 2016)

Q12. Compare and contrast the Distributed databases with the Centralised databases. (IGNOU MCA 2016& 2021)

Q13. Write short notes on the following : Distributed DBMS. (IGNOU MCA 2016)

Q14. With the help of an example, explain the process of vertical fragmentation. (IGNOU MCA 2019)

Q15. Explain the following terms with suitable example : (i) Lossless decomposition (ii) Dependency preserving decomposition. (IGNOU MCA 2020)

Q16. What are the advantages and disadvantages of distributed databases ? (IGNOU MCA 2021)

Q17. Explain Distributed database architecture. (Mumbai University MCA 2023)

**Previous Years Questions with Answer**

Q1 Explain the distributed database design concepts and its components. (RU BCA 2022)

**Answer:**

Designing a distributed database involves the creation and organization of a database system that is distributed across multiple locations or nodes. The goal is to efficiently and effectively manage data across a distributed environment while ensuring data consistency, availability, and fault tolerance. Distributed database design concepts and components include:

**Data Distribution**:

Deciding how data will be distributed across different nodes or sites is a crucial design concept. This involves partitioning the database into smaller fragments and determining which fragments should reside on each node. Data can be distributed using techniques like horizontal partitioning (data distribution by rows) and vertical partitioning (data distribution by columns).

**Data Replication**:

Data replication involves creating duplicate copies of data on multiple nodes to improve data availability and fault tolerance. Replication can be either full replication (all data is copied to all nodes) or partial replication (only specific data subsets are copied).

**Data Transparency**:

Data transparency is the ability to access data without needing to be aware of its distribution or location. Transparency can be achieved through various means, such as location transparency (the user doesn't need to know the physical location of data), naming transparency (using consistent names for data across nodes), and replication transparency (the user doesn't need to know if data is replicated).

**Data Consistency**:

Ensuring data consistency in a distributed database is challenging. It involves mechanisms for maintaining a consistent view of data across all nodes, even in the presence of concurrent updates. Techniques like two-phase commit protocols, quorum-based algorithms, and conflict resolution strategies help maintain data consistency.

**Concurrency Control**:

Managing concurrent access to data in a distributed environment is essential. Distributed systems use techniques like locking, timestamp ordering, and distributed transactions to control concurrent access while preserving data integrity.

**Data Fragmentation and Allocation**:

Deciding how to fragment data and allocate fragments to specific nodes is a fundamental aspect of distributed database design. It involves determining which data should be stored together to optimize query performance and minimize data transfer.

**Query Optimization**:

Distributed query optimization aims to improve query performance in a distributed database. This involves strategies like data placement optimization, data transfer reduction, and query parallelization.

**Data Availability and Reliability**:

Ensuring data availability and reliability is a critical concern. This includes strategies for fault tolerance, data recovery, and redundancy to minimize the impact of node failures.

**Data Access Transparency**:

Providing access transparency means that users can access data across the distributed database without needing to be aware of the underlying distribution and location. Techniques such as global schema and distributed query processing help achieve this transparency.

**Data Security and Privacy**:

Designing security mechanisms to protect data in a distributed environment is essential. Access control, encryption, and authentication are critical components of ensuring data security and privacy.

**Data Migration and Synchronization**:

When data distribution needs to be modified, data migration and synchronization techniques are employed to move data between nodes, ensuring data consistency and correctness during the process.

**Network and Communication Considerations**:

The design must take into account the network infrastructure and communication protocols used for data transfer between nodes. Bandwidth, latency, and network reliability are important factors.

**Data Recovery and Backup**:

Implementing data recovery and backup strategies is essential to protect data against data loss, hardware failures, and other disasters. This includes regular data backup and disaster recovery planning.

**Global Schema and Schema Integration**:

In a distributed environment with multiple databases, creating a global schema and resolving schema integration challenges are necessary for query processing and data consistency.

**Metadata Management**:

Managing metadata, which describes the structure and organization of data across the distributed system, is crucial for data access, query optimization, and data integration.

Distributed database design is a complex and multifaceted process that requires careful planning and consideration of various factors. The specific design decisions made depend on the organization's requirements, the nature of the data, the distribution of users, and the available technology. Effective design ensures that data remains accessible, consistent, and secure in a distributed environment.

Q2 Explain the difference between distributed database and client server architecture.(RU BCA 2022)

**Answer:**

Distributed databases and client-server architectures are both approaches used in information systems, but they serve different purposes and have distinct characteristics. Here are the key differences between distributed databases and client-server architectures:

**Distributed Database**:

**Data Distribution**:

In a distributed database, data is distributed across multiple nodes or sites, often geographically separated. Each node manages its portion of the database.

**Data Management**:

Each node in a distributed database can act as a self-sufficient database management system, capable of managing its data independently.

**Data Sharing**:

Distributed databases are designed for sharing data across multiple locations. Users can access and modify data from any node, and data can be distributed for redundancy or performance reasons.

**Data Consistency**:

Ensuring data consistency in a distributed database is challenging and typically involves mechanisms such as distributed transactions, two-phase commit protocols, and data replication.

**Scalability**:

Distributed databases are often used to handle large volumes of data and accommodate data growth. They are suitable for complex data management scenarios.

**Data Transparency**:

Data transparency is a key feature in distributed databases, where users are shielded from the complexity of data distribution and location.

**Client-Server Architecture**:

**Data Access Model**:

In a client-server architecture, client applications communicate with a central server to request and manipulate data. The server is responsible for processing client requests and managing data.

**Data Management**:

Data management in a client-server architecture is typically centralized, with the server being responsible for data storage, retrieval, and management. Clients are responsible for presentation and user interaction.

**Data Sharing**:

Data sharing is facilitated through the server. Clients request data from the server, which retrieves and sends the data to the clients. Multiple clients can access the same server.

**Data Consistency**:

Data consistency is usually easier to achieve in a client-server architecture because data management is centralized. The server can enforce consistency rules and maintain data integrity.

**Scalability**:

While client-server architectures can be scaled to a certain extent, they may face limitations as the number of clients and data requests increases. Scaling often involves enhancing the server's hardware or deploying multiple servers.

**Data Transparency**:

Data transparency in client-server architectures is typically lower than in distributed databases. Clients need to be aware of the server's location and the data access protocols used.

**Key Considerations**:

Distributed databases are designed for scenarios where data needs to be distributed across multiple locations, and data sharing and redundancy are essential.

Client-server architectures are typically used for centralized data management and client-server communication, where data can be efficiently managed by a single server.

Distributed databases can be more complex to design, implement, and maintain due to the challenges of data distribution and consistency.

Client-server architectures are simpler to set up and manage, making them suitable for many common application scenarios.

Q3 Define distributed database. (RU BCA 2021)

**Answer:**

A **distributed database** is a database system in which data is stored and managed across multiple physical or logical locations or nodes, typically connected through a network. This architecture allows organizations to efficiently manage and access data in a distributed and decentralized manner. In a distributed database, the data can be spread across different geographical locations, making it accessible to users and applications from various locations.

Key characteristics and features of distributed databases include:

**Data Distribution**: Data in a distributed database is partitioned or distributed across different nodes or sites. Each node may store a portion of the data, and the data can be organized based on various distribution strategies.

**Data Transparency**: Distributed databases often provide data transparency, which means that users can access and manipulate data without needing to be aware of the physical location of the data. The distribution details are hidden from users and applications.

**Data Consistency**: Maintaining data consistency in a distributed database is a significant challenge. Techniques like distributed transactions, two-phase commit protocols, and data replication are used to ensure that data remains consistent across all nodes.

**Data Sharing**: Distributed databases are designed for data sharing among users and applications in multiple locations. This enables collaboration and data access across an organization or network.

**Data Access**: Users and applications can access data from any node in the distributed database, provided they have the necessary permissions and access rights. Data retrieval may involve accessing data from different nodes.

**Scalability**: Distributed databases are often chosen to handle large volumes of data and to accommodate data growth. The architecture is suitable for organizations with evolving data needs.

**Fault Tolerance**: Distributed databases often include mechanisms to ensure data availability and fault tolerance. Redundancy, data backup, and recovery strategies are used to minimize the impact of node failures.

**Network Considerations**: The network connecting the distributed nodes plays a crucial role in data communication and coordination. Network performance, bandwidth, and reliability are important considerations.

**Global Schema**: In some distributed databases, a global schema is defined to provide a unified view of the data, allowing users to interact with the data as if it were centralized.

Distributed databases are commonly used in scenarios where data needs to be accessible to users and applications across different geographical locations or organizational units. They offer flexibility, improved data availability, and the ability to leverage resources from multiple locations. However, they also introduce complexity in terms of data distribution, consistency, and management. Proper design, architecture, and data distribution strategies are essential for effective distributed database implementation.

Q4 Write short note: (RU BCA 2021)

Distributed transactions

**Answer:**

**Distributed Transactions**

Distributed transactions are a fundamental concept in the realm of distributed databases and information systems. A distributed transaction is a unit of work or a series of operations that involve the modification or retrieval of data across multiple nodes or sites within a distributed database. These transactions ensure that data remains consistent, reliable, and recoverable, even in a geographically dispersed environment.

Key characteristics and concepts related to distributed transactions include:

**Atomicity**: Distributed transactions adhere to the ACID properties (Atomicity, Consistency, Isolation, Durability). Atomicity ensures that a transaction is treated as a single, indivisible unit. All its operations either complete successfully, or if an error occurs, the entire transaction is rolled back, and no changes are applied to the database. This guarantees data consistency.

**Consistency**: Distributed transactions maintain data consistency. The database is brought from one consistent state to another consistent state after the execution of a transaction, ensuring that integrity constraints are not violated.

**Isolation**: Isolation ensures that concurrent transactions do not interfere with each other. Distributed transactions use various isolation levels to control the visibility of changes made by one transaction to other transactions running concurrently.

**Durability**: Durability ensures that once a distributed transaction is committed, its changes are permanently stored and will survive system failures. Even in the event of a node or system failure, the database will recover to a consistent state.

**Two-Phase Commit (2PC)**: Distributed transactions often employ the two-phase commit protocol to coordinate the commit or rollback of a transaction across multiple nodes. The 2PC protocol ensures that all nodes reach a consensus before a transaction is committed.

**Concurrency Control**: Concurrency control mechanisms, such as locking and timestamp ordering, are used to manage concurrent access to data by multiple transactions, preventing conflicts and ensuring data integrity.

**Distributed Locking**: Distributed transactions often require distributed locking to ensure that multiple transactions do not access or modify the same data concurrently. Locks are managed across nodes.

**Replication and Data Distribution**: In a distributed database, data may be replicated or distributed across nodes. Distributed transactions must handle data access and modifications in such scenarios.

Q5discuss distributed query processing. (RU BCA 2021, 2019)

**Answer:**

**Distributed query processing** is the process of executing queries on a distributed database system, where data is stored across multiple nodes or sites. This complex and critical task involves retrieving, processing, and combining data from various nodes to satisfy a user's query. Distributed query processing is necessary for ensuring that users can access and analyze data seamlessly in a distributed environment. Here are the key aspects of distributed query processing:

**Query Optimization**:

Query optimization in a distributed database involves finding the most efficient way to execute a query. This includes determining the order in which operations should be performed, the use of indexes, and minimizing data transfer between nodes.

**Query Decomposition**:

Queries are often decomposed into subqueries that can be executed on different nodes independently. This decomposition is essential for parallel execution and data retrieval from distributed sources.

**Data Localization**:

To optimize query performance, the distributed query processor may strive to localize data access. If a query involves multiple nodes, it may attempt to execute as much of the query as possible on a single node to reduce data transfer overhead.

**Query Routing and Distribution**:

The distributed query processor determines which nodes need to be involved in the query execution based on query predicates and data distribution. It routes the subqueries to the appropriate nodes.

**Data Transfer and Communication**:

Data transfer between nodes is a significant consideration in distributed query processing. Minimizing data transfer reduces network overhead and improves query performance. Techniques like predicate pushdown and filtering are used to limit the data transferred.

**Parallel Processing**:

Distributed query processing often involves parallel execution of subqueries on multiple nodes to improve performance. Parallelism can significantly speed up query processing, especially for complex queries.

**Global Schema Mapping**:

In a distributed environment with multiple databases, global schema mapping is used to reconcile differences in data structure and attribute names across nodes. This ensures that queries are understandable and executable across the distributed system.

**Data Aggregation and Join Processing**:

Distributed query processing must handle operations like aggregation and joins that require data from multiple nodes. Techniques like distributed hash joins and distributed aggregation are used to efficiently process such operations.

**Load Balancing**:

Load balancing ensures that the workload is distributed evenly across nodes to prevent performance bottlenecks. The distributed query processor may redirect queries or data retrieval to less busy nodes.

**Data Caching**:

To reduce data transfer and improve response times, distributed query processors often implement data caching strategies. Frequently accessed data can be cached locally to reduce the need for repeated remote data retrieval.

**Distributed Query Languages**:

Special query languages and extensions (e.g., SQL extensions for distributed databases) are used to express distributed queries and take advantage of distributed features and optimizations.

**Consistency Management**:

Ensuring data consistency is a critical aspect of distributed query processing. Techniques like distributed transactions and locking mechanisms are used to manage data consistency when multiple nodes are involved in a query.

Q6 What is distribution database system? Explain types of distribution system. (RU BCA 2016)

**Answer:**

A **distributed database system** is a database management system (DBMS) that stores data across multiple sites or nodes, often geographically dispersed, and allows users and applications to access and manipulate this data seamlessly. It offers several advantages, such as improved data availability, fault tolerance, and the ability to distribute data where it's needed. There are several types of distribution systems:

**Homogeneous Distributed Database**:

In a homogeneous distribution system, all the DBMS software at different sites is the same, and the data model is consistent across all nodes. This means that all nodes use the same DBMS product and have the same database schema. Homogeneous distribution simplifies data sharing and management.

**Heterogeneous Distributed Database**:

A heterogeneous distribution system consists of multiple DBMS products, often from different vendors, at different sites. This type of distribution is more complex because it involves data integration across diverse DBMS platforms. Middleware or data translation mechanisms are often used to facilitate communication and data access between heterogeneous systems.

**Federated Database**:

In a federated database system, each site maintains its own local database, and a central component known as the federator provides a unified view of the data across all sites. Users interact with the federator, which coordinates queries and data retrieval from the individual databases. Federated databases can be heterogeneous, with different DBMS products at each site.

**Replicated Database**:

In a replicated database system, data is duplicated and stored at multiple sites or nodes. This duplication provides data redundancy and improves data availability and fault tolerance. Replication can be full, where all data is copied to all nodes, or partial, where only specific data subsets are replicated.

**Partitioned Database**:

In a partitioned database, the data is divided into partitions or fragments, and each partition is stored at a different site. This approach is often used to improve data access and distribution. Data partitioning can be horizontal (partitioning by rows) or vertical (partitioning by columns).

**Client-Server Distribution**:

In a client-server distribution system, data is managed by a central server, and client applications communicate with this server to request and manipulate data. The clients interact with the server to access data, but the data remains centralized.

**Multidatabase System**:

A multidatabase system involves multiple databases, each with its own DBMS, connected to provide a unified view of data. Users can access and query data from various databases as if they were a single, integrated database.

**Mobile and Edge Databases**:

In the context of distributed systems, mobile and edge databases are used to manage and store data on mobile devices or edge computing devices. These databases enable local data processing and storage, reducing the need for constant communication with a centralized server.

**Cloud-Based Databases**:

Cloud-based databases are hosted on cloud computing platforms and can be accessed from anywhere with an internet connection. Users and applications can interact with the database in the cloud, making data distribution seamless and scalable.

**Peer-to-Peer Databases**:

Peer-to-peer databases allow data to be distributed and shared directly between nodes (peers) without a central server. These systems are often used in decentralized and distributed networks.

Q7 Give four features of Object-Oriented Databases. (RU BCA 2018)

**Answer:**

Object-oriented databases (OODBs) are database systems designed to store, retrieve, and manage data using object-oriented principles. They offer several features that distinguish them from traditional relational databases. Here are four key features of object-oriented databases:

**Complex Data Modeling**:

OODBs support complex data modeling by allowing the storage and retrieval of complex data structures, such as objects, classes, and inheritance hierarchies. They enable the representation of real-world entities and their relationships more directly and intuitively.

**Object Identity and Persistence**:

Objects in OODBs have a unique identity, which allows them to be stored in the database and retrieved later while maintaining their identity. This feature is known as object persistence, and it ensures that objects can be saved, retrieved, and modified over time, making them suitable for modeling long-lived entities.

**Inheritance and Polymorphism**:

OODBs support inheritance, allowing objects to inherit attributes and behaviors from parent classes. This feature enables code and data reuse, making it easier to represent relationships and hierarchies. Polymorphism allows objects of different classes to be treated uniformly, enhancing flexibility and extensibility.

**Complex Query Capabilities**:

OODBs provide advanced query capabilities for navigating and querying object structures. Object Query Language (OQL) is commonly used for expressing queries in an object-oriented database. This allows complex relationships and associations to be queried efficiently.

Q8. What do you understand by Distributed DBMS? Explain its architecture. [Marks: 4] (RTU MCA 2022)

**Answer:**

A Distributed Database Management System (DDBMS) is a type of database management system that manages a distributed database. A distributed database is a collection of multiple, logically interrelated databases distributed over a computer network. The primary aim of a DDBMS is to manage the distributed databases in a manner that makes the distribution transparent to the users. This means that users can interact with the system as if it were a single, unified database rather than a collection of separate databases spread across different locations.

**Key Concepts of Distributed DBMS**

**Transparency:** Achieving a high degree of transparency in terms of data distribution, transaction processing, and system administration is a fundamental goal. This includes location transparency, replication transparency, and fragmentation transparency.

**Autonomy:** Each database in the system can operate independently, managing its own data, transactions, and security.

**Interactivity:** The system facilitates data exchange and transactions across various sites, ensuring data consistency and integrity across the network.

**Architecture of Distributed DBMS**

The architecture of a Distributed DBMS can generally be categorized into three types:

**Homogeneous DDBMS:** In this architecture, all the sites use the same DBMS product. The databases at each site can easily cooperate with each other since they share the same underlying database management system. This makes the integration and management of the database much simpler.

**Heterogeneous DDBMS:** The sites in a heterogeneous distributed database may run different DBMS products, which could lead to difficulties in transaction processing and query processing due to differences in data models, query languages, etc. The system must provide a middleware or a gateway that translates between different DBMSs and provides a uniform interface to the user.

**Federated or Multidatabase Systems:** This architecture allows for more autonomy than the homogeneous and heterogeneous systems. Each database in a federated system can operate independently, but the system provides mechanisms for sharing and integrating data. It's a collection of cooperating but autonomous component systems.

**Components of Distributed DBMS Architecture**

**Global Database Administrator (GDBA):** Responsible for the entire distributed database system's management, including schema definition for the global database.

**Local Database Administrator (LDBA):** Each site has an LDBA responsible for the local database management, dealing with local queries, transactions, and database security.

**Distributed Database Management System Software:** It includes the software systems at each site that manage the local database and handle communications and data exchange with other sites.

**Network Infrastructure:** A critical component that connects all the sites, allowing them to communicate and share data.

**Advantages of Distributed DBMS**

**Reflects Organizational Structure:** Many organizations are naturally distributed geographically, and a DDBMS aligns with this structure.

**Improved Reliability and Availability:** Data distributed across different sites can enhance the system's overall reliability and availability since the failure of one site doesn't necessarily bring down the entire system.

**Local Autonomy:** Sites can maintain a degree of autonomy, managing their data and transactions locally.

**Scalability:** It's easier to add new sites or expand existing databases in a distributed environment.

**Challenges of Distributed DBMS**

**Complexity:** Managing a distributed system, ensuring consistency, and handling failures are more complex than in centralized systems.

**Security:** Ensuring data security across the network and at all sites is more challenging.

**Data Integrity and Consistency:** Maintaining data integrity and consistency across all sites, especially in the presence of replication and concurrency, requires sophisticated protocols.

In summary, a Distributed DBMS offers a powerful solution for managing data across geographically dispersed locations, supporting the needs of distributed organizations while presenting unique challenges in terms of complexity, data consistency, and system management.

## ONLINE RESOURCES

**Practice Paper Link:** https://forms.gle/j5gP6g1eTEdqRi6P8

**QR Code:**

**Video Content:** https://www.youtube.com/playlist?list=PLzlh_31VWEFoIlw2oMU7KRz1SoBIhT3y_

**QR Code:**

# Chapter 9: Advanced Database Management Systems

## Parallel Databases

Parallel databases, also known as parallel database management systems (PDBMS), are a type of database system designed to improve performance and scalability by distributing data processing tasks across multiple processors or nodes. This parallelism allows for faster query processing, increased throughput, and efficient handling of large datasets.

In Parallel Databases, mainly there are three architectural designs for parallel DBMS. They are as follows:

Shared Memory Architecture

Shared Disk Architecture

Shared Nothing Architecture

**Shared Memory Architecture**:

In Shared Memory Architecture, there are multiple CPUs that are attached to an interconnection network. They are able to share a single or global main memory and common disk arrays. It is to be noted that, in this architecture, a single copy of a multi-threaded operating system and multithreaded DBMS can support these multiple CPUs. Also, the shared memory is a solid coupled architecture in which multiple CPUs share their memory. It is also known as

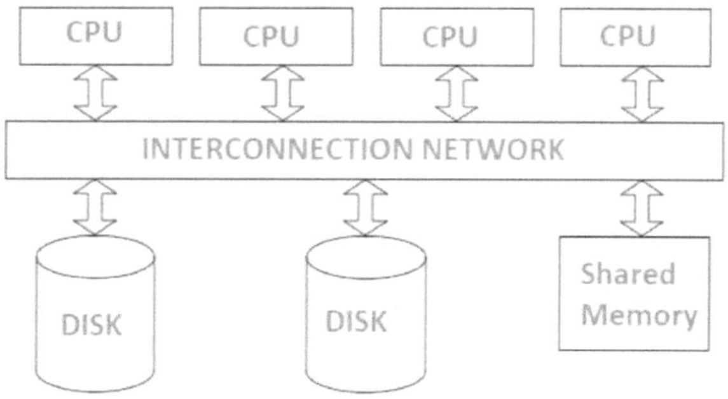


Symmetric multiprocessing (SMP). This architecture has a very wide range which starts from personal workstations that support a few microprocessors in parallel via RISC.

Advantages:

It has high-speed data access for a limited number of processors.

The communication is efficient.

Disadvantages

It cannot use beyond 80 or 100 CPUs in parallel.

The bus or the interconnection network gets block due to the increment of the large number of CPUs.

**Shared Disk Architectures:**

In Shared Disk Architecture, various CPUs are attached to an interconnection network. In this, each CPU has its own memory and all of them have access to the same disk. Also, note that here the memory is not shared among

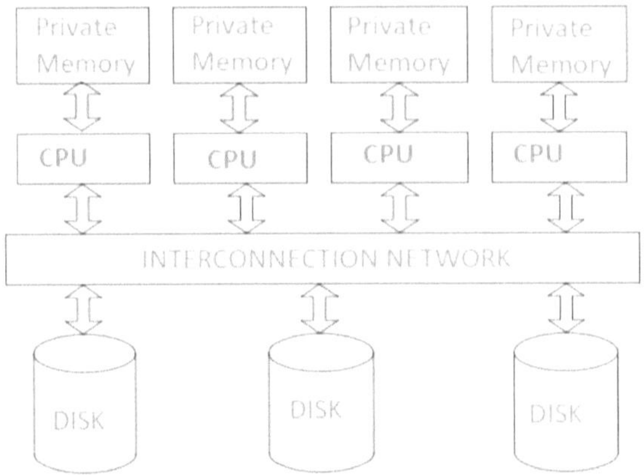


CPUs therefore each node has its own copy of the operating system and DBMS. Shared disk architecture is a loosely coupled architecture optimized for applications that are inherently centralized. They are also known as clusters.

Advantages:

The interconnection network is no longer a bottleneck each CPU has its own memory.

Load-balancing is easier in shared disk architecture.

There is better fault tolerance.

Disadvantages:

If the number of CPUs increases, the problems of interference and memory contentions also increase.

There's also exists a scalability problem.

**Shared Nothing Architecture:**

Shared Nothing Architecture is multiple processor architecture in which each processor has its own memory and disk storage. In this, multiple CPUs are attached to an interconnection network through a node. Also, note that no two CPUs can access the same disk area. In this architecture, no sharing of memory or disk resources is done. It is

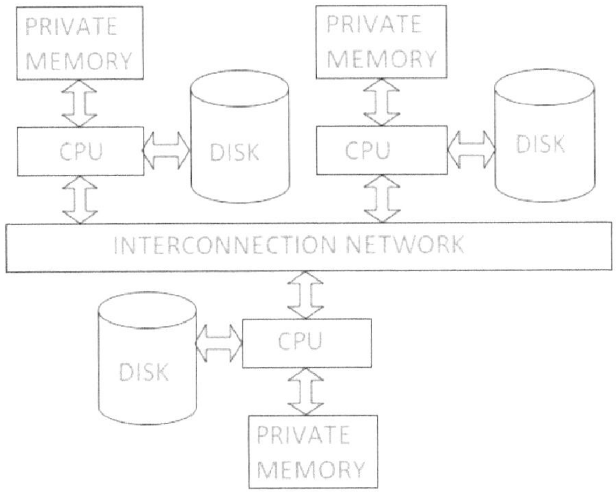

also known as Massively parallel processing (MPP).

Advantages:

It has better scalability as no sharing of resources is done

Multiple CPUs can be added

Disadvantages:

The cost of communications is higher as it involves sending of data and software interaction at both ends

The cost of non-local disk access is higher than the cost of shared disk architectures.

In summary, parallel databases leverage parallel processing and a shared-nothing architecture to enhance query performance and scalability. They are well-suited for data-intensive applications that require fast query execution, making them valuable tools for organizations dealing with large datasets and complex analytical workloads.

## Distributed Databases

A distributed database is essentially a database that is dispersed across numerous sites, i.e., on various computers or over a network of computers, and is not restricted to a single system. A distributed database system is spread across several locations with distinct physical components. This can be necessary when different people from all over the world need to access a certain database. It must be handled such that, to users, it seems to be a single database.

**Types:**

**Homogeneous Database**: A homogeneous database stores data uniformly across all locations. All sites utilize the same operating system, database management system, and data structures. They are therefore simple to handle.

**Heterogeneous Database**: With a heterogeneous distributed database, many locations may employ various software and schema, which may cause issues with queries and transactions. Moreover, one site could not be even aware of the existence of the other sites. Various operating systems and database applications may be used by various machines. They could even employ separate database data models. Translations are therefore necessary for communication across

**Data may be stored on several places in two ways using distributed data storage:**

**Replication** - With this strategy, every aspect of the connection is redundantly kept at two or more locations. It is a completely redundant database if the entire database is accessible from every location. Systems preserve copies of the data as a result of replication. This has advantages since it makes more data accessible at many locations. Moreover, query requests can now be handled in parallel. But, there are some drawbacks as well. Data must be updated often. All changes performed at one site must be documented at every site where that relation is stored in order to avoid inconsistent results. There is a tone of overhead here. Moreover, since concurrent access must now be monitored across several sites, concurrency management becomes far more complicated.

**Fragmentation** - In this method, the relationships are broken up into smaller pieces and each fragment is kept in the many locations where it is needed. To ensure there is no data loss, the pieces must be created in a way that allows for the reconstruction of the original relation. As fragmentation doesn't result in duplicate data, consistency is not a concern. various sites.

Fragmentation of relations can be done in two ways:

**Horizontal fragmentation – Splitting by rows –**

The relation is fragmented into groups of tuples so that each tuple is assigned to at least one fragment.

**Vertical fragmentation – Splitting by columns –**

The schema of the relation is divided into smaller schemas. Each fragment must contain a common candidate key so as to ensure a lossless join.

There are several different architectures for distributed database systems, including:

**Client-server architecture**: In this architecture, clients connect to a central server, which manages the distributed database system. The server is responsible for coordinating transactions, managing data storage, and providing access control.

**Peer-to-peer architecture**: In this architecture, each site in the distributed database system is connected to all other sites. Each site is responsible for managing its own data and coordinating transactions with other sites.

**Federated architecture**: In this architecture, each site in the distributed database system maintains its own independent database, but the databases are integrated through a middleware layer that provides a common interface for accessing and querying the data.

Distributed database systems can be used in a variety of applications, including e-commerce, financial services, and telecommunications. However, designing and managing a distributed database system can be complex and requires careful consideration of factors such as data distribution, replication, and consistency.

Advantages of Distributed Database System:

There is fast data processing as several sites participate in request processing.

Reliability and availability of this system is high.

It possesses reduced operating cost.

It is easier to expand the system by adding more sites.

It has improved sharing ability and local autonomy.

Disadvantages of Distributed Database System:

The system becomes complex to manage and control.

The security issues must be carefully managed.

The system requires deadlock handling during the transaction processing otherwise
the entire system may be in inconsistent state.

There is need of some standardization for processing of distributed database system.

## Object-Relational Database Management Systems (ORDBMS)

Object-Relational Database Management Systems (ORDBMS) combine the features of traditional relational databases with object-oriented concepts, providing more flexibility and expressive power for modeling complex data structures. Here's a detailed overview of ORDBMS:

**Object-Oriented Concepts:**

ORDBMS extends the relational model to include object-oriented concepts like classes, inheritance, and encapsulation.

Data in an ORDBMS can be organized into user-defined object types, which can contain both attributes (like in traditional relational databases) and methods (functions that operate on the data).

**Complex Data Types:**

ORDBMS supports complex data types, such as arrays, nested tables, and user-defined types, which allow for the modeling of structured data more effectively.

**Inheritance:**

Inheritance allows object types to inherit attributes and methods from other object types. This feature simplifies data modeling and promotes code reuse.

**Encapsulation:**

Encapsulation refers to the bundling of data (attributes) and methods (operations) into a single unit, providing better control over data access and manipulation.

**Data Abstraction:**

ORDBMS offers data abstraction, enabling developers to hide the underlying complexity of the database schema and focus on the logical structure of the data.

**Query Language Extensions:**

ORDBMS typically extends SQL with object-oriented query capabilities. For example, it allows querying data based on the structure of objects, inheritance hierarchies, and methods.

**Persistence of Objects:**

ORDBMS can store complex objects as persistent data, allowing them to be retrieved, updated, and queried like any other data in the database.

**Integration with Programming Languages:**

ORDBMS often provides language bindings and APIs for popular programming languages (e.g., Java, C++) to facilitate the development of applications that interact with the database using object-oriented constructs.

**Performance and Scalability:**

ORDBMS systems are designed for high performance and scalability. They employ indexing and caching mechanisms to optimize query execution and support large-scale applications.

**Example ORDBMS:**

PostgreSQL is a well-known open-source ORDBMS that provides extensive support for object relational features.

**Use Cases:**

ORDBMS is suitable for applications that deal with complex, structured data where traditional relational databases may struggle to model relationships effectively.

Common use cases include:

Geographic Information Systems (GIS)

Complex financial applications

Scientific data management

Multimedia databases

Content management systems

**Advantages:**

Improved modeling of complex data structures.

Enhanced data encapsulation and code reuse.

Compatibility with both object-oriented and relational programming paradigms.

Support for large-scale applications with complex data needs.

**Challenges:**

Increased complexity in data modeling and querying.

Learning curve for developers transitioning from traditional databases.

Limited standardization, leading to variations in ORDBMS implementations.

In summary, ORDBMS combines the strengths of the relational model with object-oriented principles, offering a powerful and flexible approach to data management. This makes ORDBMS suitable for applications that require advanced data modeling and complex relationships between data entities.

## Data Warehousing and Online Analytical Processing (OLAP)

Data Warehousing (DW) and Online Analytical Processing (OLAP) are integral components of modern data management and analytics. Here's an in-depth look at both:

**Data Warehousing (DW):**

**Definition:** A data warehouse is a centralized repository that stores structured, historical data from various sources, such as transactional databases, logs, and external data. It is optimized for querying and reporting.

**Key Characteristics:**

**Subject-Oriented:** Data warehouses are organized around specific subjects or themes, making it easier to analyze data within a specific context, such as sales, finance, or customer behavior.

**Integrated Data:** Data from disparate sources is transformed, cleaned, and integrated into a consistent format within the data warehouse.

**Time-Variant:** Data warehouses store historical data over time, allowing for trend analysis, time-series reporting, and comparison of data at different points in time.

**Non-Volatile:** Once data is stored in the data warehouse, it is considered non-volatile and remains unchanged. New data is added through periodic ETL (Extract, Transform, Load) processes.

**Components of a Data Warehouse:**

**ETL Process:** Data is extracted from source systems, transformed to meet data quality and consistency requirements, and loaded into the data warehouse.

**Data Warehouse Database:** The core repository for storing integrated and historical data.

**Metadata Repository:** Stores information about the data warehouse, including data lineage, definitions, and data transformation rules.

Query and Reporting Tools: Front-end tools that enable users to access and analyze data stored in the warehouse.

**Online Analytical Processing (OLAP):**

**Definition:** OLAP is a category of technology used for interactive and complex analysis of multidimensional data. It enables users to explore data from different angles, drill down into details, and generate meaningful insights.

**Key Characteristics:**

**Multidimensional Analysis:** OLAP databases are designed to handle multidimensional data, often represented in data cubes. Users can slice, dice, pivot, and drill through data to explore various dimensions and measures.

**Aggregation:** OLAP systems support aggregation functions to summarize data across dimensions. Users can view data at different levels of granularity.

**Fast Query Response:** OLAP databases are optimized for quick query response times, making them suitable for interactive analysis.

**Complex Calculations:** OLAP tools support complex calculations and calculations on aggregated data.

**Types of OLAP:**

**MOLAP (Multidimensional OLAP):** Data is stored in multidimensional cubes, and operations are performed directly on these cubes. Example: Microsoft Analysis Services.

**ROLAP (Relational OLAP):** Data is stored in relational databases, and OLAP operations are translated into SQL queries. Example: IBM Cognos.

**HOLAP (Hybrid OLAP):** Combines features of MOLAP and ROLAP, allowing users to benefit from both multidimensional and relational storage.

**Use Cases:**

**Data Warehousing:** DW is used for historical data storage and structured reporting in various domains, including finance, retail, healthcare, and manufacturing.

**OLAP:** OLAP is essential for business intelligence, data exploration, and decision support in industries where complex data analysis is critical, such as finance, marketing, and sales.

**Advantages:**

**Data Warehousing:** Provides a single source of truth, improves data quality, supports historical analysis, and enables business intelligence.

**OLAP:** Facilitates multidimensional analysis, faster query response times, and insights discovery.

**Challenges:**

**Data Warehousing:** Requires data integration efforts, storage management, and ongoing ETL processes.

**OLAP:** Complex data modeling, cube design, and query optimization can be challenging.

In summary, data warehousing and OLAP are essential components of the modern data ecosystem, enabling organizations to store, manage, and analyze data for informed decision-making and business intelligence. They play crucial roles in improving data quality, facilitating historical analysis, and supporting multidimensional data exploration.

**Star Schema:**

In a Star Schema, data is organized into a central fact table and a set of dimension tables. This design simplifies queries for business intelligence and reporting purposes because it allows for straightforward joins between the fact table and dimensions.

Components of a Star Schema:

Fact Table: This table contains quantitative and numerical data, often referred to as measures. Examples of measures could include sales revenue, profit, or quantity sold. Each row in the fact table represents a specific event or transaction.

Dimension Tables: These tables contain descriptive information about the data in the fact table. Dimensions provide context for the measures. For example, in a sales data warehouse, dimension tables could include:

Time Dimension: Contains information about dates, such as day, month, quarter, and year.

Product Dimension: Contains information about products, including product names, categories, and descriptions.

Customer Dimension: Contains information about customers, such as customer names, addresses, and demographics.

Example of a Star Schema:

Consider a retail business that wants to analyze its sales data. The Star Schema for this scenario might look like this:

Fact Table (Sales):

Columns: Date_ID, Product_ID, Customer_ID, Sales_Amount

Each row represents a sales transaction with references to dimensions.

Dimension Tables:

Time Dimension (Date):

Columns: Date_ID (Primary Key), Date, Day, Month, Quarter, Year

Product Dimension:

Columns: Product_ID (Primary Key), Product_Name, Category, Description

Customer Dimension:

Columns: Customer_ID (Primary Key), Customer_Name, Address, Age, Gender

With this Star Schema, it's easy to answer questions like "What were the total sales for a specific product category in a particular quarter?" by joining the fact table with the relevant dimension tables.

**Snowflake Schema:**

A Snowflake Schema is an extension of the Star Schema where dimension tables are further normalized into sub-dimensions or related tables, creating a more complex structure.

Example of a Snowflake Schema:

Let's take the same retail sales example but convert it into a Snowflake Schema:

Fact Table (Sales):

Columns: Date_ID, Product_ID, Customer_ID, Sales_Amount

Dimension Tables:

Time Dimension (Date):

Columns: Date_ID (Primary Key), Date

Product Dimension:

Columns: Product_ID (Primary Key), Product_Name

Product Category Dimension:

Columns: Category_ID (Primary Key), Category_Name

Product Description Dimension:

Columns: Product_ID (Foreign Key), Description

Customer Dimension:

Columns: Customer_ID (Primary Key), Customer_Name

Customer Details Dimension:

Columns: Customer_ID (Foreign Key), Address, Age, Gender

In this Snowflake Schema, we've further normalized the dimension tables, breaking down the product and customer dimensions into sub-dimensions. This can save storage space and maintain data integrity, but it may require more complex queries due to the need for multiple joins when retrieving information.

The choice between a Star Schema and a Snowflake Schema depends on factors like query performance, data integrity, and storage efficiency. Star schemas are simpler and better suited for query performance, while Snowflake schemas offer better data integrity and storage efficiency but may require more complex queries.

## Data Mining and Pre-processing

### Data Mining:

Data Mining is a process of discovering hidden patterns, trends, and insights within large datasets. It involves the use of various techniques and algorithms to extract valuable information that can aid in decision-making, prediction, and knowledge discovery. Data mining is widely used in fields like business, healthcare, finance, and marketing.Here are the key aspects of data mining in DBMS:

**Data Collection:**

Data mining begins with the collection of data from various sources. This data can include structured data from relational databases, semi-structured data from XML or JSON files, and unstructured data from sources like text documents, social media, or sensor readings.

Data pre-processing may also involve data cleaning, transformation, integration, and reduction to prepare the data for analysis.

**Data Mining Techniques and Algorithms:**

Data mining employs a wide range of techniques and algorithms to uncover patterns and insights in the data. Some common data mining techniques include:

**Classification:** Assigning data to predefined categories or classes (e.g., spam or non-spam email classification).

**Regression:** Predicting a numerical value based on other attributes (e.g., predicting house prices based on features).

**Clustering:** Grouping similar data points together based on similarity criteria (e.g., customer segmentation).

**Association Rule Mining:** Discovering relationships and patterns in data (e.g., market basket analysis).

**Anomaly Detection:** Identifying rare and unusual data points (e.g., fraud detection).

**Text Mining:** Analyzing and extracting insights from unstructured text data.

Popular algorithms for these techniques include decision trees, support vector machines, k-means clustering, Apriori algorithm, and more.

**Model Evaluation:**

After applying data mining algorithms, models need to be evaluated to assess their accuracy and performance. Evaluation metrics vary depending on the type of analysis but may include accuracy, precision, recall, F1-score, and others.

Cross-validation and splitting the data into training and testing sets are common practices for model evaluation.

**Pattern Interpretation and Knowledge Discovery:**

The patterns and insights discovered through data mining are interpreted to make informed decisions, develop strategies, or gain a deeper understanding of the data.

These insights can be used for various purposes, such as improving marketing strategies, optimizing business operations, detecting fraud, or making scientific discoveries.

**Data Visualization:**

Data mining results are often visualized using charts, graphs, and dashboards to make the insights more understandable and actionable for stakeholders.

**Challenges in Data Mining:**

**Data Quality:** Inaccurate, incomplete, or noisy data can lead to misleading results.

**Scalability:** Analyzing large datasets can be computationally intensive and time-consuming.

**Complexity:** Choosing the right algorithm and parameters can be challenging.

**Privacy and Ethical Concerns:** Handling sensitive data and ensuring privacy and compliance with regulations (e.g., GDPR) is crucial.

**Interpretability:** Complex models may be difficult to interpret and explain to non-technical stakeholders.

Data mining is a valuable tool for extracting knowledge and insights from data, and it plays a significant role in various domains, including business, healthcare, finance, and scientific research. It enables organizations to make data-driven decisions and uncover hidden opportunities or challenges within their datasets.

**Pre-processing:**

Data pre-processing is a critical phase in the data mining process, encompassing various tasks aimed at cleaning, transforming, and integrating raw data to prepare it for analysis. The primary objective of data preprocessing is to enhance data quality and tailor it to the specific data mining objectives.

**Key steps in data pre-processing include:**

**Data Cleaning:**

This initial step involves identifying and rectifying errors or anomalies in the dataset, such as missing values, outliers, and duplicate entries.

Data cleaning techniques include imputation, removal of inconsistent records, and transformation to correct discrepancies.

**Data Integration:**

Data integration entails amalgamating data from multiple sources into a cohesive dataset. This task can be intricate due to variations in data formats, structures, and semantics.

Methods like record linkage and data fusion are employed for effective data integration.

**Data Transformation:**

Data transformation involves converting the data into a suitable format for analysis. Common techniques include normalization, standardization, and discretization.

Normalization scales data to a common range, while standardization adjusts data to have zero mean and unit variance. Discretization converts continuous data into discrete categories.

**Data Reduction:**

To enhance efficiency and reduce computational complexity, data reduction methods are used to reduce dataset size while preserving pertinent information.

Techniques such as feature selection and feature extraction achieve this. Feature selection identifies relevant features for analysis, while feature extraction transforms data into a lower-dimensional space while retaining vital information.

**Data Discretization:**

Continuous data may be divided into discrete categories or intervals through data discretization. This is especially valuable for algorithms that require categorical data.

Techniques like equal-width binning, equal-frequency binning, and clustering are employed in data discretization.

**Data Normalization:**

Data normalization adjusts data to a standard range, such as between 0 and 1 or -1 and 1. It is employed to handle data with distinct units and scales.

Common normalization techniques include min-max normalization, z-score normalization, and decimal scaling.

Effective data preprocessing is indispensable in ensuring data quality and the accuracy of subsequent analysis results. The specific steps involved in data preprocessing may vary based on the data's nature and the objectives of the data mining endeavor. Performing these steps contributes to the efficiency and precision of the data mining process, ultimately leading to more accurate insights and decisions.

## Data Mining Algorithms: Association Rules, Classification, Clustering

### Association Rules

Association rules are a fundamental concept in data mining and are primarily used for discovering interesting relationships or patterns within large datasets. These rules help identify associations between items in a database, which can be useful for various applications, such as market basket analysis, recommendation systems, and more. Association rules are typically expressed in the form of "if-then" statements.

Here's how association rules work:

**Items:** In a dataset, items are individual entities or products. For example, in a retail dataset, items could represent products like "milk," "bread," "eggs," and so on.

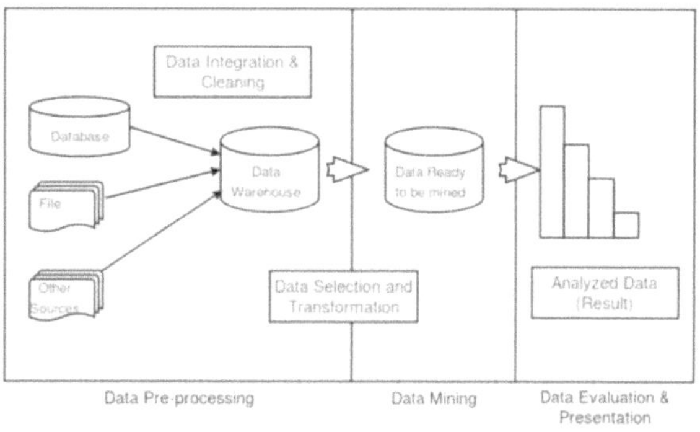

**Transactions:** Each transaction in the dataset represents a collection of items that occur together. For instance, a transaction could be a customer's shopping basket, listing the items they purchased during a single shopping trip.

**Support:** Support measures the frequency of occurrence of a specific itemset (a set of one or more items) in the dataset. It indicates how often a particular itemset appears in the transactions. High support values imply that the itemset is common in the dataset.

**Confidence:** Confidence quantifies the strength of the association between two itemsets in terms of conditional probability. It measures the likelihood that if one itemset (A) is present in a transaction, another itemset (B) will also be present. High confidence values suggest a strong association between the two itemsets.

**Lift:** Lift assesses the strength of association rules by comparing the observed support of an itemset combination with what would be expected if the itemsets were independent. Lift values greater than 1 indicate a positive association between itemsets, while values less than 1 suggest a negative association.

A typical example is a Market Based Analysis.

Market Based Analysis is one of the key techniques used by large relations to show associations between items.It allows retailers to identify relationships between the items that people buy together frequently.

Given a set of transactions, we can find rules that will predict the occurrence of an item based on the occurrences of other items in the transaction.

| TID | Items |
|---|---|
| 1 | Bread, Milk |
| 2 | Bread, Diaper, Beer, Eggs |
| 3 | Milk, Diaper, Beer, Coke |
| 4 | Bread, Milk, Diaper, Beer |
| 5 | Bread, Milk, Diaper, Coke |

Before we start defining the rule, let us first see the basic definitions.

Support Count(σ) – Frequency of occurrence of a itemset.

Here σ ({Milk, Bread, Diaper})=2

Frequent Itemset – An itemset whose support is greater than or equal to minsup threshold.

Association Rule – An implication expression of the form X -> Y, where X and Y are any 2 itemsets.

Example: {Milk, Diaper}->{Beer}

**Rule Evaluation Metrics –**

Support(s) –

The number of transactions that include items in the {X} and {Y} parts of the rule as a percentage of the total number of transaction.It is a measure of how frequently the collection of items occur together as a percentage of all transactions.

Support = σ (X+Y) \div total –

It is interpreted as fraction of transactions that contain both X and Y.

Confidence(c) –

It is the ratio of the no of transactions that includes all items in {B} as well as the no of transactions that includes all items in {A} to the no of transactions that includes all items in {A}.

Conf(X=>Y) = Supp(X\cupY) \div Supp(X) –

It measures how often each item in Y appears in transactions that contains items in X also.

Lift(l) –

The lift of the rule X=>Y is the confidence of the rule divided by the expected confidence, assuming that the itemsets X and Y are independent of each other.The expected confidence is the confidence divided by the frequency of {Y}.

Lift(X=>Y) = Conf(X=>Y) \div Supp(Y) –

Lift value near 1 indicates X and Y almost often appear together as expected, greater than 1 means they appear together more than expected and less than 1 means they appear less than expected.Greater lift values indicate stronger association.

**Classification**

Classification is a fundamental concept in data mining and machine learning that involves the process of categorizing or labeling data into predefined classes or categories based on its characteristics or attributes. The goal of classification is to build a predictive model that can automatically assign new, unseen data instances to one of these predefined classes. It is a supervised learning technique, meaning that it relies on a labeled dataset where each data instance is associated with a known class or category.

Classification is the process of classifying a record. One simple example of classification is to check whether it is raining or not. The answer can either be yes or no. So, there is a particular number of choices. Sometimes there can be more than two classes to classify. That is called multiclass classification.

**How does Classification Works?**

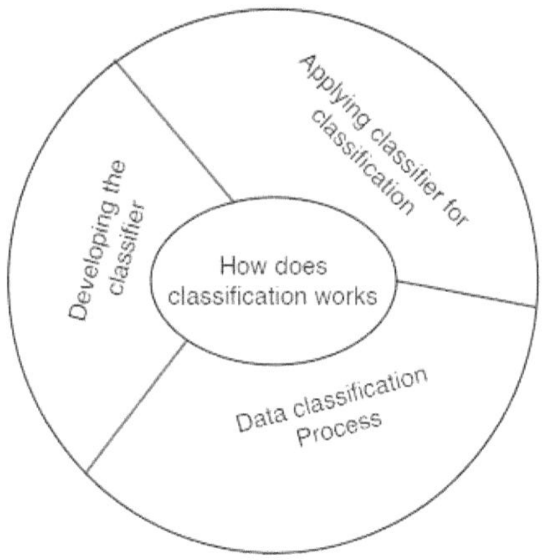


The functioning of classification with the assistance of the bank loan application has been mentioned above. There are two stages in the data classification system: classifier or model creation and classification classifier.

**Developing the Classifier or model creation**: This level is the learning stage or the learning process. The classification algorithms construct the classifier in this stage. A classifier is constructed from a training set composed of the records of databases and their corresponding class names. Each category that makes up the training set is referred to as a category or class. We may also refer to these records as samples, objects, or data points.

**Applying classifier for classification**: The classifier is used for classification at this level. The test data are used here to estimate the accuracy of the classification algorithm. If the consistency is deemed sufficient, the classification rules can be expanded to cover new data records. It includes:

Sentiment Analysis: Sentiment analysis is highly helpful in social media monitoring. We can use it to extract social media insights. We can build sentiment analysis models to read and analyze misspelled words with advanced machine learning algorithms. The accurate trained models provide consistently accurate outcomes and result in a fraction of the time.

Document Classification: We can use document classification to organize the documents into sections according to the content. Document classification refers to text classification; we can classify the words in the entire document. And with the help of machine learning classification algorithms, we can execute it automatically.

Image Classification: Image classification is used for the trained categories of an image. These could be the caption of the image, a statistical value, a theme. You can tag images to train your model for relevant categories by applying supervised learning algorithms.

Machine Learning Classification: It uses the statistically demonstrable algorithm rules to execute analytical tasks that would take humans hundreds of more hours to perform.

Data Classification Process: The data classification process can be categorized into five steps:

Create the goals of data classification, strategy, workflows, and architecture of data classification.

Classify confidential details that we store.

Using marks by data labelling.

To improve protection and obedience, use effects.

Data is complex, and a continuous method is a classification.

**What is Data Classification Lifecycle?**

The data classification life cycle produces an excellent structure for controlling the flow of data to an enterprise. Businesses need to account for data security and compliance at each level. With the help of data classification, we can perform it at every stage, from origin to deletion. The data life-cycle has the following stages, such as:

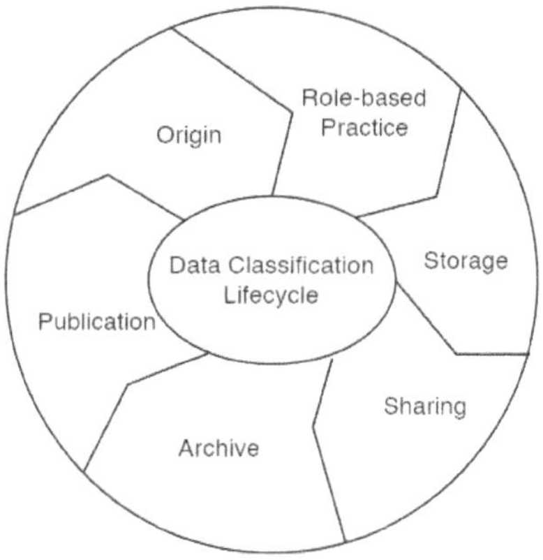


Origin: It produces sensitive data in various formats, with emails, Excel, Word, Google documents, social media, and websites.

Role-based practice: Role-based security restrictions apply to all delicate data by tagging based on in-house protection policies and agreement rules.

Storage: Here, we have the obtained data, including access controls and encryption.

Sharing: Data is continually distributed among agents, consumers, and co-workers from various devices and platforms.

Archive: Here, data is eventually archived within an industry's storage systems.

Publication: Through the publication of data, it can reach customers. They can then view and download in the form of dashboards.

**Clustering**

The process of making a group of abstract objects into classes of similar objects is known as clustering.

**Points to Remember:**

One group is treated as a cluster of data objects

In the process of cluster analysis, the first step is to partition the set of data into groups with the help of data similarity, and then groups are assigned to their respective labels.

The biggest advantage of clustering over-classification is it can adapt to the changes made and helps single out useful features that differentiate different groups.

**What is clustering in Data Mining?**

Clustering is the method of converting a group of abstract objects into classes of similar objects.

Clustering is a method of partitioning a set of data or objects into a set of significant subclasses called clusters.

It helps users to understand the structure or natural grouping in a data set and used either as a stand-alone instrument to get a better insight into data distribution or as a pre-processing step for other algorithms

**Applications of cluster analysis in data mining:**

In many applications, clustering analysis is widely used, such as data analysis, market research, pattern recognition, and image processing.

It assists marketers to find different groups in their client base and based on the purchasing patterns. They can characterize their customer groups.

It helps in allocating documents on the internet for data discovery.

Clustering is also used in tracking applications such as detection of credit card fraud.

As a data mining function, cluster analysis serves as a tool to gain insight into the distribution of data to analyze the characteristics of each cluster.

In terms of biology, It can be used to determine plant and animal taxonomies, categorization of genes with the same functionalities and gain insight into structure inherent to populations.

It helps in the identification of areas of similar land that are used in an earth observation database and the identification of house groups in a city according to house type, value, and geographical location.

**Why is clustering used in data mining?**

Clustering analysis has been an evolving problem in data mining due to its variety of applications. The advent of various data clustering tools in the last few years and their comprehensive use in a broad range of applications, including image processing, computational biology, mobile communication, medicine, and economics, must contribute to the popularity of these algorithms. The main issue with the data clustering algorithms is that it cant be standardized. The advanced algorithm may give the best results with one type of data set, but it may fail or perform poorly with other kinds of data set. Although many efforts have been made to standardize the algorithms that can perform well in all situations, no significant achievement has been achieved so far. Many clustering tools have been proposed so far. However, each algorithm has its advantages or disadvantages and can't work on all real situations.

**Clustering Methods:**

It can be classified based on the following categories.

Model-Based Method

Hierarchical Method

Constraint-Based Method

Grid-Based Method

Partitioning Method

Density-Based Method

## Web Mining and Text Mining

### Web Mining

Web mining can widely be seen as the application of adapted data mining techniques to the web, whereas data mining is defined as the application of the algorithm to discover patterns on mostly structured data embedded into a knowledge discovery process. Web mining has a distinctive property to provide a set of various data types. The web has multiple aspects that yield different approaches for the mining process, such as web pages consist of text, web pages are linked via hyperlinks, and user activity can be monitored via web server logs. These three features lead to the differentiation between the three areas are web content mining, web structure mining, web usage mining.

**Applications of Web Mining:**

Web mining is the process of discovering patterns, structures, and relationships in web data. It involves using data mining techniques to analyze web data and extract valuable insights. The applications of web mining are wide-ranging and include:

Personalized marketing:

Web mining can be used to analyze customer behavior on websites and social media platforms. This information can be used to create personalized marketing campaigns that target customers based on their interests and preferences.

E-commerce

Web mining can be used to analyze customer behavior on e-commerce websites. This information can be used to improve the user experience and increase sales by recommending products based on customer preferences.

Search engine optimization:

Web mining can be used to analyze search engine queries and search engine results pages (SERPs). This information can be used to improve the visibility of websites in search engine results and increase traffic to the website.

Fraud detection:

Web mining can be used to detect fraudulent activity on websites. This information can be used to prevent financial fraud, identity theft, and other types of online fraud.

Sentiment analysis:

Web mining can be used to analyze social media data and extract sentiment from posts, comments, and reviews. This information can be used to understand customer sentiment towards products and services and make informed business decisions.

Web content analysis:

Web mining can be used to analyze web content and extract valuable information such as keywords, topics, and themes. This information can be used to improve the relevance of web content and optimize search engine rankings.

Customer service:

Web mining can be used to analyze customer service interactions on websites and social media platforms. This information can be used to improve the quality of customer service and identify areas for improvement.

Healthcare:

Web mining can be used to analyze health-related websites and extract valuable information about diseases, treatments, and medications. This information can be used to improve the quality of healthcare and inform medical research.

**Process of Web Mining:**

Web mining can be broadly divided into three different types of techniques of mining: Web Content Mining, Web Structure Mining, and Web Usage Mining. These are explained as following below.

Web Content Mining: Web content mining is the application of extracting useful information from the content of the web documents. Web content consist of several types of data – text, image, audio, video etc. Content data is the group of facts that a web page is designed. It can provide effective and interesting patterns about user needs. Text documents are related to text mining, machine learning and natural language processing. This mining is also known as text mining. This type of mining performs scanning and mining of the text, images and groups of web pages according to the content of the input.

Web Structure Mining: Web structure mining is the application of discovering structure information from the web. The structure of the web graph consists of web pages as nodes, and hyperlinks as edges connecting related pages. Structure mining basically shows the structured summary of a particular website. It identifies relationship between web pages linked by information or direct link connection. To determine the connection between two commercial websites, Web structure mining can be very useful.

Web Usage Mining: Web usage mining is the application of identifying or discovering interesting usage patterns from large data sets. And these patterns enable you to understand the user behaviors or something like that. In web usage mining, user access data on the web and collect data in form of logs. So, Web usage mining is also called log mining.

| Points | Data Mining | Web Mining |
|---|---|---|
| Definition | Data Mining is the process that attempts to discover pattern and hidden knowledge in large data sets in any system. | Web Mining is the process of data mining techniques to automatically discover and extract information from web documents. |
| Application | Data Mining is very useful for web page analysis. | Web Mining is very useful for a particular website and e-service. |
| Target Users | Data scientist and data engineers. | Data scientists along with data analysts. |
| Access | Data Mining access data privately. | Web Mining access data publicly. |
| Structure | In Data Mining get the information from explicit structure. | In Web Mining get the information from structured, unstructured and semi-structured web pages. |
| Problem Type | Clustering, classification, regression, prediction, optimization and control. | Web content mining, Web structure mining. |
| Tools | It includes tools like machine learning algorithms. | Special tools for web mining are Scrapy, PageRank and Apache logs. |
| Skills | It includes approaches for data cleansing, machine learning algorithms. Statistics and probability. | It includes application-level knowledge, data engineering with mathematical modules like statistics and probability. |

## Text Mining

Text mining is a component of data mining that deals specifically with unstructured text data. It involves the use of natural language processing (NLP) techniques to extract useful information and insights from large amounts of unstructured text data. Text mining can be used as a preprocessing step for data mining or as a standalone process for specific tasks.

By using text mining, the unstructured text data can be transformed into structured data that can be used for data mining tasks such as classification, clustering, and association rule mining. This allows organizations to gain insights from a wide range of data sources, such as customer feedback, social media posts, and news articles.

**Areas of text mining in data mining:**

These are the following area of text mining:

Information Extraction:

The automatic extraction of structured data such as entities, entities relationships, and attributes describing entities from an unstructured source is called information extraction.

Natural Language Processing:

NLP stands for Natural language processing. Computer software can understand human language as same as it is spoken. NLP is primarily a component of artificial intelligence (AI). The development of the NLP application is difficult because computers generally expect humans to "Speak" to them in a programming language that is accurate, clear, and exceptionally structured. Human speech is usually not authentic so that it can depend on many complex variables, including slang, social context, and regional dialects.

Data Mining:

Data mining refers to the extraction of useful data, hidden patterns from large data sets. Data mining tools can predict behaviours and future trends that allow businesses to make a better data-driven decision. Data mining tools can be used to resolve many business problems that have traditionally been too time-consuming.

Information Retrieval:

Information retrieval deals with retrieving useful data from data that is stored in our systems. Alternately, as an analogy, we can view search engines that happen on websites such as e-commerce sites or any other sites as part of information retrieval.

**Conventional Process of Text Mining**

Gathering unstructured information from various sources accessible in various document organizations, for example, plain text, web pages, PDF records, etc.

Pre-processing and data cleansing tasks are performed to distinguish and eliminate inconsistency in the data. The data cleansing process makes sure to capture the genuine text, and it is performed to eliminate stop words stemming (the process of identifying the root of a certain word and indexing the data.

Processing and controlling tasks are applied to review and further clean the data set.

Pattern analysis is implemented in Management Information System.

Information processed in the above steps is utilized to extract important and applicable data for a powerful and convenient decision-making process and trend analysis.

**Procedures for Analysing Text Mining**

Text Summarization: To extract its partial content and reflect its whole content automatically.

Text Categorization: To assign a category to the text among categories predefined by users.

Text Clustering: To segment texts into several clusters, depending on the substantial relevance.

**Text Mining Process:**

The text mining process incorporates the following steps to extract the data from the document.

Text transformation

A text transformation is a technique that is used to control the capitalization of the text.

Here the two major way of document representation is given.

Bag of words

Vector Space

Text Pre-processing

Pre-processing is a significant task and a critical step in Text Mining, Natural Language Processing (NLP), and information retrieval(IR). In the field of text mining, data pre-processing is used for extracting useful information and knowledge from unstructured text data. Information Retrieval (IR) is a matter of choosing which documents in a collection should be retrieved to fulfill the user's need.

Feature selection:

Feature selection is a significant part of data mining. Feature selection can be defined as the process of reducing the input of processing or finding the essential information sources. The feature selection is also called variable selection.

Data Mining:

Now, in this step, the text mining procedure merges with the conventional process. Classic Data Mining procedures are used in the structural database.

Evaluate:

Afterward, it evaluates the results. Once the result is evaluated, the result abandon.

Applications:

These are the following text mining applications:

Risk Management:

Risk Management is a systematic and logical procedure of analyzing, identifying, treating, and monitoring the risks involved in any action or process in organizations. Insufficient risk analysis is usually a leading cause of disappointment. It is particularly true in the financial organizations where adoption of Risk Management Software based on text mining technology can effectively enhance the ability to diminish risk. It enables the administration of millions of sources and petabytes of text documents, and giving the ability to connect the data. It helps to access the appropriate data at the right time.

Customer Care Service:

Text mining methods, particularly NLP, are finding increasing significance in the field of customer care. Organizations are spending in text analytics programming to improve their overall experience by accessing the textual data from different sources such as customer feedback, surveys, customer calls, etc. The primary objective of text analysis is to reduce the response time of the organizations and help to address the complaints of the customer rapidly and productively.

Business Intelligence:

Companies and business firms have started to use text mining strategies as a major aspect of their business intelligence. Besides providing significant insights into customer behavior and trends, text mining strategies also support organizations to analyze the qualities and weaknesses of their opponent's so, giving them a competitive advantage in the market.

Social Media Analysis:

Social media analysis helps to track the online data, and there are numerous text mining tools designed particularly for performance analysis of social media sites. These tools help to monitor and interpret the text generated via the internet from the news, emails, blogs, etc. Text mining tools can precisely analyze the total no of posts, followers, and total no of likes of your brand on a social media platform that enables you to understand the response of the individuals who are interacting with your brand and content.

**Text Mining Techniques**

Information Retrieval

In the process of Information retrieval, we try to process the available documents and the text data into a structured form so, that we can apply different pattern recognition and analytical processes. It is a process of extracting relevant and associated patterns according to a given set of words or text documents. For this, we have processes like Tokenization of the document or the stemming process in which we try to extract the base word or let's say the root word present there.

Information Extraction

It is a process of extracting meaningful words from documents.

Feature Extraction – In this process, we try to develop some new features from existing ones. This objective can be achieved by parsing an existing feature or combining two or more features based on some mathematical operation.

Feature Selection – In this process, we try to reduce the dimensionality of the dataset which is generally a common issue while dealing with the text data by selecting a subset of features from the whole dataset.

Natural Language Processing

Natural Language Processing includes tasks that are accomplished by using Machine Learning and Deep Learning methodologies. It concerns the automatic processing and analysis of unstructured text information.

Named Entity Recognition (NER): Identifying and classifying named entities such as people, organizations, and locations in text data.

Sentiment Analysis: Identifying and extracting the sentiment (e.g. positive, negative, neutral) of text data.

Text Summarization: Creating a condensed version of a text document that captures the main points.

**Advantages of Text Mining**

Large Amounts of Data: Text mining allows organizations to extract insights from large amounts of unstructured text data. This can include customer feedback, social media posts, and news articles.

Variety of Applications: Text mining has a wide range of applications, including sentiment analysis, named entity recognition, and topic modeling. This makes it a versatile tool for organizations to gain insights from unstructured text data.

Improved Decision Making: Text mining can be used to extract insights from unstructured text data, which can be used to make data-driven decisions.

Cost-effective: Text mining can be a cost-effective way to extract insights from unstructured text data, as it eliminates the need for manual data entry.

Broader benefits: Cost reductions, productivity increases, the creation of novel new services, and new business models are just a few of the larger economic advantages mentioned by those consulted.

**Disadvantages of Text Mining**

Complexity: Text mining can be a complex process that requires advanced skills in natural language processing and machine learning.

Quality of Data: The quality of text data can vary, which can affect the accuracy of the insights extracted from text mining.

High Computational Cost: Text mining requires high computational resources, and it may be difficult for smaller organizations to afford the technology.

Limited to Text Data: Text mining is limited to extracting insights from unstructured text data and cannot be used with other data types.

Noise in text mining results: Text mining of documents may result in mistakes. It's possible to find false links or to miss others. In most situations, if the noise (error rate) is sufficiently low, the benefits of automation exceed the chance of a larger mistake than that produced by a human reader.

Lack of transparency: Text mining is frequently viewed as a mysterious process where large corpora of text documents are input and new information is produced. Text mining is in fact opaque when researchers lack the technical know-how or expertise to comprehend how it operates, or when they lack access to corpora or text mining tools.

**Exercise**

**Exercise 1 – MCQ**

Q 1. What is a key advantage of parallel databases?

a. Improved data security

b. Enhanced data modelling

c. Increased data processing speed

d. Simplified data integration

Q 2. OLAP is primarily used for:

a. Real-time transaction processing

b. Data storage and retrieval

c. Complex data analysis and reporting

d. Data transformation and cleansing

**Exercise 2 – True/ False**

Q 1. Data warehousing involves the collection and storage of historical data for analytical purposes, while OLAP enables complex, multidimensional analysis of this data.

Q 2. Data mining involves discovering patterns, trends, and insights from large datasets, while pre-processing is essential for cleaning and preparing data for mining.

**Exercise 3 – Small answer**

Q 1. What is the primary advantage of using a Parallel Database system?

Q 2. In a Distributed Database, what is data fragmentation?

**Exercise 4 – Long answer**

Q 1. Explain the concept of Object-Relational Database Management Systems (ORDBMS).

Q 2. Discuss the process of Data Mining and its importance in extracting valuable insights from large datasets. Provide examples of data mining techniques and algorithms commonly used in various industries.

**Answer**

**Exercise 1**

Answer 1: c, 2: c.

Answer 1: True, 2: True

**Previous Years Questions**

Q1. Why do we need to fragment a relation? What are the rules to be followed during fragmentation?(IGNOU MCA 2010)

Q2. Write a short note on: Data Pre-processing, Star, Snowflake schema, Text Retrieval Methods. (Mumbai University 2023)

Q3. Differentiate between ORDBMS and OODBMS. (Mumbai University 2023)

Q4. Define: Data Abstraction and Data Independence. (Pune University MCA 2013)

**Previous Years Questions with Answer**

Q1 What is RDBMS? (RU BCA 2022)

**Answer:**

**RDBMS** stands for **Relational Database Management System**. It is a type of database management system that is based on the principles of the relational model of data. In an RDBMS, data is organized into tables, which consist of rows and columns. Each table represents an entity, and the relationships between entities are established through keys and foreign keys.

Key characteristics and features of an RDBMS include:

**Tables**: Data is organized into tables, with each table representing a specific entity or concept. Each row in a table represents a single instance of that entity, and each column represents an attribute or property of the entity.

**Data Integrity**: RDBMS systems enforce data integrity through various constraints such as primary keys, unique keys, foreign keys, and check constraints. This ensures that the data is accurate and consistent.

**SQL (Structured Query Language)**: RDBMS systems use SQL as the standard language for querying and manipulating data. SQL provides a powerful and standardized way to interact with the database.

**ACID Properties**: RDBMS systems adhere to the ACID properties, which stand for Atomicity, Consistency, Isolation, and Durability. These properties ensure that database transactions are reliable and maintain data consistency.

**Data Normalization**: RDBMS systems support data normalization, a process that minimizes data redundancy and ensures that data is organized efficiently.

**Joins**: Relational databases allow data from different tables to be combined using SQL joins, which enables the creation of complex queries and reporting.

**Indexing**: Indexes are used to improve query performance by allowing for faster data retrieval based on specific columns.

**Security**: RDBMS systems provide robust security features, allowing administrators to control who can access, modify, and delete data in the database.

**Scalability**: Relational databases can be scaled vertically (by adding more resources to a single server) or horizontally (by distributing data across multiple servers) to handle increasing workloads.

**Multi-User Support**: RDBMS systems support multiple users and provide mechanisms for concurrent access to data while ensuring data consistency.

**Data Backup and Recovery**: RDBMS systems offer data backup and recovery features to protect data from loss or corruption.

Prominent examples of RDBMS systems include Microsoft SQL Server, Oracle Database, MySQL, PostgreSQL, and IBM Db2. These systems are widely used in various applications, including business, e-commerce, finance, and many other domains where structured data management is critical.

Q2 What is object-oriented data base? (RU BCA 2022, 2021)

**Answer:**

An **object-oriented database (OODB)** is a type of database management system (DBMS) that is designed to store and manage data using the principles of object-oriented programming. Unlike traditional relational databases, which store data in tables, OODBs store data in the form of objects, which can contain both data and the methods (functions) that operate on that data. OODBs provide a seamless way to store and retrieve complex, structured data that is representative of real-world objects and their relationships.

Key features of object-oriented databases include:

**Complex Data Modeling**: OODBs allow for the storage of complex data structures, such as objects, classes, inheritance hierarchies, and associations. This enables the representation of real-world entities and relationships in a more intuitive and natural way.

**Object Identity and Persistence**: Objects in OODBs have a unique identity, and they can be stored in the database while maintaining their identity over time. This feature is known as object persistence, and it ensures that objects can be saved, retrieved, and modified without losing their individuality.

**Inheritance and Polymorphism**: OODBs support object-oriented concepts such as inheritance and polymorphism. Inheritance allows objects to inherit attributes and behaviors from parent classes, promoting code and data reuse. Polymorphism enables objects of different classes to be treated uniformly, enhancing flexibility and extensibility.

**Encapsulation**: OODBs encapsulate data and behavior within objects. Data hiding and encapsulation principles help protect the integrity of the data and its associated methods.

**Complex Query Capabilities**: OODBs provide advanced query capabilities for navigating and querying object structures. Object Query Languages (OQL) or extensions to standard query languages are used to express queries that can traverse complex object relationships.

**Multimedia Support**: OODBs are well-suited for managing multimedia data, including images, audio, video, and other non-traditional data types.

**Consistency and Integrity**: OODBs maintain data consistency and integrity through features like transactions, constraints, and object-level locking.

OODBs are commonly used in domains where complex, structured data is prevalent, such as in computer-aided design, geographic information systems, multimedia applications, and scenarios where object-oriented programming languages are used extensively. However, they are not as widely adopted as relational databases, and their use is often limited to specific applications that benefit from their modeling capabilities.

Q3 What is data abstraction and also explain the three levels of data abstraction. (RU BCA 2022, 2016)

**Answer:**

that refers to the simplification and representation of complex systems or data to provide a high-level, user-friendly view of information. It hides the underlying complexity and details of data structures, operations, and implementation, making it easier for users and developers to work with data and systems. Data abstraction is particularly important in database systems, where it helps in managing and interacting with data efficiently.

In the context of database management, data abstraction is typically described using three levels, each offering a different perspective on the data and the database system. These three levels of data abstraction are:

**Physical Level (Internal Schema)**:

The physical level is the lowest level of data abstraction and is closest to the physical storage and organization of data on the hardware. It deals with the physical storage structures, file organization, and access methods used to store data on storage devices such as hard drives. At this level, the focus is on optimizing data storage and retrieval, including considerations like data compression, indexing, and storage structures. Database administrators and system designers are mainly concerned with the physical level.

**Logical Level (Conceptual Schema)**:

The logical level is an intermediate level of data abstraction that describes the overall structure and organization of the data in a way that is independent of the physical implementation. It defines the logical relationships between data elements, entities, and attributes. At this level, the schema provides a high-level view of the data, including tables, views, relationships, and constraints. Database designers and developers work at the logical level to create the database schema, which is often represented using Entity-Relationship Diagrams (ERDs) or similar models.

**View Level (External Schema)**:

The view level is the highest level of data abstraction and is concerned with the user perspective. It defines various user-specific or application-specific views of the data. Each user or application may have a different view of the data, showing only the portions of the database that are relevant to their specific needs. Views are created by defining queries, reports, and virtual tables to present data in a customized way. Users interact with the database at the view level through user interfaces and application programs. This level allows for data security, as users can be given access to only the views they need.

These three levels of data abstraction allow for a clear separation of concerns in database management. They provide a structured approach to database design, implementation, and usage, allowing database administrators, designers, developers, and end-users to work at the level of abstraction that is most relevant to their roles and responsibilities. This separation of concerns makes database systems more manageable, adaptable, and user-friendly.

Q4 Write short notes on: (RU BCA 2022)

Characteristics of object-oriented data model (RU BCA 2019)

State transaction

**Answer:**

**Characteristics of Object-Oriented Data Model**

The object-oriented data model is a data modeling approach that represents data as objects, classes, and their relationships, following the principles of object-oriented programming. Here are some key characteristics of the object-oriented data model:

**Objects**: In this model, data is represented as objects, which are instances of classes. Objects encapsulate both data (attributes) and behavior (methods). Each object is a self-contained entity that can interact with other objects.

**Classes**: Classes define the structure and behavior of objects. They serve as templates for creating objects. Classes can inherit attributes and methods from other classes, promoting code reuse and hierarchy.

**Inheritance**: Inheritance allows one class to inherit attributes and methods from another class. This enables the creation of hierarchies and the reuse of common data structures and behaviors.

**Encapsulation**: Objects encapsulate their data and behavior, and they expose a controlled interface for interacting with the data. This concept of encapsulation helps protect the integrity of the data and prevents unauthorized access.

**Polymorphism**: Polymorphism allows objects of different classes to be treated uniformly. It enables the use of a common interface to interact with objects, even if they belong to different classes.

**Complex Data Relationships**: The object-oriented data model is well-suited for representing complex relationships between objects. These relationships can be one-to-one, one-to-many, or many-to-many, and they are defined through associations.

**Object Identity**: Each object has a unique identity, allowing it to be uniquely identified and referenced.

**Query Language**: Object-oriented databases often use Object Query Languages (OQL) or extensions to standard query languages to retrieve and manipulate data.

**State Transaction**

A **state transaction**, often referred to as a transaction, is a fundamental concept in database management systems. It represents a unit of work or a series of database operations that must be executed atomically, ensuring the integrity and consistency of the database. The concept is often associated with the ACID properties:

**Atomicity**: A transaction is atomic, meaning that all its operations are treated as a single, indivisible unit. It either executes completely (commit) or not at all (rollback). This ensures that the database remains in a consistent state.

**Consistency**: Transactions bring the database from one consistent state to another. Integrity constraints and rules must not be violated during the execution of a transaction.

**Isolation**: Isolation ensures that the execution of one transaction is isolated from the execution of other concurrent transactions. This prevents interference between transactions and maintains data consistency.

**Durability**: Durability guarantees that once a transaction is committed, its changes are permanent and will survive system failures. Even in the event of a system crash, the committed data remains intact.

State transactions are essential for maintaining data integrity, concurrency control, and data recovery in database systems. They ensure that multiple database operations are treated as a single, reliable unit, making them a fundamental concept in database management.

Q5 Discuss the database system v/s file system. (RU BCA 2021)

**Answer:**

A **database system** and a **file system** are both methods for storing, organizing, and managing data, but they serve different purposes and have distinct characteristics. Here is a comparison of the two:

**Data Structure:**

**Database System:** A database system stores data in a structured manner using tables and relationships. Data is organized into tables with rows and columns, and the relationships between tables are defined.

**File System:** A file system stores data in files and directories. Data is often unstructured, with files containing a mix of text, binary, or other data formats.

**Data Integrity:**

**Database System:** Database systems enforce data integrity through features like constraints, foreign keys, and transactions. This ensures that the data remains accurate and consistent.

**File System:** File systems have limited built-in mechanisms for maintaining data integrity. Data consistency and validation are primarily the responsibility of the application using the file system.

**Data Retrieval:**

**Database System:** Database systems provide query languages (e.g., SQL) that enable complex data retrieval using structured queries. Users can filter, search, and analyze data efficiently.

**File System:** Data retrieval in a file system is often based on file names and directory structure. Users need to know the location and naming conventions of files to access them.

**Data Relationships:**

**Database System:** Database systems are designed for managing and representing complex data relationships through tables and associations. This allows for efficient data modeling and querying.

**File System:** File systems do not inherently support data relationships. Any relationships between data stored in files are typically managed by the application, which can be more error-prone.

**Scalability:**

**Database System:** Database systems are designed to scale and handle large volumes of data and concurrent users. They provide features like indexing and caching to optimize performance.

**File System:** File systems are generally less scalable for complex data management. As data and user requirements grow, maintaining data consistency and access control can become challenging.

**Data Security:**

**Database System:** Database systems offer robust security features with user authentication, authorization, and access controls at various levels. Data security is a primary focus.

**File System:** File systems offer basic access controls (read, write, execute) but are generally less secure than database systems. Security depends on the operating system's permissions.

**Concurrency Control:**

**Database System:** Database systems provide mechanisms for handling concurrent access to data, such as locking and transaction management.

**File System:** File systems offer limited support for concurrent access control. Handling data consistency in multi-user scenarios is more challenging.

**Query Performance:**

**Database System:** Database systems are optimized for query performance, with indexing, query optimization, and caching mechanisms.

**File System:** File systems do not offer query optimization, making it less suitable for complex data retrieval.

In summary, a database system is designed for structured data storage, data integrity, complex data relationships, and optimized data retrieval, while a file system is primarily used for storing and managing files but lacks many of the features provided by a database system. The choice between the two depends on the specific data management needs and the nature of the data being handled.

Q6 Define object database? Describe persistent programming language. What are the several approaches proposed to make the objects persistent? (RU BCA 2021, 2017)

**Answer:**

**Object Database:** An **object database** is a type of database management system (DBMS) that is designed to store, retrieve, and manage data using the principles of object-oriented programming. Unlike relational databases, which store data in tables, object databases store data in the form of objects. These objects encapsulate both data (attributes) and behaviors (methods), allowing for a more natural representation of real-world entities and their relationships. Object databases are particularly well-suited for applications where complex, structured data and object-oriented programming paradigms are prevalent.

**Persistent Programming Language:** A **persistent programming language** is a programming language that is designed to support object persistence, allowing objects to be stored and retrieved from a database in a way that maintains their identity and state across multiple program executions. Persistent programming languages are used in conjunction with object databases to build applications that require long-term data storage and retrieval, as opposed to transient, in-memory data.

**Approaches to Making Objects Persistent:** There are several approaches proposed to make objects persistent:

**Object-Oriented Databases (OODBMS):** Object-oriented databases are a direct way to make objects persistent. In an OODBMS, objects are stored and retrieved in a way that preserves their identity and state. Object databases provide a seamless way to work with persistent objects using object-oriented principles.

**Object-Relational Mapping (ORM):** ORM frameworks, such as Hibernate in Java or Entity Framework in .NET, provide a way to map objects to relational databases and make them persistent. These frameworks automatically generate SQL to store and retrieve objects. While not strictly "persistent" in the object-oriented sense, they bridge the gap between object-oriented code and relational databases.

**Serialization:** Serialization is the process of converting an object into a byte stream that can be saved to a file or a database. Deserialization is the reverse process, where an object is reconstructed from the byte stream. This approach allows objects to be saved and reloaded but may not provide the same level of identity and relationship management as OODBMS.

**Object-XML Mapping:** Some systems use XML to represent object data and relationships. This approach allows objects to be stored in XML format and then retrieved and reconstructed. It's a flexible way to make objects persistent, but it may not provide the same level of efficiency and performance as OODBMS.

**Custom Serialization and Deserialization:** Developers can implement custom serialization and deserialization logic to save and load objects to and from databases. This approach offers fine-grained control over how objects are persisted.

**Object-Cache Mapping:** In this approach, objects are cached in memory and periodically persisted to a database. Object caches (e.g., in-memory databases) provide high-performance data access and the illusion of object persistence.

**Middleware and Distributed Objects:** Middleware technologies, such as CORBA or distributed object frameworks like DCOM and Java RMI, enable objects to be distributed across multiple systems and make them persistent across networked applications.

The choice of approach depends on the specific requirements of the application, the underlying database technology, and the programming language in use. Object databases and ORM frameworks are common choices for applications that require full-fledged object persistence and relational database compatibility.

Q7 What is object-oriented database management system? Explain characteristics of OODBMS. (RU BCA 2016)

**Answer:**

An **Object-Oriented Database Management System (OODBMS)** is a type of database management system that is designed to store, manage, and retrieve data using the principles of object-oriented programming. OODBMSs are specifically tailored to handle complex data structures and the storage of objects, making them particularly suitable for applications where data structures are highly interconnected and where object-oriented concepts are integral to the software design.

Here are the key characteristics of OODBMS:

**Data Representation as Objects**: In an OODBMS, data is represented as objects, which are instances of classes. Objects encapsulate both data (attributes or properties) and behavior (methods or functions). Each object is a self-contained entity that can interact with other objects.

**Inheritance**: OODBMSs support inheritance, allowing one class (or object type) to inherit attributes and behaviors from another class. Inheritance promotes code reuse and hierarchy in data modeling.

**Complex Data Relationships**: OODBMSs excel at representing complex relationships between objects. These relationships can include one-to-one, one-to-many, and many-to-many associations, providing a more natural way to model data than traditional relational databases.

**Object Identity**: Each object in an OODBMS has a unique identity, which allows it to be referenced and manipulated consistently. Object identity is maintained, ensuring that the object can be retrieved in the same state it was stored.

**Query Languages**: OODBMSs often use Object Query Languages (OQL) or extensions to standard query languages (e.g., SQL3) for querying and retrieving data. These query languages are designed to navigate complex object structures.

**Concurrency Control**: OODBMSs include mechanisms for handling concurrent access to data, such as locking and transaction management. This ensures that multiple users or processes can work with objects simultaneously while maintaining data consistency.

**Complex Data Modeling**: OODBMSs support complex data modeling, allowing developers to create data structures that closely mirror real-world entities. This is particularly valuable in applications like computer-aided design, geographic information systems, and multimedia content management.

**Object Persistence**: OODBMSs provide object persistence, meaning objects can be stored in the database and retrieved later while maintaining their identity and state. This is essential for long-term data storage.

**Polymorphism**: OODBMSs support polymorphism, allowing objects of different classes to be treated uniformly. This promotes flexibility and extensibility in software design.

**Encapsulation**: Objects encapsulate their data and behavior, exposing a controlled interface for interacting with the data. This concept of encapsulation helps protect the integrity of the data and prevents unauthorized access.

**Application Integration**: OODBMSs are often well-integrated with object-oriented programming languages, making it seamless for developers to work with data using their preferred language.

OODBMSs are commonly used in applications where the data model closely mirrors real-world entities and their relationships, such as in scientific and engineering applications, multimedia content management, and any domain where complex data structures are prevalent. While OODBMSs offer advantages in certain contexts, it's important to carefully consider the specific requirements of your application when choosing a database management system.

## ONLINE RESOURCES

**Practice Paper Link:** https://forms.gle/XAs4TjZX12XPWGbE9

**QR Code:**

**Video Content:** https://www.youtube.com/playlist?list=PLzlh_31VWEFqKIYRcVCdVVNPUS5Ohny7A

**QR Code:**

# Chapter 10: Data Security and Privacy

## Database Security Threats

Database security threats refer to various risks and vulnerabilities that can compromise the confidentiality, integrity, and availability of data stored in a database management system (DBMS). Protecting databases from these threats is essential to ensure the safety and privacy of sensitive information

Numerous software configurations that are not correct, weaknesses, or patterns of carelessness or abuse can lead to a breach of security. Here are some of the most prevalent kinds of reasons for security attacks and the reasons.

### Insider Dangers

An insider threat can be an attack on security from any three sources having an access privilege to the database.

A malicious insider who wants to cause harm

An insider who is negligent and makes mistakes that expose the database to attack.vulnerable to attacks

An infiltrator is an outsider who acquires credentials by using a method like phishing or accessing the database of credential information in the database itself.

Insider dangers are among the most frequent sources of security breaches to databases. They often occur as a consequence of the inability of employees to have access to privileged user credentials.

### Human Error

The unintentional mistakes, weak passwords or sharing passwords, and other negligent or uninformed behaviours of users remain the root causes of almost half (49 percent) of all data security breaches.

### Database Software Vulnerabilities can be Exploited

Hackers earn their money by identifying and exploiting vulnerabilities in software such as databases management software. The major database software companies and open-source databases management platforms release regular security patches to fix these weaknesses. However, failing to implement the patches on time could increase the risk of being hacked.

### SQL/NoSQL Injection Attacks

A specific threat to databases is the infusing of untrue SQL as well as other non-SQL string attacks in queries for databases delivered by web-based apps and HTTP headers. Companies that do not follow the safe coding practices for web applications and conduct regular vulnerability tests are susceptible to attacks using these.

### Buffer Overflow is a way to Exploit Buffers

Buffer overflow happens when a program seeks to copy more data into the memory block with a certain length than it can accommodate. The attackers may make use of the extra data, which is stored in adjacent memory addresses, to establish a basis for they can begin attacks.

### DDoS (DoS/DDoS) Attacks

In a denial-of-service (DoS) attack in which the attacker overwhelms the targeted server -- in this case, the database server with such a large volume of requests that the server is unable to meet no longer legitimate requests made by actual users. In most cases, the server is unstable or even fails to function.

### Malware

Malware is software designed to exploit vulnerabilities or cause harm to databases. Malware can be accessed via any device that connects to the databases network.

**Attacks on Backups**

Companies that do not protect backup data using the same rigorous controls employed to protect databases themselves are at risk of cyberattacks on backups.

The following factors amplify the threats:

Data volumes are growing: Data capture, storage, and processing continue to increase exponentially in almost all organizations. Any tools or methods must be highly flexible to meet current as well as far-off needs.

The infrastructure is sprawling: Network environments are becoming more complicated, especially as companies shift their workloads into multiple clouds and hybrid cloud architectures and make the selection of deployment, management, and administration of security solutions more difficult.

More stringent requirements for regulatory compliance: The worldwide regulatory compliance landscape continues to increase by complexity. This makes the compliance of every mandate more challenging.

## Access Control and Authentication

Access control and authentication are essential components of database security, ensuring that only authorized users can access and manipulate the data stored in a database. The security mechanism of DBMS must include some provisions for restricting access to the data base by unauthorized users.

**Access control**

Access control is done by creating user accounts and to control login process by the DBMS. So, that database access of sensitive data is possible only to those people (database users) who are allowed to access such data and to restrict access to unauthorized persons.

The database system must also keep the track of all operations performed by certain user throughout the entire login time.

**Types of Access Control**

Obsolete access models include Discretionary Access Control (DAC) and Mandatory Access Control (MAC). Role Based Access Control (RBAC) is the most common method today, and the most recent model is Attribute Based Access Control (ABAC).

Discretionary Access Control (DAC)

With DAC models, the data owner allows access. DAC is a means of assigning access rights based on user-specified rules.

Mandatory Access Control (MAC)

MAC was developed using a nondiscretionary model, in which people are granted access based on an information clearance. MAC is a policy in which access rights are assigned based on central authority regulations.

Role Based Access Control (RBAC)

RBAC grants access based on a user's role and implements key security principles such as "least privilege" and "separation of privilege." Thus, someone attempting to access information can only access data necessary for their role.

Attribute Based Access Control (ABAC)

In ABAC, each resource and user are assigned a series of attributes. In this dynamic method, a comparative assessment of the user's attributes, including time of day, position and location, are used to make a decision on access to a resource.

**How it Works**

Let's take a look how access control works in DataSunrise.

Two-Factor Authentication

DataSunrise includes two-factor authentication mechanisms based on emails and one-time passwords (OTP) which allow to access the target database. Database users should input database's password and complete email-based or Google Authenticator based authentication to get access to the target database.

Database Access Restriction

DataSunrise features Data Security component which enables you to restrict access to a complete database or certain database objects depending on the following factors:

Database username;

Client application;

Application username;

IP address or hostname;

Operating system user;

Number of unsuccessful login attempts;

Query text.

**Authentication:**

Authentication is the process of confirmation that whether the user log in only according to the rights provided to him to perform the activities of data base. A particular user can login only up to his privilege but he can't access the other sensitive data. The privilege of accessing sensitive data is restricted by using Authentication.

By using these authentication tools for biometrics such as retina and figure prints can prevent the data base from unauthorized/malicious users.

**Authentication Factors**

As per the security levels and the type of application, there are different types of Authentication factors:

Single-Factor Authentication

Single-factor authentication is the simplest way of authentication. It just needs a username and password to allows a user to access a system.

Two-factor Authentication

As per the name, it is two-level security; hence it needs two-step verification to authenticate a user. It does not require only a username and password but also needs the unique information that only the particular user knows, such as first school name, a favorite destination. Apart from this, it can also verify the user by sending the OTP or a unique link on the user's registered number or email address.

Multi-factor Authentication

This is the most secure and advanced level of authorization. It requires two or more than two levels of security from different and independent categories. This type of authentication is usually used in financial organizations, banks, and law enforcement agencies. This ensures to eliminate any data exposer from the third party or hackers.

**Famous Authentication techniques**

Password-based authentication

It is the simplest way of authentication. It requires the password for the particular username. If the password matches with the username and both details match the system's database, the user will be successfully authenticated.

Passwordless authentication

In this technique, the user doesn't need any password; instead, he gets an OTP (One-time password) or link on his registered mobile number or phone number. It can also be said OTP-based authentication.

2FA/MFA

2FA/MFA or 2-factor authentication/Multi-factor authentication is the higher level of authentication. It requires additional PIN or security questions so that it can authenticate the user.

Single Sign-on

Single Sign-on or SSO is a way to enable access to multiple applications with a single set of credentials. It allows the user to sign-in once, and it will automatically be signed in to all other web apps from the same centralized directory.

Social Authentication

Social authentication does not require additional security; instead, it verifies the user with the existing credentials for the available social network.

## Compliance with Data Privacy Regulations (GDPR, HIPAA, etc.)

Compliance with data privacy regulations is a critical aspect of data security, especially when handling sensitive personal or confidential information. Several data privacy regulations exist globally, each with its own set of requirements and standards. Here are some key considerations for ensuring compliance with data privacy regulations:

**Know the Applicable Regulations:**

Identify which data privacy regulations are relevant to your organization based on its location and the nature of data it processes. Common regulations include the General Data Protection Regulation (GDPR) in Europe, the Health Insurance Portability and Accountability Act (HIPAA) in the United States, and many others.

**Data Classification:**

Classify the data you handle based on its sensitivity. Determine whether it contains personal, sensitive, or confidential information, as different regulations apply to different types of data.

**Consent and Transparency:**

Obtain explicit consent from individuals before collecting, processing, or storing their personal data. Be transparent about how their data will be used and for what purposes.

**Data Minimization:**

Collect only the data that is necessary for the intended purpose. Avoid collecting excessive or irrelevant information.

**Data Security Measures:**

Implement robust security measures to protect data from unauthorized access, breaches, or leaks. This includes encryption, access controls, regular security audits, and monitoring.

**Data Access Controls**:

Ensure that only authorized personnel have access to sensitive data. Implement role-based access controls and strong authentication mechanisms.

**Data Breach Response Plan**:

Develop a data breach response plan that outlines the steps to take in case of a data breach. This includes notifying affected individuals and relevant authorities, as required by some regulations.

**Data Portability:**

Some regulations, like GDPR, require that individuals have the right to request their data and transfer it to other service providers. Implement mechanisms to facilitate data portability when necessary.

**Data Retention and Deletion**:

Define clear policies for data retention and deletion. Data should not be kept longer than necessary, and individuals should have the right to request the deletion of their data.

**Data Protection Impact Assessments (DPIAs):**

Conduct DPIAs for high-risk data processing activities. This involves assessing the impact of data processing on individuals' privacy and implementing mitigating measures.

**Data Privacy Officer (DPO):**

Appoint a Data Privacy Officer or Compliance Officer responsible for overseeing data privacy compliance and ensuring that the organization adheres to relevant regulations.

**Regular Audits and Assessments**:

Conduct regular audits and assessments of your data processing practices to ensure ongoing compliance. Seek external audits or assessments if necessary.

**Documentation and Records**:

Maintain detailed records of data processing activities, consent records, and security measures implemented. This documentation may be required to demonstrate compliance during regulatory audits.

**Training and Awareness**:

Train employees and raise awareness about data privacy regulations, ensuring that they understand their responsibilities and how to handle data in compliance with the law.

**International Data Transfers**:

If your organization operates internationally, consider the regulations governing cross-border data transfers and put appropriate safeguards in place, such as Standard Contractual Clauses (SCCs) or binding corporate rules.

It's important to stay informed about changes and updates to data privacy regulations, as they can evolve over time. Failing to comply with these regulations can result in significant fines, legal consequences, and reputational damage. Therefore, organizations must prioritize data privacy as an integral part of their data security strategy.

**Exercise**

**Exercise 1 – MCQ**

Q 1. Which of the following is an example of a data security breach?

A) Regular data backup

B) Strong password policy

C) Unauthorized access to sensitive customer information

D) Data encryption

Q 2. What does GDPR stand for in the context of data privacy regulations?

A) General Data Resolution Protocol

B) Global Data Privacy Regulation

C) General Data Protection Regulation

D) Global Data Protection Resolution

**Exercise 2 – True/ False**

Q 1. Encrypting data ensures its absolute security, making it impossible for unauthorized parties to access or decipher the information.

Q 2. Privacy laws, such as GDPR (General Data Protection Regulation) in Europe, primarily apply to businesses and organizations based within the country's jurisdiction and have limited impact on international data sharing.

**Exercise 3 – One word answer**

Q 1. What security technique transforms data into a coded format to prevent unauthorized access?

Q 2. What term refers to obtaining permission from individuals to collect and use their personal data in compliance with privacy regulations?

**Exercise 4 – Small answer**

Q 1. What is data encryption, and why is it an important security measure in safeguarding sensitive information? Provide an example of a situation where data encryption would be crucial.

Q 2. Explain the concept of "data anonymization" in the context of data privacy. How does data anonymization help protect individuals' privacy while allowing for data analysis? Provide an example of when data anonymization might be applied.

**Exercise 5 – Long answer**

Q 1. Discuss the role of Access Control in data security. Explain the concepts of Role-Based Access Control (RBAC) and Mandatory Access Control (MAC), and how they contribute to safeguarding sensitive data.

Q 2. Describe privacy-preserving technologies, such as anonymization and pseudonymization. Provide examples of how these techniques can be applied to maintain data privacy while allowing data analysis.

**Answer**

**Exercise 1**

Answer 1: C), 2: C)

**Exercise 2**

Answer 1: False, 2: False

**Exercise 3**

Answer 1: Encryption., 2: Consent.

**Previous Years Questions**

Q1. Discuss the measures that are used to provide security of data in databases. (IGNOU MCA 2012)

Q2. Discuss the key control measures that are used to provide security to data in databases. (IGNOU MCA 2016)

Q3. How are database security and database integrity related? Briefly discuss the different levels of security measures which may be considered to protect the database. (IGNOU MCA 2017)

**ONLINE RESOURCES**

**Practice Paper Link:** https://forms.gle/FqcczPLL2yh7U8uDA

**QR Code:**

**Video Content:** https://www.youtube.com/playlist?list=PLzlh_31VWEFqAXtW7UsVFn7NKpeIa7I32

**QR Code:**

# Chapter 11: Data Analytics and Business Intelligence

## Data Warehouses and Data Marts

A Data Warehouse (DW) is a relational database that is designed for query and analysis rather than transaction processing. It includes historical data derived from transaction data from single and multiple sources.

A Data Warehouse provides integrated, enterprise-wide, historical data and focuses on providing support for decision-makers for data modeling and analysis.

A Data Warehouse is a group of data specific to the entire organization, not only to a particular group of users.

It is not used for daily operations and transaction processing but used for making decisions.

A Data Warehouse can be viewed as a data system with the following attributes:

It is a database designed for investigative tasks, using data from various applications.

It supports a relatively small number of clients with relatively long interactions.

It includes current and historical data to provide a historical perspective of information.

Its usage is read-intensive.

It contains a few large tables.

"Data Warehouse is a subject-oriented, integrated, and time-variant store of information in support of management's decisions."

### Characteristics of Data Warehouse

Subject-Oriented

A data warehouse target on the modeling and analysis of data for decision-makers. Therefore, data warehouses typically provide a concise and straightforward view around a particular subject, such as customer, product, or sales, instead of the global organization's ongoing operations. This is done by excluding data that are not useful concerning the subject and including all data needed by the users to understand the subject.

Integrated

A data warehouse integrates various heterogeneous data sources like RDBMS, flat files, and online transaction records. It requires performing data cleaning and integration during data warehousing to ensure consistency in naming conventions, attributes types, etc., among different data sources.

Time-Variant

Historical information is kept in a data warehouse. For example, one can retrieve files from 3 months, 6 months, 12 months, or even previous data from a data warehouse. These variations with a transactions system, where often only the most current file is kept.

Non-Volatile

The data warehouse is a physically separate data storage, which is transformed from the source operational RDBMS. The operational updates of data do not occur in the data warehouse, i.e., update, insert, and delete operations are not performed. It usually requires only two procedures in data accessing: Initial loading of data and access to data. Therefore, the DW does not require transaction processing, recovery, and concurrency capabilities, which allows for substantial speedup of data retrieval. Non-Volatile defines that once entered into the warehouse, and data should not change.

**History of Data Warehouse**

The idea of data warehousing came to the late 1980's when IBM researchers Barry Devlin and Paul Murphy established the "Business Data Warehouse."

In essence, the data warehousing idea was planned to support an architectural model for the flow of information from the operational system to decisional support environments. The concept attempt to address the various problems associated with the flow, mainly the high costs associated with it.

In the absence of data warehousing architecture, a vast amount of space was required to support multiple decision support environments. In large corporations, it was ordinary for various decision support environments to operate independently.

**Goals of Data Warehousing**

To help reporting as well as analysis

Maintain the organization's historical information

Be the foundation for decision making.

**Need for Data Warehouse**

Data Warehouse is needed for the following reasons:

Business User: Business users require a data warehouse to view summarized data from the past. Since these people are non-technical, the data may be presented to them in an elementary form.

Store historical data: Data Warehouse is required to store the time variable data from the past. This input is made to be used for various purposes.

Make strategic decisions: Some strategies may be depending upon the data in the data warehouse. So, data warehouse contributes to making strategic decisions.

For data consistency and quality: Bringing the data from different sources at a commonplace, the user can effectively undertake to bring the uniformity and consistency in data.

High response time: Data warehouse has to be ready for somewhat unexpected loads and types of queries, which demands a significant degree of flexibility and quick response time.

**Benefits of Data Warehouse**

Understand business trends and make better forecasting decisions.

Data Warehouses are designed to perform well enormous amounts of data.

The structure of data warehouses is more accessible for end-users to navigate, understand, and query.

Queries that would be complex in many normalized databases could be easier to build and maintain in data warehouses.

Data warehousing is an efficient method to manage demand for lots of information from lots of users.

Data warehousing provide the capabilities to analyze a large amount of historical data.

**Data Mart**

A Data Mart is a subset of a directorial information store, generally oriented to a specific purpose or primary data subject which may be distributed to provide business needs. Data Marts are analytical record stores designed to focus on particular business functions for a specific community within an organization. Data marts are derived from subsets of data in a data warehouse, though in the bottom-up data warehouse design methodology, the data warehouse is created from the union of organizational data marts.

The fundamental use of a data mart is Business Intelligence (BI) applications. BI is used to gather, store, access, and analyze record. It can be used by smaller businesses to utilize the data they have accumulated since it is less expensive than implementing a data warehouse.

**Reasons for creating a data mart**

Creates collective data by a group of users

Easy access to frequently needed data

Ease of creation

Improves end-user response time

Lower cost than implementing a complete data warehouse

Potential clients are more clearly defined than in a comprehensive data warehouse

It contains only essential business data and is less cluttered.

**Types of Data Marts**

There are mainly two approaches to designing data marts. These approaches are

Dependent Data Marts

Independent Data Marts

**Dependent Data Marts**

A dependent data mart is a logical subset of a physical subset of a higher data warehouse. According to this technique, the data marts are treated as the subsets of a data warehouse. In this technique, firstly a data warehouse is created from which further various data marts can be created. These data mart are dependent on the data warehouse and extract the essential record from it. In this technique, as the data warehouse creates the data mart; therefore, there is no need for data mart integration. It is also known as a top-down approach.

**Independent Data Marts**

The second approach is independent data marts (IDM) Here, firstly independent data marts are created, and then a data warehouse is designed using these independent multiple data marts. In this approach, as all the data marts are designed independently; therefore, the integration of data marts is required. It is also termed as a bottom-up approach as the data marts are integrated to develop a data warehouse.

Other than these two categories, one more type exists that is called "Hybrid Data Marts."

**Hybrid Data Marts**

It allows us to combine input from sources other than a data warehouse. This could be helpful for many situations; especially when Adhoc integrations are needed, such as after a new group or product is added to the organizations.

**Steps in Implementing a Data Mart**

The significant steps in implementing a data mart are to design the schema, construct the physical storage, populate the data mart with data from source systems, access it to make informed decisions and manage it over time. So, the steps are:

Designing

The design step is the first in the data mart process. This phase covers all of the functions from initiating the request for a data mart through gathering data about the requirements and developing the logical and physical design of the data mart.

It involves the following tasks:

Gathering the business and technical requirements

Identifying data sources

Selecting the appropriate subset of data

Designing the logical and physical architecture of the data mart.

Constructing

This step contains creating the physical database and logical structures associated with the data mart to provide fast and efficient access to the data.

It involves the following tasks:

Creating the physical database and logical structures such as tablespaces associated with the data mart.

creating the schema objects such as tables and indexes describe in the design step.

Determining how best to set up the tables and access structures.

Populating

This step includes all of the tasks related to the getting data from the source, cleaning it up, modifying it to the right format and level of detail, and moving it into the data mart.

It involves the following tasks:

Mapping data sources to target data sources

Extracting data

Cleansing and transforming the information.

Loading data into the data mart

Creating and storing metadata

Accessing

This step involves putting the data to use: querying the data, analyzing it, creating reports, charts and graphs and publishing them.

It involves the following tasks:

Set up and intermediate layer (Meta Layer) for the front-end tool to use. This layer translates database operations and objects names into business conditions so that the end-clients can interact with the data mart using words which relates to the business functions.

Set up and manage database architectures like summarized tables which help queries agree through the front-end tools execute rapidly and efficiently.

Managing

This step contains managing the data mart over its lifetime. In this step, management functions are performed as:

Providing secure access to the data.

Managing the growth of the data.

Optimizing the system for better performance.

Ensuring the availability of data event with system failures.

**Difference between Data Warehouse and Data Mart**

| Data Warehouse | Data Mart |
|---|---|
| A Data Warehouse is a vast repository of information collected from various organizations or departments within a corporation. | A data mart is an only subtype of a Data Warehouses. It is architecture to meet the requirement of a specific user group. |
| It may hold multiple subject areas. | It holds only one subject area. For example, Finance or Sales. |
| It holds very detailed information. | It may hold more summarized data. |
| Works to integrate all data sources | It concentrates on integrating data from a given subject area or set of source systems. |
| In data warehousing, Fact constellation is used. | In Data Mart, Star Schema and Snowflake Schema are used. |
| It is a Centralized System. It is a Decentralized System. | |
| Data Warehousing is the data-oriented. | Data Marts is a project-oriented. |

## OLAP vs. OLTP

| Category | OLAP (Online Analytical Processing) | OLTP (Online Transaction Processing) |
|---|---|---|
| Definition | It is well-known as an online database query management system. | It is well-known as an online database modifying system. |
| Data source | Consists of historical data from various Databases. | Consists of only operational current data. |
| Method used | It makes use of a data warehouse. | It makes use of a standard database management system (DBMS). |
| Application | It is subject-oriented. Used for Data Mining, Analytics, Decisions making, etc. | It is application-oriented. Used for business tasks. |
| Normalized | In an OLAP database, tables are not normalized. | In an OLTP database, tables are normalized (3NF). |
| Usage of data | The data is used in planning, problem-solving, and decision-making. | The data is used to perform day-to-day fundamental operations. |
| Task | It provides a multi-dimensional view of different business tasks. | It reveals a snapshot of present business tasks. |
| Purpose | It serves the purpose to extract information for analysis and decision-making. | It serves the purpose to Insert, Update, and Delete information from the database. |

## Data Visualization Tools

Graphical representation of any information or data is known as Data Visualization. This helps in segregating the data in an efficient manner by using various types of visuals such as graphs, maps, charts, maps, and visualization tools. In addition to this, with the help of a data visualization tool, the data can be presented in a very unique and understandable manner so that people who are not from a technical background can understand everything easily.

Data Visualization Tools are software platforms that provide information in a visual format such as a graph, chart, etc to make it easily understandable and usable. Data Visualization tools are so popular as they allow analysts and statisticians to create visual data models easily according to their specifications by conveniently providing an interface, database connections, and Machine Learning tools.

**Best Data Visualization Tools**

**Tableau**

Tableau is a data visualization tool that can be used by data analysts, scientists, statisticians, etc. to visualize the data and get a clear opinion based on the data analysis. Tableau is very famous as it can take in data and produce the required data visualization output in a very short time. And it can do this while providing the highest level of security with a guarantee to handle security issues as soon as they arise or are found by users.

Tableau also allows its users to prepare, clean, and format their data and then create data visualizations to obtain actionable insights that can be shared with other users.

**Looker**

Looker is a data visualization tool that can go in-depth into the data and analyze it to obtain useful insights. It provides real-time dashboards of the data for more in-depth analysis so that businesses can make instant decisions based on the data visualizations obtained. Looker also provides connections with Redshift, Snowflake, and BigQuery, as well as more than 50 SQL-supported dialects so you can connect to multiple databases without any issues.

Looker data visualizations can be shared with anyone using any particular tool. Also, you can export these files in any format immediately. It also provides customer support wherein you can ask any question and it shall be answered.

**Zoho Analytics**

Zoho Analytics is a Business Intelligence and Data Analytics software that can help you create wonderful-looking data visualizations based on your data in a few minutes. You can obtain data from multiple sources and mesh it together to create multidimensional data visualizations that allow you to view your business data across departments. In case you have any questions, you can use Zia which is a smart assistant created using artificial intelligence, machine learning, and natural language processing.

Zoho Analytics allows you to share or publish your reports with your colleagues and add comments or engage in conversations as required. You can export Zoho Analytics files in any format such as Spreadsheet, MS Word, Excel, PPT, PDF, etc.

**Sisense**

Sisense is a business intelligence-based data visualization system and it provides various tools that allow data analysts to simplify complex data and obtain insights for their organization and outsiders. Sisense believes that eventually, every company will be a data-driven company and every product will be related to data in some way. Therefore it tries its best to provide various data analytics tools to business teams and data analytics so that they can help make their companies the data-driven companies of the future.

It is very easy to set up and learn Sisense. It can be easily installed within a minute and data analysts can get their work done and obtain results instantly. Sisense also allows its users to export their files in multiple formats such as PPT, Excel, MS Word, PDF, etc. Sisense also provides full-time customer support services whenever users face any issues.

**IBM Cognos Analytics**

IBM Cognos Analytics is an Artificial Intelligence-based business intelligence platform that supports data analytics among other things. You can visualize as well as analyze your data and share actionable insights with anyone in your organization. Even if you have limited or no knowledge about data analytics, you can use IBM Cognos Analytics easily as it interprets the data for you and presents you with actionable insights in plain language.

You can also share your data with multiple users if you want on the cloud and share visuals over email or Slack. You can also import data from various sources like spreadsheets, cloud, CSV files, or on-premises databases and combine related data sources into a single data module.

**Qlik Sense**

Qlik Sense is a data visualization platform that helps companies to become data-driven enterprises by providing an associative data analytics engine, sophisticated Artificial Intelligence system, and scalable multi-cloud architecture that allows you to deploy any combination of SaaS, on-premises, or a private cloud.

You can easily combine, load, visualize, and explore your data on Qlik Sense, no matter its size. All the data charts, tables, and other visualizations are interactive and instantly update themselves according to the current data context. The Qlik Sense AI can even provide you with data insights and help you create analytics using just drag and drop.

**Domo**

Domo is a business intelligence model that contains multiple data visualization tools that provide a consolidated platform where you can perform data analysis and then create interactive data visualizations that allow other people to easily understand your data conclusions. You can combine cards, text, and images in the Domo dashboard so that you can guide other people through the data while telling a data story as they go.

In case of any doubts, you can use their pre-built dashboards to obtain quick insights from the data. Domo has a free trial option so you can use it to get a sense of this platform before committing to it fully.

**Microsoft Power BI**

Microsoft Power BI is a Data Visualization platform focused on creating a data-driven business intelligence culture in all companies today. To fulfill this, it offers self-service analytics tools that can be used to analyze, aggregate, and share data in a meaningful fashion.

Microsoft Power BI offers hundreds of data visualizations to its customers along with built-in Artificial Intelligence capabilities and Excel integration facilities.

**Klipfolio**

Klipfolio is a Canadian business intelligence company that provides one of the best data visualization tools. You can access your data from hundreds of different data sources like spreadsheets, databases, files, and web services applications by using connectors. Klipfolio also allows you to create custom drag-and-drop data visualizations wherein you can choose from different options like charts, graphs, scatter plots, etc. Klipfolio also has tools you can use to execute complex formulas that can solve challenging data problems.

**SAP Analytics Cloud**

SAP Analytics Cloud uses business intelligence and data analytics capabilities to help you evaluate your data and create visualizations in order to predict business outcomes. It also provides you with the latest modeling tools that help you by alerting you of possible errors in the data and categorizing different data measures and dimensions. SAP

Analytics Cloud also suggests Smart Transformations to the data that lead to enhanced visualizations. In case you have any doubts or business questions related to data visualization, SAP Analytics Cloud provides you with complete customer satisfaction by handling your queries using conversational artificial intelligence and natural language technology.

**Yellowfin**

Yellowfin is a worldwide famous analytics and business software vendor that has a well-suited automation product that is specially created for people who have to take decisions within a short period of time. This is an easy-to-use data visualization tool that allows people to understand things and act according to them in the form of collaboration, data storytelling, and stunning action-based dashboards. Yellowfin provides complete customer satisfaction with its five core products which have been integrated properly in order to manage analytics properly across the whole enterprise.

**Whatagraph**

Whatagraph is a seamless integration that provides marketing agencies with an easy and useful way of sharing or sending marketing campaign data with clients. With this platform, you can create the data in a way that the result is easy to understand and comprehend. This Data visualization tool has numerous customization options which can be picked virtually and help in creating reporting widgets or creating your own methods of presenting data. Whatagraph also helps in comparing data of different marketing platforms and their performance in one single report. You can try this platform for free for 30 days and after that pay $199 per month for the paid package.

Hence, these were some of the best Data Visualization tools which will help you to work efficiently without any time wastage. Also, if you want to try any of them, the trial versions are available which you can use according to your need and without any hassle.

## Extract, Transform, Load (ETL) Processes

ETL stands for Extract, Transform, Load and it is a process used in data warehousing to extract data from various sources, transform it into a format suitable for loading into a data warehouse, and then load it into the warehouse. The process of ETL can be broken down into the following three stages:

Extract: The first stage in the ETL process is to extract data from various sources such as transactional systems, spreadsheets, and flat files. This step involves reading data from the source systems and storing it in a staging area.

Transform: In this stage, the extracted data is transformed into a format that is suitable for loading into the data warehouse. This may involve cleaning and validating the data, converting data types, combining data from multiple sources, and creating new data fields.

Load: After the data is transformed, it is loaded into the data warehouse. This step involves creating the physical data structures and loading the data into the warehouse.

The ETL process is an iterative process that is repeated as new data is added to the warehouse. The process is important because it ensures that the data in the data warehouse is accurate, complete, and up-to-date. It also helps to ensure that the data is in the format required for data mining and reporting.

Additionally, there are many different ETL tools and technologies available, such as Informatica, Talend, DataStage, and others, that can automate and simplify the ETL process. ETL is a process in Data Warehousing and it stands for Extract, Transform and Load. It is a process in which an ETL tool extracts the data from various data source

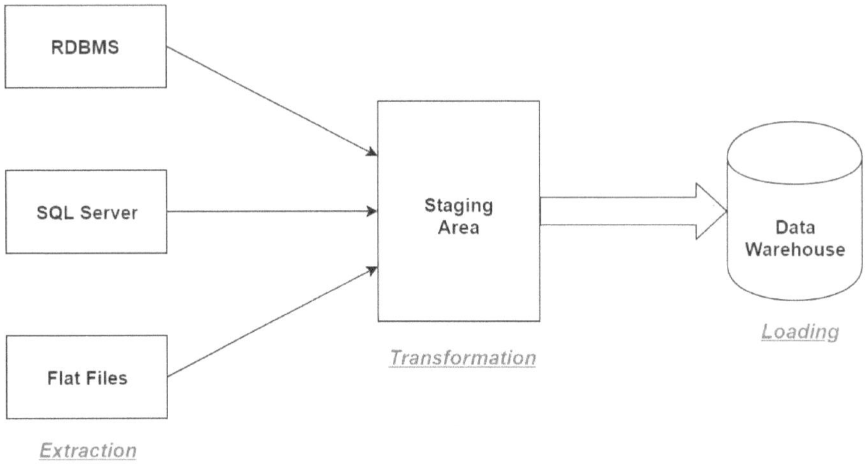


systems, transforms it in the staging area, and then finally, loads it into the Data Warehouse system.

Let us understand each step of the ETL process in-depth:

Extraction:

The first step of the ETL process is extraction. In this step, data from various source systems is extracted which can be in various formats like relational databases, No SQL, XML, and flat files into the staging area. It is important to extract the data from various source systems and store it into the staging area first and not directly into the data warehouse because the extracted data is in various formats and can be corrupted also. Hence loading it directly into the data warehouse may damage it and rollback will be much more difficult. Therefore, this is one of the most important steps of ETL process.

Transformation:

The second step of the ETL process is transformation. In this step, a set of rules or functions are applied on the extracted data to convert it into a single standard format. It may involve following processes/tasks:

Filtering – loading only certain attributes into the data warehouse.

Cleaning – filling up the NULL values with some default values, mapping U.S.A, United States, and America into USA, etc.

Joining – joining multiple attributes into one.

Splitting – splitting a single attribute into multiple attributes.

Sorting – sorting tuples on the basis of some attribute (generally key-attribute).

Loading:

The third and final step of the ETL process is loading. In this step, the transformed data is finally loaded into the data warehouse. Sometimes the data is updated by loading into the data warehouse very frequently and sometimes it is done after longer but regular intervals. The rate and period of loading solely depends on the requirements and varies from system to system.

ETL process can also use the pipelining concept i.e., as soon as some data is extracted, it can transform and during that period some new data can be extracted. And while the transformed data is being loaded into the data warehouse, the already extracted data can be transformed.

ETL Tools: Most commonly used ETL tools are Hevo, Sybase, Oracle Warehouse builder, CloverETL, and MarkLogic.

Data Warehouses: Most commonly used Data Warehouses are Snowflake, Redshift, BigQuery, and Firebolt.

**Advantages of ETL process in data warehousing:**

Improved data quality: ETL process ensures that the data in the data warehouse is accurate, complete, and up-to-date.

Better data integration: ETL process helps to integrate data from multiple sources and systems, making it more accessible and usable.

Increased data security: ETL process can help to improve data security by controlling access to the data warehouse and ensuring that only authorized users can access the data.

Improved scalability: ETL process can help to improve scalability by providing a way to manage and analyze large amounts of data.

Increased automation: ETL tools and technologies can automate and simplify the ETL process, reducing the time and effort required to load and update data in the warehouse.

**Disadvantages of ETL process in data warehousing:**

High cost: ETL process can be expensive to implement and maintain, especially for organizations with limited resources.

Complexity: ETL process can be complex and difficult to implement, especially for organizations that lack the necessary expertise or resources.

Limited flexibility: ETL process can be limited in terms of flexibility, as it may not be able to handle unstructured data or real-time data streams.

Limited scalability: ETL process can be limited in terms of scalability, as it may not be able to handle very large amounts of data.

Data privacy concerns: ETL process can raise concerns about data privacy, as large amounts of data are collected, stored, and analysed.

Overall, ETL process is an essential process in data warehousing that helps to ensure that the data in the data warehouse is accurate, complete, and up-to-date. However, it also comes with its own set of challenges and limitations, and organizations need to carefully consider the costs and benefits before implementing them.

**Exercise**

**Exercise 1 – MCQ**

Q 1. Which of the following best describes the primary goal of Business Intelligence (BI)?

a) To predict future market trends accurately.

b) To store and manage large volumes of data.

c) To turn raw data into actionable insights for informed decision-making.

d) To automate routine business processes.

Q 2What is the main objective of data visualization in Data Analytics?

a) To encrypt sensitive data.

b) To extract data from external sources.

c) To present data in a visually understandable format.

d) To create complex algorithms for data analysis.

**Exercise 2 – True/ False**

Q 1. Data Warehousing is a technology that is primarily focused on real-time data analysis and reporting.

Q 2. Data mining techniques are used in Business Intelligence to discover hidden patterns and insights within large datasets.

**Exercise 3 – One word answer**

Q 1. What is the primary goal of Data Analytics?

Q 2. What does KPI stand for in Business Intelligence?

**Exercise 4 – Small answer**

Q 1. What is exploratory data analysis (EDA) in the context of data analytics? Provide a brief explanation of its purpose and a common technique used in EDA.

Q 2. Explain the concept of Key Performance Indicators (KPIs) in Business Intelligence. Provide an example of a KPI that a retail business might use to measure its performance.

**Exercise 5 – Long answer**

Q 1. Describe the key steps involved in implementing a Business Intelligence strategy within an organization. Explain the process of data extraction, transformation, and loading (ETL), and its importance in data preparation for BI.

Q 2. Describe the key steps involved in implementing a Business Intelligence strategy within an organization. Explain the process of data extraction, transformation, and loading (ETL), and its importance in data preparation for BI.

**Answer**

**Exercise 1**

Answer 1: C), 2: C)

**Exercise 2**

Answer 1: False, 2: True

**Exercise 3**

Answer 1: Insights., 2: Insights.

**Previous Years Questions**

Q1. Differentiate the following: Agglomerative and Divisive clustering, OLAP Vs Data Mining. (Mumbai University MCA 2023)

Q2. Explain Data warehouse architecture in detail. (Mumbai University MCA 2023)

**Previous Years Questions with Answers**

Q1 What is ODL? (RU BCA 2017)

**Answer:**

**ODL**, in the context of databases and data modeling, stands for **Object Definition Language**. ODL is a language used to define the structure and characteristics of objects in an object-oriented database (OODBMS) or to specify object-oriented features in a database schema.

Key aspects of ODL include:

**Object Definitions**: ODL allows you to define classes of objects, specifying attributes (data members) and methods (member functions) for those classes. Objects of these classes are then used to represent data in the database.

**Inheritance**: ODL supports inheritance, enabling the creation of class hierarchies where child classes inherit attributes and methods from parent classes.

**Complex Data Relationships**: ODL provides mechanisms to define relationships between objects, such as associations and aggregations, which are fundamental in representing real-world data relationships.

**Data Abstraction**: ODL allows you to define abstract data types, which serve as templates for creating concrete objects.

**Data Encapsulation**: ODL supports data encapsulation, which means that the data (attributes) and behavior (methods) of an object are encapsulated within the object, and access to them is controlled through defined interfaces.

**Type Definitions**: You can define new data types in ODL, including primitive data types, structured data types, and object data types.

ODL plays a crucial role in the design and development of object-oriented databases. It helps in creating a clear and structured representation of the data to be stored in the database, reflecting the object-oriented nature of the system. ODL definitions are used by the OODBMS to create the corresponding schema and storage structures for objects in the database.

## ONLINE RESOURCES

**Practice Paper Link:** https://forms.gle/TM1sraLFeVEAtGZW9

**QR Code:**

**Video Content:** https://www.youtube.com/playlist?list=PLzlh_31VWEFqIENiPovIYj-kA_CSRC86x

**QR Code:**

# Chapter 12: Emerging Trends in Database Management

## Blockchain Databases

### What is Blockchain?

Blockchain technology stands as a leading, highly secure innovation designed to streamline transactions and asset tracking within business networks. These assets, whether tangible like real estate or intangible like intellectual property, can be efficiently monitored and traded through blockchain technology, mitigating potential hurdles and bolstering security. Consequently, it has emerged as an exceptionally secure network for tracking transactions.

Within the blockchain, data finds its home in the form of signed blocks meticulously linked together to construct an unbroken chain. To initiate any transaction, it must first pass the rigorous validation process, requiring approval from the majority of nodes within the network. Once validated, the transaction is promptly added to a block, which is then swiftly disseminated to all network nodes. This method ensures the utmost security and transparency in the realm of digital transactions.

### What is Blockchain Databases?

Blockchains and traditional databases share similarities yet differ significantly in their functionality and structure. While conventional databases organize data into tables, blockchains employ a different approach by storing data in blocks. Notably, blockchain databases are decentralized, contrasting with the centralized nature of traditional relational databases.

In essence, a blockchain serves as a distributed, decentralized ledger that securely records information within discrete blocks. It's important to note that every blockchain can be seen as a type of database, but the reverse is not true – not all databases can be classified as blockchains.

One notable distinction lies in performance, where blockchain databases tend to lag behind their traditional counterparts. This discrepancy in speed is a trade-off for the added security and decentralization offered by blockchain technology.

Blockchain databases, often referred to as blockchain technology or distributed ledger technology (DLT), represent a revolutionary approach to data management and security. They are a specialized type of database designed for recording and managing transactions across a network of computers in a way that ensures immutability, transparency, and trust without the need for a central authority.

**Blockchain vs Database**

| Parameters | Blockchain | Database |
|---|---|---|
| Control over data | Blockchain has decentralized control over the data. | The traditional database has centralized control over data. |
| Administrator | Blockchain does not require an administrator as the exact same copy of data is maintained at each node in the network. | In the database, the data is maintained by an administrator. |
| History | In Blockchain, there is real-time information but it allows one to track the history of transactions. | Traditional databases record present information only. Thus, it is not possible to trace the history of transactions. |
| Performance | Blockchains have slow performance when considered for digital transaction technology. | Relational databases outperform blockchains in terms of performance. |
| Data Integrity | Blockchains make it impossible for an attacker to tamper with data in the network without breaking the chain. | If necessary measures are not taken then it may be possible for an attacker to alter the data in databases. |
| Operations on transactions | In the blockchain, it is only possible to read or add data to the blockchain database | The database allows read, write, update, and delete operations on the data. |
| Permission | Blockchains are permissionless as anyone can access them. | Databases are permissioned as they can be accessed only by the individuals who have the right to access them. |
| Confidentiality | Blockchain is secure and confidential. | Databases are not fully confidential. |
| Recursive | Blockchains are not recursive as one cannot go back to repeat a task on any record. | Databases are recursive as one can go back to repeat a task on a particular record. |

**Different Ways to Create Blockchain Database**

There are 2 factors to consider before creating a blockchain database:

Database deployment in enterprise or consortium: It is important to determine whether the database will be used in the enterprise or consortium. In some cases, it may be possible that an enterprise is using blockchain internally for data storage and acts as a central authority governing the data. In this case, the blockchain database is centralized. But in the majority of the cases, blockchains operate in a consortium where there is no single source that owns and control data. Cryptocurrencies are one such example.

Data usage: Second most important factor to consider is how data will be used. Operational data is the data used directly by the clients connecting to the database. For example, cryptocurrencies are where there is no intermediary. Non-operational data is the one that can be accessed via an intermediary.

Considering the above 2 factors there are 4 possible ways to create a blockchain database:

Centralized With Operational Data/ Operational Blockchain Data Store With Enterprise.

Centralized With Non-operational Data/ Non-operational Blockchain Data Store With Enterprise.

Decentralized With Operational Data/ Operational Blockchain Data Store With Consortium.

Decentralized With Non-operational Data/ Non-operation Data Store With Consortium.

**Centralized With Operational Data/ Operational Blockchain Data Store With Enterprise**: When a blockchain is deployed inside an enterprise it does not need to be decentralized. Centralization simplifies the deployment and at the same time, it offers the advantages of the blockchain also compared to other databases.

This data store is useful in decision-making and operational reporting.

The database needs to be controlled by two or more administrators, each of whom will be operating from different locations.

This database provides the immutability to the documents and at the same time possibility to create and transfer assets.

This deployment provides a third-party auditor with a solid track for asset transfer.

The administrators would be responsible for reviewing the transactions whenever necessary.

In this data store, clients directly access the data without any intermediary as part of the data is stored on the blockchain.

It does prevent outside clients to access the data.

**Centralized With Non-operational Data/ Non-operational Blockchain Data Store With Enterprise**: In this case, also the blockchain database deployment is centralized and is maintained by a limited number of administrators. This approach is different in the sense that here intermediaries are set up who can access the data store and send it to clients.

In this type of blockchain database, the data is not accessed directly by the clients.

Here, clients connect to the database instances that in return connect and offload the parts of the data on the blockchain.

This approach offers better performance as less number of nodes are required to accept a transaction.

Since data is only accessible to a limited number of clients so this method adds more privacy to the blockchain database.

**Decentralized With Operational Data/ Operational Blockchain Data Store With Consortium**: In this deployment scenario, a consortium is created to remove the need for a single entity to control the database. The consortium can be made up of multiple databases.

This approach ensures that the database is decentralized.

All companies act as individual nodes and thus are responsible for maintaining the database.

Decentralization increases the immutability of the data.

For example, Supply chain management, etc.

**Decentralized With Non-operational Data/ Non-operation Data Store With Consortium**: In this deployment scenario, multiple administrators from different consortium members control the blockchain.

Intermediaries are here to help clients to access data in the database.

This approach provides increased speed and privacy as there is a limited number of clients accessing the blockchain.

For example, companies that hold personal information and sales details that might be required by the outsider parties and affiliate organizations who are not allowed to access the database directly.

When considering the utilization of Blockchain as a database, two prominent challenges emerge:

Limited Querying Capabilities: Blockchain primarily stores transactional data and doesn't excel in terms of querying capabilities. Retrieving specific information efficiently from a blockchain can be quite challenging.

Validation Delays: Block validation on a blockchain necessitates the approval of a majority of network nodes. As the number of nodes increases, the time required for validation proportionally extends.

Rather than employing blockchain as a standalone database, a more practical approach is to enhance an existing database with blockchain functionalities. This involves the integration of two distinct database layers:

Layer One: This layer incorporates a lightweight consensus protocol. It focuses on maintaining data integrity and provides robust performance for querying. Users can interact with this layer effectively to access and retrieve data.

Layer Two: In this layer, the Proof of Work (PoW) consensus mechanism comes into play. Its purpose is to store evidence of operations performed within the first layer. The integration between the two layers is facilitated through a blockchain anchoring mechanism. This mechanism effectively links the data from the first layer with the blocks in the second layer, forming a chain of evidence that validates the integrity of the data stored in the first layer.

This two-layered approach combines the efficiency of traditional databases with the security and transparency benefits of blockchain technology, offering a balanced solution for various data management needs.

Constructing a Blockchain Database presents a set of intricate challenges:

Querying Limitations: While a blockchain excels at storing transactional data, its querying capabilities are notably limited. This limitation hinders the efficient retrieval of specific information from the blockchain.

Scalability Hurdles: Public blockchains grapple with scalability issues. Expanding the network with decentralized nodes leads to increased network traffic. Paradoxically, this surge in traffic diminishes the throughput of blockchain transactions.

Low Throughput: The decentralized nature of blockchain networks, while secure, contributes to reduced transaction throughput. More nodes are mandated to approve each transaction, prolonging the process and impeding overall throughput.

Elevated Latency: Prominent blockchain networks like Bitcoin and Ethereum grapple with high latency. This delay can affect the speed and responsiveness of transactions and data processing.

Addressing these challenges is crucial to enhance the efficiency and usability of blockchain databases, especially in applications demanding rapid and scalable data management.

**Top 5 Blockchain-based Database**

BigchainDB: Ithet is a blockchain-bassed database provided by MongoDB that enables one to add decentralized and blockchain qualities to the application. It also permits the deposition of large-scale applications in numerous use cases.

Cassandra: It is an open-source NoSQL distributed database that delivers linear scalability. Cassandra is trusted by thousands of companies for high availability without compromising performance. It is a unique blockchain-based database for project purposes due to the presence of notable features.

ChainifyDB: It is a blockchain solution for databases. It provides a layer in which databases can be plugged into the ChainifyDB network. Chainify DB also synchronizes the databases.

Modex BCDB: It is a middleware software product that provides a plug-and-play approach for organizations. Modex BCDB is drawn to the plan of offering a real-time experience of data protection.

Postchain: It is a blockchain platform developed by Chromeby in Sweden. It has a network of nodes that maintain a set of data through a proof-of-authority consensus algorithm.

## Graph Databases

Graph Databases, often referred to as GDBs, introduce a distinctive approach to data storage. Unlike traditional databases that rely on tables or document-based structures, GDBs harness the power of graph structures. In this innovative paradigm, data is represented using nodes, edges, and associated properties.

In essence, nodes serve as data entities, edges signify connections or relationships between these entities, and properties provide additional information about both nodes and edges. This arrangement simplifies the retrieval of data, often requiring just a single operation.

Graph databases are a prominent category within the realm of NoSQL databases, and they excel in scenarios where relationships and complex data connections play a pivotal role. Their graph-centric architecture offers an efficient means to navigate and extract valuable insights from interconnected data points.

Representation:

The graph database is based on graph theory. The data is stored in the nodes of the graph and the relationship between the data are represented by the edges between the nodes.

**When do we need Graph Database?**

It solves Many-To-Many relationship problems

If we have friends of friends and stuff like that, these are many to many relationships. Used when the query in the relational database is very complex.

When relationships between data elements are more important

For example- there is a profile and the profile has some specific information in it but the major selling point is the relationship between these different profiles that is how you get connected within a network. In the same way, if there is data element such as user data element inside a graph database there could be multiple user data elements but the relationship is what is going to be the factor for all these data elements which are stored inside the graph database.

Low latency with large scale data

When you add lots of relationships in the relational database, the data sets are going to be huge and when you query it, the complexity is going to be more complex and it is going to be more than a usual time. However, in graph database, it is specifically designed for this particular purpose and one can query relationship with ease.

**Example**

Creating a table format for a graph database example can be challenging due to the non-tabular nature of graph databases. However, I can provide a simplified representation of a graph database example with a small dataset:

Nodes Table (Users):

| Node ID | Name | Age | Gender |
|---|---|---|---|
| 1 | Alice | 30 | Female |
| 2 | Bob | 28 | Male |
| 3 | Charlie | 35 | Male |
| 4 | David | 27 | Male |

**Edges Table (Friendships):**

| Edge ID | Source Node | Target Node |
|---|---|---|
| 1 | 1 | 2 |
| 2 | 1 | 3 |
| 3 | 2 | 4 |

In this simplified example:

The "Nodes Table" represents users and includes attributes like Name, Age, and Gender.

The "Edges Table" represents friendships between users. Each row in this table indicates a friendship (edge) between two users (nodes). The "Source Node" and "Target Node" columns specify which users are connected.

Keep in mind that this is a highly simplified representation, and real graph databases like Neo4j or Amazon Neptune can handle much more complex and interconnected data. Graph databases excel at managing and querying such interconnected data efficiently.

## Time-Series Databases

A "Time Series Database" (TSDB) is a specialized system designed to manage and retrieve data records associated with timestamps. These timestamps are crucial as they establish the chronological relationship between data points. Time series

data often consists of a continuous flow of information, such as sensor readings or stock prices throughout the day. TSDBs are engineered to efficiently store and retrieve large volumes of timestamped data, facilitating complex data analysis.

Unlike other types of datasets, time series datasets are typically characterized by their sheer size and simplicity, consisting mainly of timestamps and related data. Moreover, they do not necessarily require indefinite data retention and may exhibit fewer interconnections between data records across various tables. TSDBs leverage these unique features to excel in terms of both storage capacity and performance when compared to general-purpose databases.

A Time Series Database, also known as a TSDB, is a software system specifically designed to handle time series data. Time series data is essentially a collection of data points, each associated with a timestamp. This type of data is often encountered in scenarios like sensor readings, financial market data, or any situation where information is captured over time.

What makes TSDBs unique is their ability to efficiently store and retrieve time series data. They are optimized for fast data insertion and retrieval, making them ideal for analyzing and working with this type of data. Unlike traditional databases that store various types of data indefinitely, TSDBs are designed to handle the continuous influx of time-stamped data and can be configured to automatically remove outdated records.

One notable advantage of TSDBs is their ability to apply specialized compression techniques that work exceptionally well with uniform time series data. This sets them apart from general-purpose databases. Additionally, TSDBs can improve query performance by using tailored database indices. While they were originally employed for industrial applications with sensor data, today, TSDBs find utility in a much broader spectrum of applications due to their efficiency in handling time-based data.

**Working of Time Series Database:**

TSDBs function by recording a combination of fixed and dynamic values. One set of data points might be labelled "Oil Pressure Rig Number 1" in an oil well where numerous metrics about the rig are recorded, and the related dynamic values would be the pressure measurement and the timestamp. This sample time series data is beneficial for observing patterns in the oil pressure, which, when examined in conjunction with other parameters, may help determine whether to abandon the well or not. These data files are stored on a medium using a format that enables quick time-based reads and writes.

The sequence of the data points is a natural property of the data because all entries are timestamped. A stream processing engine that can consider the ordered data as if it were a data stream can receive the data using this order. Leveraging a quick stream processing engine is typically ideal because one of the key objectives of TSDBs is to be quick. An example of a quick stream processing engine that benefits from in-memory architecture is Hazelcast Jet. Hazelcast Jet can connect with TSDBs, allowing for the rapid processing of time series data provided by the TSDB.

**Examples of Time Series Database:**

InfluxDB

Prometheus

QuestDB

Aerospike

DataStax

GridDB

Druid

Warp 10

Trendalyze

Amazon Timestream

dataPARC

BangDB

createDB

Google Cloud Big Table

CortexDB

**Exercise**

**Exercise 1 – MCQ**

Q 1. Which of the following is an emerging trend in database management systems (DBMS)?

A) Traditional relational databases

B) Centralized data storage

C) Blockchain-based databases

D) Client-Server architecture

Q 2Which technology is commonly associated with enhancing data storage and processing capabilities in modern database management?

A) Virtual Reality (VR)

B) Quantum Computing

C) Morse Code

D) Mechanical Typewriters.

**Exercise 2 – True/ False**

Q 1. Data Warehousing is a technology that is primarily focused on real-time data analysis and reporting.

Q 2. Data mining techniques are used in Business Intelligence to discover hidden patterns and insights within large datasets.

**Exercise 3 – One word answer**

Q 1What emerging database trend focuses on storing and querying data using nodes and edges to represent complex relationships?

Q 2. Which technology, often associated with cryptocurrencies, is being explored for secure and immutable data storage in database management?

**Exercise 4 – Small answer**

Q 1. Machine Learning and Artificial Intelligence (AI) are not relevant to database management.

Q 2. Blockchain technology is primarily used for data storage and retrieval in traditional relational databases.

**Exercise 5 – Long answer**

Q 1. Describe the key steps involved in implementing a Business Intelligence strategy within an organization. Explain the process of data extraction, transformation, and loading (ETL), and its importance in data preparation for BI.

Q 2. Describe the key steps involved in implementing a Business Intelligence strategy within an organization. Explain the process of data extraction, transformation, and loading (ETL), and its importance in data preparation for BI.

**Answer**

**Exercise 1**

Answer 1: C), 2: B)

**Exercise 2**

Answer 1: False, 2: False

**Exercise 3**

Answer 1: Graph., 2: Blockchain

## ONLINE RESOURCES

**Practice Paper Link:** https://forms.gle/GQXZmTqocqC9EwPL7

**QR Code:**

**Video Content:**https://www.youtube.com/playlist?list=PLzlh_31VWEFqHAJakLR-Zt06bkBU6n9c6

**QR Code:**

# Chapter 13: Laboratory Practical's

## Experiment No: 1

**Title: Implementation of DDL commands of SQL with suitable examples**

**Create table**

**Alter table**

**Drop Table**

**Objective:**

Gain insight into the various aspects related to the design and execution of a database system.

Acquire proficiency in employing data definition language for constructing queries in a database.

**Theory:**

Oracle has many tools such as SQL * PLUS, Oracle Forms, Oracle Report Writer, Oracle Graphics etc.

SQL * PLUS: The SQL * PLUS tool is made up of two distinct parts. These are

Interactive SQL: Interactive SQL is designed for create, access and manipulate data structures like tables and indexes.

PL/SQL: PL/SQL can be used to developed programs for different applications.

Oracle Forms: This tool allows you to create a data entry screen along with the suitable menu objects. Thus it is the oracle forms tool that handles data gathering and data validation in a commercial application.

Report Writer: Report writer allows programmers to prepare innovative reports using data from the oracle structures like tables, views etc. It is the report writer tool that handles the reporting section of commercial application.

Oracle Graphics: Some of the data can be better represented in the form of pictures. The oracle graphics tool allows programmers to prepare graphs using data from oracle structures like tables, views etc.

**SQL (Structured Query Language):**

Structured Query Language is a database computer language designed for managing data in relational database management systems (RDBMS), and originally based upon Relational Algebra. Its scope includes data query and update, schema creation and modification, and data access control.

SQL was one of the first languages for Edgar F. Codd's relational model and became the most widely used language for relational databases.

IBM developed SQL in mid of 1970's.

Oracle incorporated in the year 1979.

SQL used by IBM/DB2 and DS Database Systems.

SQL adopted as standard language for RDBS by ASNI in 1989.

**Data Types:**

CHAR (Size): This data type is designed for storing character strings with a fixed length. The specified size within parentheses determines how many characters each cell can accommodate. The maximum capacity is 255 characters.

VARCHAR (Size) / VARCHAR2 (Size): These data types are used for storing variable-length alphanumeric data. They are suitable for accommodating a maximum of 2000 characters.

NUMBER (P, S): The NUMBER data type is employed for storing numerical values, including both fixed and floating-point numbers. It can handle numbers of almost any magnitude, with precision up to 38 digits. The precision (P) indicates the number of decimal places to the right of the decimal point. If the scale (S) is omitted, the default is zero. If precision is omitted, values are stored with their original precision, with a maximum of 38 digits.

DATE: This data type is used to represent date and time information. The standard format follows DD-MM-YY, such as 17-SEP-2009. To input dates in formats other than the standard one, appropriate functions can be used. Date-time data records time in the 24-hour format. When no time portion is specified, the default time in a date field is 12:00:00 am. Similarly, the default date for a date field is the first day of the current month.

LONG: Designed for storing variable-length character strings of up to 2GB, the LONG data type is also suitable for storing arrays of binary data in ASCII format. It's worth noting that LONG values cannot be indexed, and common character functions like SUBSTR cannot be applied to them.

RAW: The RAW data type is intended for storing binary data, such as digitized images or pictures. Data loaded into columns with this data type is stored without any further conversion. RAW data types can have a maximum length of 255 bytes, while LONG RAW data types can contain up to 2GB of data.

SQL language is sub-divided into several language elements, including:

Clauses, which are in some cases optional, constituent components of statements and queries.

Expressions, which can produce either scalar values or tables consisting of columns and rows of data.

Predicates which specify conditions that can be evaluated to SQL three-valued logic (3VL) Boolean truth values and which are used to limit the effects of statements and queries, or to change program flow.

Queries which retrieve data based on specific criteria.

Statements which may have a persistent effect on schemas and data, or which may control transactions, program flow, connections, sessions, or diagnostics.

SQL statements also include the semicolon (";") statement terminator. Though notrequired on every platform, it is defined as a standard part of the SQL grammar.

Insignificant white space is generally ignored in SQL statements and queries, making it
easier to format SQL code for readability.

There are five types of SQL statements. They are:

DATA DEFINITION LANGUAGE (DDL)

DATA MANIPULATION LANGUAGE (DML)

DATA RETRIEVAL LANGUAGE (DRL)

TRANSATIONAL CONTROL LANGUAGE (TCL)

DATA CONTROL LANGUAGE (DCL)

**DATA DEFINITION LANGUAGE (DDL):**

Purpose: DDL is used to define the structure and schema of a database. It allows you to create, modify, and delete database objects like tables, views, indexes, and constraints.

Examples:

CREATE TABLE: To create a new table.

ALTER TABLE: To modify an existing table's structure.

DROP TABLE: To delete a table.

CREATE INDEX: To create an index on a table.

**DATA MANIPULATION LANGUAGE (DML):**

Purpose: DML is used for manipulating data stored in the database. It allows you to insert, update, and delete data in the tables.

Examples:

INSERT INTO: To add new rows into a table.

UPDATE: To modify existing data in a table.

DELETE FROM: To remove data from a table.

SELECT: To retrieve data from one or more tables.

**DATA RETRIEVAL LANGUAGE (DRL):**

Purpose: DRL is essentially a subset of DML, specifically focused on retrieving data from the database. It's often synonymous with the SELECT statement, which is used to query the database and retrieve data based on specified criteria.

Example:

SELECT * FROM employees WHERE department = 'HR';

**TRANSACTION CONTROL LANGUAGE (TCL):**

Purpose: TCL is used to manage transactions in a database. Transactions ensure the integrity and consistency of data. TCL statements are used to control the beginning and ending of transactions and to save or discard changes made during a transaction.

Examples:

COMMIT: To save changes made during a transaction.

ROLLBACK: To discard changes made during a transaction.

SAVEPOINT: To set a point within a transaction to which you can later roll back.

SET TRANSACTION: To set properties for a transaction.

**DATA CONTROL LANGUAGE (DCL):**

Purpose: DCL is used to control access to data within the database. It deals with permissions, privileges, and security.

Examples:

GRANT: To give specific privileges to users or roles.

REVOKE: To take away specific privileges from users or roles.

DENY: To explicitly deny access to a resource.

**LAB PRACTICE ASSIGNMENT:**

Create a table EMPLOYEE with following schema:

(Emp_no, E_name, E_address, E_ph_no, Dept_no, Dept_name,Job_id , Salary)

Add a new column; HIREDATE to the existing relation.

Change the datatype of JOB_ID from char to varchar2.

Change the name of column/field Emp_no to E_no.

Modify the column width of the job field of emp table

**Questions with solutions**

Q1. Create the table with following field:

| Field | Type | Null | Key | Default | Extra |
|---|---|---|---|---|---|
| EMPNO | number(4,0) | NO | PRI | | |
| ENAME | varchar2(10) | YES | – | NULL | |
| JOB | varchar2(9) | NO | – | NULL | |
| MGR | number(4,0) | NO | – | NULL | |
| HIREDATE | date | NO | – | NULL | |
| SAL | number(7,2) | NO | – | NULL | |
| DEPTNO | number(2,0) | NO | – | NULL | |

Solution:

```
create table emp(
empno number(4,0),
ename varchar2(10),
job varchar2(9),
mgr number(4,0),
hiredate date,
sal number(7,2),
deptno number(2,0)
PRIMARY KEY (ID)
);
```

Q2. Write a SQL statement to rename the table countries to country_new.

Solution: ALTER TABLE countries RENAME country_new;

Q3. Write a SQL statement to add a column region_id after state_province to the table locations.

| Field | Type | Null | Key | Default | Extra |
|---|---|---|---|---|---|
| LOCATION_ID | decimal(4,0) | YES | | NULL | |
| STREET_ADDRESS | varchar(40) | YES | | NULL | |
| POSTAL_CODE | varchar(12) | YES | | NULL | |
| CITY | varchar(30) | YES | | NULL | |
| STATE_PROVINCE | varchar(25) | YES | | NULL | |
| COUNTRY_ID | varchar(2) | YES | | NULL | |

Solution: ALTER TABLE locations

ADD region_id INT

AFTER state_province;

| Field | Type | Null | Key | Default | Extra |
|---|---|---|---|---|---|
| LOCATION_ID | decimal(4,0) | YES | | NULL | |
| STREET_ADDRESS | varchar(40) | YES | | NULL | |
| POSTAL_CODE | varchar(12) | YES | | NULL | |
| CITY | varchar(30) | YES | | NULL | |
| STATE_PROVINCE | varchar(25) | YES | | NULL | |
| region_id | int(11) | YES | | NULL | |
| COUNTRY_ID | varchar(2) | YES | | NULL | |

# Experiment No:2

## Title: Implementation of DML commands of SQL with suitable examples

**Insert table**

**Update table**

**Delete Table**

**Objective:**

To understand the different issues involved in the design and implementation of a database system

To understand and use data manipulation language to query, update, and manage a database

**Theory:**

**DATA MANIPULATION LANGUAGE (DML)** is a crucial part of database operations, enabling users to retrieve, insert, and modify data within the database. DML commands are used by all types of database users during their regular interactions with the database. Here, we'll explore the basic DML commands with examples:

**INSERT INTO**:

Purpose: INSERT INTO is used to add new records into a relation (table).

Examples:

Inserting a single record with specified fields:

INSERT INTO student (sno, sname, class, address) VALUES (1, 'Ravi', 'M.Tech', 'Palakol');

Inserting a single record with all fields:

INSERT INTO student VALUES (1, 'Ravi', 'M.Tech', 'Palakol');

Inserting records from another relation based on a condition:

INSERT INTO std SELECT sno, sname FROM student WHERE name = 'Ramu';

Inserting multiple records with user prompts:

INSERT INTO student (sno, sname, class, address) VALUES (&sno, '&sname', '&class', '&address');

Example (User input):

Enter value for sno: 101

Enter value for sname: Ravi

Enter value for class: M.Tech

Enter value for address: Palakol

**UPDATE-SET-WHERE:**

Purpose: UPDATE-SET-WHERE is used to update the content of existing records in a relation based on a specified condition.

Example:

UPDATE student SET sname = 'Kumar' WHERE sno = 1;

**DELETE-FROM:**

Purpose: DELETE-FROM is used to remove all records from a relation while retaining the table structure.

Example:

DELETE FROM std;

**DELETE-FROM-WHERE:**

Purpose: DELETE-FROM-WHERE is used to delete specific records from a relation based on a condition.

Example:

DELETE FROM student WHERE sno = 2;

**TRUNCATE:**

Purpose: The TRUNCATE command permanently removes all data from a table, but it preserves the table's structure.

Example:

TRUNCATE TABLE student;

**Difference between Truncate & Delete: -**

By using truncate command data will be removed permanently & will not get back where as by using delete command data will be removed temporally & get back by using roll back command.

By using delete command data will be removed based on the condition where as by using truncate command there is no condition.

Truncate is a DDL command & delete is a DML command.

**To Retrieve data from one or more tables.**

SELECT FROM: To display all fields for all records. Syntax: SELECT * FROM relation_name;

Example : SQL> select * from dept;

```
DEPTNO      DNAME          LOC
--------    -----------    ----------
10          ACCOUNTING     NEW YORK
20          RESEARCH       DALLAS
30          SALES          CHICAGO
40          OPERATIONS     BOSTON
```

SELECT FROM: To display a set of fields for all records of relation. Syntax: SELECT a set of fields FROM relation_name;

Example: SQL> select deptno, dname from dept;

```
DEPTNO      DNAME
---------   ------------
10          ACCOUNTING
20          RESEARCH
30          SALES
```

SELECT - FROM -WHERE: This query is used to display a selected set of fields for a selected set of records of a relation. Syntax: SELECT a set of fields FROM relation_name WHERE condition;

Example: SQL> select * FROM dept WHERE deptno<=20;

```
DEPTNO      DNAME          LOC
------      -----------    ------------
10          ACCOUNTING     NEW YORK
20          RESEARCH       DALLAS
```

**LAB PRACTICE ASSIGNMENT:**

Create a table EMPLOYEE with following schema:

(Emp_no, E_name, E_address, E_ph_no, Dept_no, Dept_name, Job_id, Salary)

**Write SQL queries for following question:**

Insert aleast 5 rows in the table.

Display all the information of EMP table.

Display the record of each employee who works in department D10.

Update the city of Emp_no-12 with current city as Nagpur.

Display the details of Employee who works in department MECH.

Delete the email_id of employee James.

Display the complete record of employees working in SALES Department.

**Questions with Solution**

Q1. Create the following table with name countries.

| Field | Type | Null | Key | Default | Extra |
|---|---|---|---|---|---|
| COUNTRY_ID | varchar(2) | YES | | NULL | |
| COUNTRY_NAME | varchar(40) | YES | | NULL | |
| REGION_ID | decimal(10,0) | YES | | NULL | |

Solution: create table countries(

COUNTRY_ID varchar2(10),

COUNTRY_NAME varchar2(9),

REGION_ID decimal(10,0),

);

Q2. Write a SQL statement to insert one row into the table countries against the column country_id and country_name.

| Field | Type | Null | Key | Default | Extra |
|---|---|---|---|---|---|
| COUNTRY_ID | varchar(2) | YES | | NULL | |
| COUNTRY_NAME | varchar(40) | YES | | NULL | |
| REGION_ID | decimal(10,0) | YES | | NULL | |

Solution: INSERT INTO countries (country_id, country_name) VALUES('C1','India');

| COUNTRY_ID | COUNTRY_NAME | REGION_ID |
|---|---|---|
| C1 | India | NULL |

Solution: INSERT INTO countries (country_id, country_name) VALUES('C1','India');

Q3. Write a SQL statement to change the email column of employees table with 'not available' for all employees.

| EMPLOYEE_ID | FIRST_NAME | LAST_NAME | EMAIL |
|---|---|---|---|
| 100 | Steven | King | SKING |
| 101 | Neena | Kochhar | NKOCHHAR |
| 102 | Bruce | Ernst | BERNST |

Solution: UPDATE employees SET email='not available';

| EMPLOYEE_ID | FIRST_NAME | LAST_NAME | EMAIL |
|---|---|---|---|
| 100 | Steven | King | not available |
| 101 | Neena | Kochhar | not available |
| 102 | Bruce | Ernst | not available |

Q4. Write a SQL statement to delete employee from employee table having employee_id as 104.

| EMPLOYEE_ID | FIRST_NAME | LAST_NAME | EMAIL |
|---|---|---|---|
| 103 | Diana | Lorentz | DLORENTZ |
| 104 | Nancy | Greenberg | NGREENBERG |
| 105 | John | Chen | JCHEN |

Solution: DELETE From employees Where employee_id = 104;

| EMPLOYEE_ID | FIRST_NAME | LAST_NAME | EMAIL |
|---|---|---|---|
| 103 | Diana | Lorentz | DLORENTZ |
| 105 | John | Chen | JCHEN |

# Experiment No: 3

**Title: Implementation of different types of functions with suitable examples.**

**Number Function**

**Aggregate Function**

**Character Function**

**Conversion Function**

**Date Function**

**Objective:**

**NUMBER FUNCTION:**

Abs(n) :Select abs(-15) from dual;

Exp(n): Select exp(4) from dual;

Power(m,n): Select power(4,2) from dual;

Mod(m,n): Select mod(10,3) from dual;

Round(m,n): Select round(100.256,2) from dual;

Trunc(m,n): ;Select trunc(100.256,2) from dual;

Sqrt(m,n);Select sqrt(16) from dual;

**Aggregative operators**: In addition to simply retrieving data, we often want to perform some computation or summarization. SQL allows the use of arithmetic expressions. We now consider a powerful class of constructs for computing aggregate values such as MIN and SUM.

**Count**: COUNT following by a column name returns the count of tuple in that column. If DISTINCT keyword is used then it will return only the count of unique tuple in the column. Otherwise, it will return count of all the tuples (including duplicates) count (*) indicates all the tuples of the column.

Syntax: COUNT (Column name)

Example: SELECT COUNT (Sal) FROM emp;

**SUM**: SUM followed by a column name returns the sum of all the values in that column.

Syntax: SUM (Column name)

Example: SELECT SUM (Sal) From emp;

**AVG**: AVG followed by a column name returns the average value of that column values.

Syntax: AVG (n1, n2...)

Example: Select AVG (10, 15, 30) FROM DUAL;

**MAX:** MAX followed by a column name returns the maximum value of that column.

Syntax: MAX (Column name)

Example: SELECT MAX (Sal) FROM emp;

```
SQL> select deptno, max(sal) from emp group by deptno;
DEPTNO          MAX (SAL)
------------    -----------------
```

10 5000

20 3000

30 2850

SQL> select deptno, max (sal) from emp group by deptno having max(sal)<3000;

| DEPTNO | MAX(SAL) |
|---|---|
| 30 | 2850 |

**MIN**: MIN followed by column name returns the minimum value of that column.

Syntax: MIN (Column name)

Example: SELECT MIN (Sal) FROM emp;

SQL>select deptno,min(sal) from emp group by deptno having min(sal)>1000;

| DEPTNO | MIN (SAL) |
|---|---|
| 10 | 1300 |

**CHARACTER FUNCTION:**

initcap(char) : select initcap("hello") from dual;

Converts the first letter of each word in a string to uppercase and the remaining letters to lowercase.

lower (char): select lower ('HELLO') from dual;

Converts all characters in a string to lowercase.

upper (char) :select upper ('hello') from dual;

Converts all characters in a string to uppercase

ltrim (char,[set]): select ltrim ('cseit', 'cse') from dual;

Removes characters specified in the 'set' from the left side (beginning) of a string.

rtrim (char,[set]): select rtrim ('cseit', 'it') from dual;

Removes characters specified in the 'set' from the right side (end) of a string.

replace (char,search ): select replace('jack and jue','j','bl') from dual;

Replaces all occurrences of the 'search' string within a string with another specified string.

**LAB PRACTICE ASSIGNMENT:**

Create a table EMPLOYEE with following schema:

(Emp_no, E_name, E_address, E_ph_no, Dept_no, Dept_name,Job_id, Designation , Salary)

**Write SQL statements for the following query**.

List the E_no, E_name, Salary of all employees working for MANAGER.

Display all the details of the employee whose salary is more than the Sal of any IT PROFF..

List the employees in the ascending order of Designations of those joined after 1981.

List the employees along with their Experience and Daily Salary.

List the employees who are either 'CLERK' or 'ANALYST' .

List the employees who joined on 1-MAY-81, 3-DEC-81, 17-DEC-81,19-JAN-80 .

List the employees who are working for the Deptno 10 or20.

List the Enames those are starting with 'S' .

Dislay the name as well as the first five characters of name(s) starting with 'H'

List all the emps except 'PRESIDENT' & 'MGR" in asc order of Salaries.

# Experiment No: 4

**Title: Implementation of different types of operators in SQL.**

**Arithmetic Operator**

**Logical Operator**

**Comparision Operator**

**Special Operator**

**Set Operator**

**Objective:**

To learn different types of operators.

**Arithmetic Operators:**

Addition (+): This operator adds values on both sides of it.

Subtraction (-): It subtracts the right-hand operand from the left-hand operand.

Multiplication (*): Used for multiplying values.

Division (/): Divides the left operand by the right operand.

Power (^): Raises a value to a specified power.

Modulus (%): Divides the left operand by the right operand and returns the remainder.

**Logical Operators:**

AND: Allows multiple conditions in an SQL statement's WHERE clause, and all conditions must be true for the overall condition to be true.

OR: Combines multiple conditions, and if any of them is true, the overall condition is true.

NOT: Reverses the meaning of the logical operator it's used with, turning true conditions into false and vice versa.

**Comparison Operators:**

Equal (=): Checks if the values of two operands are equal.

Not Equal (!= or <>): Checks if the values of two operands are not equal.

Greater Than (>): Checks if the left operand is greater than the right operand.

Less Than (<): Checks if the left operand is less than the right operand.

Greater Than or Equal To (>=): Checks if the left operand is greater than or equal to the right operand.

Less Than or Equal To (<=): Checks if the left operand is less than or equal to the right operand.

**Special Operators:**

BETWEEN: Used to search for values within a specified range.

IS NULL: Compares a value with a NULL attribute.

ALL: Compares a value to all values in another set.

ANY: Compares a value to any value in a list according to a condition.

LIKE: Compares a value to similar values using wildcard characters (% and _).

IN: Compares a value to a list of specified values.

EXISTS: Checks for the presence of a row in a specified table that meets certain criteria.**Set Operators:**

Set operators combine the results of two queries into a single result:

Union: Returns all distinct rows selected by both queries.

Union All: Returns all rows selected by either query, including duplicates.

Intersect: Returns rows selected that are common to both queries.

Minus (or Except): Returns all distinct rows selected by the first query but not by the second query.

**LAB PRACTICE ASSIGNMENT:**

Display all the dept numbers available with the dept and emp tables avoiding duplicates.

Display all the dept numbers available with the dept and emp tables.

Display all the dept numbers available in emp and not in dept tables and vice versa.

## Questions with Solution

Consider the MOVIE DATABASE

Movies:

| Title | Director | Myear | Rating |
|---|---|---|---|
| Fargo | Coen | 1996 | 8.2 |
| Raising Arizona | Coen | 1987 | 7.6 |
| Spiderman | Raimi | 2002 | 7.4 |
| Wonder Boys | Hanson | 2000 | 7.6 |

Actors:

| Actor | Ayear |
|---|---|
| Cage | 1964 |
| Hanks | 1956 |
| Maguire | 1975 |
| McDormand | 1957 |

Acts:

| Actor | Title |
|---|---|
| Cage | Raising Arizona |
| Maguire | Spiderman |
| Maguire | Wonder Boys |
| McDormand | Fargo |
| McDormand | Raising Arizona |
| McDormand | Wonder Boys |

Director:

| Director | Dyear |
|---|---|
| Coen | 1954 |
| Hanson | 1945 |
| Raimi | 1959 |

Write following relational algebra queries for a given set of relations.

Find movies made after 1997

Find movies made by Hanson after 1997

Find all movies and their ratings

Find all actors and directors

Find Coen's movies with McDormand

Solution:

**Common notations of Relational Algebra**

**Select(σ)** The SELECT operation is used for selecting a subset of the tuples according to a given selection condition

**Projection(π)** The projection eliminates all attributes of the input relation but those mentioned in the projection list.

**Union Operation(∪)** UNION is symbolized by symbol. It includes all tuples that are in tables A or in B.

**Set Difference(-)** - Symbol denotes it. The result of A - B, is a relation which includes all tuples that are in A but not in B.

**Intersection(∩)** Intersection defines a relation consisting of a set of all tuple that are in both A and B.

**Cartesian Product(X)** Cartesian operation is helpful to merge columns from two relations.

Inner Join Inner join, includes only those tuples that satisfy the matching criteria.

**Theta Join(θ)** The general case of JOIN operation is called a Theta join. It is denoted by symbol θ.

**EQUI Join** When a theta join uses only equivalence condition, it becomes a equi join.

**Natural Join(⋈)** Natural join can only be performed if there is a common attribute (column) between the relations.

Outer Join In an outer join, along with tuples that satisfy the matching criteria.

**Left Outer Join( ⟕ )** In the left outer join, operation allows keeping all tuple in the left relation.

**Right Outer join** In the right outer join, operation allows keeping all tuple in the right relation.

**Full Outer Join** In a full outer join, all tuples from both relations are included in the result irrespective of the matching condition

Find movies made after 1997

| Title | Director | Myear | Rating |
|---|---|---|---|
| Fargo | Coen | 1996 | 8.2 |
| Raising Arizona | Coen | 1987 | 7.6 |
| Spiderman | Raimi | 2002 | 7.4 |
| Wonder Boys | Hanson | 2000 | 7.6 |

$\sigma_{myear \geq 1997}(Movies)$

| Title | Director | Myear | Rating |
|---|---|---|---|
| Spiderman | Raimi | 2002 | 7.4 |
| Wonder Boys | Hanson | 2000 | 7.6 |

Find movies made by Hanson after 1997

| Title | Director | Myear | Rating |
|---|---|---|---|
| Fargo | Coen | 1996 | 8.2 |
| Raising Arizona | Coen | 1987 | 7.6 |
| Spiderman | Raimi | 2002 | 7.4 |
| Wonder Boys | Hanson | 2000 | 7.6 |

$\sigma_{myear \geq 1997 \wedge director='Hanson'}(Movies)$

| Title | Director | Myear | Rating |
|---|---|---|---|
| Wonder Boys | Hanson | 2000 | 7.6 |

Find all movies and their ratings

| Title | Director | Myear | Rating |
|---|---|---|---|
| Fargo | Coen | 1996 | 8.2 |
| Raising Arizona | Coen | 1987 | 7.6 |
| Spiderman | Raimi | 2002 | 7.4 |
| Wonder Boys | Hanson | 2000 | 7.6 |

$\pi_{title, rating}(Movies)$

| Title | Rating |
|---|---|
| Fargo | 8.2 |
| Raising Arizona | 7.6 |
| Spiderman | 7.4 |
| Wonder Boys | 7.6 |

Find all actors and directors

Actors:

| Actor | Ayear |
|---|---|
| Cage | 1964 |
| Hanks | 1956 |
| Maguire | 1975 |
| McDormand | 1957 |

πactor(Actors):

| Actor |
|---|
| Cage |
| Hanks |
| Maguire |
| McDormand |

Director:

| Director | Dyear |
|---|---|
| Coen | 1954 |
| Hanson | 1945 |
| Raimi | 1959 |

πdirector(Directors):

| Director |
|---|
| Coen |
| Hanson |
| Raimi |

πactor(Actors) ∪ πdirector(Directors):

| Actor |
|---|
| Cage |
| Hanks |
| Maguire |
| McDormand |
| Coen |
| Hanson |
| Raimi |

Find Coen's movies with McDormand

e1 = πtitle(σactor='McDormand_ (Acts))

e2 = πtitle(σdirector=‘Coen_ (Movies))

result = e1 ∩ e2

result = e1 ∩ e2

Actors:

| Actor | Ayear |
|---|---|
| Cage | 1964 |
| Hanks | 1956 |
| Maguire | 1975 |
| McDormand | 1957 |

e1:

| Title |
|---|
| Fargo |
| Raising Arizona |
| Wonder Boys |

Movies:

| Title | Director | Myear | Rating |
|---|---|---|---|
| Fargo | Coen | 1996 | 8.2 |
| Raising Arizona | Coen | 1987 | 7.6 |
| Spiderman | Raimi | 2002 | 7.4 |
| Wonder Boys | Hanson | 2000 | 7.6 |

e2:

| Title |
|---|
| Fargo |
| Raising Arizona |

e1 ∩ e2:

| Title |
|---|
| Fargo |
| Raising Arizona |

# Experiment No: 5

**Title: Implementation of different types of Joins**

**Inner Join**

**Outer Join**

**Natural Join... etc.**

**Objective:**

To implement different types of joins

**Theory:**

The SQL Joins clause is used to combine records from two or more tables in a database. A JOIN is a means for combining fields from two tables by using values common to each.The join is actually performed by the 'where' clause which combines specified rows of tables.

Syntax:

SELECT column 1, column 2, column 3...

FROM table_name1, table_name2

WHERE table_name1.column name = table_name2.columnname;

**Types of Joins**:

Simple Join

Self-Join

Outer Join

**Simple Join:**

A simple join is the most common type of join in SQL. It retrieves rows from two tables that share a common column. There are two main categories of simple joins:

**Equi-Join**: This type of join is based on equality conditions, where a specific column from one table is matched with a specific column from another table.

Example: SELECT * FROM item, cust WHERE item.id = cust.id;

**Non-Equi-Join**: In a non-equi-join, the relationship between columns from different tables is defined using relational operators other than '='.

Example: SELECT * FROM item, cust WHERE item.id < cust.id;

**Self-Join:**

A self-join occurs when you join a table to itself. It allows you to compare rows within the same table, making it useful for scenarios where you need to compare data within a single table.

Example:

SELECT * FROM emp x, emp y WHERE x.salary >= (SELECT AVG(salary) FROM emp WHERE x.deptno = y.deptno);

**Outer Join:**

An outer join extends the result of a simple join. It returns all the rows from a simple join and additional rows from one table that don't have corresponding matches in the other table. There are different types of outer joins:

**Left Outer Join**: Returns all rows from the left table (first table) and the matching rows from the right table (second table). Rows from the left table without matches will contain NULL values for columns from the right table.

**Right Outer Join**: Similar to the left outer join but returns all rows from the right table and matching rows from the left table.

**Full Outer Join**: Returns all rows from both tables and fills in NULL values where there are no matches.

**LAB PRACTICE ASSIGNMENT:**

Consider the following schema: Sailors (sid, sname, rating, age) Boats (bid, bname, color) Reserves (sid, bid, day(date))

Find all information of sailors who have reserved boat number 101.

Find the name of boat reserved by Bob.

Find the names of sailors who have reserved a red boat, and list in the order of age.

Find the names of sailors who have reserved at least one boat.

Find the ids and names of sailors who have reserved two different boats on the same day.

Find the ids of sailors who have reserved a red boat or a green boat.

Find the name and the age of the youngest sailor.

Count the number of different sailor names.

Find the average age of sailors for each rating level.

Find the average age of sailors for each rating level that has at least two sailors.

**Questions with Solution:**

**Consider Employee table**

| EMPNO | EMP_NAME | DEPT | SALARY | DOJ | BRANCH |
|---|---|---|---|---|---|
| E101 | Amit | Production | 45000 | 12-Mar-00 | Bangalore |
| E102 | Amit | HR | 70000 | 03-Jul-02 | Bangalore |
| E103 | sunita | Management | 120000 | 11-Jan-01 | mysore |
| E105 | sunita | IT | 67000 | 01-Aug-01 | mysore |
| E106 | mahesh | Civil | 145000 | 20-Sep-03 | Mumbai |

**Perform the following**

**Display all the fields of employee table**

**Retrieve employee number and their salary**

**Retrieve average salary of all employee**

**Retrieve number of employee**

**Retrieve distinct number of employee**

**Retrieve total salary of employee group by employee name and count similar names**

**Retrieve total salary of employee which is greater than >120000**

**Display name of employee in descending order**

**Display details of employee whose name is AMIT and salary greater than 50000;**

Display all the fields of employee table

SQL> select * from employee;

| EMPNO | EMP_NAME | DEPT | SALARY | DOJ | BRANCH |
|---|---|---|---|---|---|
| E101 | Amit | Production | 45000 | 12-Mar-00 | Bangalore |
| E102 | Amit | HR | 70000 | 03-Jul-02 | Bangalore |
| E103 | sunita | Management | 120000 | 11-Jan-01 | mysore |
| E105 | sunita | IT | 67000 | 01-Aug-01 | mysore |
| E106 | mahesh | Civil | 145000 | 20-Sep-03 | Mumbai |

Retrieve employee number and their salary

SQL> select empno, salary from employee;

| EMPNO | SALARY |
|---|---|
| E101 | 45000 |
| E102 | 70000 |
| E103 | 120000 |
| E105 | 67000 |
| E106 | 145000 |

Retrieve average salary of all employee

SQL> select avg(salary) from employee;

| AVG(SALARY) |
|---|
| 89400 |

Retrieve number of employee

SQL> select count(*) from employee;

| COUNT(*) |
|---|
| 5 |

Retrieve distinct number of employee

SQL> select count(DISTINCT emp_name) from employee;

| COUNT(DISTINCTEMP_NAME) |
|---|
| 3 |

Retrieve total salary of employee group by employee name and count similar names

SQL> SELECT EMP_NAME, SUM(SALARY),COUNT(*)

FROM EMPLOYEE

GROUP BY(EMP_NAME);

| EMP_NAME | SALARY | COUNT(*) |
|---|---|---|
| Amit | 145000 | 1 |
| sunita | 187000 | 2 |
| mahesh | 115000 | 2 |

Retrieve total salary of employee which is greater than >120000

SQL> SELECT EMP_NAME, SUM(SALARY) FROM EMPLOYEE

GROUP BY(EMP_NAME)

HAVING SUM(SALARY)>120000;

| EMP_NAME | SUM(SALARY) |
|---|---|
| Mahesh | 145000 |
| sunita | 187000 |

Display name of employee in descending order

SQL> select emp_name from employee

order by emp_name desc;

| EMP_NAME |
|---|
| sunita |
| sunita |
| mahesh |
| Amit |
| Amit |

Display details of employee whose name is AMIT and salary greater than 50000;

SQL> select * from employee

where emp_name='Amit' and salary>50000;

| EMPNO | EMP_NAME | DEPT | SALARY | DOJ | BRANCH |
|---|---|---|---|---|---|
| E102 | Amit | HR | 70000 | 03-Jul-02 | Bangalore |

## Experiment No: 6

**Title: Study & Implementation of**

**Group by & Having Clause**

**Order by Clause**

**Indexing**

**Objective:**

To learn the concept of group functions

**Theory:**

**GROUP BY**: This query is used to group to all the records in a relation together for each and every value of a specific key(s) and then display them for a selected set of fields the relation.

Syntax: SELECT <set of fields> FROM <relation_name> GROUP BY <field_name>;

Example: SQL> SELECT EMPNO, SUM (SALARY) FROM EMP GROUP BY EMPNO;

**GROUP BY-HAVING :** The HAVING clause was added to SQL because the WHERE keyword could not be used with aggregate functions. The HAVING clause must follow the GROUP BY clause in a query and must also precede the ORDER BY clause if used.

Syntax:

```
SELECT column_name, aggregate_function(column_name)
FROM table_name WHERE column_name operator value
GROUP BY column_name
HAVING aggregate_function(column_name) operator value;
```

Example :

```
SELECT Employees.LastName, COUNT(Orders.OrderID) AS NumberOfOrders
FROM Orders
INNER JOIN Employees
ON Orders.EmployeeID=Employees.EmployeeID) GROUP BY LastName
HAVING COUNT (Orders.OrderID) > 10;
```

**JOIN using GROUP BY**: This query is used to display a set of fields from two relations by matching a common field in them and also group the corresponding records for each and every value of a specified key(s) while displaying.

Syntax:

```
SELECT <set of fields (from both relations)> FROM relation_1,relation_2
WHERE relation_1.field_x=relation_2.field_y GROUP BY field_z;
```

Example:

```
SQL> SELECT empno,SUM(SALARY) FROM emp,dept
WHERE emp.deptno =20 GROUP BY empno;
```

**ORDER BY**: This query is used to display a selected set of fields from a relation in an ordered manner base on some field.

Syntax: SELECT <set of fields> FROM <relation_name>

ORDER BY <field_name>;

Example: SQL> SELECT empno, ename, job FROM emp ORDER BY job;

**JOIN using ORDER BY**: This query is used to display a set of fields from two relations by matching a common field in them in an ordered manner based on some fields.

Syntax:

SELECT <set of fields (from both relations)> FROM relation_1, relation_2

WHERE relation_1.field_x = relation_2.field_y ORDER BY field_z;

Example:

SQL> SELECT empno,ename,job,dname FROM emp,dept

WHERE emp.deptno = 20 ORDER BY job;

**INDEXING**: An index is an ordered set of pointers to the data in a table. It is based on the data values in one or more columns of the table. SQL Base stores indexes separately from tables.

An index provides two benefits:

It improves performance because it makes data access faster.

It ensures uniqueness. A table with a unique index cannot have two rows with the same values in the column or columns that form the index key.

Syntax: CREATE INDEX <index_name> on <table_name> (attrib1,attrib 2….attrib n);

Example: CREATE INDEX id1 on emp(empno,dept_no);

**LAB PRACTICE ASSIGNMENT:**

Create a relation and implement the following queries.

Display total salary spent for each job category.

Display lowest paid employee details under each manager.

Display number of employees working in each department and their department name.

Display the details of employees sorting the salary in increasing order.

Show the record of employee earning salary greater than 16000 in each department.

Write queries to implement and practice the above clause.

# Experiment No: 7

**Title: Study & Implementation of**

**Sub queries**

**Views**

**Objective:**

To perform nested Queries and joining Queries using DML command

To understand the implementation of views.

**Theory:**

**SUBQUERIES:** The query within another is known as a sub query. A statement containing sub query is called parent statement. The rows returned by sub query are

used by the parent statement or in other words A subquery is a SELECT statement that is embedded in a clause of another SELECT statement

You can place the subquery in a number of SQL clauses:

WHERE clause

HAVING clause

FROM clause

OPERATORS( IN.ANY,ALL,<,>,>=,<= etc..)

**Types**

Sub queries that return several values

Sub queries can also return more than one value. Such results should be made use along with the operators in and any.

Multiple queries

Here more than one sub query is used. These multiple sub queries are combined by means of 'and' & 'or' keywords.

Correlated sub query

A sub query is evaluated once for the entire parent statement whereas a correlated Sub query is evaluated once per row processed by the parent statement.

**VIEW:** In SQL, a view is a virtual table based on the result-set of an SQL statement.

A view contains rows and columns, just like a real table. The fields in a view are fields from one or more real tables in the database.

You can add SQL functions, WHERE, and JOIN statements to a view and present the data as if the data were coming from one single table.

A view is a virtual table, which consists of a set of columns from one or more tables. It is similar to a table but it does not store in the database. View is a query stored as an object.

Syntax: CREATE VIEW <view_name> AS SELECT <set of fields>

FROM relation_name WHERE (Condition)

Example:

SQL> CREATE VIEW employee AS SELECT empno,ename,job FROM EMP WHERE job = 'clerk';

SQL> View created.

Example:

CREATE VIEW [Current Product List] AS SELECT ProductID, ProductName
FROM Products
WHERE Discontinued=No;

**UPDATING A VIEW** : A view can updated by using the following syntax :

Syntax : CREATE OR REPLACE VIEW view_name AS
SELECT column_name(s)
FROM table_name
WHERE condition

**DROPPING A VIEW:** A view can deleted with the DROP VIEW command.

Syntax: DROP VIEW <view_name> ;

LAB PRACTICE ASSIGNMENT:

Consider the following schema: Sailors (sid, sname, rating, age) Boats (bid, bname, color) Reserves (sid, bid, day(date))

Write subquery statement for the following queries.

Find all information of sailors who have reserved boat number 101.

Find the name of boat reserved by Bob.

Find the names of sailors who have reserved a red boat, and list in the order of age.

Find the names of sailors who have reserved at least one boat.

Find the ids and names of sailors who have reserved two different boats on the same day.

Find the ids of sailors who have reserved a red boat or a green boat.

Find the name and the age of the youngest sailor.

Count the number of different sailor names.

Find the average age of sailors for each rating level.

Find the average age of sailors for each rating level that has at least two sailors.

**Questions with Solution:**

For a given EMPLOYEE tables

| FNAME | LNAME | SSN | ADDRESS | SEX | SALARY | SUPERSSN | DNO |
|---|---|---|---|---|---|---|---|
| JOHN | SCOTT | RNSECE0 | BANGALORE | M | 450000 | 333445555 | 5 |
| JAMES | SMITH | RNSCSE01 | BANGALORE | M | 500000 | 888866655 | 5 |
| NEHA | SN | RNSCSE06 | BANGALORE | F | 800000 | 987664321 | 4 |
| HEARN | BAKER | RNSCSE02 | BANGALORE | M | 700000 | 888566566 | 4 |
| EDWARD | SCOTT | RNSCSE03 | MYSORE | M | 500000 | 333445555 | 5 |
| PAVAN | HEGDE | RNSCSE04 | MANGALORE | M | 650000 | 333445555 | 5 |
| GIRISH | MALYA | RNSCSE05 | MYSORE | M | 450000 | null | 1 |

Perform the Following

Creating Views (With and Without Check Option),

Selecting from a View

Dropping Views

Solution:

```
SQL> CREATE TABLE EMPLOYEE (
SSN VARCHAR2 (20) PRIMARY KEY,
FNAME VARCHAR2 (20),
LNAME VARCHAR2 (20),
ADDRESS VARCHAR2 (20),
SEX CHAR (1),
SALARY INTEGER,
SUPERSSN REFERENCES EMPLOYEE (SSN),
DNO REFERENCES DEPARTMENT (DNO));
SQL> DESC EMPLOYEE;
```

| Name | Null? | Type |
|---|---|---|
| SSN | NOT NULL | VARCHAR2(20) |
| FNAME | | VARCHAR2(20) |
| LNAME | | VARCHAR2(20) |
| ADDRESS | | VARCHAR2(20) |
| SEX | | CHAR(1) |
| SALARY | | NUMBER(38) |
| SUPERSSN | | VARCHAR2(20) |
| DNO | | NUMBER(38) |

```
INSERT INTO EMPLOYEE (SSN, FNAME, LNAME, ADDRESS, SEX, SALARY)
VALUES ('RNSECE01','JOHN','SCOTT','BANGALORE','M', 450000);
INSERT INTO EMPLOYEE (SSN, FNAME, LNAME, ADDRESS, SEX, SALARY)
VALUES ('RNSCSE01','JAMES','SMITH','BANGALORE','M', 500000);
INSERT INTO EMPLOYEE (SSN, FNAME, LNAME, ADDRESS, SEX, SALARY)
VALUES ('RNSCSE02','HEARN','BAKER','BANGALORE','M', 700000);
INSERT INTO EMPLOYEE (SSN, FNAME, LNAME, ADDRESS, SEX, SALARY)
VALUES ('RNSCSE03','EDWARD','SCOTT','MYSORE','M', 500000);
INSERT INTO EMPLOYEE (SSN, FNAME, LNAME, ADDRESS, SEX, SALARY)
VALUES ('RNSCSE04','PAVAN','HEGDE','MANGALORE','M', 650000);
```

INSERT INTO EMPLOYEE (SSN, FNAME, LNAME, ADDRESS, SEX, SALARY)
VALUES ('RNSCSE05','GIRISH','MALYA','MYSORE','M', 450000);
INSERT INTO EMPLOYEE (SSN, FNAME, LNAME, ADDRESS, SEX, SALARY)
VALUES ('RNSCSE06','NEHA','SN','BANGALORE','F', 800000);
INSERT INTO EMPLOYEE (SSN, FNAME, LNAME, ADDRESS, SEX, SALARY)
VALUES ('RNSACC01','AHANA','K','MANGALORE','F', 350000);
INSERT INTO EMPLOYEE (SSN, FNAME, LNAME, ADDRESS, SEX, SALARY)
VALUES ('RNSACC02','SANTHOSH','KUMAR','MANGALORE','M', 300000);
INSERT INTO EMPLOYEE (SSN, FNAME, LNAME, ADDRESS, SEX, SALARY)
VALUES ('RNSISE01','VEENA','M','MYSORE','M', 600000);
INSERT INTO EMPLOYEE (SSN, FNAME, LNAME, ADDRESS, SEX, SALARY)
VALUES ('RNSIT01','NAGESH','HR','BANGALORE','M', 500000);

**Creating View**

The query that defines the sales_staffview references only rows in department 5. Furthermore, the CHECK OPTION creates the view with the constraint (named sales_staff_cnst) that INSERT and UPDATE statements issued against the view cannot result in rows that the view cannot select.

**1. Creating Views (With and Without Check Option)**

SQL> CREATE VIEW sales_staff AS
SELECT fname, ssn, dno
FROM employee
WHERE dno =5
WITH CHECK OPTION CONSTRAINT sales_staff_cnst;
View created.

**Selecting from a View**

SQL> select * from sales_staff;

**Drop View**

SQL>DROP VIEW sales_staff;

# Experiment No: 8

## Title: Study & Implementation of different types of constraints

**Objective:**

To practice and implement constraints

**Theory:**

**CONSTRAINTS:**

Constraints are used to specify rules for the data in a table. If there is any violation between the constraint and the data action, the action is aborted by the constraint. It can be specified when the table is created (using CREATE TABLE statement) or after the table is created (using ALTER TABLE statement).

**NOT NULL**: When a column is defined as NOTNULL, then that column becomes a mandatory column. It implies that a value must be entered into the column if the record is to be accepted for storage in the table.

Syntax:

CREATE TABLE Table_Name (column_name data_type (size) NOT NULL, );

Example:

CREATE TABLE student (sno NUMBER(3)NOT NULL, name CHAR(10));

**UNIQUE:** The purpose of a unique key is to ensure that information in the column(s) is unique i.e. a value entered in column(s) defined in the unique constraint must not be repeated across the column(s). A table may have many unique keys.

Syntax:

CREATE TABLE Table_Name(column_name data_type(size) UNIQUE, ….);

Example:

CREATE TABLE student (sno NUMBER(3) UNIQUE, name CHAR(10));

**CHECK**: Specifies a condition that each row in the table must satisfy. To satisfy the constraint, each row in the table must make the condition either TRUE or unknown (due to a null).

Syntax:

CREATE TABLE Table_Name(column_name data_type(size) CHECK(logical expression), ….);

Example:

CREATE TABLE student (sno NUMBER (3), name CHAR(10),class CHAR(5),CHECK(class IN('CSE','CAD','VLSI'));

**PRIMARY KEY**: A field which is used to identify a record uniquely. A column or combination of columns can be created as primary key, which can be used as a reference from other tables. A table contains primary key is known as Master Table.

It must uniquely identify each record in a table.

It must contain unique values.

It cannot be a null field.

It cannot be multi port field.

It should contain a minimum no. of fields necessary to be called unique.

Syntax:

CREATE TABLE Table_Name(column_name data_type(size) PRIMARY KEY,

....);

Example:

CREATE TABLE faculty (fcode NUMBER(3) PRIMARY KEY, fname CHAR(10));

**FOREIGN KEY:** It is a table level constraint. We cannot add this at column level. To reference any primary key column from other table this constraint can be used. The table in which the foreign key is defined is called a detail table. The table that defines the primary key and is referenced by the foreign key is called the master table.

Syntax: CREATE TABLE Table_Name(column_name data_type(size)

FOREIGN KEY(column_name) REFERENCES table_name);

Example:

CREATE TABLE subject (scode NUMBER (3) PRIMARY KEY, subname CHAR(10),fcode NUMBER(3), FOREIGN KEY(fcode) REFERENCE faculty );

**DEFAULT :** The DEFAULT constraint is used to insert a default value into a column. The default value will be added to all new records, if no other value is specified.

Syntax:

CREATE TABLE Table_Name(col_name1,col_name2,col_name3 DEFAULT '<value>');

Example:

CREATE TABLE student (sno NUMBER(3) UNIQUE, name CHAR(10),address VARCHAR(20) DEFAULT 'Aurangabad');

LAB PRACTICE ASSIGNMENT:

Create a table called EMP with the following structure.

Name Type

----------------------------

EMPNO NUMBER (6)

ENAME VARCHAR2 (20)

JOB VARCHAR2 (10)

DEPTNO NUMBER (3)

SAL NUMBER (7,2)

Allow NULL for all columns except ename and job.

Add constraints to check, while entering the empno value (i.e) empno > 100.

Define the field DEPTNO as unique.

Create a primary key constraint for the table(EMPNO).

Write queries to implement and practice constraints.

# Experiment No: 9

## Title :

## Study and Implementation of Database Backup & Recovery Commands.

## Study and Implementation of Rollback, Commit, Save point.

**Objective:**

To understand the concept of administrative commands

**Theory:**

A transaction is a logical unit of work. All changes made to the database can be referred to as a transaction. Transaction changes can be made permanent to the database only if they are committed a transaction begins with an executable SQL statement & ends explicitly with either rollback or commit statement.

**COMMIT**: This command is used to end a transaction only with the help of the commit command transaction changes can be made permanent to the database.

Syntax: SQL> COMMIT;

Example: SQL> COMMIT;

**SAVE POINT:** Save points are like marks to divide a very lengthy transaction to smaller once. They are used to identify a point in a transaction to which we can latter role back. Thus, save point is used in conjunction with role back.

Syntax: SQL> SAVE POINT ID;

Example: SQL> SAVE POINT xyz;

**ROLLBACK:** A role back command is used to undo the current transactions. We can role back the entire transaction so that all changes made by SQL statements are undo (or) role back a transaction to a save point so that the SQL statements after the save point are role back.

Syntax: ROLLBACK (current transaction can be role back)

ROLLBACK to save point ID;

Example: SQL> ROLLBACK;

SQL> ROLLBACK TO SAVE POINT xyz;

LAB PRACTICE ASSIGNMENT:

Write a query to implement the save point.

Write a query to implement the rollback.

Write a query to implement the commit.

# Experiment No: 10

**Title: Creating Database/ Table Space**

**Managing Users: - Create User, Delete User**

**Managing Passwords**

**Managing roles: - Grant, Revoke**

**Objective:**

To understand the concept of administrative commands

**Theory:**

DATABASE is collection of coherent data. To create database we have :

Syntax: CREATE DATABASE <database_name>Example : CREATE DATABASE my_db;

**TABLESPACE:**

The oracle database consists of one or more logical storage units called tablespaces. Each tablespace in an Oracle database consists of one or more files called datafiles, which are physical structures that confirm to the operating system in which Oracle is running.

Syntax:

CREATE<tablespace name> DATAFILE'C:\oraclexe\app\oracle\product\10.2.0\ server \<file name.dbf 'SIZE 50M;

Example:

Create tablespace te_cs DATAFILE 'C:\oraclexe\app\oracle\product\10.2.0\ server\usr.dbf 'SIZE 50M;

**CREATE USER:**

The DBA creates user by executing CREATE USER statement.

The user is someone who connects to the database if enough privilege is granted.

Syntax:

SQL> CREATE USER < username> -- (name of user to be created)

IDENTIFIED BY <password> -- (specifies that the user must login with this password)

SQL> user created

Eg: create user James identified by bob;

(The user does not have privilege at this time, it has to be granted.These privileges determine what user can do at database level.)

**PRIVILEGES:**

A privilege is a right to execute an SQL statement or to access another user's object. In Oracle, there are two types of privileges

System Privileges

Object Privileges

System Privileges : are those through which the user can manage the performance of database actions. It is normally granted by DBA to users.

Eg: Create Session,Create Table,Create user etc..

Object Privileges : allow access to objects or privileges on object, i.e. tables, table columns. tables,views etc..It includes alter,delete,insert,select update etc.

(After creating the user, DBA grant specific system privileges to user)

**GRANT:**

The DBA uses the GRANT statement to allocate system privileges to other user.

Syntax:

SQL> GRANT privilege [privilege.... ... ] TO USER ;

SQL> Grant succeeded

Eg: Grant create session, create table, create view to James;

Object privileges vary from object to object.An owner has all privilege or specific privileges on object.

SQL> GRANT object_priv [(column)]

ON object

TO user;

SQL>GRANT select, insert ON emp TO James;

SQL>GRANT select ,update (e_name,e_address)

ON emp TO James;

**CHANGE PASSWORD:**

The DBA creates an account and initializes a password for every user.You can change password by using ALTER USER statement.

Syntax:

Alter USER <some user name>

IDENTIFIED BY<New password>

Eg: ALTER USER James

IDENTIFIED BY sam

**REVOKE:**

REVOKE statement is used to remove privileges granted to other users.The privileges you specify are revoked from the users.

Syntax:

REVOKE [privilege....]

ON object

FROM user

Eg:

REVOKE create session,create table from James;

REVOKE select ,insert ON emp

FROM James

**ROLE:**

A role is a named group of related privileges that can be granted to user.In other words, role is a predefined collection of previleges that are grouped together,thus privileges are easier to assign user.

SQL> Create role custom;

SQL> Grant create table, create view TO custom;

SQL> Grant select, insert ON emp TO custom;

Eg: Grant custom to James, Steve;

**LAB PRACTICE ASSIGNMENT:**

Create user and implement the following commands on relation (Emp and Dept).

Develop a query to grant all privileges of employees table into departments table.

Develop a query to grant some privileges of employees table into departments table.

Develop a query to revoke all privileges of employees table from departments table.

Develop a query to revoke some privileges of employees table from departments table.

## ONLINE RESOURCES

**Practice Paper Link:** https://forms.gle/PGEzWK7WZXaBHgYf7

**QR Code:**

**Video Content:** https://www.youtube.com/playlist?list=PLzlh_31VWEFq40n4m6HhJIEosd7ol_BKm

**QR Code:**

# Chapter 14:Viva Questions

**What is SQL?**

Structured Query Language

**What is database?**

A database is a logically coherent collection of data with some inherent meaning, representing some aspect of real world and which is designed, built and populated with data for a specific purpose.

**What is DBMS?**

It is a collection of programs that enables user to create and maintain a database. In other words it is general-purpose software that provides the users with the processes of defining, constructing and manipulating the database for various applications.

**What is a Database system?**

The database and DBMS software together is called as Database system.

**Advantages of DBMS?**

Redundancy is controlled.

Unauthorized access is restricted.

Providing multiple user interfaces.

Enforcing integrity constraints.

Providing backup and recovery.

**Disadvantage in File Processing System?**

Data redundancy & inconsistency.

Difficult in accessing data.

Data isolation.

Data integrity.

Concurrent access is not possible.

Security Problems.

**Describe the three levels of data abstraction?**

There are three levels of abstraction:

Physical level: The lowest level of abstraction describes how data are stored.

Logical level: The next higher level of abstraction, describes what data are stored in database and what relationship among those data.

View level: The highest level of abstraction describes only part of entire database

**Define the "integrity rules"**

There are two Integrity rules.

Entity Integrity:States that —Primary key cannot have NULL value‖

Referential Integrity:States that —Foreign Key can be either a NULL value or should be Primary Key value of other relation.

**What is extension and intension?**

Extension - It is the number of tuples present in a table at any instance. This is time dependent.

Intension -It is a constant value that gives the name, structure of table and the constraints laid on it.

**What is Data Independence?**

Data independence means that —the application is independent of the storage structure and access strategy of data‖. In other words, The ability to modify the schema definition in one level should not affect the schema definition in the next higher level.

Two types of Data Independence:

Physical Data Independence: Modification in physical level should not affect the logical level.

Logical Data Independence: Modification in logical level should affect the view level.

NOTE: Logical Data Independence is more difficult to achieve

**What is a view? How it is related to data independence?**

A view may be thought of as a virtual table, that is, a table that does not really exist in its own right but is instead derived from one or more underlying base table. In other words, there is no stored file that direct represents the view instead a definition of view is stored in data dictionary. Growth and restructuring of base tables is not reflected in views. Thus the view can insulate users from the effects of restructuring and growth in the database. Hence accounts for logical data independence.

**What is Data Model?**

A collection of conceptual tools for describing data, data relationships data semantics and constraints.

**What is E-R model?**

This data model is based on real world that consists of basic objects called entities and of relationship among these objects. Entities are described in a database by a set of attributes.

**What is Object Oriented model?**

This model is based on collection of objects. An object contains values stored in instance variables within the object. An object also contains bodies of code that operate on the object. These bodies of code are called methods. Objects that contain same types of values and the same methods are grouped together into classes.

**What is an Entity?**

It is an 'object' in the real world with an independent existence.

**What is an Entity type?**

It is a collection (set) of entities that have same attributes.

**What is an Entity set?**

It is a collection of all entities of particular entity type in the database.

**What is an Extension of entity type?**

The collections of entities of a particular entity type are grouped together into an entity set.

**What is an attribute?**

It is a particular property, which describes the entity.

**What is a Relation Schema and a Relation?**

A relation Schema denoted by R(A1, A2, …, An) is made up of the relation name R and the list of attributes Ai that it contains. A relation is defined as a set of tuples. Let r be the relation which contains set tuples (t1, t2, t3, ...,tn). Each tuple is an ordered list of n-values t=(v1,v2, ..., vn).

**What is degree of a Relation?**

It is the number of attribute of its relation schema.

**What is Relationship?**

It is an association among two or more entities.

**What is Relationship set?**

The collection (or set) of similar relationships.

**What is Relationship type?**

Relationship type defines a set of associations or a relationship set among a given set of entity types.

**What is degree of Relationship type?**

It is the number of entity type participating.

**What is DDL (Data Definition Language)?**

A data base schema is specified by a set of definitions expressed by a special language called DDL.

**What is VDL (View Definition Language)?**

It specifies user views and their mappings to the conceptual schema.

**What is SDL (Storage Definition Language)?**

This language is to specify the internal schema. This language may specify the mapping between two schemas.

**What is Data Storage - Definition Language?**

The storage structures and access methods used by database system are specified by a set of definition in a special type of DDL called data storage- definition language.

**What is DML (Data Manipulation Language)?**

This language that enable user to access or manipulate data as organized by appropriate data model.

Procedural DML or Low level: DML requires a user to specify what data are needed and how to get those data.

Non-Procedural DML or High level: DML requires a user to specify what data are needed without specifying how to get those data.

**What is DML Compiler?**

It translates DML statements in a query language into low-level instruction that the query evaluation engine can understand.

**What is Relational Algebra?**

It is a procedural query language. It consists of a set of operations that take one or two relations as input and produce a new relation.

**What is Relational Calculus?**

It is an applied predicate calculus specifically tailored for relational databases proposed by E.F. Codd. E.g. of languages based on it are DSL, ALPHA, QUEL.

**What is normalization?**

It is a process of analyzing the given relation schemas based on their Functional Dependencies (FDs) and primary key to achieve the properties

Minimizing redundancy

Minimizing insertion, deletion and update anomalies.

**What is Functional Dependency?**

A Functional dependency is denoted by X Y between two sets of attributes X and Y that are subsets of R specifies a constraint on the possible tuple that can form a relation state r of R. The constraint is for any two tuples t1 and t2 in r if t1[X] = t2[X] then they have t1[Y] = t2[Y]. This means the value of X component of a tuple uniquely determines the value of component Y.

**When is a functional dependency F said to be minimal?**

Every dependency in F has a single attribute for its right hand side. We cannot replace any dependency X A in F with a dependency Y A where Y is a proper subset of X and still have a set of dependency that is equivalent to F. We cannot remove any dependency from F and still have set of dependency that is equivalent to F.

**What is Multivalued dependency?**

Multivalued dependency denoted by X Y specified on relation schema R, where X and Y are both subsets of R, specifies the following constraint on any relation r of R: if two tuples t1 and t2 exist in r such that t1[X] = t2[X] then t3 and t4 should also exist in r with the following properties

t3[x] = t4[X] = t1[X] = t2[X]

t3[Y] = t1[Y] and t4[Y] = t2[Y]

t3[Z] = t2[Z] and t4[Z] = t1[Z]

where [Z = (R-(X U Y)) ]

**What is Lossless join property?**

It guarantees that the spurious tuple generation does not occur with respect to relation schemas after decomposition.

**What is 1 NF (Normal Form)?**

The domain of attribute must include only atomic (simple, indivisible) values.

**What is Fully Functional dependency?**

It is based on concept of full functional dependency. A functional dependency X Y is fully functional dependency if removal of any attribute A from X means that the dependency does not hold any more.

**What is 2NF?**

A relation schema R is in 2NF if it is in 1NF and every non-prime attribute A in R is fully functionally dependent on primary key.

**What is 3NF?**

A relation schema R is in 3NF if it is in 2NF and for every FD X A either of the following is true X is a Super-key of R.

A is a prime attribute of R. In other words, if every non prime attribute is non-transitively dependent on primary key.

**What is BCNF (Boyce-Codd Normal Form)?**

A relation schema R is in BCNF if it is in 3NF and satisfies additional constraints that for every FD X A, X must be a candidate key.

**What is 4NF?**

A relation schema R is said to be in 4NF if for every Multivalued dependency X Y that holds over R, one of following is true

X is subset or equal to (or) XY = R.

X is a super key.

**What is 5NF?**

A Relation schema R is said to be 5NF if for every join dependency {R1, R2, ..., Rn} that holds

R, one the following is true

Ri = R for some i.

The join dependency is implied by the set of FD, over R in which the left side is key of R.

**Define DCL?**

The DCL language is used for controlling the access to the table and hence securing the database. DCL is used to provide certain privileges to a particular user. Privileges are rights to be allocated.

## ONLINE RESOURCES

**Practice Test Paper Link:** https://forms.gle/hj2AiVvBgRk52FTB8

**QR Code:**

**Video Content:**https://www.youtube.com/playlist?list=PLzlh_31VWEFoWH2tSlGBidOCNhe-ePdh-

**QR Code:**

## ADDITIONAL RESOURCE: Online Resources

**Introduction to Database Management System:**https://youtu.be/SwB6RTAQ-o0

**QR Code:**

**IGNOU MCA/BCA June 2023 DBMS Solved paper:**https://youtu.be/P5edlFTMm6Q

**QR Code:**

**Database Management quick Introduction:**https://youtu.be/0giJSc9vBKU

**QR Code:**

**IGNOU MCA/BCA June 2012 DBMS Solved paper:**https://youtu.be/hXkPT9eQgTk

**QR Code:**

**Microsoft SQL Server Introduction:**https://youtu.be/ea8J7PsfaEc

**QR Code:**

**How to install MySQL:**https://youtu.be/drGz7of1xHQ

**QR Code:**

**MySQL- Quick Introduction:**https://youtu.be/-7NOhrJoDko

**QR Code:**

### Database Management System Playlist

**Link :https://www.youtube.com/playlist?list=PLzlh_31VWEFo6OJyr2J8Gc6e9-beyDiPB**

**QR Code:**

## YouTube Videos Playlists for all Chapters

**CHAPTER 1 Link:** https://www.youtube.com/playlist?list=PLzlh_31VWEFpHf2teQUBkgicMGxz1s3vV

**QR Code:**

**CHAPTER 2 Link:** https://www.youtube.com/playlist?list=PLzlh_31VWEFqlTQ77B1DrjW-3sVOWrXE-

**QR Code:**

**CHAPTER 3 Link:** https://www.youtube.com/playlist?list=PLzlh_31VWEFrMmNTIGE7i4E0mcqQOaiY7

**QR Code:**

**CHAPTER 4 Link:** https://www.youtube.com/playlist?list=PLzlh_31VWEFqPevKzR_1UgioCBDHVSTnA

**QR Code:**

**CHAPTER 5 Link:** https://www.youtube.com/playlist?list=PLzlh_31VWEFoFVGYleZ8kkXloq2XqaRWk

**QR Code:**

**CHAPTER 6 Link:** https://www.youtube.com/playlist?list=PLzlh_31VWEFr7Vqg60ws_vmGVa1a6PE9-

**QR Code:**

**CHAPTER 7 Link:** https://www.youtube.com/playlist?list=PLzlh_31VWEFoXkU4ET9iBpaYefWMqpeHq

**QR Code:**

**CHAPTER 8 Link:** https://www.youtube.com/playlist?list=PLzlh_31VWEFoIlw2oMU7KRz1SoBIhT3y

QR Code:

**CHAPTER 9 Link:** https://www.youtube.com/playlist?list=PLzlh_31VWEFqKIYRcVCdVVNPUS5Ohny7A

QR Code:

**CHAPTER 10 Link:** https://www.youtube.com/playlist?list=PLzlh_31VWEFqAXtW7UsVFn7NKpeIa7I32

QR Code:

**CHAPTER 11 Link:** https://www.youtube.com/playlist?list=PLzlh_31VWEFqIENiPovIYj-kA_CSRC86x

QR Code:

**CHAPTER 12 Link:** https://www.youtube.com/playlist?list=PLzlh_31VWEFqHAJakLR-Zt06bkBU6n9c6

QR Code:

**CHAPTER 13 Link:** https://www.youtube.com/playlist?list=PLzlh_31VWEFq40n4m6HhJIEosd7ol_BKm

QR Code:

**CHAPTER 14 Link:** https://www.youtube.com/playlist?list=PLzlh_31VWEFoWH2tSlGBidOCNhe-ePdh-

QR Code: